CACHE LEVEL

3

Early Years Educator

FOR THE WORK-BASED LEARNER

Penny Tassoni

Contributors: Louise Burnham and Carolyn Meggitt

HODDER
EDUCATION
AN HACHETTE UK COMPANY

Upon successful completion of this qualification, learners will be awarded the NCFE CACHE Level 3 Diploma for the Early Years Workforce (Early Years Educator) 601/2629/2. This CACHE branded qualification is certified by the Awarding Organisation, NCFE.

Orders: please contact Bookpoint Ltd, 130 Milton Park, Abingdon, Oxon OX14 4SB. Telephone: (44) 01235 827720. Fax: (44) 01235 400454. Lines are open from 9.00–5.00, Monday to Saturday, with a 24 hour message answering service. You can also order through our website www.hoddereducation.co.uk.

British Library Cataloguing in Publication Data

A catalogue record for this title is available from the British Library

ISBN 9781471808067

First Published 2014

Impression number 10 9 8 7

Year 2018

Copyright © Penny Tassoni, 2014

Hachette UK's policy is to use papers that are natural, renewable and recyclable products and made from wood grown in sustainable forests. The logging and manufacturing processes are expected to conform to the environmental regulations of the country of origin.

Cover photo © Katrina Brown/Alamy

Typeset in 10.5/14 Palatino Light by Integra Software Services Pvt. Ltd, Pondicherry, India

Printed in Italy

Contents

Acknowledgements

Penny Tassoni

I would like to thank The 197 Early Years Nursery, Kingston Upon Thames and Alpha Ark Nursery for inspiring me and ensuring that I keep in touch with the issues of the day. I would also like to thank Nicola Amies, Director of Early Years, Bright Horizons Family Solutions for her interesting thoughts and ideas. Finally, my thanks go once again to the Tassoni Team for their continued support.

Louise Burnham

I would like to thank Stephen Halder and Sundus Pasha for their support with this project, as well as the staff and children at Clare House Primary School in Beckenham for their wonderful inspiration.

The publisher would like to thank all the staff, children and families at Vanessa Nursery School, Kate Greenaway Nursery School and Children's Centre, Godinton Day Nursery, Ark Alpha Nursery and Bright Horizons Family Solutions for their help with many of the photographs, taken by Jules Selmes, Andrew Callaghan, and Justin O'Hanlon. A special thanks to Michele Barrett, Jenni Hare, Julie Breading, and Susan Goodbrand for all their assistance with organising the photo shoots.

Photo credits

Page 6: © Dean Mitchell/Fotolia; page 7: © Crown copyright material is reproduced with the permission of the Controller of HMSO and Queen's Printer for Scotland. Courtesy of the Foods Standards Agency; page 34: ©RomainQuéré/Fotolia; page 103: ©aerogondo/Fotolia; page 242: © Woodapple/Fotolia; page 260: ©Patrick Eden/Alamy; pages 86, 136, 142, 177, 199, 238, 258, 294, 302, 334, 396: © Andrew Callaghan; pages 22, 135: © Justin O'Hanlon; all other photos © Jules Selmes.

How to use this book

This book contains all the units you need to master the skills and knowledge for the new CACHE Level 3 Diploma for the Early Years Workforce (Early Years Educator), and is divided into three themes:

1 Health and well-being
2 Legislation, frameworks and professional practice
3 Play, development and learning for school readiness

This book should be taught in conjunction with the most up-to-date Level 3 Early Years Educator Work-Based specification document, available from **www.cache.org.uk**. You should also refer to the most up-to-date EYFS document available on the **www.gov.uk** website. References to parents are intended to include other carers as well.

Key features of the book

LO4 Understand childhood immunisation

Understand all the requirements of the new qualification with clearly stated learning outcomes and assessment criteria fully mapped to the specification.

AC 4.1 Reasons for immunisation

Learning outcomes

By the end of this unit, you will:

1 Understand the impact of food and nutrition on children's health and development.

Prepare for what you are going to cover in the unit.

Key term

nutrients Foods that contain chemicals that the body requires.

Understand important terms.

Reflect

Write about how you support healthy eating in your own setting. Think about how well you role

Learn to reflect on your own skills and experiences.

In practice

Write about how you have worked with a child with additional needs in your setting.

Apply your knowledge in the work setting.

In your setting

What strategies does your setting use to promote healthy eating at meal times?

Develop your professional skills in the work setting with these questions and tasks.

Case study

Harry's mother has written a note to say that he did not want to eat his breakfast. Harry's key

See how concepts are applied in settings with real life scenarios.

Test yourself

Give five reasons why physical exercise is good for children.

Short tasks and knowledge-based questions to help enhance your understanding of assessment criteria.

Research it!

1 Find out more about the 5 a day campaign. Visit **www.nhs.uk/livewell/5aday/ Pages/5ADAYhome.aspx**.

Enhance your understanding of topics with research-led activities encouraging you to explore an area in more detail.

Tips when reflecting on an activity

You should consider the following points when reflecting on your activity. These apply to both indoor and outdoor activities:

Helpful tips to develop your professional skills.

Assessment

For this unit you will need to complete a variety of tasks. Some of these tasks will focus on whether you have acquired the knowledge needed to

Information guiding you through what you will need to learn from each unit to meet the assessment criteria.

Useful resources

'Eating well for under 5s in child care' by Dr Helen Crawley (2006) The Caroline Walker Trust: **www.cwt.org.uk/pdfs/Under5s.pdf**

Includes references to websites, books and other various sources for further reading and research.

Introduction

Welcome to this book, which has been written to accompany the CACHE Level 3 Diploma for the Early Years Workforce. Congratulations also for deciding to develop further your knowledge and practice with children.

Working professionally with young children is a demanding role. It is now recognised that the first few years of a child's life can significantly impact on their later health, learning and well-being. There is research that indicates that adults who work with children need a good knowledge of child development, how children learn and sensitivity, as well as the everyday practical skills. It is also recognised that working with young children in the early years sector is a profession in its own right and this is reflected in the title of your Level 3 qualification.

To help you achieve your qualification, the book has been written to follow the units and there are many features included in each unit that should help you to link theory to your everyday practice, know where to find out more or to help you approach the assessments. These features are explained on pages vi–vii.

Once you have achieved your qualification, you should have gained the skills and experience needed to work effectively with young children and their families. With this qualification, you can work in a range of different early years settings including nurseries and pre-schools, or develop your own business as a childminder or a nanny, for example. You may also be able to use this qualification as a steppingstone onto other qualifications or into other associated career paths (subject to their admission requirements).

Good luck with this qualification and good luck with your career in early years.

Structure of this qualification

To complete this qualification, you will study 23 units which are divided across three themes:

● Theme 1 Health and well-being
● Theme 2 Legislation, frameworks and professional practice
● Theme 3 Play, development and learning for school readiness

Each unit is divided into 'learning outcomes'. Some learning outcomes focus on knowledge and will often start 'To know' or 'To understand' while other learning outcomes focus on practice, which begin with 'Be able to'. When you look at a unit, you will also see that under each learning outcome there are assessment criteria. The assessment criteria indicate what knowledge or practice you will need to be able to demonstrate.

This may seem complicated, but most learners find that once they have completed one unit, it all falls into place. This book should help you as each chapter follows the structure of the units of the qualification. You will find that the learning outcomes are explained with an introduction and then the information needed to meet each assessment criteria is included.

How the qualification is assessed

To gain this qualification, you will be allocated an assessor who will guide you through the assessments. The qualification requires you to complete a variety of assessments including written assignments as well assessments of your practice with children. As part of the assessment process, you will also need to complete a longitudinal study. This is an important assessment as through its completion you will be able to show that you can link the knowledge that you have gained during the qualification to your work with children.

Health and well-being

Unit 1.1 Support healthy lifestyles for children through the provision of food and nutrition

Unit 1.2 WB Support healthy lifestyles for children through exercise

Unit 1.3 WB Support physical care routines for children

Unit 1.4 WB Promote children's emotional well-being

Unit 1.5 Understand how to support children who are unwell

Unit 1.1 Support healthy lifestyles for children through the provision of food and nutrition

What was your favourite food when you were little? Do you still like it now? Interestingly many of our food preferences as adults are linked to childhood. It is for this reason that the foods that early years settings provide are healthy and balanced. In this unit, we will look at the importance of food on children's development as well as the impact on children if they have a poor diet. We also think about how best to meet children's individual nutritional needs and how you might play a part in promoting healthy eating.

Learning outcomes

By the end of this unit, you will:

1 Understand the impact of food and nutrition on children's health and development.
2 Understand how food choices impact on health and development during pre-pregnancy, pregnancy and breastfeeding.
3 Understand the nutritional needs of children.
4 Understand the impact of poor diet on children's health and development.
5 Understand individuals' dietary requirements and preferences.
6 Be able to support healthy eating in own setting.

LO1 Understand the impact of food and nutrition on children's health and development

Have you ever seen posters encouraging you to eat more healthily? Or heard that children in the UK are increasingly overweight? In this section, we look at what is meant by healthy eating and the advice and legal requirements that early years settings have to follow.

AC 1.1 Healthy eating

The term 'healthy eating' is often used and so it is worth exploring what it actually means. Healthy eating is about making food choices that will provide the body with what it needs to keep healthy. At a simple level, the human body is a machine that needs certain **nutrients** and energy to keep it going. Nutrients and energy all come from food and drink.

→ In LO3 on page 6, we look at the different types of nutrients that the body needs.

> **Key term**
>
> **nutrients** Foods that contain chemicals that the body requires.

AC 1.2 National and local initiatives to promote healthy eating

To help families and also early years settings provide healthy foods for children, there is a range of different initiatives. Some have been organised directly by the Department of Health; others by organisations such as the School Food Trust, which has been partly funded by the government, as well as ones that are funded by local authorities.

Difficulties with initiatives

Providing information for families is actually quite difficult and when evaluating initiatives it is worth considering some of the following points:

- Families may not have internet access or may not know to visit the websites or pick up the leaflets.
- The style of the websites or leaflets may not be sufficiently interesting.
- Not all parents may have the literacy skills to understand the information.
- Some of the suggestions for recipes or food may not be suitable for families on a tight budget.
- Some families may not be in areas where shops stock the types of food shown on the websites.

5 a day campaign

This initiative was funded and organised by the Department of Health. Its aim is to encourage everyone to eat more fruit and vegetables. The idea is that everyone should eat at least five portions of fruit and vegetables a day as these are thought to reduce the risk of cancer and also prevent people from becoming overweight.

Schools fruit and vegetables scheme

As part of the 5 a day scheme, children aged 4–6 years are entitled to a free piece of fruit or vegetable while they are at school. This is usually given at snack time. The idea is that by giving children opportunities to taste fruit and vegetables, they will become more used to the taste and so ask for them at home.

Start4Life

This initiative provides parents with information about how to have a healthy pregnancy and to keep children under five healthy. It is funded by the Department of Health and organised by the National Health Service.

Change4Life

This initiative encourages families and adults to think about making healthy choices, including taking exercise and healthy eating.

Food labelling – traffic light system

To help families make healthier food choices, supermarkets and food manufacturers have

Figure 1.1.1 Children should be given plenty of opportunities to try fruit and vegetables

introduced food labelling systems. There is a variety of different food labels, but the one that is most common is called the traffic light systems. On the front of the packaging, the amounts of sugar, fat and salt are labelled as red, amber or green. The idea is that families can see whether or not a food is healthy. From 2016, there will be regulations in place that make it compulsory for nutritional information to be provided on food packages.

Community food schemes

In some local areas, there are opportunities for families to buy fruit and vegetables at a reduced cost. These schemes are often funded by the local authority, but are organised by volunteers.

Growing food

In some areas, residents are being encouraged to grow their own food. There are often community garden and allotment projects.

Research it!

1 Find out more about the 5 a day campaign. Visit www.nhs.uk/livewell/5aday/Pages/5ADAYhome.aspx.
2 Find out more about the information and advice on healthy eating from the Start4Life website: www.nhs.uk/start4life.
3 Find out more about the information and advice on healthy eating from the Change4Life website: www.nhs.uk/change4life.

4 Visit two different supermarkets. Look at how food is labelled. How easy is it to identify which packaged foods are healthy?
5 Find out about local initiatives in your area. Visit your local NHS community clinic or carry out an internet search using the name of your nearest town+food+initiative.

AC 1.3 Food and drink requirements under current frameworks

There are some food and drink requirements that have been put in place to ensure that children are given healthy food by early years settings and schools.

Early Years Foundation Stage (EYFS)

The EYFS is divided into two parts. The first part looks at the education programme. As part of the education programme, children are meant to learn about making healthy food choices. The second part of the EYFS deals with keeping children safe and healthy. In this second part, there is a requirement for early years settings to provide nutritional food appropriate to the age of the children and also make fresh water available at all times. There is also a requirement to ensure that food is prepared hygienically and that staff have the skills and knowledge to do this.

Key Stage 1

While there are no specific guidelines in the National Curriculum in relation to food, there are national school food standards which are compulsory for most schools to use when providing food and drink. The national standards include the need for schools to provide fruit and vegetables at meal times and also

to restrict foods that are high in fat, sugar and salt. The national standards have been criticised because they do not apply to schools that run as academies or to independent schools.

LO2 Understand how food choices impact on health and development during pre-pregnancy, pregnancy and breastfeeding

Did you know that it is harder for a couple to start a family if they have a poor diet? Or that some babies are born with medical conditions because their mother lacked a certain mineral? It may seem amazing, but food plays an important part in the healthy development of babies. In this section, we look at how diet can affect conception, pregnancy and also breastfeeding.

AC 2.1 The impact of food choices on health and development

What we eat at different times of life can have an impact on our short-term and long-term health. In theory, a poor diet can also have an effect on the future health of any babies that women go on to have.

During pre-pregnancy

Women and men need to have a healthy diet if they wish to start a family. It seems to make a difference not just for the baby's health but also to becoming pregnant. It is important for women to try to be a healthy weight for their height as this also makes it easier to conceive.

During pregnancy

It is recommended that women thinking of becoming pregnant take a folic acid supplement and also eat plenty of green vegetables, such as cabbage, sprouts and spinach. This is because, in the first few weeks of pregnancy, lack of folic acid can cause a medical condition in babies called spina bifida.

In the first few months of pregnancy, women should also avoid consuming high levels of drinks containing caffeine, such as energy drinks and coffee. This is because it increases the risk of miscarriage. Later in pregnancy, there is a range of foods to be avoided, including unpasteurised cheeses, uncooked eggs and undercooked meat, as these can cause infections and food poisoning.

It is also recommended that women do not over-eat or under-eat during pregnancy. Eating for two is therefore a myth. While some weight gain is normal, women are encouraged to eat healthily to ensure they remain fit and well.

As well as the advice to eat healthily during pregnancy, women are advised not to drink alcohol. A condition known as foetal alcohol syndrome is caused by alcohol and affects the development of the baby's brain.

During breastfeeding

Women who breastfeed need to drink plenty of fluid and make sure that they eat plenty of foods that are calcium rich. This is because extra calcium is needed during pregnancy and breastfeeding. Women also need to eat slightly more, but still healthily, so as to make sure that there is enough milk for the baby. As with pregnancy, women should avoid high-risk foods associated with food poisoning, such as raw eggs or undercooked meat.

In practice

Prepare a poster that provides information about the effects of a poor diet on the developing baby and child.

LO3 Understand the nutritional needs of children

Do you remember adults telling you to eat up your greens? You might have wondered what all the fuss was about. In this section, we look at the

Figure 1.1.2 Mothers who breastfeed need plenty of fluid and calcium-rich food

importance of a balanced diet for children of all ages, including weaning babies and why it is important to make sure that children are given fruit and vegetables

AC 3.1 The nutritional value of the main food groups

A healthy diet consists of a wide range of foods. To help people make healthy food choices, foods are divided into several groups. Food from the first four groups shown in Table 1.1.1 should be taken at each meal or during the course of the day. Foods that contain high levels of fat, sugar and salt should be kept to a minimum. Table 1.1.1 shows the different food groups and how these foods provide different nutritional benefits.

Table 1.1.1 Nutritional benefits of different food groups

Fruit and vegetables	Contain vitamins and minerals. Fruit and vegetables are thought to be important for overall health. They also help digestion.
Bread, pasta, rice, potatoes	Contain carbohydrates, which are important for slow-burning energy. Also contain vitamin B and some minerals.
Milk and dairy foods	Contain protein, which is needed for growth and repair of cells. Also provide some energy as well as vitamins and calcium. Calcium is important for healthy teeth and bones.
Meat, eggs, fish, poultry, beans and pulses	Contain protein, which is needed for growth and repair of cells, as well as providing some energy. They also contain important minerals. Beans and pulses also contain carbohydrates.
Foods high in fat, salt or sugar, e.g. chips, sweets, chocolate, ice cream	Foods high in fat, sugar or salt but low in protein, vitamins and minerals should be avoided as they can cause children and adults to become overweight. While some fat, salt and sugar is important for a healthy diet, these can be found naturally in the other food groups.

The eatwell plate

Use the eatwell plate to help you get the balance right. It shows how much of what you eat should come from each food group.

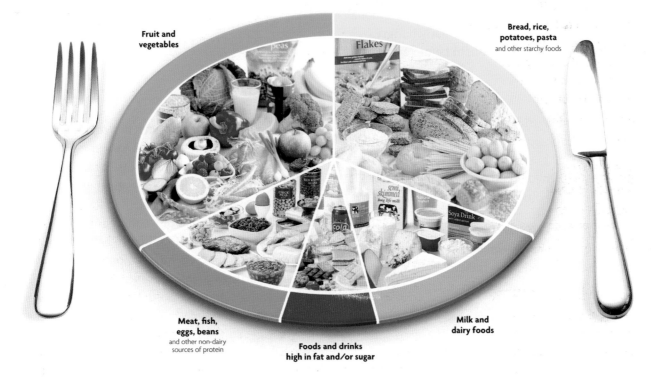

Figure 1.1.3 The eatwell plate helps adults understand how much of each food group they should be eating

AC 3.2 The nutritional needs of babies until they are fully weaned

Over the past few years, there have been changes to the way that babies are fed and weaned. It is now recommended that babies are breastfed until they are six months old before they are weaned. If mothers do not breastfeed, it is suggested that babies are given formula milk, which should be made up and given in the quantity suggested by the baby's health visitor.

It is important that babies begin the process of weaning at six months because, unless babies are bottle fed, their natural store of the mineral iron will have run out. Iron is important for the blood as it helps to carry oxygen around the body.

Early weaning

Weaning babies earlier than six months is not advised as babies' digestive systems are thought not to be sufficiently mature. It is thought that early weaning may result in allergic reactions and also skin conditions such as eczema. In exceptional cases, where a baby seems particularly hungry, medical advice should be sought before weaning takes place.

Vitamin D

Vitamin D is important for the formation of babies' and young children's bones. With the exception of babies who are bottle fed, it is now advised that all babies and children up until the age of five are given vitamin D drops.

Foods to be avoided

Until babies are fully weaned at 12 months, they should not be given cow's milk to drink because this can cause digestive problems. Other foods that babies should not be given until they are fully weaned include:

- honey
- salt
- liver
- uncooked eggs
- fruit juice or sugary drinks
- sugary foods.

Research it!

Find out more about babies' nutritional needs by visiting www.eatwell.gov.uk.

AC 3.3 Weaning programmes

There are three stages in weaning. Each stage is important as it helps babies to learn the skills of eating and also introduces new tastes and foods. This means that deciding what babies need will depend on the stage of weaning that they have reached. Early years settings also have to work in partnership with parents when drawing up a weaning programme. This is because some babies may have special dietary needs or their parents may have dietary preferences.

→ For more on special dietary needs, see page 14.

Table 1.1.2 shows the stages of weaning along with examples of the types of foods that might be given to babies.

Baby-led weaning

While we have looked at conventional weaning from six months, some parents like to use a system of weaning known as 'baby-led weaning'. Baby-led weaning still begins at six months but instead of babies being fed by adults, they are given food and allowed to explore it and tackle it in the way that they want. This method of weaning is controversial. Parents and professionals who use baby-led weaning claim that it is more empowering for children and also that it prevents fussy eaters. Critics of this approach claim that, as some babies may not have the skills to feed themselves, they may not get sufficient nutrition. They also claim that babies are more likely to choke. On a practical level, everyone does agree that it is messy and that meal times take longer because babies tend to play with their food.

Table 1.1.2 Stages of weaning

Stage	Description	Foods
Puréed and mashed foods: from six months	At first, foods are puréed so that the baby can learn to swallow them, but then foods are mashed. Babies learn to take food from a spoon. Foods are introduced one by one so as to identify any foods that might cause an allergic reaction. Baby rice or fruit and vegetables are the first food groups to be introduced. Babies are introduced to drinking from a cup. Babies should not be given cow's milk to drink but it can be used in cooking. Breast milk or formula feeds are still needed.	Mashed or soft fruit and vegetables Baby rice or cereal mixed with breast or bottled milk Cooked meat that is soft, e.g. chicken or fish Pasta, rice and noodles Dairy products, yoghurt and cheese
Soft finger foods, mashed and chopped foods: from 8–9 months	Babies are given foods that they need to chew slightly. This action helps develop the tongue and mouth movements. Babies are given a wider range of foods with different textures and should be moving to having three meals a day, with a gradual reduction in the number of milk feeds.	Foods can be mixed so that babies are having mini meals. Babies need a wide range of foods from all of the different food groups.
Finger foods: 12 months	Babies learn to chew in this stage, which helps to develop further the tongue and mouth movements. Babies also learn to feed themselves by picking finger foods. This encourages their fine motor coordination. Cow's milk can be used as a drink.	Babies should be gaining their food intake from solid food and so will not need milk feeds any more. Babies should be encouraged to drink water or cow's milk from a cup with meals.

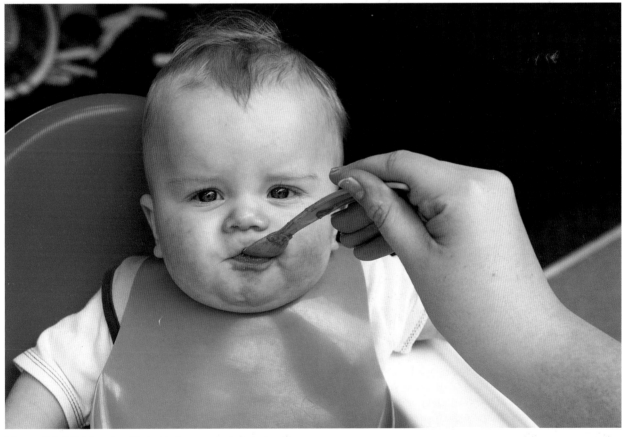

Figure 1.1.4 Babies should start to be weaned at six months

AC 3.4 Children's nutritional requirements

As children grow, their nutritional requirements vary because over time they need more energy. These needs are shown in Table 1.1.3. This usually comes from slightly larger portion sizes. It is important to give children correct portion sizes so as to prevent them from becoming either underweight or overweight. Interestingly, children can become overweight even if they are given healthy foods.

Table 1.1.3 Nutritional requirements of different age groups

Age	Nutritional needs	Foods to avoid
1–2 years	<ul><li>Need three meals a day plus nutritional snacks</li><li>Full-fat milk and dairy products should be offered</li><li>Milk consumption should be no more than 400 ml a day (two-thirds of a pint)</li><li>Vitamin D supplement required</li><li>Five portions or tastes of fruit and vegetables a day</li><li>Approximate energy requirement in calories: about 1,000 kcal</li></ul>	<ul><li>Low-sugar and artificially sweetened foods and drinks</li><li>Ready-to-drink cartons of juice or squash as these are high in calories and are acidic, which can cause dental decay</li><li>Foods that are made for adults, e.g. to lose weight, for sport or to reduce cholesterol, such as special margarines, sports drinks and caffeine drinks</li><li>Chilled, ready meals and take-away meals as these are high in salt and fat</li><li>Crisps and savoury snacks as these are too high in salt and are not sufficiently nutritious</li><li>Bran cereals and high-fibre foods as they fill children up too quickly</li></ul>
2–3 years	<ul><li>Need three meals a day plus nutritional snacks</li><li>If children are not underweight, semi-skimmed milk and low-fat products should be offered</li><li>Milk consumption should be no more than 350 ml a day</li><li>Five small portions of fruit and vegetables a day</li><li>Vitamin D supplement required</li><li>Approximate energy requirement in calories: 1,230 kcal</li></ul>	
3–5 years	<ul><li>Need three meals a day plus nutritional snacks</li><li>Milk consumption should be no more than 300 ml a day</li><li>Vitamin D supplement required</li><li>Salt in foods should be restricted to 2–3 g a day</li><li>Five portions of fruit and vegetables a day</li><li>Approximate energy requirement in calories: 1,480 kcal</li></ul>	
5–7 years	<ul><li>Need three meals a day plus nutritional snacks</li><li>Five portions of fruit and vegetables a day</li><li>Salt in foods should be restricted to 3 g</li><li>Approximate energy requirement in calories: 1,600 kcal</li></ul>	

AC 3.5 Strategies to encourage healthy eating

It is thought that our food preferences are linked to the foods that we enjoy during childhood. Experts therefore believe that, during early childhood, children should be given a wide range of foods, especially fruit and vegetables, so that they develop a taste for them.

Weaning

During the weaning process, babies should be given a wide range of fruit and vegetables as this introduces them to different textures and tastes.

Colour

It has been shown that children eat more healthily if they are given a wide range of foods of different colours, especially fruit and vegetables.

Choice and self-service

Where children are able to choose foods (assuming that they are all healthy) and also serve themselves, they are more likely to try out new foods. They are also more likely to learn to stop eating when they feel full.

Presentation

Children are more likely to be interested in healthy food if it is attractively presented. In many early years settings, foods are put into attractive serving dishes or are arranged in ways that look interesting.

> **In your setting**
>
> What strategies does your setting use to promote healthy eating at meal times?

Involvement

As soon as children are able to walk, they should be involved in the preparation of food or meal times. They can carry things to the table, serve themselves or take part in cooking. Being involved, especially in the cooking process, seems to make

Figure 1.1.5 Presenting food in attractive ways can make it more appealing to young children

children keener to taste new foods or to try foods that they previously disliked.

Repetition

Some green vegetables are naturally bitter and so are less likely to be enjoyed by children. The sensation of bitterness can be reduced if children keep trying them. This is why foods should be regularly offered so that over time children can learn to enjoy them.

Providing healthy snacks and drinks

While young children do need snacks, as their stomach capacity is smaller than that of adults, the types of snacks on offer need to be healthy. They may include fruit, vegetables or 'mini meals', such as cheese with biscuits. It is important, however, that when planning menus the calorie content of snacks is taken into consideration. Snacks should always be nutritious and this is why biscuits and cakes are not usually advised. Figure 1.1.6 shows examples of healthy snacks that can be provided as part of a healthy diet.

> **In your setting**
>
> Make a list of the snacks that are served over the course of a week. How healthy are they?

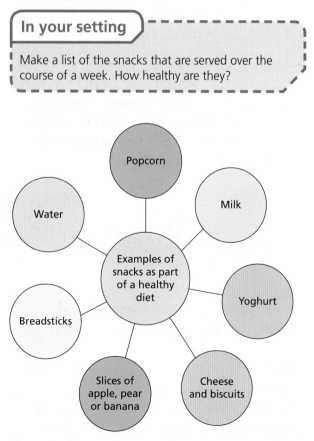

Figure 1.1.6 Examples of snacks as part of a healthy diet

LO4 Understand the impact of poor diet on children's health and development

Have you ever heard of rickets? Rickets is a bone disease that used to be quite rare but has come back because of a lack of vitamin D in the diet. It is a good example of what happens if the body does not get sufficient nutrients. In this section, we look at the impact of a poor diet on children's health and overall development.

AC 4.1 The impact of poor diet on children's health and development

Children need a healthy diet so that they can stay healthy and develop well. Children who do not have a healthy diet are likely to be disadvantaged in a variety of ways.

Short-term impact on children's health

A poor diet can affect children's health and development in the short term. Fighting off colds and other infections is the job of the **immune system**. A poor diet can affect the body's ability to fight off infection.

Anaemia

A mineral called iron is very important in our diets. Iron is needed to make red blood cells, which in turn carry oxygen around the body. Lack of iron causes a medical condition called **anaemia**, which if left untreated can become very serious. The signs of anaemia include severe tiredness and lack of energy. Babies who are anaemic may not, for example, have the strength to learn to crawl or walk. Iron is found in meat, poultry, some fish, beans and brown rice. It can also be found in some green leafy vegetables, such as watercress. Meals with iron-rich foods should also contain foods high in vitamin C, such as fruit and vegetables. This is because the body absorbs iron more easily when vitamin C is present.

Key terms

anaemia A disease caused by a lack of iron.

immune system Processes in the body designed to fight infection.

Behaviour and concentration

Children need to have a good, varied diet, but they also need to have food at regular intervals. It has been well researched that children who do not have breakfast are more likely to have difficulties in concentrating and managing their behaviour before lunch. This is because the brain needs energy to work well.

Activity levels

Where children do not have a good diet, they may be less inclined to be active. This could be because they do not have sufficient calories in their diet or their diet lacks certain minerals or vitamins. In the case of children who become overweight, this is because movement requires more effort. If children are not sufficiently active, this in turn affects their ability to practise fine and gross motor skills.

Digestive problems

Children's ability to digest foods can be affected by what they eat. A lack of water as well as fruit and vegetables in a diet can cause **constipation**. Some diets may also cause **diarrhoea**, especially if children are not given foods that require chewing.

Key terms

constipation Difficulty in passing a bowel movement.

diarrhoea Bowel movements that are liquid rather than solid.

Long-term impact on children's health

There are several ways in which a poor diet can affect children's long-term health and development. Surprisingly, in some cases, the impact of a poor diet can continue into adulthood.

Bones and teeth

A diet lacking in calcium can cause long-term problems with bones and teeth that can continue into adulthood. A lack of calcium can cause weaknesses in the teeth and bones. In later life, a disease called osteoporosis can cause older people's bones to fracture more easily.

Tooth decay

If a diet has included too many sugary foods, including fruit juices, there is a danger of tooth decay. While young children's milk teeth might be affected, the adult teeth sitting under the gum can also become decayed. This can result in these teeth needing to be removed.

Obesity

There is a link between young children who become overweight and later obesity. This is partly due to eating habits, but also because fat cells in the body are activated. Being obese as an older child or adult can put strain on the joints, heart and other organs of the body. It also makes it harder to take exercise and be active. There are also other effects of obesity, which can include depression and low self-esteem.

Brain development

During childhood, children's brains are developing. A very poor diet can affect this brain development and in theory may lower children's academic attainment if they remain continually **malnourished**.

Key term

malnourished A diet lacking in some of the minerals, vitamins and other nutrients required by the body.

LO5 Understand individuals' dietary requirements and preferences

Have you noticed in your setting that some children are not allowed certain foods? There is a range of reasons why this might be the case. In this section, we look at the different reasons

Figure 1.1.7 These children's bones are strong because they have a healthy diet

why children may need special diets or have certain requirements. We will also look at the importance of keeping records of children's dietary needs.

AC 5.1 Special dietary requirements and the importance of keeping and sharing coherent records

Reasons for special dietary requirements

Allergies

Some children have food allergies. A child with a food allergy will have a sudden and potentially serious reaction if they come into contact with certain foods. In some cases, the food allergy may be so serious that it affects the child's breathing and therefore can be fatal. Common food allergies include nuts, milk, wheat and eggs. When children have a food allergy, it is important that the food they eat does not come into contact with the food to which they are allergic. Therefore, their food may have to be prepared separately. As food allergies can have serious consequences, no risks can be taken with a child who has a known allergy.

Intolerances

Food intolerances are different from food allergies and are not life threatening. Reactions often come a few hours after eating the food and common symptoms include skin reactions or digestive problems. Common food intolerances include wheat and dairy products.

Medical conditions

Some children have medical conditions that affect what they are able to eat. Two common medical conditions are diabetes and coeliac disease.

Diabetes

Diabetes is a disease caused by the body not being able to produce a hormone called insulin. Insulin is important because, when food is digested, it is turned into glucose. The job of insulin is to help convert the glucose into energy, which can then be used by cells. If there is insufficient insulin, the body starts to shut down. In contrast, if there is too much insulin, organs in the body can become damaged. It is therefore a serious medical condition. There are two types of diabetes:

- Type 1 diabetes is an inherited condition and is the one that you are most likely to come across in very young children. People with type 1 diabetes cannot produce insulin and so injections of insulin are given usually before meal times.
- Type 2 diabetes used to be associated with older people who were overweight, but it has become more common in younger people. Type 2 diabetes can often be managed by diet alone.

Where a child has been diagnosed with diabetes, you should make sure that you know about their diet and also the timings of their meals. It is important that children with diabetes have regular meals and snacks.

Research it!

Find out more about diabetes by downloading a copy of 'Supporting children with Type 1 diabetes in school and early years settings' from Diabetes UK www.diabetes.org.uk.

Coeliac disease

Coeliac disease is a condition whereby the body attacks itself if it comes into contact with gluten. Gluten is found in wheat, barley and rye. Foods with wheat include bread and pasta. Coeliac disease can be serious because it affects the body's ability to absorb other nutrients from food and also it can damage the intestine. Children with coeliac disease must not be given any foods that contain gluten.

Religious requirements

Some families practise religions that have dietary laws. In some religions, pork cannot be eaten, while in others, beef is prohibited. Religions such as Judaism and Islam also specify how meat, including beef and chicken, should be prepared. It is important to find out from families about their religious food

requirements and avoid making any assumptions. This is because some families vary as to the extent to which they follow religious teachings.

Social and cultural requirements

Some families have dietary requirements that are based on social and cultural circumstances. They may be vegetarians, for example, and not eat any meat or fish. Some families may want food to be sourced locally or meat, eggs and poultry to be free range.

The importance of keeping and sharing records

All early years settings are required to keep records about children's dietary needs and share these with people involved in their care. Records have to be kept up to date to ensure that information remains accurate. Good record keeping is important for a variety of reasons, as follows.

Allergies and food requirements

Most early years settings avoid serious incidents caused by food allergies by creating systems to prevent a child being given the wrong foods. It is usual for photographs of children to be put up in the kitchen to remind staff about which children have allergies or particular food requirements. Early years settings also work with parents to check on a regular basis that their child's food requirements are still accurate.

Provision of babies' bottles

Records are also kept regarding making up and giving babies bottles of feed. Checks have to be made to ensure that babies are given the correct formula as different babies will have different types of milk. After each feed, the amount taken by the baby is recorded and sent home so that parents know how much feed their child has had.

Food intake

It is important that information is shared about children's food intake, especially children who have diabetes, where it is important for everyone to know how much food has been taken. Parents and early years settings will also share information if older children have not eaten as well as usual.

Case study

Harry's mother has written a note to say that he did not want to eat his breakfast. Harry's key person reads this information and decides to offer Harry a snack earlier than usual. Harry eats this and also eats well at lunch. Harry's key person writes a note in the home book to let his mother know this.

1 Why was it important that Harry's mother shared information about Harry's food intake?
2 Why did the key person bring forward Harry's snack?
3 Why is it important that Harry's mother knows that he has eaten during the day?

AC 5.2 The role of the early years practitioner and individual dietary requirements

There are several ways in which an early years practitioner can meet children's individual dietary needs, depending on the setting in which they work.

Working with parents

The starting point for meeting children's individual dietary needs is to work with parents. As well as being good practice, this is also a legal requirement of the EYFS. Finding out about individual children's dietary needs and preferences is usually the role of the key person. This is because the key person has responsibility for working closely with the child and their parents. When children first come into the early years setting, the key person will record any dietary needs. Over time, this information will be updated.

Preparation of food

In most early years settings, early years practitioners prepare snacks for children. In some early years settings, practitioners will also plan and prepare meals. This is common in childminding settings and also where early years practitioners work as nannies. When early years practitioners are involved in the preparation of food, it is important that they check that each child is given the type of food that they need. When preparing food for children with allergies, early years practitioners should make sure that the food to which the children are allergic is not prepared at the same time or they should prepare their food in a separate part of the kitchen using different utensils to avoid any possibility of contamination.

Preparation of babies' feeds

Most early years settings that take babies will make up their feeds. When making up feeds, it is important for the correct feed to be given and in the correct quantity. The manufacturer's instructions should also be followed. In addition, good hygiene, including sterilisation procedures, should be followed.

Serving of food

In most early years settings, early years practitioners are involved in the serving of food to children. They have to check that each child is given the food that they need. In some settings, children with particular dietary needs have their foods served on certain coloured plates as a reminder for staff. While serving food to children, it is important that individual children are not made to feel different and so comments about their food differences need to be kept to a minimum. Wherever possible, food should also be served in ways that do not necessarily flag up that children have dietary differences.

In your setting

Do you serve any food to children in your setting? What steps are taken to ensure that children with dietary requirements are given the correct food?

Recording of food intake

As we saw earlier, an important role of the early years practitioner is to maintain records of food intake, especially for babies and for children with medical conditions such as diabetes. These records must then be shared with parents.

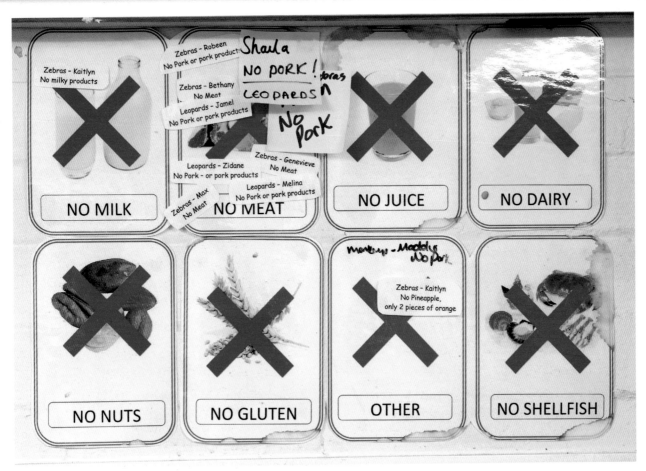

Figure 1.1.8 Staff should be aware of all the children's dietary requirements in the setting

AC 5.3 The benefits of working in partnership with parents/carers

It is important for everyone who works with children to develop a strong partnership with the child's parents. When it comes to the provision of food and drink, this is particularly important. By finding out about children's individual needs, we show parents that we care about their children and respect their wishes. For children with significant medical conditions or allergies, such as diabetes or a nut allergy, by working closely with parents we can reassure them that their child will be safe. This in turn will allow the child to benefit from the play and educational opportunities on offer. A good relationship with parents also enables information to be shared with the setting – for example, if the child has not eaten breakfast or is fussy about certain foods.

Referring parents

Another benefit of having a good relationship with parents is that they are more likely to talk to us about any difficulties that they are having around meal times. While early years professionals are not trained in nutrition and so cannot provide advice, they can signpost parents to other services or professionals who may be able to help.

LO6 Be able to support healthy eating in own setting

Do you tend to snack or do you eat properly at meal times? Ideally, you should aim to eat healthily when you are with children. In this section, we look at how you can support healthy eating in the setting where you work.

Figure 1.1.9 A good relationship with parents is essential for meeting children's needs

AC 6.1 Planning activities to support healthy eating

There are many activities that we can use with children to help them become interested in healthy eating. These activities link to the EYFS as there is an aspect called 'Health and self-care' within 'Physical development'. This aspect is about teaching children to stay healthy and includes healthy eating.

→ In Unit 3.1, we look at the steps involved in planning activities. You may find it useful to visit this section.

Table 1.1.4 shows some activities that are commonly used to help children become interested in healthy eating. It is important though when choosing activities to think about the age and stage of children to ensure that they can participate in them. A good example of this is cooking activities. There are some cooking activities that are easier than others. If you decide to cook with children, you

should first check whether any children have food allergies and also ensure that the food being cooked is healthy.

AC 6.2 Implementing activities to support healthy eating

Once you have planned the activity and have talked it through with your placement supervisor, the next step is to implement it. For cooking activities, you should first think about a risk assessment, which might include dangers associated with any cooking utensils or equipment, as well as hygiene steps that will need to be taken. It is also important to think carefully about the timing of activities as tired or overexcited children may not benefit from or enjoy the activities. During all activities, it is important to monitor children's reactions and to think about whether the activity is working. Table 1.1.5 shows some of the points to consider when implementing the activities that we looked at earlier.

Table 1.1.4 Activities to support healthy eating

Outing to a shop to buy fruit and vegetables	This allows children to see the different range of fruit and vegetables on offer and afterwards they can taste them.
Visit to a local farm or allotment	This allows children to see where food comes from.
Planting fruit and vegetables	This helps children to learn about growing fruit and vegetables and is a good way of encouraging them to try out new foods.
Making a fruit smoothie	This is a simple cooking activity that young children can help with.
Cutting up or mashing bananas and mixing with natural yoghurt	This is a simple cooking activity that does not require any special equipment and so is suitable for very young children.
Making a vegetable pizza	This activity can help children to try out new, healthy toppings, such as courgettes or sweetcorn. Pizza bases can be bought or made with the children.
Creating a salad	This is a simple activity which is good in warm weather. Children can choose different vegetables to put into their salad. They can wash tomatoes and lettuce, chop cheese into cubes or add spoonfuls of ready-chopped vegetables, such as cucumber.
Making bread	This is a good activity for introducing children to brown bread. It can be done by hand or with a bread maker.
Cooking simple dishes, e.g. baked potato, boiled eggs and toast	Making simple dishes is a good activity for older children who, under supervision, can make healthy light meals.

Table 1.1.5 Implementing activities to support healthy eating

Outing to a shop to buy fruit and vegetables	Talk to the children about the fruit and vegetables that they can see. Take time to see which fruit and vegetables children already know. With the children, choose some fruit and vegetables to buy and encourage them to try out new ones. Afterwards, with the children, wash, prepare and, if needed, cook the fruit and vegetables.
Visit to a local farm or allotment	Talk to children beforehand to find out what they already know about farms and/or the growing of food. Use this information to help you work out what points to draw children's attention to when you visit the farm or allotment. Take plenty of photographs so that afterwards children will be able to talk about food and farming.
Planting fruit and vegetables	Look out for some seeds or plants that will grow well and preferably quickly. Check that they are suitable for your setting. Make sure that the soil is properly prepared or, if you intend to use containers, that they drain well and are sufficiently large. Make sure that each child has their own plant or seeds but always plant some extra. Encourage children afterwards to take care of them by watering them. Encourage children to eat 'their produce'.
Cooking activities **Making a fruit smoothie** **Cutting up or mashing bananas and mixing with natural yoghurt** **Making a vegetable pizza** **Creating a salad** **Making bread** **Cooking simple dishes, e.g. baked potato, boiled eggs and toast**	Check that none of the children has a food allergy, intolerance or other dietary requirement that will prevent them from joining in. Show children how to wash their hands and put on aprons, and make sure that you role model this. For cooking activities to be successful, work in pairs or very small groups with children. Keep children active by making sure that they all have something to do most of the time. Talk to children about what they are doing and about healthy food.

AC 6.3 The practitioner's role in supporting healthy eating

There are several ways that we can support healthy eating when we are with children. One of the most important ways that adults can support healthy eating is by being a good role model. This means eating with children and showing that you enjoy healthy foods. Ideally, you should eat the same meals as them, but when this is not possible, children should see that you eat a balanced diet with plenty of fruit and vegetables. Children should not see you eat cake, chocolate or crisps as these foods are not suitable for children.

Attitudes

Children learn a lot about food from the attitudes of adults, including the things that are said about food. Ideally, children should learn that healthy food is something to enjoy rather than endure. It is therefore suggested that children are not told that they must eat up their main meal before having a dessert. The reason behind this is that children may learn that the main meal is 'boring' and that the part of the meal that is to be enjoyed is the pudding. Provided that the dessert or pudding is healthy – for example, fruit or yoghurt – there is no reason why children should not be offered it.

Involvement of children

Adults also have to think about how they help children to make choices about food and be involved in its preparation and serving. Meal times should be friendly and fun, so adults have to think about how they create a climate where this happens. Rules such as 'no talking' at meal times are therefore not appropriate, neither are situations where children are forced to eat foods when they have said that they are full.

> **Reflect** ?
>
> Write about how you support healthy eating in your own setting. Think about how well you role model healthy eating as well as how you support children to be involved at meal times.

AC 6.4 Recommendations for healthy eating in your setting

In this unit, we have looked at the many ways in which early years settings might encourage healthy eating. In this section, you need to think about whether your setting could benefit from any further information or use or develop current strategies to further promote healthy eating. To help you with this, here are some areas on which you might like to focus.

Using current information

Think about to what extent your setting is aware of current healthy eating guidelines and sources of information such as the Children's Food Trust or the Caroline Walker Trust.

Parents

Think about how often information about children's dietary needs and preferences is exchanged with parents. You might also like to think about how your setting helps parents to find about current guidelines for healthy eating.

Meal times

To what extent are the meals that are served helping children to eat healthily? Think about whether children have access to at least five portions of fruit and vegetables a day. Are children encouraged to self-serve and get involved in the preparation of meals?

Snacks

To what extent are snacks seen as being part of children's overall food intake? Are snacks healthy, i.e. nutrient-rich, low in salt and sugar?

Activities

To what extent are children involved in the preparation of food? Are cooking activities regularly planned that will help children to try out new foods?

Assessment

For this unit you will need to complete a variety of tasks. Some of these tasks will focus on whether you have acquired the knowledge needed to support your practice with children. In preparation for these you will need to do some research into the latest government guidelines in relation to children's nutrition, as well as the EYFS food and drink requirements and national and local initiatives. You need to make sure that you understand the way in which food and drink supports children's health and is also important for conception and pregnancy. The websites below may help you in this.

You will have to reread or research information linking to the nutritional value of food groups and children's nutritional requirements, including babies' and weaning.

You should also be sure that you know why it is important to meet children's individual needs and why practitioners should work closely with parents.

As well as showing that you have gained the necessary knowledge from this unit, you will also need to show that you are able to support healthy eating in your setting. You will need to think about an activity that you can plan and implement. You could use the suggestions on page 18.

A good tip is to try out your idea first and be ready to adapt it according to the responses that you gain from the children. You will also need to think about how more generally you could support healthy eating in your setting. You could use the information on pages 20 to help you with this.

Useful resources

'Eating well for under 5s in child care' by Dr Helen Crawley (2006) The Caroline Walker Trust: **www.cwt.org.uk/pdfs/Under5s.pdf**

Eat Better, Start Better resources available on the children's food trust website: **www.childrensfoodtrust.org.uk/pre-school/eat-better-start-better**

Start 4 life resources from the National Health Service: **www.nhs.uk/start4life**

Unit 1.2 WB Support healthy lifestyles for children through exercise

Do you remember playing on the swings or throwing a ball? You probably did not realise it at the time, but you were actually taking exercise! Exercise is good for us all, but it is particularly important in early childhood. In this unit, we look at how important it is for children to take exercise and also how we might help children to take exercise as part of their play and learning.

Learning outcomes

By the end of this unit, you will:

1 Understand children's need for exercise.
2 Be able to support children's exercise in indoor and outdoor spaces.

LO1 Understand children's need for exercise

AC 1.1 The benefits of exercise for children

There are many benefits of physical exercise and activity for young children. In this section, we look at the health benefits of exercise.

→ In Unit 3.11, we look at how physical development supports children's learning and specific physical skills. You may find it useful to read this unit alongside the present one.

Figure 1.2.1 shows the health benefits associated with exercise.

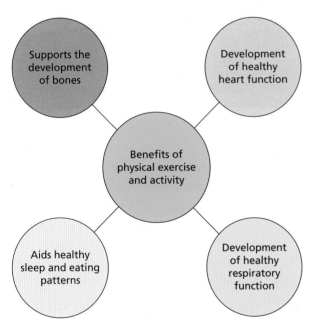

Figure 1.2.1 Benefits of physical exercise and activity

Development of healthy heart function

Children's hearts are still developing. Children need exercise in order that their heart grows and develops healthily. If children do not have sufficient exercise, they are more likely to develop heart disease in later childhood and into adulthood.

Development of healthy respiratory function

Children's lungs are still developing. Exercise helps to build healthy lungs and so builds children's stamina. Healthy lung function is important because our lungs provide oxygen to the body.

Aids healthy sleep and eating patterns

Children need exercise as part of a healthy lifestyle. When children take exercise, especially outdoors, they are more likely to feel tired at bedtime and also hungry at meal times.

Supports the development of bones

Physical exercise which involves running, walking or other weight-bearing movements helps build strong bones. This is important for later life and for children to grow.

> **Test yourself**
>
> Give five reasons why physical exercise is good for children.

AC 1.2 The outdoor access requirements of current frameworks

Spending time outdoors is a key way in which children can take exercise, especially as young children enjoy playing outdoors. In the EYFS, there is a clear requirement for children to spend time each day outdoors as part of the Safeguarding and Welfare requirements. While there is no direct requirement for schools to ensure outdoor access, in reality all schools have outdoor spaces for children at playtime and also for PE lessons.

The requirements of current frameworks for regular exercise for children

Both the EYFS and Key Stage 1 frameworks expect children to take exercise. In the EYFS, this is part of the area of learning and development called 'Physical development'. While the term 'exercise' is not used as such, it is implicit in the skills that children need to gain in order to achieve or work towards the early learning goal for this area of learning and development. The importance of physical development is reflected in the fact that it is one of the three **prime areas of learning and development**. Prime areas are ones that are considered to be a priority when planning for children's play and learning.

Figure 1.2.2 Physical activity has a wide range of benefits for children

In the National Curriculum at Key Stage 1, children are required to take regular exercise as it forms the subject area known as PE (physical exercise). By the end of Key Stage 1, children should have gained a range of skills such as running, jumping, throwing and catching. These are all associated with taking exercise.

> **Key term**
>
> **prime areas of learning and development**
> Areas of development which are seen by the EYFS as being a priority as they support children's later development.

AC 1.3 National and local children's exercise initiatives

There are some concerns that many children today are not taking sufficient physical exercise. It is thought that this is the reason why one in five children currently entering the reception year are overweight and also why increasing numbers of children are showing

early signs of heart disease at the end of their primary education. There are, therefore, several national initiatives in place. Some have been organised by the health service, others are organised by interested organisations. There are many factors to consider when evaluating how effective initiatives might be at encouraging children to take more exercise:

- Equipment: not all early years settings and schools have the equipment that they need to promote exercise. For initiatives to work well, they need to consider this.
- Space: some early years settings and schools have limited space. Initiatives have to be realistic when suggesting activities.
- Knowledge of adults: some adults have more skill than others when it comes to encouraging children to take exercise. Initiatives need to take this into consideration.
- Presentation of information: it is important that information about any initiatives is easy to find and also to understand. If

information is only available on the internet, early years settings and schools might not find out about it. Information also has to be attractively presented.

Table 1.2.1 shows some of the initiatives that are available at the time of writing.

Reflect ?

Choose one of the organisations from Table 1.2.1 or another national initiative that you know about and find out how they work to promote exercise in children. Consider how effective their work might be.

Local initiatives

Local authorities and primary care trusts also provide local initiatives for children and their families. Many local initiatives are targeted at helping the whole family take exercise as there is a concern that many adults are not doing sufficient physical activity. There is research to suggest that children are more likely to develop positive attitudes towards exercise if their parents take regular exercise.

Figure 1.2.3 Throwing is one of the skills that children should have gained by the end of Key Stage 1

Table 1.2.1 Current initiatives that promote exercise

Start Active, Stay Active www.gov.uk/government/publications/start-active-stay-active-a-report-on-physical-activity-from-the-four-home-countries-chief-medical-officers	This is a report by the Chief Medical Officer that looks at the importance of physical activity and sets national guidelines for physical activity for babies and children as well as adults.
Change4life	This is a National Health Service initiative aimed at all adults as well as children and their families. The comprehensive website provides advice as well as ideas for activities to help children and their families keep fit.
Live Well www.nhs.uk/livewell	Live Well is a part of the NHS website. It provides advice about exercise for children and also has downloadable resources and guidelines about exercise for young children.
Sport England www.sportengland.org	Sport England aims to encourage more children and adults to take up sport. As part of their work, they provide funding and advice to schools.
Play England www.playengland.org.uk	This organisation campaigns for better play opportunities for all children. As part of their work, they organise projects such as 'street play', which encourages communities to create safe places where children can play outdoors in the street.

Figure 1.2.4 Young children need plenty of opportunities to be outdoors and active

Research it!

Find out what initiatives are available in your local area. Try visiting your local leisure centre to see what is available, as well as visiting your local council's website.

Reflect

Choose at least one local initiative to evaluate. Consider how effective it might be at promoting exercise to children.

AC 1.4 The benefits of working with parents/carers

As we will see in Unit 1.5, it is important for everyone working with children to work closely with their parents/carers. In terms of supporting children's exercise, it is important to work with parents and carers for several reasons. Parents and carers will know whether there are any medical conditions or disabilities that might affect children's ability to join in any activities. They can also talk to their child's key person about what skills and interests the child has at home when it comes to physical activity. Equally, early years settings can provide information to parents about the importance of exercise and individual children's interests and skill levels. There are many ways in which settings might provide this type of information, as Table 1.2.2 on the next page shows.

LO2 Be able to support children's exercise in an indoor and outdoor space

Do you remember playing chase or having fun on an obstacle course? While children enjoy playing by themselves and so exercising, they also benefit from activities organised by adults.

Table 1.2.2 Providing information about exercise

Displays of information	Some early years settings put up displays that provide information about the importance of exercise and how it contributes to children's learning and development.
Leaflets	It is common to see early years settings displaying leaflets or notices that provide information about local facilities and opportunities for exercise.
Sharing information about individual children	In early years settings, it is usual for a child's key person and parents to talk together about the child's development. As part of these regular discussions, early years settings explain to parents the value of exercise and also the types of activities that children enjoy.
Photographs and film clips	To help parents understand their children's level of skill and interests, many key persons will show film clips and photographs. They may also use these to give parents ideas of what they might be able to do with their child at home.

In this section, we look at the types of activities that you can plan for children, both indoors and outdoors.

➡ As exercise and physical development are interlinked, you might also like to read this section alongside Unit 3.11, where further ideas for activities can be found.

AC 2.1 Planning activities for exercise both indoors and outdoors

When planning an activity, the starting point is the children's age and stage of development and also their interests.

➡ On page 317 in Unit 3.11, there is detailed information about children's usual patterns of physical development, which should help you to plan activities accurately.

Stamina

While vigorous activity is good for children, it is important to plan activities that allow children to rest from time to time. This is needed because children's patterns of exercise are different from adults'. While adults are capable of sustained exercise, children tend to take exercise in bursts. One minute a two-year-old may run ahead; two minutes later the same child will want to be carried, before wanting to run again. This 'off–on' approach to exercise is important to accept and should be built into the way that you plan activities.

> **In your setting**
>
> Observe a child aged two to five years playing outdoors for 30 minutes. Note how much of their time is spent resting and how much time is spent engaged in vigorous physical activity. How does this link to the earlier information about children's stamina?

Participation

Young children are active and also impulsive. This is particularly important to remember when working with children under three years old. It means that a long instruction or waiting a while before taking part in a game or activity is unlikely to work well. Most early years settings therefore work with pairs or small groups of children at a time.

Risk assessment

As part of your plans, you should think about how to keep children safe. This is done by thinking about any potential risks or hazards involved in the activity.

➡ In Unit 2.3, we look at this in more detail.

The most common risks involved in exercise are children falling over, colliding with each other or falling off equipment. When activities involve throwing, you should also recognise that young children's ability to aim or be aware of others is limited.

Table 1.2.3 shows some examples of activities that encourage exercise indoors and outdoors, although you might decide to choose one of the activities from Unit 3.11.

Figure 1.2.5 An activity to support children's exercise can be as simple as helping a child to walk along a raised surface

Case study

Ronya, a learner on placement, has decided that the two year olds that she works with would benefit from an obstacle course. She takes a lot of different equipment out of the shed outdoors and makes an obstacle course. She creates a ramp out of pieces of wood and bridges by putting wooden planks onto car tyres. She does this without looking at the state of the equipment or thinking about the children's stage of physical development. She does not take time to check that the pieces of wood that she has put onto some car tyres are stable. The children are very excited when they see it. One child clambers onto the wooden plank, but it falls off as the wood slips off from the tyre. Another child gets a splinter from one of the other wooden planks as it is not in a good condition.

1 Explain the importance of risk assessment when planning physical activities.
2 Why is it important to think about children's stage of development when planning physical activities?
3 Explain what Ronya should have done differently.

Table 1.2.3 Activities that encourage exercise

Indoors	Outdoors
Parachute games	Games such as 'What's the time, Mr Wolf?'
Dancing to music	Obstacle courses
Games such as musical chairs or musical statues	'Throw the wellington'
Obstacle courses	Kicking balls into a net
Indoor skittles	Tricycle and wheeled-toy circuit

AC 2.2 Implementing activities to support exercise in indoor and outdoor spaces

When implementing an activity that involves children exercising, there is a range of factors to consider before and during the activity. Here are some tips that might be helpful when implementing the activity.

Resources

Consider whether you have sufficient resources to hand and try to avoid situations where children become bored because they are waiting.

Safety

You should constantly be thinking about safety. This is because exercise usually involves movements and children might collide, fall over or throw something in a dangerous way. You should assess the risks of the activity beforehand and then be alert to any possible dangers during the activity

Monitoring children's health

During all exercise, you should monitor the children's reactions and skin colour carefully. You should know beforehand which children have medical conditions, such as asthma – you should have found out about their symptoms from parents or the child's key person and what you should do if they show any of these symptoms. Being aware of children during exercise is particularly important outdoors – children may become cold during winter or overheated in the summer. By looking at children's reactions and skin colour, you should be able to detect whether children need a break.

> **In your setting**
>
> Are there any children in your setting that have medical conditions that might affect the way they can take exercise?

Supervising children

During exercise, children are likely to feel good. This can lead them to become overconfident or overexcited. You should keep an eye out for children who are becoming overexcited or are starting to take risks. It is therefore worth adapting the activity to ensure that children have time to calm down or so you can intervene to remind older children of possible risks.

Supporting children

As well as supervising children, you should also look for opportunities to support children to learn skills or encourage them to try out new things. Some children need more help or time than others and so it is important for us to think about individual children's needs.

> **In practice**
>
> Write about how you implemented an activity indoors and also one outdoors. Write about the factors you thought about when implementing the activity. Were there any children who needed additional support or encouragement?

AC 2.3 Reflecting on activities

It is important to reflect on our work with children, particularly during or after an activity. This helps us to think about how we can further help individual children, but it also helps us to learn how to plan and implement more effective activities.

> **Tips when reflecting on an activity**
>
> You should consider the following points when reflecting on your activity. These apply to both indoor and outdoor activities:
>
> - Did each child participate in the activity?
> - What did each child gain from the activity?
> - Did any children need significant support during the activity?
> - Was the activity sufficiently challenging?
> - Was the activity sufficiently interesting and enjoyable for each child?
> - How good was your preparation for the activity?
> - Were there any issues that you had not considered?
> - How did you monitor children's safety?

Figure 1.2.6 During activities, it is important to monitor children at all times

AC 2.4 Providing inclusive indoor and outdoor provision in your own setting

Taking exercise is essential for all children and so looking for ways to help all children participate in some way is important. An inclusive provision is one in which there is plenty of choice for children so that every child has the opportunity to take some type of exercise. An inclusive provision also looks to reduce or remove barriers that might prevent children from being able to join in. In the case of children who have disabilities, this might mean working with other professionals, such as the sensory impairment team, to find out how best to support a child with sight problems. In some cases, it might also mean that specific equipment, such as a specially designed swing, should be found to help a child take exercise.

In early years settings that have babies and toddlers alongside older children, an inclusive provision is also one that is mindful about meeting the youngest children's exercise needs. It might be that, in the garden, an area is created which encourages babies to pull themselves to stand or sit. Ride-on toys may also be on offer for toddlers who are not yet ready for tricycles.

Finally, in addition, an inclusive provision considers whether some children are being put off from participating by the attitudes and actions of other children – for example, an older child might take a ball away from a younger one, saying that balls are only for big children.

You may like to consider the following points when evaluating your own setting's provision and making recommendations:

- What range of equipment is available for different age ranges, both indoors and outdoors?
- How much time is available for children to take part in physical exercise?

- How do staff ensure that all children are able to participate in planned activities?
- Do you liaise with other professionals in order to meet individual children's needs?
- Do you monitor children's participation in physical exercise?

In practice

Write about how your setting works to create an inclusive provision. Write about which aspects work well and also where you think improvements or further developments could be made.

Assessment

For this unit you will need to complete a variety of tasks. Some of these tasks will focus on whether you have acquired the knowledge needed to support your practice with children. In preparation for assessment you will need to begin by finding out about the latest guidelines and initiatives for children's exercise. You also need to know about the benefits that children gain from taking exercise. A good starting point for finding out more about exercise is the National Health Service (**www.nhs.gov.uk**) website and also the British Heart Foundation website (**www.bhf.org.uk**).

To find out more about local initiatives consider visiting your local sports or leisure centre and also library. You could also look at websites run by your local authority, city or town. You also need to be able to explain the importance of working in partnership with parents and the benefits that this brings. As well are revising the information in this book, you could also talk to your placement supervisor or manager about what they think the benefits are.

As well as showing that you have gained the necessary knowledge for this unit, you will need to show that you are able to support children during exercise both indoors and outdoors. Your assessor will want to see that you can plan, implement and reflect on at least two activities, both indoors and outdoors. You should begin by thinking carefully about what physical activities would be suitable for the age of children you are working with. You should also think about what children are interested in as well as the type of equipment and resources that are available. You should also talk to your placement supervisor as they may give you advice and ideas. It is a good idea to give your activity a trial run so that you are confident when your assessor observes you. This will also allow you to practice your skills of reflection.

Finally, you should take time to think about your setting's approach to encouraging physical exercise. To do this you will need to revise the information within the unit and relate it to your setting

Useful resources

Books

Cooper, L. and Doherty, J., (2010) *Physical Development (Supporting Development in the Early Years Foundation Stage)*, Continuum

Hughes, B. (1996a), *Play Environments: A question of quality*. PLAYLINK.

Meggitt, C. (2012), *An Illustrated Guide to Child Development* (3rd edn). Oxford: Heinemann.

Pound, L., (2013) *Quick Guides for Early Years: Physical Development* Hodder Education

UK Physical guidelines for early years **www.bhfactive. org.uk/userfiles/Documents/guidelineswalkers.pdf**

Organisations for the UK

JABADAO

A national charity that works in partnership with the education, health, arts and social care sectors to bring about a change in the way people work with the body and movement: **www.jabadao.org**

British Heart Foundation National Centre (BHFNC)

The BHF publishes the UK Physical Activity Guidelines for Early Years: **www.bhfactive.org.uk**

Organisations for England

Learning, Playing and Interacting: Good practice in the Early Years Foundation Stage

A toolkit to support early years practitioners' work with advice on pedagogy, practice and assessment: **www. nationalstrategies.standards.dcsf.gov.uk/ earlyyears**

Start4Life and Play4Life (Department of Health)

The early years section of the Department of Health's (DH) Change4Life campaign, aimed at health care and childcare professionals. Active play resources are available which can be downloaded from **www.dh.gov.uk** (search Start4Life).

Play England
www.playengland.org.uk

Unit 1.3 WB Support physical care routines for children

Do you remember needing help to wash your hands or clean your teeth? There are many different physical care routines that take place in early years settings. In this unit, we look at the different physical care needs of children at different ages, including sleep and rest, as well as the importance of taking steps to prevent the spread of infection. We also look at the role of childhood immunisation in preventing infection as well as how to help children learn the skills to care for themselves.

Learning outcomes

By the end of this unit, you will:

1 Understand the physical care needs of children.
2 Be able to use hygienic practice to minimise the spread of infection.
3 Understand rest and sleep needs of children.
4 Understand childhood immunisation.
5 Be able to support children in personal physical care routines.

LO1 Understand the physical care needs of children

Have you ever watched a two year old clean their teeth? The chances are that you will have seen them eating the toothpaste off the brush rather than actually doing any brushing! Young children need adults to support their physical care and in this section we look at how adults do this and why it is important to work with parents.

AC 1.1 The role of the early years practitioner in physical care

Physical care routines keep children healthy. They also prevent infection and so they are an important part of what happens in early years settings. It is good practice for physical care routines to be seen as learning opportunities rather than just activities in themselves. In LO5, we look at some examples of how this might be done. It is also important that, wherever possible, children are encouraged to be involved in their own care so that, over time, they can learn the skills to become independent.

Nappy changing

Nappy changing is essential in order to prevent babies and toddlers from developing skin infections. It has to be done in a hygienic way so as to prevent the spread of bacteria and viruses. This means that all early years settings should provide disposable aprons and gloves. These should always be worn. Nappies should always be placed in a designated bin and the adult should always wash their hands before and afterwards. Many settings change babies and toddlers on a raised surface, so the adult must never leave the child unattended in case they fall.

Adults also have to make the experience as pleasant for children as possible. This can be done by talking to the child, giving the child

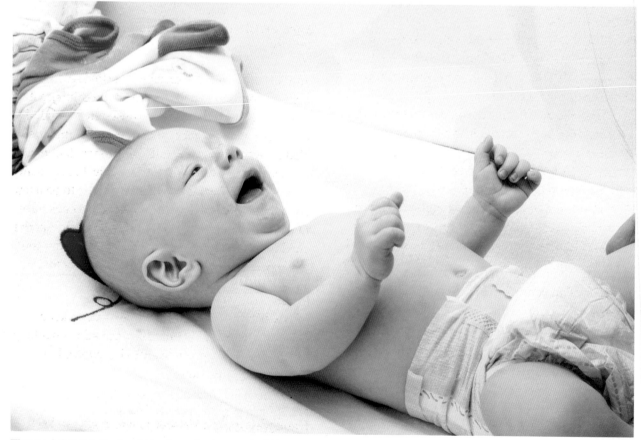

Figure 1.3.1 Adults should try to make nappy changing as enjoyable for the child as possible

something to play with or look at and involving the child before and afterwards.

Nappy changing is a skill that is best learnt by watching someone else before attempting it yourself. One of the hardest parts is remembering to talk to the baby or child at the same time. Here are some of the key steps in the nappy-changing process.

Steps in nappy changing

1 Clean the changing mat.
2 Check that everything is to hand and that you know which products are suitable for the child.
3 Talk to the child and either carry or lead them to the changing table.
4 Wash hands and put on disposable gloves and apron.
5 Remove/undo the child's clothing and move them so that they will be away from the soiled nappy.
6 Remove soiled nappy and fold it in on itself. If the bin is in reach, put it in the bin immediately; otherwise put the nappy out of reach of the child.
7 Clean the genital area thoroughly by using either baby wipes or cotton wool dipped in water. Make sure that wiping takes place from front to back when changing a girl.
8 When the area is dry, put on barrier cream if parents have requested it and then put on the clean nappy.
9 Re-clothe the child and take them from the changing mat to a place of safety.
10 Clean the changing mat thoroughly. Remove and dispose of gloves and aprons.
11 Wash hands and, if appropriate, make a record of the time of the nappy change along with any comments, e.g. early signs of nappy rash.

Toilet training

There is no exact age when children are ready to move from nappies to using a potty or toilet. Each child is different, although most children are clean and dry by three years. The skill of the adult is to work with parents to recognise when the child is ready. The signs of a child being ready are mainly physical as the bladder has to be sufficiently mature.

If children are trained before they are ready, there is a danger that they will become frustrated or upset and overall the process will take longer. Figure 1.3.2 shows the signs of children being ready to move out of nappies.

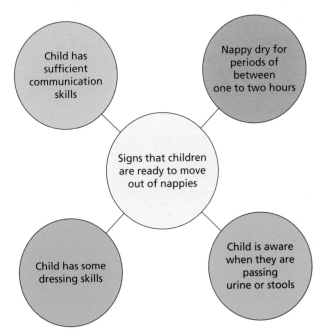

Figure 1.3.2 Signs that children are ready to move out of nappies

The role of the adult is to show the child where the potty or toilet is and then to let the child use it independently. If children are constantly reminded to go, they may not pick up on the signals that their bladder sends when it is full. This can result in more accidents. It is also important for adults to stay calm because, at the beginning, there are likely to be a few accidents. Parents and early years practitioners have to work together. They need to agree on whether the child is ready to be toilet trained and then, after the first day, talk about how well the child is coping.

Washing and bath time

Most early years settings will only need to keep children's faces and hands clean, but adults working in home-based care are likely to be involved in washing and bath time.

Hand and face washing

Hand washing is a key way in which we can keep children free from infection. It is important that children's hands are thoroughly washed throughout the day but particularly:

- before eating or touching food
- after going to the toilet
- after playing outdoors
- after touching animals
- after blowing their nose
- after playing with sensory materials.

As with nappy changing, it is useful to learn from others how to help children when washing their hands and faces.

Wash a face by using a soft cloth. It is important to make face wiping as pleasant as possible. Always tell children what you are about to do and never wipe a baby's or child's face from behind. Try using downward strokes and as soon as possible encourage children to wipe their own faces. If possible, make a game out of it.

Wash hands by checking the water temperature first and interlink your hands and the child's. You should use warm water and soap. Afterwards always rinse and dry children's hands thoroughly.

Shower time and bath time

The role of the adult will be first to talk to parents about their preferences and how they usually bathe their child. This is important as some parents do this in the morning, others in the evening. As we will see in AC 1.3, it is also important to find out from parents what types of products they use and also whether they have developed any routines so that we can continue them – for example, the child always pulls the plug out of the bath.

When adults are responsible for washing and bath time, one of their roles is to keep children safe. There are three immediate risks during washing and bath time, as follows.

Danger of scalding

This can be prevented by checking the temperature of the water before children enter the shower or the bath. It is good practice to fill the bath with

some cold water before adding any hot water so that if the child slips or decides to get in, there is no danger of scalding. When children are in showers, it is important to supervise them carefully to prevent them from playing with the knobs that control the temperature.

Danger of drowning

Children can drown in very small amounts of water. Although there is a risk of children drowning in a shower, this risk is greater in a bath. It is essential that children are actively supervised when they are in the shower or the bathroom.

Falls

If water gets onto the floor, children are in danger of slipping and falling. Adults therefore should have cloths to hand to wipe up any spills.

Care of skin

Caring for children's skin is important as it acts as an important barrier to prevent infection from entering the body. As well as hand washing and washing of faces, it is important to protect skin from the sun as this can cause long-term damage to the skin. At the time of writing, it is advised that babies and young children have only limited exposure to sunlight of around ten minutes. The rest of the time, they need to be kept out of strong sunshine. This means that either their skin should be kept covered or suncream should be applied. As with all skin care, parents need to agree to the application of suncream and, in most early years settings, they will be responsible for supplying it.

Research it!

There are some concerns that children are lacking in vitamin D because of lack of exposure to sunlight. Find out what the current recommendations are for exposure to sunlight on the NHS website in the Live Well section under the topic 'Summer health', at: www.nhs.uk/Livewell/Summerhealth/Pages/vitamin-D-sunlight.aspx.

Care of teeth

There are two key factors that affect the health of children's teeth: diet and cleaning. This means that adults in early years settings must think about the food that they provide and check that it will not, or is not likely to, cause tooth decay. Foods and drinks that are high in sugar are therefore not suitable. As well as foods and drinks high in sugar, the way that food is served can also make a difference. Ideally, children's teeth need a complete rest between meals and snacks. While water is fine for children to keep sipping, fruit juices or squashes are not because they contain acid, which causes decay if the teeth are repeatedly exposed to them. The second way in which dental decay is prevented is through regular brushing, twice a day. Most parents will be responsible for the brushing of their children's teeth, but in home-based care and also in settings that provide breakfast, adults will need to clean children's teeth. It is thought that children are not ready to thoroughly clean their own teeth until they are between six and nine years old. So, while children may want to have a go at brushing, an adult will always have to take over.

1 Find out from parents what type of toothpaste to use.
2 Get the child to sit comfortably in a position where their head can tilt back.
3 For children under three, put a smear of toothpaste onto the brush, but for children aged three to six a little more can be used, but no more than a pea-sized amount.
4 Start on one side of the mouth and methodically and gently brush all the teeth.
5 Make sure that you are brushing away from the gum line so as not to push any bacteria into the gums.
6 Once you have brushed, encourage the child to spit out any excess toothpaste.
7 Allow children to have a go at brushing either before you start or afterwards.

Care of hair

Most early years settings will not have responsibility for the care of children's hair unless they offer home-based care, e.g. childminders or nannies. In LO5, we look at how you might help children with their hair. While many early years settings will not be responsible for combing and styling children's hair, they are likely to keep an eye out for head lice. Head lice are parasites that live on the scalp and draw blood from the scalp. They are very common in early years settings where they spread very easily because children are often in close contact with each other. As head lice can move onto adults' hair, it is important for you to check your own hair regularly and tie it back if it is long.

Signs of a head lice infestation include:

● itchiness of the scalp
● white flecks on strands of hair which do not move if touched – these are the empty egg cases, often called 'nits'
● scabs or blood spots on the scalp where the head lice have bitten
● sight of a head louse.

The nits in hair are often easier to spot than the head lice.

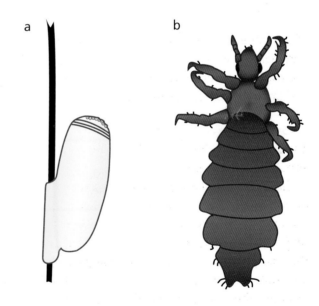

Figure 1.3.3 (a) a nit; (b) a head louse

What should happen if a child has head lice?

If an adult suspects that a child has a case of head lice, they should inform the parents. There are several ways of treating head lice and it will be the parents' responsibility to do this. Early years settings will also put up a sign warning parents to look out for signs of head lice in their children.

Meal times

The role of the adult at meal times is to ensure that children are given food that is nutritious and to ensure that meal times are enjoyable. We looked at meal and snack times in Unit 1.1 and you should revisit this unit. The adult may also have to help children in a range of ways, by:

- encouraging children to try new tastes
- encouraging children to serve themselves
- providing children with bowls, beakers and cutlery that will help them to feed themselves
- encouraging children to use cutlery and to feed themselves
- supervising children in case of a reaction to food or choking
- cutting some foods into smaller sizes in order to allow children to manage.

AC 1.2 Situations that require non-routine physical care

There may be times when children have additional needs, including medical conditions, that may require non-routine physical care.

> **Key term**
>
> **emollient cream** A product that moisturises skin and is used in the treatment of eczema.

AC 1.3 Working in partnership with parents/carers

It is essential for early years settings to work closely with parents to ensure that individual children's care needs are met. This is a requirement of the EYFS and is normally the responsibility of the key person. It is good practice before children start at a setting to find out about individual children's care needs and discuss these with parents.

Allergies

Young children have sensitive skin and so talking to parents is important when using products such as soap, shower gel or creams when nappy changing or washing. In the same way that children can have an allergic reaction to personal care products, as we saw in Unit 1.1 they can also have allergies to foods. This means that it is important to listen and act on information that parents share with us about their children's needs.

Preferences

Some parents will have preferences about the types of products that are used. They may, for example, want their children only to have products made by a certain manufacturer. It is usual for parents to bring in products that they want their children to be given.

Cultural and religious reasons

You may also find that parents want their children cared for in certain ways based on cultural or

Table 1.3.1 Situations in which non-routine physical care is required

Blowing noses	When children have colds, they will need their nose to be wiped. It is important to help children learn to blow their own nose. To prevent infection, disposable tissues should be used and hands should be washed.
Emollient cream	Some children who have eczema may need adults to put emollient cream on their hands and/or their bodies to keep their skin moisturised.
Nappy changing for older children	While most children are not in nappies after the age of three years, some children who have medical conditions or disabilities may still need to be in nappies. When older children are in nappies, additional washing is likely to be required.
Feeding	While most children can feed themselves, some children with complex medical needs may need to be fed by an adult.
Changing and washing children after toileting accidents	When children are being toilet trained and, for some time afterwards, adults may need to change and wash them if they have wet or soiled themselves.

Figure 1.3.4 A good relationship with parents/carers is vital when caring for children

religious reasons. It is not uncommon for families to shower rather than to bathe or to do all washing under running water.

LO2 Be able to use hygienic practice to minimise the spread of infection

Have you noticed that staff in your setting tend to wear disposable gloves? This is one of the many important methods used to prevent the spread of infection. In this section, we look at how to ensure that your practice is hygienic in a range of different situations.

AC 2.1 Using hygienic practice

Hand washing

As we have already seen earlier, hand washing is a key way to prevent infection from spreading. Many bacteria, germs and fungi thrive on our hands and are also passed across onto others' hands, toys, surfaces and food. Hand washing is therefore seen as one of the most important ways of preventing infection from spreading. Good hand washing will also prevent you from becoming ill.

There are many situations in which you should wash and dry your hands, even if you are in a hurry or if they look clean. We have already looked at when children should wash their hands.

➔ For more on when children should wash their hands, see page 36.

Adults should also wash their hands after changing nappies and before handling food. As we will see when looking at food hygiene, you should also wash your hands at certain times during the food preparation process.

The step-by-step diagram in Figure 1.3.5 shows you how to wash your hands thoroughly using hot water and soap.

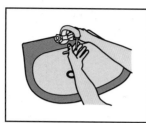

1 Wet hands with water

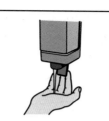

2 Apply enough soap to cover all hand surfaces

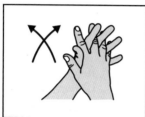

3 Rub hands palm to palm

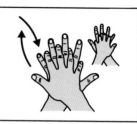

4 Right palm over back of left hand with interlaced fingers and vice versa

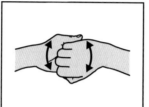

5 Palm to palm with fingers interlaced

6 Backs of fingers to opposing palms with fingers interlocked

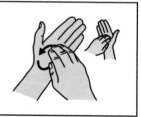

7 Rotational rubbing of left thumb clasped in right palm and vice versa

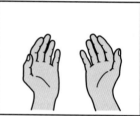

8 Rotational rubbing, backwards and forwards with clasped fingers of right hand in left palm and vice versa

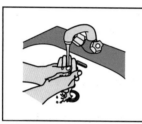

9 Rinse hands with water

10 Dry hands thoroughly with a single-use towel

11 Use towel to turn off tap

12 Your hands are now safe

Figure 1.3.5 It is important to know how to wash your hands thoroughly when working with children

In practice

Keep a record during a session of when and why you washed your hands. Explain what the consequences of not washing your hands might be.

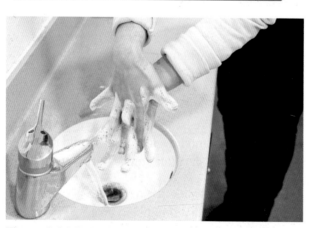

Figure 1.3.6 Hand washing reduces the risk of infection spreading

Food hygiene

Good food hygiene can reduce the possibility of food poisoning. Food poisoning can be very dangerous for babies and young children. If you are preparing or serving food, your employer should show you how to do this hygienically or send you on a food hygiene course. There are many different aspects to good food hygiene.

→ Food safety is also discussed in Unit 2.3, page 113.

Hand washing

As we have already seen, bacteria and viruses can thrive on hands and so in theory can contaminate food. This is why you should always wash your hands before preparing or serving food. In addition, you should wash your hands after you have touched any raw meat, poultry or fish during the cooking process, as well as when your hands become dirty.

Apron on, hair back

It is important that an apron is worn when cooking and that hair is tied back. This is another way of preventing infection from spreading.

Covering cuts

If you have any cuts on your hands, these have to be covered up with a plaster. Blue plasters are usually used in kitchens where food is prepared for children.

Clean surfaces

Throughout the food preparation process, you should keep the surfaces clean. You should also use separate chopping boards and dishes for raw meat, poultry and fish.

Storage of food

You should always store food according to the manufacturer's instructions. Instructions will include when food should be thrown away after being opened as well as best-before dates. For food that needs refrigerating or freezing, it is important to check the temperature of the fridge or freezer. One of the most important things when refrigerating food is to make sure that food that has already been cooked or that will be eaten uncooked is kept away from raw meat, poultry and fish. This is because raw meat, fish and poultry contain bacteria. It is also important to wrap foods to prevent them from becoming contaminated with raw foods.

Reheating food

Most early years settings do not reheat food because there is a higher danger of food poisoning, unless they are using ready meals. If food is reheated, it should be reheated only once. It should be reheated until it is clearly piping hot and is actually being cooked.

Washing fruit and vegetables

Fruit and vegetables should always be washed, and in some cases peeled, before being given to children.

Cooking meat, fish, poultry and eggs thoroughly

Meat, fish, poultry, especially chicken, and eggs all have to be cooked thoroughly. This is because they are naturally high in bacteria. Due to this, it is also important that special care is taken during storage and preparation to keep them away from other foods.

Research it!

Find out about good food hygiene by reading the Food Standards Agency booklet 'Safer food, better business for childminders' at: http://food.gov.uk.

Formula feed

Formula feed is milk that is given to babies instead of breast milk. There are different types of formula feed – powdered milk, which is made up with boiling water, and formula feed that comes ready-made. It is important that formula feed is prepared hygienically. This is because if the milk, the bottle or the teat is contaminated, the bacteria will be swallowed by the baby. As babies' immune systems are still developing, this can cause them to become very ill.

To prevent the risk of food poisoning, there has been a significant change in the approach used to make up powdered formula feed. Whereas previously several bottles were made up in advance, today it is recommended that no formula feed made from powdered milk should be made up ahead of time.

To ensure that formula feed is made up hygienically, you should always follow the manufacturer's instructions. These include the need to wash hands thoroughly at the start of the process and ensuring that all equipment, including teats and bottles, has been thoroughly sterilised.

Research it!

Find out the latest guidelines in relation to preparing powdered formula feed by visiting www.nhs.uk/Conditions/pregnancy-and-baby/pages/making-up-infant-formula.aspx.

In practice

Prepare a step-by-step poster showing how formula feed should be prepared hygienically. You could illustrate your poster with photographs or pictures.

Dealing with spillages safely

It is important that any spillages, including toileting accidents or where a child has been sick, are dealt with hygienically to prevent the spread of germs. Here is a step-by-step guide for dealing with spillages safely:

1   Remove any children from the area.
2   Put on disposable gloves and an apron.
3   Get appropriate cleaning products to disinfect the area as well as some paper towels and a plastic bag.
4   Use the paper towels to mop up any liquid or to scoop any solids. Put the soiled paper towels into the plastic bag as you go.
5   Once the floor has been partially cleaned, put some disinfectant onto a paper towel or disposable cloth and wipe up the area.
6   Put the cloth or paper towels in the plastic bag.
7   Dry the area with the paper towels.
8   Throw away the plastic bag in the appropriate waste bin.
9   Remove apron and gloves and throw these away.
10 Afterwards, wash hands thoroughly.

Safe disposal of waste

Early years settings other than childminders and nannies are required to dispose of bodily waste separately. This means that there are separate bins both indoors and outdoors for items such as nappies, soiled paper towels and anything that has been in contact with blood, faeces, vomit or urine. These bins are often yellow or are distinguished from ordinary waste paper bins. They will have lids on them, again to prevent the spread of infection. If you work in a setting where waste is disposed of in separate bins, you must use them, as this will be part of the setting's health and safety policy.

In home-based settings, it is good practice to use separate bins for items of bodily waste. These should have lids on them and be emptied regularly, with the contents being moved to an outdoor bin in a secure area.

You should never let children play with waste bins, even though they might be interested in them.

In your setting

What system is in place in your setting to dispose of waste?

Using correct personal protective equipment

There is a range of items that early years settings use to protect children and adults from disease and infections. Under the Health and Safety Act of 1974, you have a duty to use them if they are provided. The two items that you are most likely to use are disposable gloves and disposable aprons. These should be used every time you change a nappy or come into contact with blood – for example, from a cut or vomit. You should also use these items to clean toilets and any spillages involving urine, faeces or vomit. Afterwards, you should always remove the gloves and the apron immediately – do not walk around with them on. You should also wash your hands as this will give you added protection.

In practice

Write about when you use protective equipment in your setting to prevent the spread of infection.

Cleaning and sterilisation processes

All settings have to be kept clean. This is a requirement of the EYFS as it ensures the safety of the children as well as the staff.

Cleaning

Who does the general cleaning depends very much on the setting. In many large group care settings, a caretaker or cleaner will come and clean at the end of the day. In other settings, including smaller group care and home-based care, it may be the responsibility of the adults.

In addition to general cleaning, which includes mopping floors and vacuuming carpets, most adults during the session will also need to maintain the cleanliness of areas, including toilets, the kitchen and the tables where the children eat. Table 1.3.2 shows what is usually cleaned in early years settings.

Sterilisation

Sterilisation is a process by which bacteria, viruses and germs are removed from items. There are several methods of sterilising: exposing objects to high temperatures or soaking them in a chemical mixture. Sterilisation is usually used for items that babies use for feeding or with items that they play with. Figure 1.3.7 shows which items are usually associated with sterilising.

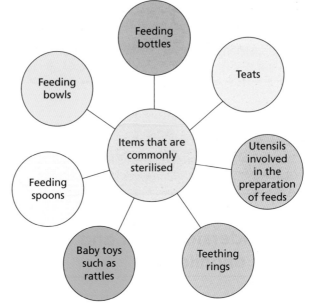

Figure 1.3.7 Items that are commonly sterilised

Table 1.3.2 Cleaning in early years settings

What?	When and how is it cleaned?
Basins and taps	Daily and when needed.
Toilets	Cleaned thoroughly each day and immediately after any accident. Disinfectant should be used.
Nappy changing mats	Wiped down with disinfectant after each use.
Bins	Emptied daily and washed out. Bins should be lined to prevent spread of infection.
Carpets	Daily.
Floors	Daily with hot water and detergent. Disinfectant to be used if there has been a toileting accident or sickness.
Tables and chairs	Daily with disposable cloths.
Bedding	Every few days or immediately if soiled. Machine washed at a minimum of 60°C.
Soft toys	Weekly. Should be machine washed at 60°C.
Plastic toys	Should be cleaned weekly with a weak solution of bleach. Should be sterilised if used with young babies.
Water trays/containers	Water changed after use. Tray should be dried to prevent mould if not in use.
Water toys	Washed with a weak solution of bleach from time to time. Should always be dried when not in use to prevent mould.
Sand tray indoors	Should be changed regularly. Tray should be washed and dried when sand changed.
Sand outdoors	Raked daily. Should be kept covered when not in use.
Play dough	Should be frequently changed. Children should wash hands before and after use.

LO3 Understand rest and sleep needs of children

Have you seen a young child who is irritable and clearly tired? Sleep and rest are important for children's overall health. In this section, we look at the difference between sleep and rest and also the need for sleep and rest for children at different ages.

AC 3.1 The rest and sleep needs of children at different ages

Rest and sleep are two different things. Rest is about times when the body can relax and stay fairly still but the brain remains active and continues to concentrate on what is happening. Sleep, on the other hand, allows both the body to rest and the brain to change its pattern of activity. Another key difference is that, during sleep, the body produces hormones that are responsible for a variety of functions, especially growth. Over the past few years, there have been concerns that some children are not sleeping sufficiently. Figure 1.3.8 shows the impact on children's development if they are not sleeping sufficiently.

Children's need for sleep

How much sleep children need varies between individual children. A good indicator that babies and children need more sleep is their mood. Babies and children are more likely to be irritable, impulsive and find it hard to concentrate when

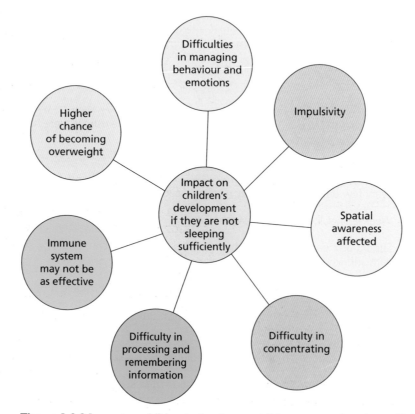

Figure 1.3.8 Impact on children's development if they are not sleeping sufficiently

they are not sleeping sufficiently. Children should wake up from a nap and from a good night's sleep refreshed. Babies and toddlers also need naps as part of their daily requirement for sleep and some children carry on needing naps until they are four years old. As children become older, not only do they sleep less, but their sleep is more likely to be taken in a single block at night.

Sleep patterns

How and when children fall asleep tend to be a result of the habits that they have developed. Most children get into a habit of being tired at a certain time and so this is why, in early years settings, it is important to find out the sleep routines of individual children. As well as timing, some children find it hard to self-settle. They may be rocked to sleep or have an adult sitting with them at night. This can mean that, without these conditions, children cannot manage to fall asleep easily.

Research it!

Find out about how to help children develop good sleep habits.

Finding out how much sleep is required at specific ages

As children vary in their sleep requirements, it is hard to pinpoint exactly how much sleep a child should have at a particular age. We know that children, like adults, will often have days where they sleep half an hour more and others when they sleep less. This is why looking at whether children are showing signs of tiredness is important as well as just keeping an eye on whether the amount of sleep they have is not radically different to that shown in Table 1.3.3.

To find the sleep requirements of a particular age of child, you can use Table 1.3.3 to add up the total amount of sleep that is needed over 24 hours and work out the approximate accordingly. For example, to find the sleep requirements of a six week old, add up the total sleep needed for a four week old (15.5 hours of sleep) and do the same for the three month old (15 hours). It is therefore likely that

a child of six weeks will need around 15 hours 10 minutes. In the same way, if a two year old needs 13 hours of sleep and a three year old needs 12 hours of sleep, you might expect that at two and half years, many children would need somewhere around 12.5 hours, although do remember that this would be an approximate guide.

Table 1.3.3 shows typical ranges for sleep over a 24-hour period and includes naps. Where children do not have naps, they are likely to need more sleep at night. You can see from the table that children's sleep requirements reduce over time, but compared to an adult, who needs between seven and eight hours, they remain quite high.

Table 1.3.3 Sleep requirements over a 24-hour period

Age	Day-time	Night-time
One week	8 hours	8.5 hours
Four weeks	6.75 hours	8.75 hours
Three months	5 hours	10 hours
Six months	4 hours	10 hours
Nine months	2.75 hours	11.25 hours
Twelve months	2.5 hours	11.5 hours
Two years	1.25 hours	11.75 hours
Three years	1 hour	11 hours
Four years		11.5 hours
Five years		11 hours
Six years		10.75 hours
Seven years		10.5 hours

Source: Based on recommendations by the Millpond Children's Sleep clinic, cited on the NHS website.

Reflect

- If a three-month-old baby needs 15 hours of sleep in a 24-hour period and a six-month-old child needs 14 hours, approximately how much sleep do you think a four-month-old child might need?
- If a three year old needs 12 hours of sleep in a 24-hour period and a four year old needs 11.5 hours of sleep, approximately how much sleep would a three and a half year old need?

Figure 1.3.9 Children are likely to need daytime naps until they are around three years old, but children do vary in their sleep requirements

In your setting

How does your setting provide for children who need to sleep?

Case study

Harry is three years old. The nursery has noticed that towards the end of the afternoon, he is often irritable and has tantrums. In the afternoon, he looks tired and often rolls around on the cushions. Today he has not wanted to join in any activities and has been particularly uncooperative. He also looks very tired. His key person talks to his parent about his mood and behaviour. She asks how well Harry is sleeping. The parent says that, since the arrival of his baby sister, Harry has been waking up several times in the night.

1 What is the link between Harry's behaviour and mood and his sleep patterns?
2 How much sleep is Harry likely to need in a 24-hour period?
3 Why might it be important for Harry to have a nap in the afternoon?

Children's need for rest

Children need times when they can be still and calm. Most children naturally do this if the right environment and opportunities are available. How much rest children need depends on individual children and how much physical and mental stimulation they need. Children who seem very sluggish and need to rest a lot may actually need more sleep. Figure 1.3.10 shows some examples of activities that can help children to rest.

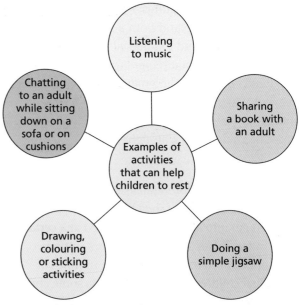

Figure 1.3.10 Examples of activities that can help children to rest

In practice

Ask your placement supervisor if you can note down the sleep and rest patterns of two children of different ages in your setting. How much sleep and rest does each child have during the session? If you can, find out from parents about how much sleep each child has at night.

AC 3.2 Safety precautions regarding sudden infant death syndrome

Sudden infant death syndrome, which is also more commonly known as 'cot death', occurs when babies die in their sleep without any warning. While the causes of sudden infant death syndrome are not fully understood, there are some steps that parents and early years settings can take to reduce the risk of it occurring. It is now good practice to make sure that, when babies are put down to sleep, the following measures are taken:

- Babies should be put on their back to sleep, with their feet touching the end of the cot. This is called the 'feet to foot' position (see Figure 1.3.11).
- Cot duvets should not be used as they can cause a baby to overheat.
- Blankets should be tucked in at shoulder level so as to avoid the baby's head becoming covered.

- Babies should be put down to sleep in cool rooms of around 16–20°C.
- Babies should not be in smoky environments or held by anyone who has just been smoking. (After smoking, it takes 20 minutes for an individual's oxygen levels to return to normal and so a baby who is being held by someone who has just been smoking is likely to inhale some of the toxic substances found in cigarettes.)

Figure 1.3.11 The 'feet to foot' position

Test yourself

1 In what position should babies be placed in a cot?
2 At what temperature should the room where babies sleep be kept?

LO4 Understand childhood immunisation

Do you remember having your jabs? While most children hate injections, the immunisation programme that it is offered to children plays an important role in preventing serious diseases from spreading. In this section, we look at the importance of immunisation in early childhood and also the reasons why not all children will have been immunised.

AC 4.1 Reasons for immunisation

Up until the middle of the last century, large numbers of babies and toddlers died before their third birthday as a result of contracting various infectious diseases, including tuberculosis, typhoid and diphtheria. Others survived the illness but were left with long-term disabilities, including deafness. The breakthrough in preventing deaths in early childhood came with the use of antibiotics, improved hygiene and living conditions but also because vaccines were developed which gave children immunity to the diseases. Vaccines work by giving the body a safe version of the disease so that the body's immune system can develop antibodies to protect itself. These antibodies mean that, if the child is later exposed to the disease, they are ready to fight it.

Another reason why immunisation is considered so important is that, in theory, diseases can be eradicated when a large number of the population has been vaccinated. This is because there are fewer opportunities for the disease to spread and so eventually it dies out. Examples of such diseases are polio, which is no longer found in the UK, and small pox, which has been globally eradicated. Interestingly, as few families now remember how dangerous some of these diseases are, there are concerns that some people may not recognise the importance of immunising their children against them.

Table 1.3.4 The NHS vaccination schedule

Two months	Five-in-one (DTaP/IPV/Hib) vaccine against diphtheria, tetanus, whooping cough (pertussis) and polio and hib, which can cause pneumonia
	Pneumococcal (PCV) vaccine (a bacteria that can cause pneumonia and meningitis)
	Rotavirus vaccine (an infection that causes diarrhoea and sickness)
Three months	Five-in-one (DTaP/IPV/Hib) vaccine, second dose
	Meningitis C
	Rotavirus vaccine, second dose
Four months	Five-in-one (DTaP/IPV/Hib) vaccine, third dose
	Pneumococcal (PCV) vaccine, second dose
12–13 months	Hib/Men C booster, given as a single jab containing meningitis C (second dose) and Hib (fourth dose)
	Measles, mumps and rubella (MMR) vaccine, given as a single jab
	Pneumococcal (PCV) vaccine, third dose
Two and three years	Annual flu vaccine
Three years four months	Measles, mumps and rubella (MMR) vaccine, second dose
	Four-in-one pre-school booster, given as a single jab, containing vaccines against diphtheria, tetanus, whooping cough (pertussis) and polio

Figure 1.3.12 Immunisation plays a crucial role in keeping children healthy

AC 4.2 The immunisation schedule

The National Health Service provides free vaccinations for children as part of the national immunisation programme. It is a mark of success that some of the diseases against which children are vaccinated are rarely diagnosed in children today, although they remain a potential threat. Table 1.3.4 shows the immunisation schedule offered by the NHS. Most children will be vaccinated at their local family GP practice.

AC 4.3 Why some children are not immunised

There is a range of reasons why some children are not immunised, such as, medical conditions, temporary delay and parental choice.

Medical conditions

Most babies and children are able to be vaccinated. However, there are some groups of children with pre-existing medical conditions who may not be able to be vaccinated. This includes children who have epilepsy which is not under control, as well as children who have a known allergy to some key components of the vaccine, notably eggs.

Temporary delay

Some parents will be advised to temporarily delay a particular vaccine if the parents or health professionals agree that the child is already unwell, especially with a fever. Wherever possible, the advice is always to vaccinate as soon as possible because of the dangerous nature of the illnesses being vaccinated against.

Parental choice

Some parents choose not to have their children vaccinated for a variety of reasons. This includes concerns about how vaccines have been developed using animals and also that some vaccines are cultivated using eggs. In some cases, parents do not believe that vaccination is an effective tool or they calculate that their child is not at risk. There have also been some high-profile stories about vaccinations causing other medical conditions in children, particularly in respect of the mumps, measles and rubella vaccine (MMR). While there is plenty of medical research to show that the vaccines are safe, and allergic reactions are rare, some parents still choose not to vaccinate their children.

> **Research it!**
>
> Find out why there were concerns about the MMR vaccine and how it has affected take-up of the vaccination by visiting the Health Protection Agency's website and navigating to the General Information webpage on MMR at: **www.hpa.org.uk**.

Figure 1.3.13 Adults should talk to children about the importance of sleep and rest

LO5 Be able to support children in personal physical care routines

Do you remember having your face wiped by an adult? The chances are that you did not like it, unless of course the adult was gentle and made it fun. In this section, we look at how you might support children during personal physical care routines.

AC 5.1 Supporting children's personal physical care routines

Supporting children in physical care routines does require practice as well as knowledge. Most importantly, we should always be looking for ways to maintain children's dignity and privacy. Wherever possible, we should encourage children to be involved in the process so that over time they can develop the skills needed to become independent. It is also essential that physical care routines are not separated from children's learning. This means it is good practice to see physical care routines as opportunities for interacting with children and drawing their attention to concepts such as number or size. Table 1.3.5 shows some of the things that you should think about when carrying out personal physical care routines and how you might support children's learning.

→ In LO1, we looked at the role of adults during these physical care routines. You should reread this section before you take part in physical care routines.

> **In your setting**
>
> Ask if you can take part in each of the personal care routines shown in Table 1.3.5. Make sure that you follow your setting's policies and procedures. Write about how you took part in each of the care routines. Try to explain how you maintained children's dignity and also helped them to benefit from the learning opportunity.

Table 1.3.5 Supporting children in personal physical care routines

Care routine	Ways of supporting children	Learning opportunities
Nappy changing	<ul><li>Encourage children to make movements while undressing and dressing.</li><li>Put up mobiles so that children have something to look at during nappy changes.</li><li>Encourage toddlers to find their clean nappy and bring it to the changing area.</li></ul>	<ul><li>Interact with babies and toddlers.</li><li>Sing rhymes to them during nappy changes.</li><li>Talk to toddlers about clean and dirty.</li></ul>
Toileting	<ul><li>Encourage children to do as much undressing by themselves.</li><li>Give children privacy, e.g. partially closing a door.</li><li>Encourage children to wash their own hands when they have finished.</li></ul>	<ul><li>Talk about how washing hands prevents germs.</li></ul>
Hand washing	<ul><li>Encourage children to wash their own hands.</li><li>Model hand washing.</li><li>Encourage children to dry their own hands.</li></ul>	<ul><li>Talk about when it is important to wash hands and why.</li><li>Look at how water goes down the plughole.</li></ul>
Bath or shower time	<ul><li>Encourage children to dress and undress according to their skill level.</li><li>Help children to do as much washing as possible.</li><li>Encourage children to dry themselves but 'finish off' to ensure that children are fully dry.</li></ul>	<ul><li>Provide a range of water toys so children can explore scooping and pouring.</li></ul>
Skin	<ul><li>Encourage children to put on suncream according to their skill level.</li><li>Encourage children to dress to go outdoors.</li><li>Allow children to choose the order in which they get dressed, e.g. sunhats before shoes.</li></ul>	<ul><li>Talk to children about the weather and link this to the clothes we wear or the use of suncream.</li></ul>
Hair	<ul><li>Look for ways of helping children to be involved, e.g. watching their hair being brushed in a mirror.</li><li>Encourage children to do as much as they can according to their skill level.</li><li>With children who have long hair, encourage them to choose different styles.</li></ul>	<ul><li>Encourage children to count how many strokes of the comb or hairbrush will be needed.</li><li>Talk to children about how people have different types and colours of hair.</li></ul>
Teeth	<ul><li>Encourage children to put toothpaste onto the toothbrush.</li><li>Use a mirror so that children can see when you are cleaning their teeth.</li><li>Allow children to spend a little time cleaning their own teeth as well.</li></ul>	<ul><li>Talk to children about what we use our teeth for.</li><li>Count children's teeth with them in front of the mirror.</li></ul>
Meal times	<ul><li>Encourage children to self-feed wherever possible.</li><li>Allow children to serve their own food (provided it is nutritious).</li><li>Encourage children to choose where they wish to sit.</li></ul>	<ul><li>Use this time for children to talk together.</li><li>Point out the colours and textures of the food.</li></ul>
Rest/sleep	<ul><li>Encourage children to reflect on how being tired makes them feel.</li><li>Allow children to choose the stories that you will share with them before bedtime.</li><li>Allow children enough time to self-settle.</li><li>Give children a choice of 'rest' activities, including sharing stories with them.</li></ul>	<ul><li>Talk to children about why sleep and rest are important.</li></ul>

Assessment

For this unit you will need to complete a variety of tasks. Some of these tasks will focus on whether you have acquired the knowledge needed to support your practice with children.

Your starting point will be to look at the latest guidelines and tips for good practice in relation to the physical care for children. A good start is to look at the National Health Service website where you will find the latest guidelines relating to skincare as well as sleep and latest advice regarding immunisation.

You should also look at the latest guidelines for minimising cot death, which you can find by looking at the Lullaby Trust website. You should also reflect on the importance of why early years practitioners need to work closely with parents in relation to all aspects of children's physical care.

In addition to the knowledge that you need to show for this unit, your assessor will also want to watch you work with children during physical care routines. You should make sure that you can show that your knowledge about best practice is shown in the way that you work. This will include minimising the spread of infection during physical care routines such as meal times, nappy changing and toileting. As with most aspects of working with children, practice does make perfect, so make sure that before your assessor visits, you have had sufficient experience of taking part in physical care routines with children. You could ask your placement supervisor to watch you work first.

Useful resources

Organisations

Birth to five

This is a guide to parenting in the early years and has 150 pages of NHS-accredited information, videos and interactive tools: **www.nhs.uk/Planners/birthtofive**

The Lullaby Trust

This organisation offers confidential support to family, friends and carers affected by the sudden and unexpected death of a baby or toddler: **www.lullabytrust.org.uk**

Unit 1.4 WB Promote children's emotional well-being

For children to thrive, they need to feel safe, relaxed and happy. To create an environment where this can happen, adults working with children need to understand how best to promote children's emotional well-being. In this unit, we look at children's emotional needs, including during transitions and significant events, and consider how adults working with children can promote their emotional well-being.

Learning outcomes

By the end of this unit, you will:

1 Understand children's needs in relation to emotional well-being.
2 Understand the requirements for promoting emotional well-being in relation to current frameworks.
3 Understand the needs of children during transition and significant events.
4 Be able to promote the emotional well-being of children in own setting.

LO1 Understand children's needs in relation to emotional well-being

Have you noticed that most young children when they are scared head straight for their parents or those looking after them? They may want a hug or to just stay close to them. This is normal behaviour for young children, and even adults at times! In this section, we look at why adults are so important in relation to young children's **emotional well-being**.

> ## Key term
>
> **emotional well-being** An umbrella term that covers many aspects of emotional development, including relationships, self-esteem, happiness and resilience.

AC 1.1 Theoretical perspectives of emotional well-being

The term emotional well-being is relatively new. It covers many aspects, including relationships, how we view ourselves and also how we cope under stress or in a difficult environment.

Psychological perspectives

Most psychologists believe that children's emotional well-being comes principally from their relationships with adults in the earliest years of their life. These relationships are known as attachments. From feeling loved and nurtured by their parents and also those who play a significant role in their lives, they can go onto develop other relationships as well as manage the more difficult challenges that life brings. Strong and positive relationships with adults also seem to play a part in developing children's self-esteem and resilience.

➡ We look at this in Unit 3.12 and you should read this section along with pages 330–49 to deepen your understanding of this area.

Attachment theories

We now know that children need strong relationships with their parents and other key people in their lives to support their well-being. The importance of these attachments has not always been recognised, but today they are seen as being central to children's emotional well-being.

Behaviourist model of attachment

Up until the 1950s, it was thought that babies and young children would automatically attach to those who fed and cared for their physical needs. This is often dubbed 'cupboard love' and was a behaviourist model. The behaviourist model relies on the theory that children are likely to repeat an action if there is a positive reinforcement, such as a reward or praise, or something is offered that a child wants or needs.

➡ See also page 282.

In the behaviourist model of attachment, children should in theory develop the strongest relationship with the person who feeds them because the food acts as a positive reinforcement. This theory in relation to attachment is no longer thought to be accurate as a result of an experiment known as 'Harlow's monkeys'.

Harlow's monkeys: attachment is not cupboard love

Harry Harlow wanted to show that attachment was not 'cupboard love' and so devised an experiment with monkeys, who have similar needs for attachment as humans. Baby monkeys were put in a cage with man-made monkeys. One of the man-made monkeys was made from wire mesh. It gave out food. The other man-made monkey was covered in a towelling cloth but did not give out food. During the experiment, the baby monkeys spent nearly all of their time clinging onto the 'cloth' monkey, only going to the other, wire, monkey for food.

> ## In your setting
>
> If someone other than a key person feeds a baby, have you noticed that the baby will still want to be with his/her key person afterwards?

John Bowlby – theory of attachment

One of the classic theories of attachment was provided by John Bowlby in the late 1950s. For a number of years, he had been aware that there was a link between children's mental health and later outcomes in life and children's needs to be with their parents. During the Second World War, he, along with other eminent doctors, wrote a letter to protest against children under five years being evacuated and thus separated from their families.

In 1951, he published a book called *Maternal Care and Mental Health,* in which he was able to show the importance of early relationships to children's later mental health. He also showed that there were serious effects on children when they were separated from their main carers, usually mothers, at this time.

Bowlby's work influenced other researchers, including Mary Ainsworth and James and Joyce Robertson.

→ See page 56.

The main features of Bowlby's theory are as follows:

- Babies need to form one strong attachment, usually to their mother, in the first year of their lives.
- Babies and young children are at risk of psychological damage if they either do not form a strong attachment or if there is prolonged separation from the attachment in the first four years of life.
- Babies and young children need more than just having their physical care needs met in order to thrive.
- Babies and young children show **separation anxiety** if they are separated from their main attachments.

Key term

separation anxiety A term used to describe the stages of distress that occur if a baby or child is separated from their primary attachment.

Separation anxiety

One of the key features of attachment theory is that most children show a pattern of distress when they cannot be with their primary attachment. This seems to begin from around seven months. Bowlby and his colleagues, James and Joyce Robertson, identified three phases. The final phase, 'detachment', is associated with children who are not reunited with their primary carer for a significant amount of time, such as six weeks.

Table 1.4.1 Phases of attachment

Phase	Features
Protest	Children may scream, try to escape, kick and show anger.
Despair	Children show calmer behaviour, almost as though they have accepted the separation. They may be withdrawn and sad. Comfort behaviour, such as thumb sucking or rocking, may be shown.
Detachment	Children may appear to be 'over' the separation and start to join in activities. The child is actually coping by trying to 'forget' the relationship – hence the title 'detachment'. The effects of detachment may be longer lasting as the child may have learnt not to trust people they care for.

Quality of attachment matters – the strange situation

While we now accept that attachment is important in the first year of babies' lives, a colleague of Bowlby, Mary Ainsworth, went on to investigate whether the quality of attachment matters to children's well-being and whether some attachments are better than others. To test this, an experiment known as the 'strange situation' was set up. Today this experiment would not be allowed as it caused babies and their mothers temporary distress.

The strange situation experiment

To test how strong attachments were, a mother and baby were shown into a room. Then the experiment, which was divided into eight parts, began.

1 Parent and baby enter room.
2 Parent remains inactive; baby is free to explore room.

3 Stranger joins parent and infant.
4 Parent leaves room.
5 Parent returns, settles baby and stranger leaves.
6 Baby is alone in the room.
7 Stranger returns and interacts with baby.
8 Parent returns again and stranger leaves.

Ainsworth and her colleagues focused on the babies' reactions during each part of the experiment, noting how distressed the babies became, but also how easily they could be comforted either by the parent and/or by the stranger.

They categorised babies' behaviour and therefore the quality of the attachment with the parent into three types:

- **Type A – anxious-avoidant**: Baby largely ignores parent, shows little signs of distress when parent leaves and continues to play. Baby ignores or avoids parent on their return. Baby dislikes being alone, but can be comforted by stranger.
- **Type B – securely attached**: Baby plays while parent is present, but shows visible distress when parent leaves and play is reduced. Baby is easily comforted on return of parent and carries on playing. The baby cries when alone because parent is not there, but can be partly comforted by a stranger. Reactions towards stranger and parents are markedly different.
- **Type C – anxious-resistant**: Baby is wary and explores less than other types. Baby is very distressed when parent leaves and actively resists stranger's attempts to comfort. Baby wants immediate contact with parent on return but is ambivalent, showing frustration and anger alongside clinginess – for example, they may want to be held but then immediately struggle to get down.

Why are some children more securely attached than others?

Ainsworth came to the conclusion that the quality of attachment depended on the parenting that the baby received. Where parents were able to sense and predict their babies' needs and frustrations, the babies showed type B behaviour, i.e. securely attached. This meant that they were able to explore and play, knowing that their parent was a safe base.

Figure 1.4.1 Toddlers rely on their parents to be a safe base

Should parents leave their young children with others?

If you have read this so far, you may be thinking that perhaps parents should never leave their children in early years settings. Happily, further research has shown that, provided the babies and children are left with someone with whom they have a strong attachment, they can cope for short periods in the absence of their primary attachments. The research that shows this was provided by James and Joyce Robertson, who were colleagues of John Bowlby. In the early 1960s, they began a study which showed how, with good substitute foster care, children could cope with separations when their parents went into hospital. Their work provides the basis for the key person system that is used today in early years settings.

→ We look at the key person system on page 59.

Research it!

The Robertsons made a series of films showing phases of separation anxiety and their work in providing substitute care. Read about these films by visiting www.robertsonfilms.info.

Case study

Jonas is two years old. His mother has been rushed to hospital. No family members are available to look after him and so a neighbour has said she will keep an eye on him. He does not know this neighbour very well. When he sees his mother being taken away in the ambulance, he screams. During the next hour, he screams and, despite the neighbour's best efforts, he does not calm down. As well as crying, he bangs the front door and tries to get out. When his father comes to pick him up, he immediately calms down and hugs him. A few minutes later, he is playing with the neighbour's cat.

1 What stage of separation anxiety was Jonas showing?
2 Why was his father able to calm him down?
3 Why is it important that children in early years settings get to know their key person before their parents leave?

AC 1.2 The process of bonding, attachment and developing secure relationships

It is important to understand how children develop relationships with adults because, as we have seen, the quality of children's relationships seems to play a major role in their emotional well-being. The terms 'bonding' and 'attachment' are often used together, but in this section we will use the term 'bonding' in terms of how parents build a relationship with their newborn babies.

Bonding

Bonding is a process which, for most parents, is very instinctive and powerful and which nature has designed to ensure the survival and protection of the vulnerable newborn child.

The process of parents bonding with their children begins before babies are born. From around the 16th week of pregnancy, mothers first begin to feel the kicking and movements of their babies. At first, these movements are slight but, as the pregnancy progresses, these can be seen as well as felt. With modern technology, parents are also likely to see photographs of their babies as a result of scans. By 26 weeks, babies are also responding and recognising their mother's voice and may sometimes respond to their father's too. Once the baby is born, touch plays an important part in the bonding process, which is why parents are encouraged to hold and cuddle their baby immediately after birth and why mothers are encouraged to breastfeed wherever possible. Nature primes babies to stop crying when they are held and also to stare into the eyes of their parents or caregivers when they are being fed. Interestingly, nature is also responsible for the production of hormones, during birth and shortly afterwards, that prime mothers to fall in love with their babies.

Over the following few weeks, the bonding process continues as babies start to smile and also stop crying when they hear their parents' voices. In some ways, bonding is a cycle whereby parents respond positively to their baby and then the baby settles and may coo or smile. This in turn helps parents to gain confidence and also enjoy their baby more.

Factors affecting bonding

While, for most parents, bonding is straightforward, there can be some factors that affect early bonding.

● **Post-natal depression** is thought to be caused by an imbalance of hormones and can affect the mother's ability to bond with the baby.
● **A difficult birth** can affect the mother's ability to respond to the child, especially if she is in pain or has been traumatised by the birth.
● **Premature birth** may lead to the parents not being able to touch or feel their baby as much as would otherwise be expected.
● **Babies with additional needs** may not feed easily or soothe when parents pick them up. This can cause parents to lose confidence and become more anxious, which in turn affects babies' responses.

Attachment

The process by which babies develop attachments with their parents and key family members is gradual. Table 1.4.2 shows the process by which children attach to their parents and also start to develop other attachments. Primary or specific attachments are usually lifelong and very important to the child, such as relationships with parents and close family members. Secondary attachments include relationships with their key person as well as friendships with other children.

In your setting

Ask your placement supervisor if you can talk to two parents of children in your setting. Ask each parent to name the people with whom their child would settle and would be happy with if they had to leave them for a couple of hours.

The process of developing secure relationships

It takes a while for children to develop secure relationships with adults who are not their parents or primary attachments. As shown in Table 1.4.2, from eight months, babies and children start to know who 'their' adults are and, unless they are supported, seem to be naturally wary of other adults.

The starting point for building a secure relationship is to understand that babies and young children will take their cue from watching their parents' reactions. This is known as 'social referencing'. If parents are friendly and relaxed towards a 'new' adult, the child is likely to be less wary. At first, many babies and toddlers will simply observe the new adult from the safety of their parent's side. Once the child has done this, they are more likely to gradually start to make eye contact and interact with the new adult. Play is often a good medium for this interaction. Interestingly, it can take many hours before children under the age of three are happy to be left alone with the 'new' adult. The process of building new relationships is often slightly faster with children older than three years. This is because the 'stranger danger' instinct is less pronounced.

Table 1.4.2 The process of attachment

Age	Stage	Features
Six weeks–three months	Indiscriminate attachments	Babies begin to be attracted to human faces and voices. First smiles begin at around six weeks.
Three months–seven/eight months	Indiscriminate attachments	Babies are learning to distinguish between faces, showing obvious pleasure when they recognise familiar faces. They are happy to be handled by strangers, preferring to be in human company than left alone – hence the term 'indiscriminate' attachments.
Seven/eight months	Specific/primary attachments	At around seven or eight months, babies begin to miss key people in their lives and show signs of distress – for example, crying when their parent leaves the room. Most babies also seem to develop one particularly strong attachment – often to the mother. This is often referred to as a primary attachment. Babies also show a wariness of strangers, even when in the presence of their 'key people'. This wariness may quickly develop into fear, if the stranger makes some form of direct contact with the baby – for example, by touching them.
From eight months	Multiple attachments	After making specific attachments, babies then go on to form multiple attachments provided that their specific attachments are there to act as a safe base. This is an important part of the socialisation process.

Signs that children have developed a secure relationship

Children who have a secure relationship with an adult will often show active signs of wanting to be with that adult. They will often seek them out in a range of situations:

● at the start of a session
● for reassurance if they are unsure of a situation
● to share an achievement or news
● for a cuddle or a hug
● if the adult is doing something interesting
● when they are tired.

In addition, babies and toddlers will also want to keep their 'adult' within their sight and will often make frequent eye contact with them.

AC 1.3 Impact of secure relationships

The impact of secure relationships on children is very significant. Having a strong bond with their parents, key carers and, in early years settings, their key persons seems to be important for many aspects of children's emotional well-being.

● **Protective against depression**: children who have strong relationships are less likely to develop depression in childhood and in later life.

Figure 1.4.2 This child has a special relationship with their key person

- **Stress**: children who have strong, secure relationships seem to be less affected by stress and find it easier to cope with change.
- **Friendships and relationships**: children who have secure relationships find it easier to make friends and to understand others' thoughts and feelings.
- **Behaviour**: children who have secure relationships seem to find it easier to manage their emotions in line with their age and stage of development and so are more likely to show expected behaviour.
- **Confidence**: children who have secure relationships are more likely to have stronger self-identity, which in turn supports the development of confidence and self-esteem.

LO2 Understand the requirements for promoting emotional well-being in relation to current frameworks

Have you ever been somewhere new for the first time and felt quite lost? To make children feel safe and know that there is someone there for them, early years settings are required to ensure that every child has a designated adult who will have a special relationship with them. In this section, we look at the role of this person, who is referred to as a key person or key worker.

AC 2.1 The key person and promoting emotional well-being

It has been good practice for a while for all early years settings to have a key person system in place. A key person (sometimes referred to as a key worker) is someone who builds up a significant and special relationship with the child and their parents. This relationship is a close one and allows the child to cope and feel emotionally secure in the absence of their parents. The role of the key person is so important that it is something that inspectors check when they visit early years settings. In England, it is also a legal requirement and so, in theory, an early years setting that does not have a key person system in place is breaking the law.

Role of the key person

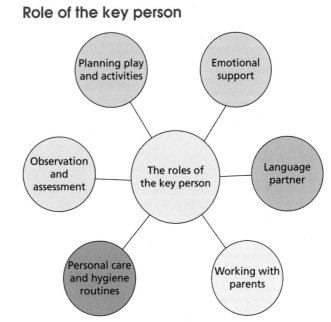

Figure 1.4.3 Roles of the key person

Emotional support
This is the main role of the key person. They must develop a close relationship with the child, which from the child's perspective should feel as if they are with a 'favourite relative'. It is usual for key persons to greet the child warmly, which may include a hug, spend time with them during the day and be ready at any point to give the child additional reassurance.

Language partner
We know that babies and young children need a lot of adult interaction to help with their communication and language skills. Where children have a strong relationship with their key person, they are more likely to interact and so this can help children's language.

Personal care and hygiene routines
As part of their role, it is good practice for the key person to change the nappies of their key children and, in the case of babies, feed them. With toddlers and slightly older children, it is good practice for a child's key person to sit with them at snack and meal times.

Working with parents
An important role for a key person is also to establish a good working relationship with the

child's parents. This usually starts during the settling-in process. This relationship is important because, by working closely together, information can be shared and the child's needs can be met. Children are also more likely to settle when they can see that their parents and their key person seem to have a strong relationship.

→ See page 57.

In England, the key person also has the role of supporting parents to help their children's development at home.

→ We look at this particular role of the key person in more detail in Unit 2.5.

Observation and assessment

The key person is normally the person who considers children's development and uses this information to feed back to the parents and also to the team in group care settings.

Planning play and activities

The key person is likely to be involved in planning play and activities as they will know what their children enjoy doing. They will also spend time playing with their child so that the relationship can remain secure.

Co-key person/buddying

In some settings, where members of staff work part time or where children have a long day in the setting, it is usual for a buddying or co-key person system to be in place. This means that children may have two adults who act as key persons and so, when one is off on annual leave or on a break, the other key person can take over.

In your setting

Find out how the key person system works in your setting.

Figure 1.4.4 The key person must also develop a good relationship with the child's parents

LO3 Understand the needs of children during transition and significant events

Can you remember starting at a new school or perhaps moving home? You might remember feeling worried. In this section, we look at how we might help young children to cope with changes in their lives.

AC 3.1 Transitions and significant events that a child may experience

There is a range of situations and events that most children will have to cope with. One of these is of course coming into an early years setting. It is important to understand the types of transitions and events with which children will need help. See Table 1.4.3.

AC 3.2 Potential effects of transition and significant events on a child's life

When children face a transition or a significant event, there can be effects on their short- and long-term behaviours.

Short-term effects

Many adults believe that children are able to adapt easily to new situations and so do not take seriously the effect of transitions and significant events, such as moving school, moving home or the arrival of a sibling. While children who experience transitions will, in the long run, be able to cope, there are likely to be short-term effects, including the following.

Regression

When children are struggling to cope with a situation, they may revert to an earlier stage of development. A two year old who was out of

Table 1.4.3 Types of transitions and events that a child may experience

Transition or event	Description
Moving between settings and carers	Many children are cared for in more than one early years setting during the week or even during the day. For example, they may go to a nursery in the morning and a childminder in the afternoon.
Starting and moving through day care	Children who start in day care may experience transitions as they move from one section to another – for example, from the toddler room to the pre-school room.
Moving to school	Moving to school is a significant change. At school, there are more children and adults and it is usually a much larger space.
Birth of a sibling	When a new sibling arrives, children have to adapt to the change in family structure.
Moving home	Some children will move home during their early years.
Living outside the family home	Some children may not always live with their parents. They may live with extended family, with grandparents or in foster care. This might occur for a variety of reasons, including family breakdown.
Family breakdown	Some children may have to cope with their family structure changing because of the separation of their parents or some sort of breakdown in relationships between family members.
Loss of significant people	Sadly, some children may lose a member of their family or someone close to them.

nappies may start to have many toileting accidents or a three year old whose speech was clear might start to talk using a babyish style.

Physical well-being

Many children's physical well-being is affected in the short term by transitions. Their immune system may not be as effective and they are likely to have more infections than usual. This is because stress affects the immune system. In addition, it is common for children to have disturbed sleep patterns or they may refuse to go to bed. They may also become fussier eaters or not have much of an appetite.

Emotional effects

Transitions also affect children's emotional regulation. They are likely to become upset more easily than usual and may be tearful or angry. They may also withdraw or become aggressive.

Long-term effects

Some transitions and significant events can have long-term effects on children. This usually happens when children have not been supported before, during and after a transition or a significant event. In some cases, the long-term effects can impact on children's lives. These effects are listed in Table 1.4.4.

AC 3.3 The role of the early years practitioner and planned transitions

Many of the transitions that children will experience are ones that can be planned for. They include the arrival of a child into a setting or a child moving on to school. There are many ways in which early years practitioners can prepare children for these transitions and, as we will see, a key way is to make sure that information is shared between those involved in the transition. While this is important, it is worth noting that parents have to give permission for information about their child to be shared with others.

Work closely with the family

It is important to work closely with the family so that information can be shared to avoid any misunderstandings and also to agree a strategy as to how best to prepare the child.

Work closely with other settings

Where a child is moving from one setting to another, it is helpful if the settings work closely together. By doing this, accurate information can be given to the parents and also the child. The early years practitioner will also understand how

Table 1.4.4 Long-term effects of transitions or significant events

Self-confidence	Some children's self-confidence can be affected by transitions and events. This affects their ability to make friends as well as their ability to cope with new challenges.
Depression	If untreated, depression can become a long-term problem for children and may affect their ability to make relationships and enjoy life.
Anger	Some children become very angry as a result of events and, if the anger is supressed or they do not learn to manage it, they may become aggressive adults.
Relationships	Some transitions or events cause children to lose trust in adults or other children. This may cause them to find it hard to make meaningful relationships later in life.
Self-harming and abusive behaviours	Some children who have not been able to express their pain may later use self-harming and abusive behaviours, such as cutting themselves or taking drugs, as a way of dealing with it.
Antisocial behaviours	Some children who have not been able to express their frustration or pain, or who have been let down by adults, may go on to show antisocial behaviours.
Underachievement	A consequence of some significant transitions and events is underachievement at school. There is a range of reasons why this might happen, including inability to focus at school while the child is experiencing other difficulties.

the other early years setting works and be able to prepare the child accordingly.

Work closely with other professionals

Some children will also be gaining support from other professionals and so it is important to work closely with them too. A good example of this is where a child attends a speech and language centre and is due to move to mainstream nursery or where a child has been in foster care and will be moving home again.

Planning activities

Early years practitioners can also help children prepare for transitions by planning activities that will help them understand more about the transitions that they are about to undergo. Practitioners may choose a book about moving home or the arrival of a new baby. Through the planning of activities, the early years practitioner can prompt children to talk and ask questions about the transition and reassure them.

Visiting new settings or carers

In cases where children are moving setting or carer, the role of the early years practitioner is to introduce the child to the new setting or carer. By being with the child, the early years practitioner acts as a safe base so that the child can explore the new setting and get to know the new carer.

AC 3.4 The early years practitioner and supporting children during transition and significant life events

While, ideally, children should be prepared for transitions and life events, unfortunately this is not always the case. A child's parent may be involved in an accident requiring hospitalisation or a child might be suddenly removed from their parents by social services because of concerns over their welfare. Whatever the circumstances, children will need to be supported during a transition or significant life event. The early years practitioner will play an important role in this, especially if they are the child's key person.

Working closely with others, including families

As with preparing a child for a planned transition, wherever possible, the early years practitioner will need to work closely with others who are involved with the child. This may mean talking to a social worker, previous carer and family members. As with preparing a child for a planned transition, there are rules about confidentiality and, with very few exceptions, information must not be shared about a child without a parent's consent.

→ Also see page 144.

Spending time with a child

Many children who are going through transitions or significant life events need to spend more time with their key person. The role of the early years practitioner in such cases is to be there for the child and to sensitively respond to their mood. Children may or may not want to talk about what they are feeling and so taking the lead from the child is important.

Allowing children to express emotions

It is usual for children to show a range of emotions during transitions and significant life events. While it is always tempting to 'cheer up' children, it is now known that instead adults should acknowledge how children feel and allow them to feel sad or angry. For young children, this might mean looking for safe materials and activities to allow them to do this, including using sensory materials such as dough, paint and water.

Seeking further support

Some life events are so significant and potentially traumatic for children that they are likely to need additional support from other professionals. A child who has seen a parent murdered, for example, is likely to need the help of a specially trained professional to work through their feelings and emotions. It is therefore an important role of the early years professional to find out more about how they can help a child or, with permission, to refer a child to a specialist service.

LO4 Be able to promote the emotional well-being of children in own setting

When you go somewhere new, what helps you to settle in quickly and relax? In this section, we look at how to identify the needs of children in relation to emotional well-being and practical ways in which we might support their emotional well-being.

AC 4.1 The emotional well-being of children in your setting

One of the skills of the early years practitioner is to identify and to understand the needs of the children that they work with. This is a particular responsibility of the key person as they spend time building a relationship with the child and also the parents. There are many ways of identifying the needs of children.

Working with parents

Where there is a good relationship with parents, information is likely to be shared. This may include parents telling practitioners about how the child responds at home as well as any changes in home circumstances. This is important as it can help the practitioner understand more about the child's needs.

Observation of the child

Early years practitioners are also able to identify individual needs by carefully watching them.

They may, for example, notice that a child tends to be quiet for the first hour of a session or that a child often gives up when faced with a challenge. Practitioners may also notice changes in the way children respond to others, such as a child who used to enjoy playing with other children but who now prefers to play alone. Noting changes is important because it may indicate that the child needs additional support. By observing children, practitioners can then think about how best to respond to their needs. Table 1.4.5 gives some examples of points that are worth noting when observing children.

In practice

Using some of the observation points in Table 1.4.5, observe a child in your setting. Use the information gained to consider what emotional needs the child might have.

AC 4.2 Supporting emotional well-being

There are a number of ways in which early years practitioners can work to support children's emotional well-being. To do this well, early years practitioners have to think about the age and stage of a child's development and adapt their practice accordingly. Interestingly, many of the ways that adults can support some aspects of children's emotional well-being are interlinked, as Table 1.4.6 shows.

Reflect

Look at the different ways in which the adult can support children's emotional well-being. Reflect on the skills that the adult needs and consider to what extent you have mastered them.

AC 4.3 Planning activities to promote emotional well-being

One of the ways that we can support children's emotional well-being is by planning activities. There are many different types of activities to choose from

Table 1.4.5 Observing children

Observation point	What it might mean
Does the child show signs of joy or pleasure during a session?	Children who do not seem happy and relaxed may need more time with their key person in order to feel secure.
Does the child seem anxious at times?	Children who appear anxious may need additional reassurance or guidance.
Is the child able to persevere at an activity when it becomes challenging?	Children who find it hard to persevere may have other things on their mind that are distracting them. They may need help to talk about them. Some children who find it hard to persevere may need an adult to mentor them during the activity.
Does the child seem to enjoy the company of other children?	Most children enjoy watching others or, in the case of children over three years, enjoy playing with them. Children who do not enjoy the company of others may need an adult to help them play with others.
How much reassurance does the child need during a session?	Children who need a lot of reassurance may need additional time with their key person. They may need to be praised for 'having a go'. They may also be helped by knowing what is about to happen next.
Is the child confident to try out new activities, materials and resources?	Some children may take time before exploring or trying out new activities. They may need an adult to reassure them and to acknowledge their efforts.

Table 1.4.6 Ways to support children's emotional well-being

Aspect	Role of the adult
Support independence Build resilience and perseverance Build confidence Support self-reliance	• Acknowledge children's attempts at being independent – for example, a baby trying to feed himself. • Provide materials and resources that will allow children to access them and tidy them away easily. • Recognise children's achievements, however small, and acknowledge when children have tried to be independent or have persevered. • Provide resources that require a little perseverance – for example, construction blocks and jigsaws – and coach children where necessary. • Create routines that encourage independence – for example, collecting own plate, serving own food, wiping own face. • Be positive when children have tried to do something for themselves, even if not always successfully – for example, spilt drinks or toys put back in the wrong place.
Equip children to protect themselves	• When toileting and nappy changing, treat children with dignity and encourage them to do as much as they can independently. With older children, give opportunities for privacy. • Show children that you respect that they have rights over their bodies – for example, not patting children on the head or insisting that they should come for a cuddle.
Build relationships between children	• Provide materials that will allow toddlers to play alongside each other (e.g. water, gloop). • Provide activities where children come together with an adult (e.g. cooking, parachute games). • Play simple games so that children from three years can learn to take turns (e.g. picture lotto). • Praise and encourage children when they are playing/cooperating. • Encourage older children to resolve their own squabbles

Table 1.4.7 Activities that promote children's well-being

Type of activity	How they promote children's well-being
Books and stories	These can help children talk about their feelings or be used to support children through a transition.
Puppets	These can encourage children to talk and to think about what they are feeling.
Sensory materials (e.g. dough, sand and water)	These are often used to help children express emotions, including anger.
Painting and drawing	Older children often find it helpful to draw or paint out their feelings or what has happened to them.
Role play	Many children act out their feelings or what has happened to them.
Making music	Singing or making sounds with instruments can help children to feel positive and also to express their emotions, including anger, in a positive way.

depending on the needs of the child. Table 1.4.7 shows some common examples of activities that are used in early years settings.

Factors to consider when planning an activity

There are a number of factors to consider when planning activities for children.

→ You can find more information on planning activities on this page.

Age and stage of development

These are important because otherwise the child might not enjoy the activity or benefit from it.

Interests of the child

It is important to think about what might appeal to the child. Some activities that work well are based on children's interests or on other activities that the child has previously enjoyed.

Outcome

It is important to think about which aspect of a child's emotional well-being you are hoping to promote – for example, confidence, expressing emotion or coping with a transition.

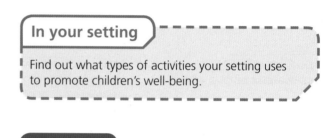

In your setting

Find out what types of activities your setting uses to promote children's well-being.

In practice

Planning an activity

Think of a child or group of children that would benefit from a planned activity. Observe their interests and stage of development.

Think about an activity that would promote their emotional well-being.

AC 4.4 Implementing activities to promote emotional well-being

Once an activity has been planned, the next step is to implement it. There are plenty of things to consider when implementing an activity.

1 Where will the activity take place?
2 Do you have the resources to hand?
3 Have you checked that this is a good time for the activity to take place?
4 How will you introduce the activity?
5 How will you ensure that the child or children can participate?

In addition, during the activity, you will need to keep monitoring the responses of the child or children. This will help you to adapt the activity or your style of working if needed. It will also help you to assess whether the child or children are enjoying the activity and gaining from it. Monitoring the responses of the children will also help you to consider when the natural life of the activity is nearing its end.

Once you have completed the activity, you should also think about what the next steps might be for the child or children. It may be that their interest in the activity was high and so it might be worth repeating it, or it might be that the activity needs to be adapted. In some cases, the impact of an activity may not be immediately apparent as sometimes children need time or repetition of the activity in order for it to make a difference.

AC 4.5 The role of adults in promoting emotional well-being in the setting

There are a number of ways that adults can support children's emotional well-being. It is important to consider these and also to reflect on how well you manage these.

In practice

Look at each of the ways in which adults can support children's emotional well-being. Giving examples, write about your strengths and weaknesses. Also write about how you might improve further.

Table 1.4.8 Evaluating own role when promoting children's well-being

Responding sensitively to children	Do you note children's mood?
	Do you listen carefully to children without being distracted?
Acknowledging children's feelings	Do you acknowledge children's emotions (e.g. feeling sad), rather than ignore them?
	Do you allow children to express their feelings (e.g. paint a black picture) or do you always try and distract them?
Responding positively to children	Do you smile and show positive body language?
	Do you show that you care about the children through the way you talk?
Providing opportunities to be independent	Do you give children time to try things for themselves rather than take over?
	Do you allow children to make mistakes so that they can learn (e.g. shoe on wrong foot)?
Empowering children	Do you encourage children to do as much as they can during physical care routines (e.g. washing hands, toileting)?
	Are you respectful of children during physical care routines (e.g. allowing privacy)?
Providing opportunities for children to enjoy being with others	Do you plan activities that are appropriate for pairs or small groups of children to be together?
	Do you allow children time to settle their own disputes or do you always take over immediately?
	Do you acknowledge and, where appropriate, praise children for showing cooperative behaviours?
	Do you model cooperative behaviours?

Assessment

For this unit you will need to complete a variety of tasks. Some of these tasks will focus on whether you have acquired the knowledge needed to support your practice with children. There are many links between this unit and Unit 3.12, so a good starting point will be to read the sections in Unit 3.12 that relate to theories of attachment. You should also revisit the impact of secure relationships on children's well-being.

The role of the key person is an important component of this unit. You need to understand how the key person role is linked to the current early years framework and its importance to children's emotional development.

For this you can download a copy of the Statutory Framework for the Early Years Foundation Stage and read the paragraphs that inform current practice. You can gain an up-to-date copy of the EYFS by visiting **www.dfe.gov.uk** or **www.foundationyears.org. uk**. Another key component of this unit is about transition. You will need to know the different types of transitions that children undertake and how adults can support these.

As well as tasks that are linked to the knowledge outcomes in this unit, you will also need to prepare for your assessor to watch you working with children. You will need to show that the way you work with children helps them to build independence, self-reliance, confidence and other such characteristics that support children's emotional well-being.

Before your assessor comes it is worth asking your placement supervisor to give you feedback about the way you interact and support children in a range of different situations. Finally, for this unit you need to plan an activity that will support children's emotional well-being. The starting point when planning activities is of course to think carefully about the age and stage of children. Examples of activities for different ages and stages of children have been given in this unit and so these could be used to give you some ideas.

Useful resources

Films

Siren Films

High-quality DVDs showing the importance of attachments and key people in the EYFS.

www.sirenfilms.co.uk

Books and articles

Bowlby, J. (1969), *Attachment and Loss. Vol. I: Attachment*. London: Hogarth Press.

Bruce, T. (2005), *Early Childhood Education and Care* (3rd edn). London: Hodder Arnold.

Elfer, P. and Dearnley, K. (2007), 'Nurseries and emotional well-being: Evaluating an emotionally containing model of continuing professional development', *Early Years: An International Journal of Research and Development* 27(3): 267–79.

Dearnley, K., Elfer, P., Grenier, J., Manning-Morton, J. and Wilson, D. (2008) 'Appendix 1: The key person in reception classes and small nursery settings', in *and Emotional Aspects of Development: Guidance for Practitioners Working in the Early Years Foundation Stage*. Nottingham: DCSF Publications, available at http://nationalstrategies.standards.dcsf.gov.uk/node/132720.

Freud, A., in collaboration with Dorothy Burlingham (1973) *The Writings of Anna Freud. Vol. III: Infants Without Families [and] Reports on the Hampstead Nurseries, 1939–1945*. New York: International Universities Press.

Isaacs, S. (1945), *Childhood and After: Some Essays and Clinical Studies*. London: Agathon Press.

Winnicott, D.W. (1964), *The Child, the Family and the Outside World*. London: Penguin Books.

Unit 1.5 Understand how to support children who are unwell

Do you remember being sick as a child? For children it can be frightening as well as unpleasant. In this unit, we look at the how to support children who are unwell, including recognising childhood illnesses and when children are becoming poorly, as well as how we might care for children when they are for ill. We look at how some diseases are reported to health authorities as they are considered to be significant. While most children's illnesses are temporary and not severe, there are some children who may have long-lasting medical conditions or who need to go into hospital. In this unit, we also look at how we might support these children.

Learning outcomes

By the end of this unit, you will:

1 Know common childhood illnesses.
2 Know the signs of ill health in children.
3 Understand legal requirements for reporting notifiable diseases.
4 Understand the role of the early years practitioner in minimising ill health in children.
5 Understand care routines when a child is ill.
6 Understand how to support children for planned hospital admission.
7 Understand the therapeutic role of play in hospitals.
8 Understand the role of the early years practitioner when supporting children who are chronically ill.

LO1 Know common childhood illnesses

Do you remember waking up with a rash or a sore throat? While some of the more serious childhood illnesses are now rare, children still become poorly with different infections. In this section, we look at the common childhood illnesses, their symptoms and also their treatment.

AC 1.1 Identifying common childhood illnesses

It is important for adults working with children to know about the different childhood illnesses that children might get. Table 1.5.1 shows the most common childhood illnesses, along with their signs and symptoms.

AC 1.2 Signs and symptoms of common childhood illnesses

It is helpful if adults working with children can recognise the signs and symptoms of common childhood illnesses and identify those which may be serious. Having said this, it is important for adults working with children to remember that they are not doctors and nurses and, where there is any concern about a child's health, parents should be notified quickly and advised to seek medical attention. Table 1.5.1 shows the usual signs and symptoms, although it is worth remembering that children do vary. For example, some children may only have three or four chickenpox spots to start with, while others may have more of a rash.

Table 1.5.1 Common childhood illnesses

Infection	Signs and symptoms	
Chickenpox (varicella) Incubation time: 2–3 weeks	• Pink spots that turn to blisters, usually starting on head and behind ears • Slight fever and headache	• Spots in crops and very itchy • Children feel unwell
German measles (rubella) Incubation time: 2–3 weeks	• Slight fever • Rash of tiny red-pink spots – not very itchy • Rash starts on face and neck and spreads to body	
Measles Incubation time: 10–14 days	• Child feels unwell • Tiny greyish spots in mouth and throat • Cold-like symptoms, runny nose, red eyes, sneezing • Blotchy red rash starts behind ears and on face • Sensitivity to light	
Hand, foot and mouth Incubation time: 3–5 days	• High fever • Cough • Mouth ulcers	• Loss of appetite • Sore throat
Impetigo bullous Incubation time: 4–10 days	• Fluid-filled blisters appear on the chest • Blisters spread quickly but are not painful or itchy	
Impetigo non-bullous	• Red sore around the nose and mouth	• Sores burst leaving yellow-brown crusts
Ear infection	• Temperature • Child feels unwell • Babies and toddlers may rub or pull at their ear	
Influenza	• Sudden onset, unlike a cold, which is more gradual • Fever • Headache • Children feel very unwell, e.g., tiredness, aching muscles, sore throat • Dry, chesty cough	

→

Table 1.5.1 Common childhood illnesses (contd.)

Infection	Signs and symptoms
Scabies	• Tiny rash caused by a parasite burrowing into the skin • Very itchy rash • Babies may develop blisters on their feet
Scarlet fever Incubation time: 2–5 days	• Begins with sore throat, headache and fever • Rash begins with red blotches that turn into a fine pink-red rash that feels like sandpaper
Diarrhoea and vomiting (food poisoning and norovirus)	• Diarrhoea • Vomiting
Common cold	• Raised temperature • Sneezing and runny nose
Whooping cough Incubation time: 6-20 days	• Symptoms at first are mild and are cold-like, e.g., sneezing, runny nose, but a dry irritating cough • Child may feel unwell and have a slight temperature • Later symptoms are more serious • Bouts of intense coughing which bring up thick phlegm • Vomiting after coughing • Tiredness and exhaustion as a result of the coughing

Meningitis (bacterial and viral)	• This can be a fatal disease with a very rapid onset
	• Early symptoms:
	  • Severe headache
	  • Fever
	  • Cold hands and feet, shivering
	• Later symptoms:
	  • Nausea and vomiting
	  • Drowsiness and unresponsiveness
	  • Unusual crying
	  • Rapid breathing rate
	  • Unable to tolerate bright light
	  • Blotchy red rash that does not fade or colour when a glass is pressed against it

Mumps
Incubation time: 14–25 days (often 17)
	• Early symptoms:
	  • Headache
	  • Joint pain
	  • Fever
	• Followed by swelling of glands (underneath ears)

Tonsillitis	• Sore throat • High temperature • White pus-filled spots on tonsils • Headache

AC 1.3 Treatments for common childhood illnesses

Depending on the type of illness, children will need different types of treatment. Where illnesses are caused by a virus, such as chickenpox and flu, the usual course of action is to make sure that children have sufficient rest and drink enough to avoid dehydration. Where children are prescribed antibiotics, it is essential that the course of treatment is completed. Table 1.5.2 shows some of the treatments for the common illnesses.

Table 1.5.2 Treatments for common childhood illnesses

Infection	Treatment
Chickenpox	• No specific treatment. • Paracetamol to relieve fever and calamine lotion and cooling gels to ease itching may be given.
German measles	• No specific treatment but paracetamol can be given to reduce temperature. • Children must be kept away from pregnant women because, if this disease is caught during pregnancy, it can harm the baby.
Measles	• Paracetamol can be given to reduce fever. • Children may prefer to be in a darkened room. • Plenty of drinks should be offered.
Hand, foot and mouth	• No specific treatment. • Offer plenty of fluids and also soft foods to make eating easier.
Impetigo bullous and non-bullous	• Antibiotic cream or tablets.
Scabies	• Insecticidal cream will be prescribed by a doctor. • Family members will need to be treated.
Scarlet fever	• Treatment with antibiotics. • Paracetamol to relieve fever.
Meningitis (bacterial)	• Hospitalisation and treatment with antibiotics.
Meningitis (viral)	• Hospitalisation may be required along with treatment with anti-viral drugs.
Mumps	• No specific treatment but plenty of drinks should be offered and also paracetamol to reduce pain or fever. • Soft foods to be offered as children will have difficulty in swallowing.
Influenza	• No specific treatment, but paracetamol can be given to reduce fever. • Plenty of drinks should be offered.

Diarrhoea and vomiting (food poisoning and norovirus)	• Plenty of drinks to be provided, but not fizzy drinks or fruit juices.
	• Food can be introduced once vomiting has stopped. Foods high in carbohydrates, such as pasta, bread and rice, are recommended.
	• Medical attention to be sought if:
	  • there is persistent vomiting without diarrhoea
	  • there is blood or mucus in stools
	  • diarrhoea symptoms have not improved after seven days.

Common cold	• No specific treatment. • Plenty of drinks should be offered.
Ear infection	• Antibiotics may be given if the doctor feels it is necessary.
Whooping cough	• Antibiotics given as soon as possible. • Babies under 12 months may be hospitalised.
Tonsillitis	• No specific treatment but paracetamol may be given to reduce fever. • Plenty of drinks and soft foods should be offered.

AC 1.4 Exclusion periods

To prevent the spread of infection, all early years settings and schools will have a policy about when children who have been ill are able to return. These are known as exclusion periods. The source of information about these exclusion periods at the time of writing is Public Health England (PHE) and in turn local authorities or individual settings will devise their own policies. Table 1.5.3 shows the exclusion periods that are currently advised by PHE.

Table 1.5.3 Exclusion periods as advised by PHE

Infection	Recommended exclusion period
Chickenpox	Five days from onset of rash
German measles	Six days from onset of rash
Hand, foot and mouth	None
Impetigo	Until lesions are crusted or healed, or 48 hours after commencing antibiotic treatment
Influenza	Until recovered
Measles	Four days from onset of rash
Scabies	None
Scarlet fever	Children can return 24 hours after commencing appropriate antibiotic treatment
Diarrhoea and vomiting (food poisoning and norovirus)	48 hours from last episode of diarrhoea or vomiting
Common cold	None
Whooping cough	Five days from start of antibiotic treatment or 21 days from onset of illness if antibiotics not used
Meningitis (bacterial)	Until recovered
Meningitis (viral)	None
Mumps	Five days from onset
Tonsillitis	None

LO2 Know the signs of ill health in children

Have you noticed that some children tend not to want to eat or are very irritable just before they fall ill? In this section, we look at how to identify the signs that children are becoming poorly. We also look at situations in which children may need medical intervention.

AC 2.1 The signs and symptoms of ill health

When children are beginning to fall ill, there will often be signs and symptoms that their immune system is fighting an illness. It is important to recognise these so that children can be given opportunities to rest and receive medical attention and also for them to be separated from other children in order to prevent the spread of infection.

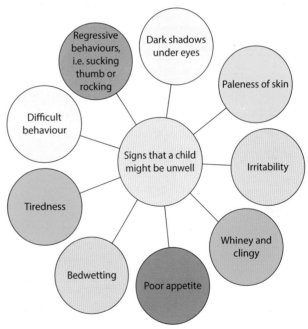

Figure 1.5.2 Signs that a child might be unwell

Common symptoms

As well as the signs that children are starting to become unwell, we should also be looking out for symptoms that show that the immune system is trying to fight something. Common symptoms include a raised temperature or fever, headache, sore throat and, in the case of illnesses such as chickenpox, a rash.

Test yourself

List five signs that might indicate that a child is becoming unwell.

In practice

Make a leaflet explaining to a new member of your workplace team how to identify children who may be unwell and the procedures that they should follow.

AC 2.2 When medical intervention is necessary

There are some signs and symptoms that children might show which mean that immediate medical attention is needed. It is important that if ever you are concerned, you err on the side of caution. This is because babies' and young children's immune systems are still developing and so an infection can quickly take hold. In the case of some diseases, such as meningitis, these can be fatal. Table 1.5.4 lists the signs and symptoms that indicate when immediate medical attention should be sought.

Table 1.5.4 Signs and symptoms when medical attention should be sought

Temperature	• Raised temperature of 38°C if the child is under three months • Raised temperature of 39°C if the child is three to six months • High temperature with quietness and lack of responsiveness • Convulsions
Breathing	• Difficulty in breathing • Fast breathing • Grunting when breathing
Skin colour and rash	• Spotty purple-red rash • Turning blue • Skin mottled colour • Very pale
Responsiveness	• Lack of response • Floppiness • Hard to wake up • Difficulty in staying awake
Other	• High-pitched cry • Continuous cry • Neck stiffness • Not drinking for more than eight hours • Repeated vomiting • Bile-stained vomiting (green) • In babies, bulging fontanelle (soft part at top of skull)

LO3 Understand legal requirements for reporting notifiable diseases

Have you ever had scarlet fever or mumps? If you have, your family doctor and also your school would have had to let the authorities know. In this section, we look at which diseases are notifiable and how these are reported.

AC 3.1 Notifiable diseases

There are some diseases which doctors and early years practitioners are required by law to report to either the local authority or their local health protection team. This is either to prevent the disease from spreading, as in the case of meningitis, or to provide information about disease trends, such as whooping cough.

All the current notifiable diseases, many of which are extremely rare.

- Acute encephalitis
- Acute infectious hepatitis
- Acute meningitis
- Acute poliomyelitis
- Anthrax
- Botulism
- Brucellosis
- Cholera
- Diphtheria
- Enteric fever (typhoid or paratyphoid fever)
- Food poisoning
- Haemolytic uraemic syndrome (HUS)
- Infectious bloody diarrhoea
- Invasive group A streptococcal disease
- Legionnaires' disease
- Leprosy
- Malaria
- Measles
- Meningococcal septicaemia
- Mumps
- Plague
- Rabies
- Rubella
- SARS
- Scarlet fever
- Smallpox
- Tetanus
- Tuberculosis
- Typhus
- Viral haemorrhagic fever (VHF)
- Whooping cough
- Yellow fever

However, as the list of notifiable diseases can change and procedures for reporting diseases can change, it is important to keep up to date with the latest guidelines. Visit the Public Health England website to find out more about current notifiable diseases: www.gov.uk/government/organisations/public-health-england.

AC 3.2 The process for reporting notifiable diseases

When a child has a notifiable disease, their family GP will fill in a form that will be sent to the local health protection team. For early years settings, there is a requirement that, if children have a serious illness, the early years setting must inform Ofsted within 14 days. This is usually the responsibility of the manager or, if the manager is not available, the deputy. In addition, the early years setting is also required to get into contact with their local health protection unit. This can be done by calling the health protection team directly.

> **In your setting**
>
> Find out who in your setting would be responsible for reporting a notifiable disease.

LO4 Understand the role of the early years practitioner in minimising ill health in children

Do you remember as a child sitting waiting for a parent to collect you because you were unwell? This was probably done to minimise the risk of your germs passing to other children. In this section, we look at how early years practitioners can minimise ill health in children.

AC 4.1 Minimising ill health in children

When children are ill, it is important that we find ways to prevent the spread of infection and also help children to recover quickly.

Preventing the spread of infection

As we saw in Unit 1.3, there are many ways to prevent the spread of infection, including using disposable gloves and aprons when dealing with bodily fluids and making sure that adults maintain good hand washing procedures. In addition, adults should wash their hands after touching children who are clearly poorly, but also before washing or giving medicine.

Preventing secondary infections

Sometimes when children are ill, they are more likely to pick up another infection because their immune system is weak. There is a range of measures that you can take to prevent secondary infections, and these are discussed below.

Hygiene

As we have already seen, hand washing is very important in reducing the risk of infection. As well as adults caring for children, visitors too should be encouraged to wash their hands. The environment in which children are being cared for also needs to be hygienic. This means that bed linen should be changed every few days and children's pyjamas and underwear should be changed each day. The room itself should be kept clean so that the risk of any further infections is reduced.

Mobility

It is beneficial for children to spend a little time sitting up or moving, even for a few minutes, when they are unwell. This is important to ensure good circulation.

Good ventilation

Opening a window slightly reduces the amount of viruses and bacteria in the air for children to breathe.

Encouraging children to rest

Children are more likely to recover if they sleep and rest. While, at first, children who are poorly are likely to want to do this, later as children are becoming better, they may not be willing to rest. It is therefore a good idea to think about some interesting activities for children that are not physically demanding – for example, jigsaw puzzles, playing cards or sharing books.

Providing a good-quality diet

What children eat can speed up their recovery. Food that is high in protein (meat, eggs, fish, chicken and pulses) is considered to be beneficial to health, along with fruit and vegetables. This is because protein is known to repair cells. Fruit and vegetables also have minerals and vitamins in them. In addition, if children have not been eating well, a medical practitioner may recommend supplementing their diet with vitamin and iron tablets.

Minimising contact with other people

While it is helpful for children to have visitors, it is important that children are not in contact with anyone who is poorly themselves. If children have been very poorly, the number of different contacts should be minimised as each visitor increases the risk of infection.

LO5 Understand care routines when a child is ill

Do you remember being bored when you were poorly, but not well enough to get up? In this section, we look at how we might support care routines when a child is ill.

AC 5.1 The needs of an ill child

Most early years practitioners will not have responsibility for children when they are ill as children usually want to be with their parents. However, some early years practitioners, such as nannies, may provide care when children are unwell.

The importance of maintaining a routine

When children are ill, it is helpful if a routine is followed as this can give them security. This means that having a set breakfast, lunch, dinner and bedtime is important, unless a child is very seriously ill, in which case a routine may be totally suspended.

Food

Many children will go off their food when they are poorly and this is not a cause for concern. Soft food is easier to eat for children who are unwell, so foods such as mashed potato, yoghurt and soups can work well, especially if children have sore throats. While we should encourage children to eat, it is often best to offer them small quantities regularly.

Providing drink

It is important for all children who are ill to drink sufficiently. This is to prevent dehydration, which can cause medical complications. Ideally, children should be offered drinks hourly and these can include water, milk or diluted fruit juices. Where children have diarrhoea, water is considered to be the best option, although babies should be offered their usual milk feeds.

Personal care

It is important to keep children clean when they are ill and so the personal care routines that we looked at in Unit 1.3 should still be completed. This is to prevent the risk of skin infections but also to keep them feeling comfortable and fresh. Many children may also have toileting accidents when they are not well and so these should be dealt with sensitively. It is important during personal care routines to use disposable tissues and wipes to prevent infection.

Rest and sleep

One of the key ways in which the body fights infection and responds to illness is through sleep and rest. In Unit 1.3, we looked at children's usual patterns and needs for rest and sleep, but when children are ill they are likely to want to sleep and rest more. It is important to follow children's needs for sleep and rest, although ideally it is helpful if the usual routine of bedtime is kept. Once children start to feel better, they are likely to want to be more active and sleep less. It is important to recognise when to follow their lead, but to understand that they may quickly tire and so need to rest or sleep.

Emotional well-being

Children need a lot of reassurance when they are ill as they are at their most vulnerable. They may show clinginess and want extra cuddles and reassurance. Some children will also want an adult to sit with them while they fall asleep or for their bed to be moved so that they can hear an adult. It is also worth recognising that events such as bouts of coughing or vomiting are frightening for children and they may need an adult to help them talk about these. Children may also need adults to acknowledge how they are feeling.

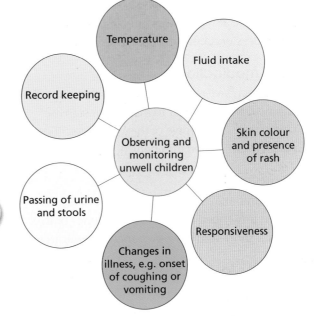

Figure 1.5.3 Observing and monitoring unwell children

> **Reflect**
>
> Did you ever experience a situation as a child when you wanted adults to listen to you and to acknowledge how you were feeling?

Dignity and respect

As with all aspects of physical care, we need to maintain children's rights to dignity and respect. This should underpin how we talk to children, listen to them and also how we carry out physical care routines, such as washing and undressing them. As part of children's right for dignity, we should try to give them as much privacy as possible and also encourage them to do as much of their personal care as is practicable.

Observation and monitoring

It is important that children who are unwell are carefully observed and monitored. This is because children's health can change quickly and so a child who seemed fine at the start of the day may become increasingly poorly as the day progresses. This can be as a result of the way that the illness is progressing or it may be that other medical complications are developing. Children should therefore be observed and monitored even when they are asleep. Figure 1.5.3 shows what you should observe and monitor.

If you are sharing the care of a child with a parent or another professional, it is important to keep records detailing such things as the child's temperature, how much fluid they have had and also how the child has been feeling during the day.

> **Case study**
>
> Lucien is two years old. He has chickenpox and is feeling unwell. His mother has asked you to keep an eye on him for two hours while she has a break. His skin is still itchy. He is not very hungry, although he will eat chopped-up bananas. He is quite clingy and does not want to be left alone. He needs some encouragement to drink.
>
> 1 Make a list of Lucien's care needs.
> 2 For each care need, explain why it is important.
> 3 Explain what information will need to be shared with Lucien's mother when she returns home.

AC 5.2 Procedures for storing, giving and recording medication

It is common to find that some children in early years settings need medication. As a result, all early years settings will have a range of procedures covering the administration of medicines. In the EYFS, there are specific legal requirements in place that early years settings have to follow.

There is a range of reasons why children might need medication.

Occasional use

Some children need medication occasionally while they are in the early years setting. They may have a long-term medical condition such as asthma but only need to use their reliever inhaler when they feel breathless or are having an asthma attack.

Regular medication

Some children have medical conditions that require regular medication in order to manage or stabilise their condition. An example of this would be children with diabetes who need injections of insulin regularly.

Temporary use

Some children may need medication because they have been prescribed a course of antibiotics or eye drops for a short-term illness or medical condition.

Procedures for storage of medication

All settings have to have procedures in place for the safe storage of medicines. These have to conform to the COSHH regulations.

→ See Unit 2.3 for more on the COSHH regulations.

This means that, with a few exceptions, all medicines have to be locked away to keep them out of reach of children. Most early years settings have a cupboard that is locked, in which they keep medicines. There are some exceptions, though. Some medicines, such as **inhalers** used to relief asthma attacks and **Epi-Pens**, may be kept in places that are quicker for adults to access as these are potentially life-saving medicines. Inhalers and Epi-Pens should still be kept out of reach of children. Some medicines require refrigeration. Settings still have to ensure that children cannot access these, either by installing a safety gate in the kitchen or by putting the medicines in a container that can be locked.

Key terms

inhaler A device used to deliver medication to the lungs.

Epi-Pen A device used to inject adrenaline when a child is having a severe allergic reaction.

In your setting

Find out where your setting keeps children's medication, including inhalers for asthma.

Figure 1.5.4 All medication should be stored safely

Procedures for administration of medication

As well as procedures for the storage of medication, there are also procedures for giving medicine to children. There are clear requirements for this in the EYFS. The key points on these procedures are as follows:

- In early years settings, medication should usually only be given that has been prescribed by a nurse, doctor, dentist or pharmacist.
- For each medication that is to be given to a child, there must be written parental permission in place.
- You must have training to give a medicine that requires technical or medical knowledge – for example, an Epi-Pen or insulin injection.

In addition, most settings will insist that medicines come in their original packaging or container. This means that, if necessary, settings can find out more about the medication and its side effects, as well as check that it was intended for the child.

All early years settings should have policies and procedures about how they administer medicines. It is quite common to find that it is the responsibility of the first aider to administer all medicines.

Practical procedures to follow when administering medicines

- Read the label on the medicine carefully to check:
  - the name of the child
  - the dosage that should be given and how it should be administered
  - the expiry date of the medication (this is important because, if the medicine has expired, it may not be effective or safe)
  - the instructions about when and how it should be given (e.g. 'an hour before food' or 'shake before use').
- For liquid medicines, always use the measure that comes with it and wash it first.
- Pour medicines with the label away from you to prevent drips, which could make it difficult to read the label later.

In your setting

What are the procedures in place to give children medicines in your setting? Who usually administers them?

Case study

Daisy Swift is four years old. She has asthma and has a blue inhaler (Ventolin), which she needs if she has an asthma attack or if she looks out of breath. One afternoon, at three o'clock, she is playing outdoors and running around. After ten minutes, her key person notices that she is starting to wheeze and looks out of breath. She quickly finds the inhaler, which is always kept close by, and checks that it is Daisy's and is in date. Daisy has two puffs of the inhaler and after five minutes goes back to her game.

1 Why was it important that Daisy's inhaler was easily accessible?
2 Why did the key person check that it belonged to Daisy?
3 Why is it important that the key person checks the expiry date of the inhaler?

Procedures for record keeping with regard to medication

The EYFS requires that each time a medication is given, a record is kept. It is also a requirement that parents are informed at the end of the session or day that medication has been given. Information that is usually recorded includes:

- the date and time when medication was given
- the name of the child
- the name of the medication that was given
- the quantity of the medication that was given
- the reason for the medication being given
- any side effects
- the name and signature of the person who gave the medication.

In practice

Ask your placement supervisor if you could copy the form used to record the administration of medicines to children. Look at the earlier case study and fill in the form as if you had given the medication to Daisy.

AC 5.3 Procedures to be followed in a setting when a child is taken ill

There may be times when a child becomes ill in an early years setting. When this happens, the following procedures are likely to be followed:

- Child is reassured, but moved away from the other children to prevent spread of infection.
- Child's condition is assessed and continues to be monitored.
- Parents are called so that they can make arrangements to collect their child. (Where parents cannot be contacted, the early years setting will call other contact names that have been given by the parents.)
- In a situation where there are concerns that a child's condition is deteriorating, immediate medical attention will be sought.

LO6 Understand how to support children for planned hospital admission

Did you go into hospital as a child? It can be quite scary for children if they are not prepared. In this section, we look at how early years practitioners can support children before they go into hospital.

AC 6.1 Supporting a child preparing for a stay in hospital

Going into a hospital can be frightening for children so most hospitals work with parents to prepare children for this. Many hospitals use booklets and also film clips to help children understand what will happen when they are in hospital. Some hospitals will also let children look around beforehand. When it comes to the role of the early years practitioner, their main duty is to work closely with the parents and, where appropriate, the hospital to decide on how best to prepare the child. This is important because, if all the adults do not work closely together, children may get mixed messages about what will happen when they are in the hospital and this can make the child more anxious.

Preparing children for a planned admission

There are many strategies involved in preparing children for hospital. It is important to remember that children need accurate information so that they are prepared for what will happen to them. This means that you should always find out as much as you can about the procedure that the child

will be having. Children will also need plenty of opportunities to talk through their feelings and their concerns. How exactly adults can help children prepare for a hospital admission depends on a range of factors.

Timing of the admission

In some cases, families will be told that a child is due for an admission but no definite date is given, while other times, a definite date is already booked.

Age of the child/level of understanding

How adults prepare children will depend on their age and also level of understanding. Very young children may find it harder to understand the concept of 'hospital' unless they visit one or learn about it from a film clip. They may need longer to process information and may need repeated activities such as stories.

Previous experiences of being in a hospital

Some children have had repeated stays in hospital. Provided these have been positive, children are likely to be more relaxed and will need less preparation. For other children, going into hospital will be a new experience and it will be important for children to feel positive about it.

Level of anxiety of parents

All children are quick to pick up on the level of anxiety of their parents and close family members. When adults are very anxious around children, it tends to make children fearful too.

Table 1.5.5 shows some of the ways in which children might be prepared for a planned admission.

Figure 1.5.5 Early years practitioners should help prepare children for a planned hospital admission

Table 1.5.5 Preparing children for a planned admission

Stories and books involving hospitals	Children can be introduced to the work of hospitals and the concept of children staying in hospital through books and stories. These can be read to children ahead of the planned admission. Time should be spent exploring what the characters in the stories might feel like and what they might not like.
Visiting the hospital	Where appropriate, a visit to the hospital beforehand can be useful.
Film clips and images of hospitals	It can be helpful for children to see realistic images of hospitals and also of the people who work in them.
Role play	Role play can be used as a way to help children understand what will happen to them in hospital. Adults will need to lead the play at first.
Creating a scrapbook	It can be worth creating a scrapbook telling the story of their admission into hospital. The idea of the scrapbook is to help children think of their operation or admission as a journey. In the scrapbook might be an appointment card and a photograph of the hospital.

LO7 Understand the therapeutic role of play in hospitals

Did you know that play is used to help children in hospitals? A playroom with toys can be found in nearly every children's ward. In this section, we look at the role of therapeutic play to support children's recovery.

AC 7.1 The therapeutic role of play in helping children recover

We will see in Theme 3 how play is important for children's overall development and learning. When children are in hospital, play is also used to help them recover, to help them come to terms with the experiences they have and also as a way of helping them to express emotions. It is also used to help children gain skills that they may have lost or need to develop. Play is also helpful for children because, although they are in an environment that may feel unfamiliar and which they cannot control, through play children can take control of what they do. This can make them feel more confident. Play can also help staff understand what children are thinking as many children will talk as they are playing. When staff see or hear children say something of significance, they will often make a note of it so that any issues can be addressed.

Most **paediatric wards** will have a playroom, toys and also qualified staff to help children play. As children will often be tired or resting, children can play at their own pace and the therapist will often follow children's leads. To help children come to terms with their experiences, there are usually opportunities for role play and props may include items that children will have seen, such as syringes, bandages and medical uniforms.

Where children are unable to leave their bed, toys and activities will be brought to them. The choice of these toys and activities will be based on the child's age and also their interests.

Key term

paediatric ward The ward on a hospital that specialises in nursing children.

LO8 Understand the role of the early years practitioner when supporting children who are chronically ill

Some children in early years settings will need additional support from practitioners because they have a chronic health condition. This section looks at the responsibilities early years practitioners have when supporting children, including their own need for training and development, working in partnership with others and demonstrating inclusive practice.

AC 8.1 The responsibilities of the early years practitioner

Some children who are in early years settings may have chronic health conditions. A chronic health condition means one that is long term. Figure 1.5.6 shows some common chronic health conditions that may affect children.

Training and development

In order to care properly for children with a chronic medical condition, it is important to fully understand what the condition is and also any signs that might be significant – for example, a child becoming disorientated or a change in their skin colour. Some children also need specific medication and it will be important for early years practitioners to know how to properly administer it and under what circumstances. Early years practitioners may gain this knowledge either directly from the medical practitioners

Case study

Jade is four years old. She is in hospital because she has had pneumonia. In the last couple of days, she has been well enough to go to the playroom. The paediatric play therapist has watched as Jade has dressed up as a nurse and cared for a dolly. She knows that Jade became distressed last week when she was given a bed bath. She asks Jade if it is time for the dolly to have a bed bath and when Jade says yes, she brings over some wipes and a cardboard bowl. Jade talks to the dolly and tells the dolly not to cry because she will be gentle. She also tells the dolly that she will only be able to go home

when she is not being naughty. The paediatric play therapist notes this down and later on talks to the nurse who is acting as the child's named nurse.

1 Why does the nurse encourage Jade to give the dolly a bed bath?
2 Why was it important for the paediatric play therapist to pick up on Jade's comments to the dolly?
3 Explain how play is helping Jade to cope with her experiences in hospital.

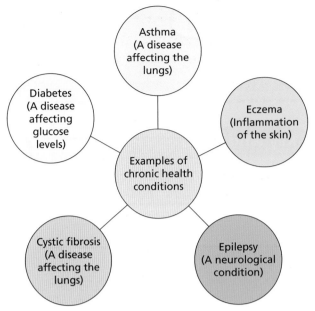

Figure 1.5.6 Chronic health conditions

supporting the child (e.g. nurse or doctor) or from the parent. In addition, to find out more information and also sometimes to gain further training, it can be worth contacting the relevant voluntary organisation, such as Asthma UK or Diabetes UK, as they are set up to support parents and professionals.

Partnership working

Partnership working means sharing information with and gaining information from parents and a range of different professionals. This is very important when working with children with medical conditions who may need careful monitoring or medicines/procedures.

Research it!

Look at two of the following websites and read the sections that are aimed at professionals to find out more about the medical conditions and how to support children:

- www.asthma.org.uk
- www.diabetes.org.uk
- www.epilepsy.org.uk
- www.cysticfibrosis.org.uk

As you may find yourself working for the first time with a child who has a certain illness, it is important not to be afraid of saying that you are unfamiliar with terms that are being used or how to use any equipment. Being honest in these situations can prevent misunderstandings which might affect the child's health.

→ For more information about the principles of partnership working, you should also look at Unit 2.5.

Inclusive practice

It is essential to work in ways that are inclusive when you work with children who have chronic medical conditions.

→ You might like to read this section alongside Unit 3.13.

Labelling the child

It is important to remember that, while a child might have a medical condition, the medical condition should not be what defines the child. This is why terms such as 'asthmatic child' or 'diabetic child' are not considered to be good practice because they literally put the disease before the child.

Sensitivity

Children who have medical needs often want adults to be sensitive and discreet. A child with medical needs may not want other children in the setting knowing that it is time for a treatment or to have attention drawn to their medical condition.

Access

It is important that thought is given to how children can be included in activities and to avoid situations where children have to sit out or are not invited to take part. This may mean adapting activities to suit children – for example, creating a stop/start game so that a child with asthma will have time to rest between bursts of activity or ensuring that a recipe for cooking does not have any ingredients that will mean that a child who has a severe allergy cannot take part.

Support for self

There may be times when you feel that you need support as caring for a child with a chronic illness can bring its own stresses. This is likely to be the case if you care for a child with a condition that is **life limiting**, such as cystic fibrosis, or when you have been with a child during a serious episode, such as an asthma attack or a child with diabetes losing consciousness. Gaining support may mean talking to a sympathetic colleague or line manager or gaining a referral by talking to your own family doctor.

In your setting

Find out how your setting works to ensure that children who have chronic medical conditions feel included.

Key term

life limiting When a medical condition reduces the life expectancy of a child.

Assessment

This unit is a knowledge-based unit so the tasks will focus on how much you know and understand. Your assessor may give you a case study, questions or may engage you in a professional discussion. It will be important that you have revised your knowledge before taking an assessment.

This unit looks at common childhood diseases as well as the immunisation programme. As advances in medical knowledge and treatment can change practices, it is important that you begin by using checking that you have the latest information. A good reputable source of information about medical conditions is the National Health Service's website (**www.nhs.gov.uk**), or you could gain information from your local family doctor or medical centre.

Start out by researching common childhood illnesses, their signs and symptoms, and their treatments. You also need to know the signs and symptoms that children are likely to show as they are fighting infection and when medical intervention is needed. There are two assessment criteria that consider notifiable diseases.

This is an area where practice does change. To gain up-to-date information, you should visit Public Health, England's website (**www.phe.gov.uk**) and look to see which disease are notifiable and the reporting process.

The final sections of the unit look at the role of the early years practitioner. You will need to know how to prevent illness and there are links here to Unit 1.3 which is worth revising. In addition, you need to show you can explain how you might help a child who is ill in relation to caring for them and administering medication. The administering of medication is an area where there are statutory requirements. You should therefore look at the statutory requirements within the statutory framework for the Early Years Foundation Stage.

You also need to know how you would support a child who is due to go into hospital and the importance of play in hospitals. The unit ends with a learning outcome about the responsibilities of early years practitioners who are working with children who have chronic medical conditions.

Useful resources

Organisations

Action for Sick Children

The UK's leading health charity, specially formed to ensure that sick children always receive the highest standard of care possible. Provides useful information for parents and professionals on all aspects of healthcare for children: **www.actionforsickchildren.org.**

Contact a Family

This website is for families who have a disabled child and those who work with disabled children or who are interested to find out more about their needs: **www.cafamily.org.uk**

Health Play Staff

Aims to promote the physical and emotional wellbeing of children and young people who are patients in hospital, hospice or receiving medical care at home: **www.nahps.org.uk**.

The Royal Society for Public Health

www.rsph.org.uk

Legislation, frameworks and professional practice

Unit 2.2 Understand legislation relating to the safeguarding, protection and welfare of children

Unit 2.3 WB Use legislation relating to the health and safety of children

Unit 4.1 Engage in professional development is also part of Theme 2. This is covered on pages 395–409.

Unit 2.4 WB Follow legislation relating to equality, diversity and inclusive practice

Unit 2.5 WB Working in partnership

Unit 2.2 Understand legislation relating to the safeguarding, protection and welfare of children

Safeguarding children's welfare means protecting them from physical, emotional and sexual abuse, and neglect. It also means helping children to grow into confident, healthy and happy adults.

Learning outcomes

By the end of this unit, you will:

1 Understand legislation and guidelines for the safeguarding, protection and welfare of children.
2 Understand policies and procedures for the safeguarding, protection and welfare of children.
3 Understand how to respond to evidence or concerns that a child has been abused or harmed.
4 Understand the purpose of serious case reviews.

LO1 Understand legislation and guidelines for the safeguarding, protection and welfare of children

Keeping children safe – everyone's responsibility

There is one aspect of work with babies, toddlers and young children that must always come first: the requirement to keep them safe, and to protect them from significant harm. All this work with children and families falls under the umbrella term of safeguarding.

AC 1.1 Current legislation and guidelines

> ### Key term
>
> **guidelines** This refers to the local authority's published supporting document for practitioners when looking at issues of safeguarding, welfare and child protection. This will be up to date with current legislation and in line with the guidance and procedures of the Local Safeguarding Children's Board (LSCB). It should also contain information about how to share sensitive information with others as well as how the early years practitioner can keep themselves safe.

Working Together to Safeguard Children (2013)

This document applies to those working in education, health and social services as well as the police and the probation service. It is relevant to those working with children and their families in the statutory, independent and voluntary sectors. The document covers the following areas:

- a summary of the nature and impact of child abuse and neglect
- how to operate best practice in child protection procedures
- the roles and responsibilities of different agencies and practitioners
- the role of Local Safeguarding Children Boards (LSCBs)

- the processes to be followed when there are concerns about a child
- the action to be taken to safeguard and promote the welfare of children experiencing, or at risk of, significant harm
- the important principles to be followed when working with children and families
- training requirements for effective child protection.

All early years practitioners should read *Working Together to Safeguard Children* in order to understand the principles and to perform their roles effectively. However, those who work regularly with children and young people and who may be asked to contribute to assessments of children and young people in need should read the relevant sections.

The new *Working Together to Safeguard Children* (2013) streamlines previous guidance documents to clarify the responsibilities of professionals towards safeguarding children and to strengthen the focus away from processes and onto the needs of the child. It replaces:

- *Working Together to Safeguard Children* (2010)
- *Framework for the Assessment of Children in Need and their Families* (2000), and
- 'Statutory guidance on making arrangements to safeguard and promote the welfare of children under section 11 of the Children Act 2004' (2007).

➡ See also Theme 1, for more on health and well-being, and also Section 3 of the EYFS statutory guidance.

'What to do if you're worried a child is being abused' (2006)

This is a guide for professionals working with children which explains the processes and systems contained in *Working Together to Safeguard Children* and *Framework for the Assessment of Children in Need and their Families*.

Protection of Children Act 1999

As a further safeguard to children's welfare, this Act requires childcare organisations (including any organisation concerned with the supervision of children) not to offer employment involving regular contact with children, either paid or unpaid, to any person listed as unsuitable to work with children on the Department of Health list.

The Disclosure and Barring Service (DBS)

The Disclosure and Barring Service helps employers make safer recruitment decisions and prevent unsuitable people from working with vulnerable groups, including children. (It replaces the Criminal Records Bureau [CRB] and Independent Safeguarding Authority [ISA].) The DBS acts as a central access point for criminal records checks for all those applying to work with children and young people.

The Children Act 2004

This Act placed a duty on local authorities and their partners (including the police, health service providers and the youth justice system) to cooperate in promoting the well-being of children and young people and to make arrangements to safeguard and promote the welfare of children.

The Act put the new Local Safeguarding Children Boards on a statutory footing (replacing the non-statutory Area Child Protection Committees), and gave them powers of investigation and review procedures which they use to review all child deaths in their area, as required by the *Working Together to Safeguard Children* statutory guidance. The Act also revised the legislation on physical punishment by making it an offence to hit a child if it causes mental harm or leaves a lasting mark on the skin. This repealed the section of the Children and Young Persons Act 1933 which provided parents with the defence of 'reasonable chastisement'.

In practice

Make sure you are familiar with the current safeguarding requirements in your area. Do they meet the legislation and advised guidelines? Could they be improved in any way?

AC 1.2 Policies and procedures on safeguarding, protection and welfare of children

All early years settings in the UK must be registered by the appropriate organisation and are also regularly inspected. Each of the home countries of the UK has its own system for registering and inspecting settings. All settings must demonstrate (through policies and codes of practice) how they intend to ensure that they meet the legal, regulatory requirements. All workplace policies and codes of practice must be drawn up within the framework of current legislation.

Key term

policy A safeguarding policy is a statement that makes it clear to staff, parents and children what the organisation or group thinks about safeguarding, and what it will do to keep children safe.

In addition to the **policy**, each early years setting will need clear procedures about what to do when there is a concern about a child. These should include:

- keeping a clear, written record of any concern identified
- reporting any concerns to a line manager, or the designated member of staff who is responsible for safeguarding, who will then decide what (if any) further action is required
- guidelines about how and whether to discuss the concern with the child and/or family.

Policies and codes of practice are usually kept in the staff room or manager's office. It is the employer's duty to ensure that each member of staff knows about the policies and procedures within the setting.

However, it is your responsibility to ensure that you have read and understood the documents. If you come across any policy matter that you are unsure about, you should know where to find the relevant document in order to find out what is expected of you in practice.

Legal requirements for all settings

All early years settings and schools must nominate a member of staff to oversee safeguarding and child protection. This person must be specifically trained to undertake this role. The whole team (including volunteers and students) must work together to promote children's welfare and keep them safe. The whole team will need regular training and updating, and it is best practice that such training provides staff with time to explore different experiences, attitudes and opinions as steps towards agreeing policy and practice.

Every adult working in the setting must be a *suitable person* to work with young children, and must have a full DBS clearance. This includes students on placements and regular volunteers.

➡ For more on DBS clearance, see page 88.

In practice

Find out what the legal term 'suitable person' means in relation to the care of young children.

Familiarise yourself with the safeguarding policy in your placement.

AC 1.3 How current legislation and guidelines inform policy and procedure

There is one aspect of work with babies, toddlers and young children that must always come first: the requirement to keep them safe, and to protect them from significant harm. All early years settings are bound by the laws described above – and by the many laws relating to health and safety.

➡ See Unit 1.2.

Schools and early years settings are places where children spend a considerable amount of their lives. Early years practitioners are some of the most important adults that young children will come into contact with. As a staff team, they can create an atmosphere and ethos which profoundly affect the child's experience of being cared for, listened to, valued, guided and stimulated. Early years settings and schools therefore play a considerable part in promoting children's best interests.

Safeguarding children in early years settings and schools

An early years setting or school keeps children safe by:

- having effective procedures around safe recruitment, management and its general operating policy; for example, if children are encouraged to speak out when they feel unhappy or uncomfortable, they will be much less vulnerable to abuse
- ensuring that children's intimate care – nappy changing, toileting, dressing and undressing – is coordinated by a key person. This reinforces the child's right to privacy, and the child would not then expect that just anyone could take them aside and undress them.

LO2 Understand policies and procedures for the safeguarding, protection and welfare of children

AC 2.1 The roles and responsibilities of the early years practitioner

Key term

roles and responsibilities Working within organisational policies and procedures.

Safeguarding systems
Common Assessment Framework (CAF)
The Children Act 2004 requires different agencies – for example, across education, health, children's social care and housing – to cooperate in the best interests of children and young people. The CAF provides a structure to facilitate this cooperation. (Although the CAF is specific to England, the same approach of working together is recommended in all the countries of the United Kingdom.)

Shared assessment

One of the many difficult issues when working with vulnerable children and families is making an assessment of what the needs of the child and the family are. In the example we will consider here, a health visitor may notice that a three-year-old girl presents as slightly more prone to infections than is usual, and appears a little low in energy. Her development may seem satisfactory in terms of number of words spoken and understood, walking and running, and building with blocks in the clinic.

However, the early years practitioners working with the child may have noticed that she appears sociable at first, but is not able to play with or alongside other children. It may have been observed that, while the child remains playing in areas of the nursery for some time, this involvement is only superficial and she is merely repeating the same actions over and over again.

As a result of these concerns, the child's key person could arrange to meet with the parents and the health visitor to discuss the extent to which the child is:

- healthy
- safe from harm
- learning and developing well
- socialising and making positive relationships with others
- not significantly impaired by the effects of poverty.

Team Around the Child (TAC)

This type of meeting is called Team Around the Child. There is a pre-assessment checklist for the CAF which early years practitioners can consult before calling such a meeting. It is important to remember that meetings like this, and the process of drawing up a CAF, are voluntary. Early years practitioners should only proceed with the **informed consent** of parents.

> ### Key term
>
> **informed consent** When anyone, child or adult, is given sufficient information to be able to make a genuine decision to say 'yes' or 'no' to a request.

Using our example of the three-year-old girl, in such a meeting the mother might explain that her child sometimes gets very little sleep at night because her older brother, with whom the girl shares a room, has disabilities and needs care through the night. The mother might explain that the family is feeling overwhelmed and very stressed, and that there is little time for positive attention for her daughter.

By bringing together the information from the health visitor, the early years practitioner and the parent, an assessment of needs can be made in the following areas:

- development of the child
- parents and carers
- family environment.

This assessment, and the action plan based on the assessment, will be recorded on a standard CAF form, or electronically (the eCAF). In this case, the possible benefits of the CAF could be:

- a referral to the Children's Centre family support service, in order to investigate whether the family could be entitled to disability carers' allowance with respect to the older sibling
- a local voluntary group offering to provide respite care for several hours a week so that the older brother can be cared for while the rest of the family have some time together
- an application for more suitable housing, supported by the different agencies.

The parent will be asked to nominate a lead professional to coordinate this plan. With the CAF, the parents will not constantly need to fill out different forms and repeat the same information to different agencies.

It is possible that, without this support, the child's development and play could have fallen further behind that of her peers in nursery, leading to her becoming more isolated and unhappy. The stress of the family's situation could have led to the child's needs being neglected at home. In a small number of cases, stress of this kind can lead to mistreatment of one or both children.

There are no specific mandatory laws in the UK that require professionals to report any suspicions they may have of child abuse to the authorities. In Northern Ireland, however, it is an offence not to report an arrestable crime to the police, which by definition includes crimes against children. In England, government guidance *Working Together to Safeguard children* (DCSF, 2013) states that:

Everybody who works or has contact with children, parents and other adults in contact with children should be able to recognise, and know how to act upon, evidence that a child's health or development is or may be being impaired – especially when they are suffering, or likely to suffer, significant harm.

The guidelines also state that all staff members who have or become aware of concerns about the safety or welfare of a child or children should know:

- *who* to contact in what circumstances, and *how*, and
- *when* and *how* to make a referral to local authority children's social care services or the police.

If there are any child welfare concerns, 'relevant information about the child and family should be discussed with a manager, or a named or designated health professional or a designated member of staff depending on the organisational setting'.

Following the procedures for safeguarding children

All the legislation and guidance in recent decades, including the Children Act 2004, make it clear that the child's interests must come first. All professionals must work together to promote the child's welfare before all else. For example, imagine that you found out that a father has slapped his child on the face, leaving a mark. You may have developed a very close relationship with this parent and you may be very sympathetic to the difficulties he is experiencing. You may feel that this incident is a 'one-off', that he genuinely loves and cares for the child, and that he would be devastated if you did not keep this to yourself. All the same, you are required to put the child's interests before your feelings about the family.

→ The actions you might take are discussed later in this chapter. See page 92.

Media and online safety, including the use of cameras and mobile phones

You will also need to ensure that you follow your setting's policy for media and online safety and ensure that you keep yourself safe as well as the children. Many setting policies now prohibit the use of personal cameras and mobile phones and the setting should provide their own, which are exclusively for your work with children and which stay in the setting or when you are working with the children. This is because you should not have any images of children on your own equipment, such as cameras, computers and phones. You should also ensure that any helpers or volunteers who may accompany children during trips or setting visits are aware of the policy.

In practice

Look at your setting's policy for online safety and the use of cameras and mobile phones. What are your responsibilities under the policy? How does the setting ensure that all members of staff are aware of the policy?

Test yourself

Explain your role and responsibilities in relation to the safeguarding, protection and welfare of children within your setting. Would you know whom to contact and how to report any concerns you have?

AC 2.2 Reporting and the responsibility to meet safeguarding, protection and welfare requirements

Duty of care

All adults, whether paid or unpaid, who work with or on behalf of children have a duty of care in that they are accountable for the way they exercise their authority, manage risk, use resources and otherwise act to safeguard children. In carrying out their work, the child's welfare must be paramount.

This means that they have a duty to:

- keep children safe, and protect them from sexual, physical and emotional harm and neglect
- treat children with dignity and respect at all times
- take reasonable steps to ensure children's safety and well-being; failure to do so may be regarded as neglect
- ensure that confidential information about children is only shared when it is in the child's interests to do so.

→ See page 93 for further information about confidentiality.

These duties are fulfilled by:

- developing respectful and caring relationships between adults and children
- consistently behaving as a professional adult in ways that demonstrate integrity, maturity and good judgement.

Safeguarding children

- All adults working with children have a statutory duty of care to safeguard children, and children's welfare is paramount.
- Everybody involved in an early years and childcare setting needs to be clear about their roles and responsibilities around safeguarding.
- All adults should receive safeguarding information as part of their induction, appraisal and supervision.
- Everybody involved in the early years and childcare setting must attend appropriate safeguarding training and ensure learning is embedded in practice.

- All settings must have safeguarding policies and procedures in place that are reviewed in line with local and national guidance and legislation.

Research it!

Look at a copy of the statutory guidance for the EYFS. Under Section 3, you will find the safeguarding and welfare requirements. Make notes on the different areas of the requirements, in particular 'Child Protection and Suitable People'.

In your setting

- What are your responsibilities for reporting information on possible abuse to a senior colleague or external agency?
- How and to whom should you pass on information from a child's personal disclosure of abuse? For example, what are your responsibilities for providing information on the disclosure to a senior colleague or external agency?

AC 2.3 The boundaries of confidentiality

Confidentiality and 'need to know'

In general, you must keep sensitive information confidential. If information circulates too freely, parents can feel very exposed and vulnerable. They may stop sharing information with staff.

Allegations made against staff

Schools and early years settings are usually some of the safest places for children to be. However, sadly there have been incidents when children have been harmed or abused by the adults who work with them and care for them. Cases include the discovery in 2009 that a nursery nurse, Vanessa George, had sexually assaulted and made and distributed indecent pictures of some of the children in her care.

Generally, an early years setting or school keeps children safe by having good procedures around safer recruitment, management and its general operating policy; for example, if children are

Tips for confidentiality

- **Where appropriate, seek consent before you share information** – you might find out on a home visit that a child's mother has a serious mental health difficulty, which is well managed by medication and therapy. However, the medication can make her feel rather tired first thing in the morning, and she tells you that she can struggle to take on information or hold a conversation then. So you might say, 'I'll need to tell my manager this, but shall we also let the staff team know, so they can talk with you at the end of the day and not in the morning?' The parent can then give or withhold consent freely.
- **Never disclose any information about a child's welfare in an inappropriate way** to people outside the setting or school – for example, you would not tell friends or family about a child protection conference you had attended.
- **Put the child's interests first** – if sharing information will help to ensure a child's safety, you must do this. In nearly all cases, you would start by explaining to the parent why you wish to share the information and how this would help the child. If a parent refuses, ask for advice and guidance from the named person for safeguarding or the manager/head of the setting. If a parent says something like, 'I did smack her round the head, but you won't tell anyone will you? They'll take her into care,' you will need to explain clearly that you are legally required to pass on information like this.

encouraged to speak out when they feel unhappy or uncomfortable, they will be much less vulnerable to abuse. Children's intimate care – nappy changing, toileting, dressing and undressing – should be coordinated by a **key person**. This means that children do not have the experience that anyone can take them aside and undress them, and their right to privacy is upheld. It is good practice, where developmentally appropriate, to ask children to consent to offers of intimate care and to give them as much control as possible. So you might say to a toddler in the toilet, 'Would you like me to help pull your pants down?' rather than just going ahead and doing it.

Key term

key person system A system within an early years setting in which care of each child is assigned to a particular adult, known as the key person. The role of the key person is to develop a special relationship with the child, in order to help the child to feel safe and secure in the setting. The key person will also liaise closely with each child's parents.

However, no system alone can protect children: what matters, beyond good policies and procedures, is that adults are confident to raise concerns, and that children are encouraged to say if they are unhappy or uncomfortable with anything that happens to them.

All early years settings and schools are required to have a policy to deal with allegations made against staff. This will cover cases where a child makes a disclosure, or an adult is seen or overheard behaving in an inappropriate way. But there are other examples that might give rise to a concern, without a specific allegation being made:

- a child who seems fearful of a particular member of staff
- a member of staff seeming to try to develop a very close relationship with a child – for example, offering small presents and special treats, or arranging to meet the child outside the setting or school
- a parent expressing a general concern about how a member of staff relates to their child, without being able exactly to say what is wrong.

In cases like these, you will need to discuss your concerns with the named person for safeguarding. Discussions like these are awkward, but it is important to share any concerns you have – the child's welfare is paramount.

In your setting

Explain the boundaries of confidentiality in relation to the safeguarding of children. Find out about your setting's policy and procedures with regard to the confidentiality of information in child protection matters.

AC 2.4 The benefits of partnership working

Partnership working is important to ensure that children's and young people's welfare is safeguarded regardless of where they are and who is looking after them. For example, where children receive education and care in more than one setting, early years practitioners must ensure continuity and coherence by sharing relevant information with each other and with parents or carers.

Different professionals and agencies should work together to help the child and family early on when there are difficulties. They should not wait until something serious happens before taking action. For example, a health visitor might notice that a mother is getting very stressed by the behaviour of her toddler and is struggling to cope. **Early intervention** might involve talking to the mother, showing sympathy, and perhaps finding some support for her at the local Children's Centre or setting up a programme of home visits. This would be much better than waiting to see if the situation becomes worse before doing anything. Although there is still a common view that social workers swoop in to take children away from their families, in reality, the vast majority of social work is about helping different agencies work together to support the family, so that the child's safety and well-being are assured.

Key term

early intervention This approach seeks to offer extra help and support to a family before the child starts to lag behind in development or experience neglect or abuse. Early intervention is about working cooperatively with parents and carers, giving them a chance to make choices about which services they need.

Initial assessment

An initial assessment is undertaken by specialist children's social workers in response to referrals made by, for example, schools, doctors, nurses and early years settings. The initial assessment informs the decision of what to do next. Possible decisions include the following:

- **Offering services to support the child and family**, if it is judged that the child is not at immediate risk of harm but is at risk of poor developmental outcomes.
- **Urgent action to protect the child from harm** (e.g. apply for a court order to take the child into care). Social workers cannot take children away from their parents: only the courts can direct this. However, a police officer can take a child into police protection in an emergency.
- **Holding a strategy discussion.** This would happen where the assessment indicates that the child may be suffering significant harm. Other professionals, like GPs, health visitors, teachers and early years practitioners, who know the child and family may be invited to this discussion. Specialist police officers must always be represented in strategy discussions. Where appropriate, a child protection conference will be arranged.

It is important to remember that staff in early years settings and schools should *not* investigate possible abuse or neglect. The role of the early years practitioner is to refer concerns to children's social care, contribute to the initial assessment and attend meetings as requested.

The initial assessment can lead to:

- further work and assessment being undertaken by specialist children's social workers (called the **Core Assessment**)
- help being offered to the child and family on a voluntary basis, usually coordinated under the CAF
- a **Child Protection Conference** being convened. Key staff working with the family, and the child's parents, will be invited to this conference. The meeting will be organised by an independent chair who has not previously been involved in the case in any way, and who reports to the Director of Children's Services.

Child Protection Conference

The Child Protection Conference seeks to establish, on the basis of evidence from the referral and the initial assessment, whether the child has suffered illtreatment, or whether their health or development has been significantly impaired as a result of physical, emotional or sexual abuse or neglect. A professional judgement must be made about whether further illtreatment or impairment is likely to occur. It is possible to hold a Child Protection Conference pre-birth if there are significant concerns that the newborn baby will be at risk of immediate harm (for example, in a family where there has been significant previous child abuse, or where a mother has abused drugs or alcohol during pregnancy).

If this is established, then the child will be made the subject of an inter-agency **child protection plan**. The child's early years setting or school should be involved in the preparation of the plan. The role of the school or early years setting to safeguard the child, and promote their welfare, should be clearly identified. Examples of this role might include:

- carefully monitoring the child's heath or well-being in the setting on a daily basis
- making referrals to specialist agencies, e.g. educational psychology
- offering support and services to the parents, e.g. a parenting class run at the setting
- monitoring the child's progress against the planned outcomes in the agreed plan.

Case study

One of your key children is subject to an inter-agency child protection plan, under the category of neglect. During the day, you notice that the child looks rather grubby. Other children are avoiding him because he smells.

1 How would you talk to the parent at the end of the day?
2 What information would you pass on to the child's social worker?

Key term

Core Group A group made up of the child (if appropriate), family members and professionals who are responsible for developing and implementing the child protection plan.

The Core Group

The Core Group of professionals and the child's parents must meet within 10 working days of a child being made subject to a child protection plan. The group will be called together by the child's social worker in the role of the lead professional (sometimes called the key worker), and will then meet regularly as required. This group should include a member of staff from the child's early years setting or school. The Core Group develops the child protection plan into a more detailed working tool, outlining who will do what and by when. Both this working plan and the overall child protection plan should be based on the assessments undertaken by the specialist social worker and others, and should address the issues arising in relation to:

- the child's developmental needs
- parenting capacity
- family and environmental factors.

There should be a review child protection conference within three months of the initial conference. Further reviews should be held at least every six months while the child remains subject to a child protection plan.

The plan may be ended if it is judged that there have been significant improvements to the well-being and safety of the child. These improvements might have taken place as a result of:

- a change in circumstances (for example, the abusing parent has moved out of the family home and no longer has unsupervised contact with the child)
- the family responding positively to the requirements set out in the plan, and following advice given
- the child being given the medical or other treatment they need.

At this stage, there might be no further involvement from Children's Services, or the family may continue to be offered further help and support by the different agencies, usually coordinated under the CAF. This only happens once Children's Services are satisfied that their involvement is not required because the child is no longer considered to be 'in need'.

Test yourself

1 What is the Common Assessment Framework (CAF) and how can it help children and their families?

2 Who can take children into protective care if they are in immediate danger?

3 Why might a child be made subject to an inter-agency child protection plan?

4 If early years practitioners suspect a child is being abused, should they investigate their concerns?

LO3 Understand how to respond to evidence or concerns that a child has been abused or harmed

AC 3.1 Child protection and safeguarding

What is safeguarding?

For some children, universal services such as early years education and health visiting are not enough to ensure their healthy, safe and happy development. These children might, for periods of time, be vulnerable. They may experience emotional difficulties, fall behind in their development or learning, or suffer the adverse effects of poverty, poor housing or ill health. The CAF exists to support children and families with appropriate help and advice for a brief period.

Child protection is a part of safeguarding and promoting welfare.

- It refers to the activity that is undertaken to protect specific children who are suffering, or are likely to suffer, significant harm.
- There are also *children in need*, who are judged to be unlikely to reach or maintain a satisfactory level of health or development unless they are offered additional services. This group includes children with disabilities.
- Finally, there are children who are subject to an **inter-agency child protection plan**. These children are judged to be at risk of significant harm without the provision of additional

services, as well as close and careful monitoring by specialist children's social workers.

All this work with children and families falls under the umbrella term of **safeguarding**.

In the Department for Education (DfE) document *Working Together to Safeguard Children* (March 2013), safeguarding and promoting the welfare of children are defined as:

- protecting children from maltreatment
- preventing impairment of a child's health or development
- ensuring that children grow up in circumstances consistent with the provision of safe and effective care, and
- taking action to enable all children to have the best outcomes.

This unit offers concise, useful and accurate information about safeguarding. If you have any doubts or concerns about a child, however trivial you might think they are, we strongly advise you to speak to the manager or head teacher of the early years setting or school where you are working. Always ask for information and guidance.

Key terms

inter-agency protection plan If a child's health or development has been significantly impaired as a result of physical, emotional or sexual abuse or neglect, an inter-agency protection plan may be drawn up. The plan will identify the steps that the family needs to take to safeguard the child, with the support of Children's Services and other agencies. The child's safety, health, development and well-being will be regularly monitored throughout the plan.

safeguarding This term includes: all the steps you would take in an early years setting or school to help children to feel safe and secure; protecting children from neglect or abuse; ensuring that children stay safe, healthy and continue to develop well.

Definitions of abuse and neglect

Abuse and neglect are forms of maltreatment of a child. Somebody may abuse or neglect a child by inflicting harm, or by failing to act to prevent harm. *Children may be abused in a family or in an institutional or community setting, by those known to them or, more rarely, by a stranger, for example, via the internet. They may be abused by an adult or adults, or another child or children.*

Source: Working Together to Safeguard Children: A Guide to Inter-agency Working to Safeguard and Promote the Welfare of Children (DCSF 2010)

There are four categories of abuse: physical, emotional and sexual abuse, and neglect. These are outlined on the following pages.

Physical abuse

Physical abuse is the most apparent form of child abuse. It includes any kind of physical harm to a child, which can include hitting, shaking, throwing, poisoning, burning or scalding, drowning and suffocating.

Physical harm may also be caused when a parent or carer fabricates the symptoms of illness in a child, or deliberately induces illness – for example, giving a child so much salt that he or she becomes very ill, so that medical staff think the child has a gastric illness or a brain condition.

Emotional abuse

Emotional abuse is difficult to define and can be difficult to detect. It involves continual emotional mistreatment which results in significant damage to the child's emotional development. The child may come to feel worthless, unloved, inadequate or valued only if they meet the expectations or needs of another person. Emotional abuse includes the following:

- The parent having expectations that are well outside what is suitable for the child's age and development. This includes unreasonable expectations, like continuously trying to force a child to achieve more, and then constantly criticising the child for his or her failures. At the other end of the spectrum, some parents may fail to stimulate their child adequately – for example, keeping a two-year-old in a playpen with only a couple of baby toys.
- Preventing a child from participating in normal social interaction with other children, either

by keeping the child at home, or by taking the child out but being so overprotective, fearful or controlling that the child cannot join in.
- Failing to protect the child from witnessing the mistreatment of others – for example, cases of domestic violence.

All children will experience some emotional difficulties as part of the ordinary processes of growing up. It becomes abusive if the result is significant damage to the child's emotional development. All cases of child abuse will include some degree of emotional abuse.

Sexual abuse

Sexual abuse involves forcing or encouraging a child to take part in sexual activities. The child may or may not be aware of what is happening. Activities may involve physical contact – for example, rape, including forced anal sex or oral sex – or non-penetrative acts like touching or masturbation.

The abuse may include non-contact activities, such as involving children in looking at or in the production of sexual images online or on mobile phones, watching sexual activities or encouraging children to behave in sexually inappropriate ways.

Neglect

Neglect means that the parent persistently fails to meet the child's basic physical needs, psychological needs or both. The result is that the child's health or development is significantly impaired.

Neglect can occur during pregnancy if the mother abuses drugs or alcohol, which can have serious effects. Neglect of babies and young children includes the failure to:

- provide adequate food, clothing and shelter
- keep the child safe from physical and emotional harm or danger
- supervise the child adequately, including leaving the child with inadequate carers
- make sure the child is seen promptly by medical staff when ill
- respond to the child's basic emotional needs.

In addition to these categories, children may also be affected by domestic abuse.

Domestic abuse

This type of abuse takes place when one adult in a relationship exercises control over another in an actual or threatened way. It can cover physical, emotional, psychological or sexual abuse. It may affect children if they regularly witness harm or the threat of harm from one parent or parent's partner to the other. It is also more likely to mean that children themselves are being abused if they are in a household where domestic abuse takes place.

AC 3.2 Signs, symptoms, indicators and behaviours for concern

Early years practitioners are good at recognising when all is not well with a child. Historically, the biggest difficulty has not been in recognising problems, but in communicating concerns to others (including the child's parents) and acting on them. Often practitioners worry about the consequences of passing on information, and worry that it might lead to the family being split up. It is important to remember that, in the vast majority of cases, the different services will work with the family to ensure the child's safety. But the decision about what is best for the child should be made by a trained social worker, acting on the best possible information. When practitioners feel worried but do not communicate their concerns to others, a child can be put in danger.

The National Society for the Prevention of Cruelty to Children (NSPCC) states: 'Children and young people often find it very difficult to talk about the abuse they are experiencing. So adults have a vital role to play in looking out for the possible signs.'

The following section draws on the NSPCC's guide *Learn How to Recognise the Signs of Child Abuse*. It is not always possible to be completely certain that a child is being abused, but there are signs and indicators that all early years practitioners should look out for:

- a baby or toddler who is always crying
- a child who often has injuries or bruises
- a child who is often very withdrawn: withdrawn children are not simply quiet or shy – they shrink from adult attention, lack interest in their surroundings and try to occupy themselves without being noticed
- a child who is often in very dirty clothes, looks unwashed for a period of time or is very smelly
- a child who is frequently very hungry
- a child who is often inappropriately dressed for the weather or time of year: this would include children who often come to the setting in thin T-shirts, shorts or dresses through the winter; it would also include children who come into the setting on a hot day in very warm clothes
- any indication that a child is being left home alone, or left unsupervised in risky circumstances at home
- a child who does not receive the medical treatment he or she needs
- a child who is mocked, sworn at, constantly joked about and made to feel foolish or useless
- a child who expresses fear about particular adults, or seems reluctant to be picked up by a particular adult or afraid to be left alone with that person
- a child with very strong mood swings – anxiety, depression, uncontained anger or severe aggression
- a child whose sexual knowledge, use of sexual words or sexual behaviour is not appropriate for their age or development
- a child who is witnessing domestic violence
- a child who is witnessing significant drug or alcohol abuse.

There may be valid explanations for some of these signs. Equally, there are many other indications of possible abuse, and other circumstances that could be unsafe for a child. The NSPCC advises: 'The most important thing to remember is that if you have a gut feeling that something is not right, **trust your judgement** and take action.'

Reflect

Go through the NSPCC list above and identify which of these types of abuse may be indicated by the various signs:

- domestic abuse
- neglect
- physical abuse
- emotional abuse
- sexual abuse.

Research it!

You can read the full NSPCC guide *Learn How to Recognise the Signs of Child Abuse* at www.nspcc.org.uk.

In practice

Remember that when practitioners feel worried but do not communicate their concerns to others, a child can be put in danger. Make sure to:

- use your observational skills to learn how to recognise the indicators that may cause concern
- understand what is expected behaviour for children, and
- be aware of any unusual signs and symptoms that could indicate abuse.

If possible, arrange to attend a course to further your understanding of this complex subject.

AC 3.3 Actions to take if harm or abuse is suspected and/or disclosed

Allegations

Sometimes a child may allege information that leads you to think that he or she is being abused. With young children, this may happen in a number of ways. A child might tell you something directly: 'Mummy and daddy went out yesterday, and me and Scarlet were scared because we were all alone.' Or a child might use play to communicate – for example, you might observe a child in the home corner shouting at and slapping one of the dolls.

In all cases, your role when a child alleges is to listen very carefully and show concern. Reaffirm that it is good for the child to tell you things that are worrying or upsetting him or her. Say that you believe the child. If you are not sure about something the child has said, then ask for clarification: 'I'm not sure I quite understood – did you say it was your arm that hurts?'

However, there are also some things that you must not do. You must not question or cross-examine a child or seem to put words into a child's mouth. So you would not ask a question like 'Does this happen every day?' because the child might just agree with you, or repeat your words. You are there to listen and observe – you are not an investigator.

A child may make an allegation to anyone – his or her key person, the caretaker, the dinner supervisor, a student on placement. For that reason, it is very important that everyone who comes into contact with children has training on safeguarding and knows what to do if they have any reason to be worried about a particular child.

Key term

disclosure A safeguarding allegation means the giving out of information that might commonly be kept secret, usually voluntarily or to be in compliance with legal regulations or workplace rules. (Allegation used to be known as disclosure.) For example, a child tells an adult something that causes him or her to be concerned about the child's safety and well-being.

Procedure for when abuse is suspected

If a child alleges (makes an allegation) to you, or if you are worried for one or more of the reasons listed by the NSPCC (see page 98):

- Make a note that is as exact as you can make it, recording exactly what the child said, and anything you noticed (signs of an injury, child seeming upset, stressed, angry or ashamed while talking to you). If you have had ongoing concerns, summarise what these are; again, be as accurate as you can.
- Discuss your concerns as a matter of urgency with the named member of staff for safeguarding, however busy that person seems to be.

In most cases, the named member of staff will discuss the concerns with the parent and then make a judgement about what to do next. You should be told what action (if any) is being taken, and why. Responses might include:

- no action – for example, in a case where a parent gives a reasonable explanation for their child's injury or behaviour

- advice given – for example, a parent is advised on what sort of clothes will keep their child warm enough in winter; staff can then check that the child is appropriately dressed on subsequent days
- support offered – for example, a parent might agree that she is finding it difficult to manage the child's behaviour, and might welcome the offer of support from a parenting group or an appointment with a clinical psychologist
- referral to family support at the local Children's Centre – this will provide structured support and help for the family on a voluntary basis; a similar type of referral might be made to a specialist social work team (Disabled Children's Team, Domestic Violence Project)
- referral to children's social care (social services) – if the named person judges that the child is at risk of significant harm, a written referral will be made to children's social care.

If you have raised a concern and you think that the action being taken is inadequate, meet the named person again. Explain your opinion, referring to what you have observed or heard. Although such conversations are very difficult, they are essential if we are to uphold the principle that the child's welfare and safety come first.

If you are a student, discuss your concerns in confidence with your tutor. Any worried adult is also entitled to contact children's social care or the NSPCC directly. If you have reason to believe your concern is not being acted on, you should do this.

Test yourself

Revise the main points of the last pages by answering the following questions:

1 What are the four categories of child abuse?
2 What should you remember to do if a child alleges to you? What should you avoid doing?
3 Why would early years staff share concerns about a child's welfare or well-being with the child's parents, rather than just keeping a record or making a referral?

AC 3.4 The rights of children and parents/carers when harm or abuse is suspected or alleged

When a child is suspected of being abused, then the primary concern will be to ensure that the child is protected from further abuse and the child's welfare is paramount.

The rights of children

In cases of alleged abuse or harm, a child has the following rights:

- to be protected against significant harm
- not to be subjected to repeated medical examinations or questions following suspected abuse
- to be involved in decisions that are being made about them
- to be kept fully informed of processes involving them, while also being allowed to express their own views and opinions.

Wherever possible, the child may be allowed to remain in their family home, and protection will be achieved by working with the child's parents or carers without the need to remove the child. However, if they are suffering from physical or sexual abuse, then they will be removed from their home to protect them from any further harm.

The rights of parents

The rights of parents are modified by their responsibilities towards their children. In cases of alleged abuse or harm to a child, parents or carers have a right to be informed about what is being said and to contribute their own views and opinions. However, if the child is suffering significant harm, then the parents or carers have no immediate rights.

AC 3.5 The responsibilities of the early years practitioner in relation to whistleblowing

Whistleblowing

Whistleblowing is an important aspect of safeguarding where staff, volunteers and students are encouraged to share genuine concerns about a colleague's behaviour. The behaviour may not be child abuse but the colleague may not be following the code of conduct or could be pushing the boundaries beyond normal limits.

Whistleblowing is very different from a complaint or a grievance. The term 'whistleblowing' generally applies when you are acting as a witness to misconduct that you have seen and that threatens other people or children.

The Public Interest Disclosure Act 1998, known as the Whistleblowing Act, is intended to protect the public interest by providing a remedy for individuals who suffer workplace reprisal for raising a genuine concern, whether it is a concern about child safeguarding and welfare systems, financial malpractice, danger, illegality or other wrongdoing.

The statutory guidance from the DfE, *Working Together to Safeguard Children*, makes it clear that all organisations that provide services for, or work with, children must have appropriate whistleblowing procedures. They must also have a culture that enables concerns about safeguarding and promoting the welfare of children to be addressed by the organisation. The concern may relate to something that is happening now, that has happened in the past or that you think could happen in the future.

All staff, volunteers and students should be aware of, and follow, their setting's whistleblowing policy and procedures.

Examples of whistleblowing in early years settings

Sometimes a person inside an organisation knows that something is going wrong and is being covered up. This could affect the safety and well-being of children. Examples of this in early years settings and schools include the following:

- A member of staff has reported a number of concerns about a child's welfare. The child's parents are on the management committee of the nursery, and the manager says, 'They are not the sort of people who would harm their child.'

- There are consistently too few staff on duty in the nursery. When the local authority comes to visit, supply staff are hired, and during an Ofsted inspection, management and office staff are brought into the room so that legal ratios are met.

In cases like these, it is very important that action is taken before there is a serious incident. If a member of staff has spoken to the manager, head teacher or other appropriate person and made clear that a situation is dangerous and illegal, and no action is taken, it is necessary to 'blow the whistle' and report the concerns directly to an outside body, such as the local Children's Services, Ofsted or the NSPCC.

If you act to protect children or to keep them safe, you are clearly protected by the law. In general, employees who blow the whistle are legally protected against being bullied, sacked or disciplined, if they have acted in good faith.

Research it!

Search online for 'Protection of whistleblowers' or find out more at **www.direct.gov.uk**.

Test yourself

Make sure you know the answers to the following questions:

1 What is whistleblowing?
2 Why should you ask a parent for consent before sharing confidential information with another professional?
3 Under what sort of circumstances would you share information without consent?

LO4 Understand the purpose of serious case reviews

AC 4.1 The need for serious case reviews

In England, the LSCB must undertake a serious case review (SCR) after a child dies and abuse or neglect is believed to be a factor. In addition, serious case reviews are considered in all cases where:

Figure 2.2.1 Children need to be cared for by suitably qualified staff

- a child has sustained a potentially life-threatening injury through abuse or neglect, or
- a child has sustained serious and permanent impairment of health or development through abuse or neglect, or
- important lessons for inter-agency working could be learnt.

The government requires that every agency that had a role and responsibility for the child should contribute to the SCR by having an individual management report. The reports are then collated by an overview report author, who must be independent of any of the agencies that had involvement with the child and family. This is all overseen by a review panel of senior staff from the agencies which had no prior involvement with the child or family or decisions taken. The SCR overview report is presented to the Local Safeguarding Children Board, which decides what recommendations are to be acted upon and tracked.

Their purpose is to:

- establish whether there are lessons to be learnt from the case about the way in which professionals and statutory and/or voluntary agencies work together to safeguard children
- improve inter-agency working and thus provide better safeguards for children.

Research it!

Research the incidence of serious case reviews in your part of the UK. Explain why and when serious case reviews are required.

AC 4.2 How serious case reviews inform practice

The key purpose of undertaking SCRs is to enable lessons to be learnt from cases where a child dies or is seriously harmed and abuse or neglect is known, or suspected, to be a factor. In order for these lessons

Figure 2.2.2 Serious case reviews take place to inform practice after a child dies or is seriously harmed in circumstances where abuse or neglect is believed to be a factor

to be learnt as widely and thoroughly as possible, professionals need to be able to understand fully what happened in each case, and most importantly, what needs to change in order to reduce the risk of such tragedies happening in the future.

Test yourself

Using the information in this section, give three examples of how serious case reviews inform early years practice.

Case study

A serious case review

The serious case review into Little Stars nursery in Birmingham highlighted the failings that allowed Paul Wilson to abuse a child in his care. Paul Wilson was found guilty of raping a child in Little Stars nursery in 2010 and he also admitted 47 counts of 'grooming' teenage girls over the internet. Wilson, whose mother had previously been a manager at the nursery, though not at the time of the attacks, had abused the toddler on at least two occasions. Ofsted had received an anonymous complaint from a staff member about Wilson's behaviour towards the girl, who the review said was from a vulnerable background. It included him cuddling the child, rocking her for hours at a time, wrapping her in a blanket and refusing to leave her. He also spent time with her to the exclusion of others.

The review found that weak safeguarding practices within the nursery had created an environment where factors that might have deterred Wilson from abusing the child were missing.

In the above case, the SCR made eight recommendations based on its findings:

1 Colleges providing early years qualifications should ensure students' application and understanding of child protection procedures have been properly evaluated.
2 Ofsted should ensure the review's findings on safeguarding practices are used in the training of inspectors.
3 Ofsted and Birmingham Children's Services should work together on child protection concerns in early years settings to coordinate intervention.
4 Early years development workers should receive safeguarding training, which includes how to raise concerns about a colleague's conduct.
5 Birmingham Safeguarding Children Board should review local internet safety education campaigns to ensure people are aware of the dangers of internet chat rooms.
6 Information from the setting where a child is subject of an assessment by children's social care must be incorporated into assessments.
7 Early years settings should adhere to safer recruitment's best practice, to prevent unsuitable people working with children and young people.
8 Organisations that complete individual management reviews must provide evidence that action has been taken to address individual and management practice below expected standards.

The lessons to be learnt from the review are that:

● those in charge of settings caring for children must ensure there are strong, clear practices and systems to minimise the risk of abuse
● staff should listen to and ask about children's experiences rather than just speak to adults
● safeguarding children is a job for everyone, and every single person who looks after or cares for children needs to know how to recognise when something is not right and what to do about it, and have confidence they will get the right response when they do act.

Assessment

This is a knowledge-based unit and your assessor will need to see that you know and understand the issues involved in the safeguarding and protection and welfare of children. You may be given a range of tasks that may include case studies.

The starting point for this unit is to look at the current legislation and guidelines that are in place. You can do this by visiting the Department of Education's pages on the **gov.uk website**. From here you should do a search using the keywords 'safeguarding children'. As every setting is required to have a member of staff who is responsible for safeguarding and child protection, you should also talk to that person in your work setting. You should find out about local guidelines as well as the policies and procedures in your setting for if you have concerns about a child or about another staff member. As confidentiality is important in relation to safeguarding and child protection, it will also be worth talking about this to the member of staff who has responsibility for this area.

A key aspect of this unit are the signs and symptoms that might act as indicators that a child is in danger or is being harmed. You will therefore need to revise these carefully and also how the partnership model is used to safeguard children. Finally, you should be familiar with the purpose of serious case reviews and why they are used to inform practice.

Useful resources

Books

Lindon, J. (2009) *Safeguarding Children and Young People*, London: Hodder Education.

Munro, E. (2011) *The Munro Review of Child Protection: Final Report. A Child-centred System*, London: Department for Education.

Documents

Early Years Foundation Stage Statutory Framework: Section 3, 3.1–3.3 inclusive.

The Early Years Foundations for Life, Health and Learning: An Independent Report on the Early Years Foundation Stage to Her Majesty's Government: **www.gov.uk/government/publications/the-early-years-foundations-for-life-health-and-learning-an-independent-report-on-the-early-years-foundation-stage-to-her-majestys-government**.

Working Together to Safeguard Children – the government's guide to inter-agency working to safeguard and promote the welfare of children: **www.gov.uk/government/publications/working-together-to-safeguard-children**.

Organisation

National Society for the Prevention of Cruelty to Children (NSPCC)

The NSPCC campaigns against cruelty to children, and runs ChildLine, the free, confidential helpline for children and young people. The NSPCC also offers services to support children and families, and can investigate cases where child abuse is suspected: **www.nspcc.org.uk**.

Unit 2.3 WB Use legislation relating to the health and safety of children

Adults working in early years settings have many responsibilities. One of these is the duty to keep children safe. In this unit, we look at the legal requirements that settings must follow as well as the policies and procedures that are put in place. We also look at how we can keep children safe as well as the importance of taking a balanced approach to health and safety. Finally, we look at what needs to happen in the event of an accident, incident or emergency.

Learning outcomes

By the end of this unit, you will:

1 Understand legislation and guidelines for health and safety.
2 Understand policies and procedures for health and safety.
3 Be able to manage risk within an environment which provides challenge for children.
4 Be able to identify, record and report accidents, incidents and emergencies.

LO1 Understand legislation and guidelines for health and safety

How would you feel if, while you were working, you turned on a light, were electrocuted and then your boss told you that it was bad luck? Happily, in the United Kingdom, there is a lot of health and safety legislation designed to keep the public, employees and also children safe. In this section, we look at the key legislation and guidelines that are in place.

AC 1.1 Current legislation and guidelines

To keep children and also all adults in early years settings safe, there are several pieces of **legislation** and guidelines that early years settings have to follow. Here, we look at some of the key pieces of legislation and guidelines that early years settings are following at the time of writing. Interestingly, as you will see, a lot of legislation is workplace related, although there are some pieces of legislation that are specifically about early years settings. The most relevant laws relating to health and safety in the childcare setting are listed in Table 2.3.1.

Table 2.3.1 Current laws relating to health and safety in the childcare setting

Health and Safety at Work Act 1974	Employers must take reasonable steps to protect the health and safety of their staff but also visitors – for example, by providing protective clothing and keeping the building safe. Employers with more than five employees must have a written health and safety policy. Employees have a duty to keep themselves and others safe through their actions and also to report any safety issues. They must, for example, follow guidance on handling equipment and must not work in a way that puts others in danger.
Health and Safety (First Aid) Regulations 1981	This deals with first aid in workplaces and includes the need to have a first aid box and also to have members of staff who are trained first aiders.
The Manual Handling Operations Regulations 1992	These regulations are about preventing injuries or accidents when members of staff are lifting objects or people. They include: • the need for risk assessments to take place • the need for staff to be trained to lift safely • the requirement for equipment to be provided when needed.
The Reporting of Injuries, Diseases and Dangerous Occurrences Regulations 1995 (RIDDOR)	These regulations require employers to report any injuries, diseases or serious accidents to the Health and Safety Executive. Employers must keep a record of incidents.
The Control of Substances Hazardous to Health Regulations 2002 (COSHH)	A range of regulations about the use and storage of chemicals and other substances that could be dangerous, including the need to carry out risk assessments and manage storage.
The Regulatory Reform (Fire Safety) Order 2005	There are many fire regulations. These regulations require employers to: • carry out risk assessments specifically identifying and minimising fire hazards • have equipment to fight fires and have procedures to evacuate the building • have a person in charge of fire safety • have equipment to fight fires.
The Food Hygiene (England) Regulations 2006	These are regulations to ensure food safety, including: • the need for some early years settings that provide food to be registered • the need for staff who handle food to be trained in food hygiene • the need for premises and the way that food is stored and prepared to be hygienic.

In your setting

Health and safety in the workplace

Can you see how health and safety legislation relating to the workplace is reflected in your work placement?

- Are you required to wear disposable aprons and gloves for some tasks?

- Is there a book where any accidents, incidents or injuries to staff have to be recorded?
- Are you expected to report any hazards or dangers?
- Do you have a person responsible for health and safety?

Test yourself

Health and safety legislation

Look at each of the following pictures and work out which pieces of legislation they may relate to.

Legislation that is specific to early years settings is shown in Table 2.3.2.

Table 2.3.2 Legislation specific to early years settings

Childcare Act (England) 2006	The Childcare Act applies mainly to England, but similar legislation is in place for the other countries. The Act made the Safeguarding and Welfare requirements outlined in the EYFS statutory framework legally binding. These include the need for settings to: <ul><li>have a health and safety policy and to carry out risk assessments</li><li>to keep records of accidents, incidents and emergencies and to report these to Ofsted when they are serious</li><li>to have a no smoking policy</li><li>to have staff trained in paediatric first aid</li><li>to train staff in evacuation procedures</li><li>to train all staff involved in food preparation and handling</li><li>to check the identity of visitors and to only allow people named by parents to collect children</li><li>to meet the minimum staff–child ratios as stated in the EYFS statutory framework</li><li>to meet the minimum space requirements per child as stated in the EYFS statutory framework.</li></ul>

LO2 Understand policies and procedures for health and safety

The term '**policies** and **procedures**' might sound boring, but if you were in a crowded restaurant and someone shouted that there was a fire, you would probably want the staff to direct you to the nearest exit and to keep everyone calm. Their action would probably be as a result of knowing the policies and procedures for evacuating the building. In this section, we look at the policies and procedures that can be found in early years settings.

AC 2.1 Policies and procedures on health and safety

All early years settings are required to have a range of policies on health and safety. They are usually written down to help parents, staff and others understand how an early years setting intends to keep children safe. An example of this would be a child collection policy that might state that children can only be collected at the end of the session by parents or named people. In order to implement the policy, settings will also create a set of procedures for staff and others to follow. For example, there will be a procedure to follow if a parent wants another adult to collect their child at the end of the day.

Procedures are important to follow because they have been designed to find ways of keeping children and often adults safe. If there were no procedures to follow in the event of a fire, some children might be left behind and no one may have thought about calling the fire service!

AC 2.2 How legislation and guidelines inform day-to-day work

There are many ways in which legislation and guidelines affect what happens in early years settings. Look at Table 2.3.3 and see if you recognise any of the examples from your work placement.

Table 2.3.3 How legislation informs day-to-day practice

Legislation	Example of how it informs day-to-day practice
Health and Safety (First Aid) Regulations 1981	First aid boxes are provided. EYFS safeguarding and welfare requirements: There are always first aiders present with a current or up-to-date paediatric first aid qualification.
The Manual Handling Operations Regulations 1992	Staff are trained in how to lift children, and equipment, such as sand trays, is on wheels.
The Reporting of Injuries, Diseases and Dangerous Occurrences Regulations 1995 (RIDDOR)	Accidents, incidents and emergencies are recorded in a staff book. EYFS safeguarding and welfare requirements: Accidents, incidents and emergencies are recorded and parents are informed as soon as possible afterwards.
The Control of Substances Hazardous to Health Regulations 2002 (COSHH)	Cleaning materials are kept in locked cupboards. Disposable gloves and aprons are provided for cleaning.
The Regulatory Reform (Fire Safety) Order 2005	Fire exits are kept clear and are clearly marked. EYFS safeguarding and welfare requirements: There are regular fire practices.
The Food Hygiene (England) Regulations 2006	Fridges and freezers are kept at correct temperature and are checked weekly. Separate places for cooked and uncooked foods to be stored in fridge. Kitchen is kept clean. EYFS safeguarding and welfare requirements: Staff are trained in food handling.
Childcare Act 2006/EYFS safeguarding and welfare requirements	
Staff–child ratios	Bank staff or the manager will step in where required in the case of staff absence to ensure ratios are maintained.
No smoking policy	No smoking is allowed anywhere on the premises.
Visitors	Visitors are asked to sign in and to identify themselves.
Safety of children at end of session	Staff check that children go home with parents or named people.

AC 2.3 Procedures for registration and collection of children

It is essential that everyone follows the policies and procedures in the setting. This is why, when you first start a work placement, time is spent going through the policies and why you will be shown procedures to follow – for example, washing hands before preparing food or asking visitors to sign in. If you are not sure what a procedure is or you have difficulty in following it, you should always get help. Adults working with children also have a responsibility to say if they think that a procedure needs to be changed because it is no longer effective.

Registration of children

One important procedure that all early years settings are required to have in place is the registration of children as they enter the setting. This is important in case of a fire or other emergency so that adults know how many children need to be evacuated. It is also important for administrative reasons. Most settings register children as they arrive, with the time and date.

Collection of children

While registering children is important, so too are the collection arrangements. As we saw in LO1, it is a legal requirement of the EYFS for early years settings to have policies in place to ensure the safe collection of children. When it is time for children to go home, only the named person is allowed to take them unless parents have given written permission for someone else to take them. Staff will normally 'hand over' the children to the named person, who might be the child's parent but also their childminder. They will also update the attendance register to show that the child has now left, which means that, in the event of an evacuation, the number of children evacuated tallies with the number on the register.

> **In your setting**
>
> - What are the procedures for registering children at the start of each session in your setting?
> - What are the procedures for the collection of children?

> **In practice**
>
> Ask your placement supervisor if you can observe the procedures for registering and collecting children.

Plan environments that support children's health and safety

Imagine that you were looking for childcare for your child or for a baby sister or brother. Do you think that you might worry if you visited a setting where there were a couple of broken windows and where children were playing with matches? Of course, this is not likely to happen, but it does remind us that safety is very important and needs to be thought about when planning environments.

Factors to consider when planning healthy and safe environments

Early years settings have to create environments that are healthy and safe. There are many factors that have to be taken into consideration in order to do this.

Individual needs, age and abilities of children

One of the most important things to consider when planning an environment is the age/stage and the needs of the children who will be using it.

> **In your setting**
>
> For each of the following age groups, write down some of the key safety measures that are taken in your setting:
>
> - 0–1 year
> - 1–3 years
> - 3–5 years.

> **Test yourself**
>
> - Give two reasons why two year olds will need closer supervision than four year olds.
> - Why is it important that toys and resources for babies are not very small?

The needs of parents/carers

Some parents and carers may have needs that will affect health and safety when they are on the premises. They may, for example, not be able to hear a fire alarm or may have mobility problems that will make it harder for them to evacuate the building without support. Some parents may also bring other children with them into the setting when they are dropping off or collecting their child (e.g. a baby in a pushchair). While the supervision of these children remains with the parents, it is important to create environments and routines that take this into account – for example, an area for parents to wait with age-appropriate toys for their children.

The function and purpose of environments and services offered in relation to health and safety

Duty of care

The term 'duty of care' means that early years settings are responsible for the health, safety and well-being of not just the children but everyone who works in the setting or comes into it. Duty of care also applies to the general public, who might be hit by a ball that is kicked out of a school playground. Duty of care requires that early years settings have to take reasonable steps to prevent accidents or incidents from occurring. In practical terms, it means not only focusing on the needs of children, but also thinking about other issues, such as the maintenance of the building, hazards caused by activities and potential threats posed by others.

Case study

Duty of care

High Grove Infant School has a large playground where parents wait at the end of the school session. There is a system in place to ensure that children only go home with their parents or named person. A climbing frame has been recently added to this area. The head teacher has noticed that toddlers waiting with their parents to pick up their siblings are starting to climb on it. He is concerned that, because the climbing frame is not designed for younger children, an accident might occur.

1 Why does the school have duty of care towards the toddlers who are not pupils of the school?
2 Suggest how the head teacher might ensure that toddlers are kept safe while they are on the premises.

The desired outcomes for babies and young children

One thing that we should never lose sight of is that babies and children need a wide range of resources and activities in order to support their development. When planning an environment, it is important to think about the physical location of things – for example, ensuring that a water tray is positioned so that spills can be wiped up easily and that the water can be changed between sessions.

On page 116, we look at the types of activities that support babies and young children's development, the potential hazards associated with these and how these can be managed.

Lines of responsibility and accountability

When early years settings plan an environment, they also have to think about the procedures that they will put in place to make sure that everyone knows their responsibilities and who they must report to.

We look at this on page 121.

Identify hazards to the health and safety of children, colleagues and visitors

Most people are surprised about the number of potential hazards that there are in early years settings. Happily though, accidents and incidents are very rare and most hazards can be avoided, and easily managed. It is important, though, to know what to look for.

Physical hazards

On page 119, we look at some of the key accidents and incidents that might take place in early years settings and the hazards associated with them.

In terms of children, there are specific hazards that we have to be aware of associated with play and resources (see Table 2.3.4 on the following page).

Research it!

For each of the hazards identified in Table 2.3.4, research and make a suggestion as to how the risk could be minimised.

There are also some outdoor activities and resources that can cause hazards for children, as shown in Table 2.3.5 on the following page.

In your setting

How does your setting manage each of the outdoor hazards shown in Table 2.3.5?

Table 2.3.4 Hazards associated with play and resources

Indoor activities	Hazards
Water play	• Drowning • Slipping on wet floor • Danger of water being contaminated if not regularly changed
Sand play	• Sand might go in eyes • Slipping on sandy floors
Playing with dough	• Dough being eaten, which may not be hygienic/may contain too much salt • Infection might be spread if children do not wash their hands
Art and craft activities, e.g. pens, pencils, paintbrushes/mark-making, scissors	• Poking in eye • Cuts from scissors
Playing with dressing-up clothes – belts and similar items	• Strangulation as children pretend to take a dog for a walk • Belt going in eyes and face
Cooking activities	• Danger of knives, hot stoves and ovens • Allergies

Table 2.3.5 Hazards associated with outdoor activities

Outdoor activities	Hazards
Slides/climbing frames	• Falls caused by children pushing each other, or children losing balance
Swings	• Falls as a result of a child losing balance • Children walking in the path of a swing may have a bang on head
Wheeled toys, such as tricycles	• Falls as a result of a child losing control • Collisions with other children
Fencing/gates	• Children leaving the premises unnoticed • Strangers entering
Water activities	• Drowning • Slipping on wet floor • Danger of water being contaminated if not regularly changed
Sand	• As for indoors, plus the possibility of contamination from animal faeces
Plants	• Poisoning • Poke in eye from sticks

Security

If you are in a work placement or have visited one, you have probably already found out that security is taken seriously. It is good practice for there to be gates, buzzers and a signing-in book. Much of this security was put into place following a serious incident in a school in Dunblane, Scotland. There are three reasons why security is important:

• to prevent children from leaving the premises unnoticed
• to prevent adults, including estranged parents who may not have custody, from abducting children
• to prevent adults who may threaten or attack children and adults, including visitors, from gaining access.

In your setting

Security

Find out about the measures that are in place in your setting to monitor people coming in and also to prevent children from going missing.

In practice

Write about your role in preventing children from going missing in your setting.

Potential fire hazards

A fire affects the safety of everyone in the setting, including any visitors or parents who happen to be there. Figure 2.3.2 shows the possible fire hazards. Are there more fire hazards indoors or outdoors?

In your setting

Do you know where the smoke alarms are in your setting?

Food safety

Food poisoning can be fatal for babies and young children because their immune systems are not as developed as those of adults. Most food poisoning is avoidable. It is a requirement that everyone handling food or even serving has some training. Early years settings also have to make sure that children who have any food allergies are given only foods that are suitable for them. They also have to make sure that foods that could potentially cause choking are not given to babies. Table 2.3.6 on page 115 shows some examples of food safety hazards.

In practice

If you are involved in serving children's snacks or meals, write a list of the steps that you take to prevent food poisoning or to prevent causing an allergic reaction.

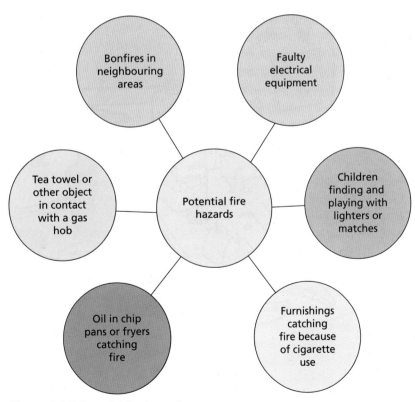

Figure 2.3.2 Potential fire hazards

Test yourself

Look at the drawing below. How many hazards can you find that might result in food poisoning?

Figure 2.3.3 Spot the food safety hazards

Table 2.3.6 Examples of food safety hazards

Hazard	Implication
Food not stored at correct temperature	Bacteria can develop
Meat/fish/poultry/eggs not sufficiently cooked	Bacteria may remain
Hands not washed before and during food preparation	Bacteria spread from hands and onto food or from food to hand via the hands
Raw meat/poultry/fish/eggs come into contact with foods that are not going to be cooked	Foods become contaminated
Food is not reheated to sufficiently high temperatures/food is reheated more than once	Bacteria on food are not destroyed/bacteria may build up
Bottles given to babies are not sterilised or manufacturer's instructions on how to make up feeds are not followed	Bacteria may remain
Bottles of baby milk are not given straight away	Bacteria can develop
Grapes, nuts or other unsuitable items are given to babies	May cause choking
Children are given food to which they have an allergic reaction	Allergic reaction could occur, and could prove fatal

LO3 Be able to manage risk within an environment which provides challenge for children

When you were a child, did you play on a tricycle or climbing frame? What if everyone was so worried about health and safety that these activities were banned? In this section, we look at why it is important for adults working with children to take a sensible approach to managing health and safety issues.

AC 3.1 The importance of a balanced approach to risk management

While everyone recognises that preventing accidents is important, it is necessary to find a balance whereby children can still play, explore and be active. We also know that children have to experience a range of situations and activities in order that they can learn. This means, for example, that if children are never allowed to use scissors because of fears that they may cut themselves, they will not develop the skills to use them. In the same way, if children have never experienced running on an uneven surface, they are more likely to fall

Figure 2.3.4 What is more important: that the children are learning a new skill or that they might fall off?

over later. Most settings therefore try to create an environment which is safe, but where children can experience new opportunities and learn new skills. This means that, while children may have an occasional graze or bruise from time to time, serious accidents are extremely rare.

In your setting

In your work placement, observe how serious accidents are avoided, but how children still have opportunities to explore, gain new skills and play in the following ways:

- using tools – for example, forks, scissors, hole punches, pencils
- using sensory materials – for example, water, sand, dough
- developing physical skills – for example, climbing, jumping and balancing.

AC 3.2 How to carry out a risk assessment in your own setting

A risk assessment is a five-step process used to prevent possible accidents from occurring because it makes people reflect on possible hazards and how to overcome them. In some cases, as a result of a risk assessment process, a piece of equipment, outing or activity may not get the go-ahead because it is deemed to be too risky. Early years settings carry out written risk assessments, although the forms that they use will vary from setting to setting.

Risk assessments are not difficult to carry out, but like most things they become easier with practice and the starting point is to understand the inherent risks associated with the age of children and also materials and environments.

Risks associated with different ages/stage of children

One of the most important things to consider when carrying out a risk assessment is the ages/stage of children involved in the activity. This is because they will not only have different

needs, but they will also play and explore in different ways. A good example of this is the way that, up until around 18 months, most babies and toddlers will automatically put objects into their mouths. This means that, in planning the environment, only toys and resources that are not choking hazards can be put out. Table 2.3.7 shows the potential risks associated with children's ages and how the risks might be managed.

It is also worth bearing in mind that some children will have additional needs on top of those related to their age/stage that will affect how we keep them safe. A child who has limited sight, for example, will need areas where they may walk to be kept free of objects. A child who has hearing difficulties will need adults to remember that they may not hear instructions or warnings.

→ Look back at Tables 2.3.4 and 2.3.5 on page 112 for the hazards associated with different indoor and outdoor activities.

Carrying out a risk assessment

Risk assessments are an important part of early years practice. While you will find that your setting will have many written risk assessments in place, it is good practice to constantly be risk assessing while you are involved in an activity.

The following example shows things to consider if you were risk assessing an activity using play dough.

Step 1: Identify potential hazards and who may be at risk.

- A child might have an allergic reaction because of the flour in the dough.
- The children might eat the dough.
- It might not be suitable for children with a skin condition, such as eczema.
- The dough might spread infection as children would be handling it.

Table 2.3.7 Risks associated with different ages/stages of children

Age/stage	Needs	Managing the risk
Babies: non-mobile	• May start to wriggle or roll and so may fall off surfaces, e.g. during nappy changing • Takes all objects to the mouth to explore • Immune system very vulnerable so food poisoning can be fatal	• Close supervision is required • Only objects and toys safe to go into the mouth should be given • Toys and resources must be frequently cleaned after use • Food hygiene must be a priority
Babies: mobile	• Mouthing objects • Will pick up small objects left on the floor using pincer grasp • Holds onto furniture to pull to standing position • Immune system very vulnerable so food poisoning can be fatal	• Close supervision and tidying away of small toys or objects that older children might have left • Furniture has to be stable • Objects left on furniture have to be safe • Toys and resources must be frequently cleaned after use • Food hygiene must be a priority
Toddlers	• Extremely active • Love to climb, throw and explore • Move fast • May not understand or remember instructions/warnings • Try to imitate older children • Have impulsive and limited understanding of danger	• Close supervision is required • Opportunities for physical activity • Keep unsuitable resources/substances out of reach or locked
3–5 years	• May copy adults' actions and are physically more capable now • May become engaged in superhero play or copy actions from films • Excited by challenges and trying new things	• Good supervision is required • Adults to act as role models • Provision of exciting, but safe, activities

Figure 2.3.5 It is important to keep areas safe for all children

Step 2: Consider steps to minimise or eliminate the hazards.

- Ask parents about possible allergic reactions or suitability for skin conditions.
- Use a dough recipe that contains salt and ensure that children wash their hands afterwards.
- Supervise the activity to prevent children from eating the dough.

Step 3: Evaluate the potential risk caused by the hazards.

- Risk of accident or incident once steps are taken is small.

Step 4 (for written risk assessments): Record your findings – most early years and schools will have a form to complete this.

Step 5 (for written risk assessments): Monitor and review – once a risk assessment has been completed, it should be regularly checked and, if needed, changed.

AC 3.3 Monitoring and reviewing of health and safety risk assessments

For the risk assessment process to be effective, early years settings have to keep monitoring that the steps recommended to prevent an accident are being taken and also that these steps are still effective. This means that settings will review risk assessments regularly and always when there is a change of circumstances or if an accident or incident has occurred.

Case study

Flower Garden Nursery regularly takes children to visit the local library. A risk assessment has been done which covers taking children out in the rain as well as the sun and also assesses the risks according to the ages of the children being taken out. The outing requires children to cross the road at a pelican crossing. Today, roadworks have started for a week. The pelican crossing is out of action.

1 Why is a new risk assessment needed?
2 Identify the potential hazard now the pelican crossing is closed.
3 What might be the result of the risk assessment?

AC 3.4 Helping children manage risk

One of the ways in which we can help children to be safe is by teaching them to think about hazards and risks. We can do this by drawing children's attention to a potential hazard, such as an uneven surface, and explain what they will need to do to manage the risk. As children become older and so more experienced, we might start to ask them what the potential hazards are and encourage them to manage the risk themselves.

In practice

Give an example of how you have helped a child to identify a possible risk and supported them to manage it – for example, using a sit-and-ride toy or a pair of scissors.

AC 3.5 The importance of your role in managing risk

As we have seen, there is a tension between keeping children safe and allowing them to have fun, explore their environment and develop skills. You must think about your own role when managing risk. This would include acting as a good role model because children do copy our actions. It might also include keeping an eye out for hazards, such as toys or objects on the ground, and supervising children carefully.

Supervising children

Supervising children is quite a skill. You need to think about hazards, but you also need to make sure that children can learn skills and enjoy whatever they are doing. If you are new to early years, it is worth watching other adults to see when they intervene and also how they remind children of potential hazards. One of the best ways of supervising is to join in with children's play. If you do this, you should always remember that you are the adult, not a child, and that you must not encourage them to do anything that is unsafe, either by making them overexcited or by doing something that children may copy.

Reflect

Your role when managing risk
Think about how you have actively kept children safe while allowing them to learn and explore, indoors and outdoors.

LO4 Be able to identify, record and report accidents, incidents and emergencies

Did you ever have an accident while you were at nursery or school? You might remember that staff had to fill in a report afterwards. In this section, we look at how to complete records in the event of accidents, incidents and emergencies.

AC 4.1 Recording accidents, incidents and emergencies

From time to time in early years settings, there will be an accident, incident or emergency. While they do happen from time to time, they are not usually part of everyday work with children. Let's start off by looking at what we mean by accidents, incidents and emergencies.

Accidents

These are injuries that might occur to adults or children. They include falls, scalds, poisoning and choking. Accidents become emergencies when:

- a child is unconscious and/or has no pulse
- a child is not breathing or has difficulty in doing so
- a child's lips and face swell (e.g. following a bee sting)
- there is severe bleeding
- a child's leg or arm is sticking out at an unnatural angle
- a child has a severe burn
- a child has had a blow to the head and is drowsy/has difficulty seeing/is sick or feeling nauseous.

In such cases, immediate medical attention is needed and a 999 call should be placed.

Incidents

There is a range of ways of responding to incidents. Table 2.3.8 shows some of the usual responses to different types of incidents, although you should always find out the procedures for the setting where you are on work placement.

When incidents become emergencies

Incidents become emergencies when there is a danger that a situation is or is becoming a serious threat to well-being or life. A missing child who cannot be found quickly, for example, becomes an emergency situation and the police should be called to assist the search.

Emergencies

An emergency can be defined as a life-threatening situation or a potential life-threatening situation. We have seen that emergencies usually arise from accidents and incidents.

Completing records

All accidents, incidents and emergencies have to be recorded accurately. This is important because serious accidents and incidents also have to be reported to inspectorates and agencies, such as Ofsted or the Health and Safety Executive, who will investigate further. In the case of accidents, parents also need to know what has happened and so early years settings will report any injury, however minor, to parents. Most forms require the following information:

- time and date of accident/incident/emergency
- details of the accident/incident/emergency, including its cause and the names of those injured
- how the accident/incident/emergency was responded to and by whom
- name and signature of the person reporting the accident/incident/emergency.

In your setting

Forms to be filled in
In your setting, find out what forms have to be filled in for:

- accidents
- incidents
- emergencies.

Table 2.3.8 Responses to different types of incidents

Incident	Likely actions to take
Missing child	Follow the setting's procedures, which will include reporting the missing child to the line manager immediately, systematically searching the premises and alerting police and parents if necessary.
Aggressive behaviour of a child	Steer other children away from the scene. Talk softly to the child while removing objects that could be thrown or cause a danger to the child. Report incident to the line manager or key person.
Gas leak	Phone 999 or 112 if you are first on the scene and if safe to do so. Follow the evacuation procedure (e.g. take register with you). Use closest exit available, provided that it is away from the incident.
Fire	
Bomb threat	
Threatening behaviour of an adult (e.g. parent/ visitor/intruder)	Stay calm but tell children to move away if you are first on the scene. Encourage adult to move into office or space away from children. Assess situation as to whether it is safe/necessary to call 999 or 112. In serious situations, evacuate the building or move children to a room or cupboard that can be locked.
Flooding	Phone 999 or 112 if you are first on the scene and if safe to do so. Consider evacuation if still safe to do so. If not, move children to higher ground or upstairs. Call for help.

Figure 2.3.6 What would you do if this child went missing?

In practice

In your setting, ask if you can practise filling in an accident form. You could do this by making a copy of the form and then filling it in. Ask your placement supervisor to give you feedback afterwards.

Following an accident, incident or emergency

It is important to understand the usual lines of reporting within a setting as sometimes it will not be one of your duties to complete the accident, incident or emergency records. In other cases, after an accident, incident or emergency, further action may need to be taken. Table 2.3.9 shows the different roles and responsibilities in early years settings.

In practice

Draw a diagram that shows the lines of reporting and responsibility in your work placement for:

- one incident
- one accident.

Table 2.3.9 Lines of reporting and responsibility in the event of accidents, incidents and emergencies

Staff member	Responsibility	May need to report to:
Student on placement/ volunteer	To follow policies or procedures and to summon further assistance in the event of an accident, incident or emergency.	Whoever is acting as placement supervisor or, in the event of an emergency, any member of staff
Member of staff with a current paediatric first aid qualification	To provide immediate assistance in the event of a medical emergency. They may provide direction to others – for example, ask them to call for an ambulance.	Medical teams in the event of a child needing medical attention
Health and safety officer/ fire officer	To ensure that the health and safety/ fire policy is being followed and to advise the manager as to how to make improvements. Should act on reports by members of staff about faulty equipment and potential hazards.	Depends on setting but usually deputy, manager or head teacher
Deputy	To take on the responsibilities in the absence of the manager. To take specific responsibilities for health and safety in some roles.	Manager
Manager/head teacher	To ensure the smooth running of the setting. To ensure that all policies relating to health and safety are being followed.	Parents in the event of a serious injury, incident or emergency Director/owner/governors
Director/owner/governors	To take on legal responsibility in the event that an accident, incident or emergency is the fault of the setting.	Health and Safety Executive Ofsted

Assessment

In order to achieve this unit you are likely to be given a variety of tasks. Your starting point should be to look at legislation relating to health and safety. While this has been given in this unit, it will be worth visiting the Health and Safety Executive's website (**www.hse.gov. uk**) to look for the latest regulations. You should also look at the latest statutory framework for the early years foundation stages and read carefully through the safeguarding and welfare requirements.

Every early years setting is required to have a member of staff who is responsible for health and safety. It is worth talking to this person as well as revisiting your settings' procedures for the registration of children, collection of children and for carrying out risk assessments.

As well as tasks that demonstrate your knowledge of health and safety in your setting, you will need to show your assessor that you know how to and can carry out risk assessments. You must be able to explain why it is important to take a balanced approach to risk management give some examples of this in practice. It will be important to practise conducting a risk assessment before your assessor visits and gaining feedback from your placement supervisor or the nominated person for health and safety.

Finally, you need to show that you can complete records in the event of accidents, incidents or emergencies. To practise this you could ask if you could be shown how accidents, incidents or emergencies are recorded in your setting.

Useful resources

Organisations

Health and Safety Executive (HSE)

HSE is the national independent watchdog for work-related health, safety and illness: **www.hse.gov.uk**.

RIDDOR

RIDDOR puts duties on employers, the self-employed and people in control of work premises (the Responsible Person) to report certain serious workplace accidents, occupational diseases and specified dangerous occurrences (near misses): **www.hse.gov. uk/riddor**.

Ofsted

Ofsted is the Office for Standards in Education, Children's Services and Skills. Ofsted inspects and regulates services which care for children and young people, and those providing education and skills for learners of all ages: **www.ofsted.gov.uk**.

Unit 2.4 WB Follow legislation relating to equality, diversity and inclusive practice

Equality, inclusion and anti-discriminatory practice refer to moral and legal obligations and rights for people working in and using public services. As an early years practitioner, you have a role to play in ensuring that, in all aspects of your work, every person is given real opportunities to thrive, and that any barriers that would prevent them from reaching their full potential are removed. The principles of equality and inclusion are at the heart of work with children and young people in every kind of setting.

Learning outcomes

By the end of this unit, you will:

1 Understand how legislation, policies and procedures inform equality, diversity and inclusive practice.
2 Be able to use information, advice and support to promote equality, diversity and inclusion.
3 Be able to work in ways which support equality, diversity and inclusive practice.

LO1 Understand how legislation, policies and procedures inform equality, diversity and inclusive practice

What are meant by **equality** and **diversity** in early years settings? You will need to be aware of how legislation impacts on early years settings and what it means for the early years practitioner. This section looks at the kinds of policies and procedures that settings should have in place and how they affect our work with young children.

Key terms

equality Allowing the same access for every child and family to full participation for all services.

diversity The differences in values, attitudes, cultures, beliefs, skills and life experiences of each individual in any group.

inclusive practice The process of ensuring the equality of learning opportunities for all children and young people.

AC 1.1 Legislation, policies and procedures relating to equality, diversity and inclusive practice

Legislation and codes of practice

The laws and codes of practice relating to equality, diversity and discrimination are listed in Table 2.4.1.

In addition to understanding legislation, you will also need to be aware of your setting's policies and procedures relating to equality, diversity and **inclusive practice**. All settings must demonstrate (through policies and codes of practice) how they intend to ensure that they meet the legal, regulatory requirements. All workplace policies and codes of practice must be drawn up within the framework of current legislation. A code of practice is not a legal document, but it does give direction and cohesion to the organisation for which it has been designed. Policy documents cover areas of ethical concern and good practice.

Table 2.4.1 Legislation and codes of practice relating to equality, diversity and discrimination

Legislation and codes of practice	Relevant points	How it affects practice
The Equality Act (2010)	The Equality Act 2010 replaces all previous equalities legislation, bans unlawful discrimination and helps achieve equal opportunities in and outside the workplace. All early years settings, whether in the statutory, voluntary, independent or private sectors, including childminders, must comply with the Act. The Equality Act 2010 makes sure that people with particular characteristics are protected from discrimination. These are the protected characteristics: ● age ● disability ● gender reassignment ● marriage and civil partnerships ● pregnancy or maternity ● race ● religion or belief ● sex ● sexual orientation (gay, lesbian or bisexual).	The Equality Act sets out the different ways in which it is unlawful to treat someone, such as direct and indirect discrimination, harassment, victimisation and failing to make a reasonable adjustment for a disabled person.

Table 2.4.1 Legislation and codes of practice relating to equality, diversity and discrimination   (contd.)

Legislation and codes of practice	Relevant points	How it affects practice
The Special Educational Needs and Disability Act 2001	The Special Needs and Disability Act 2001 is supported by the SEN code of practice and strengthens the right of children with disabilities to attend mainstream educational facilities. It was supported by the Code of Practice 2002.	More children with SEN and disabilities start to attend mainstream schools and nurseries. More specialist staff and/or additional training may be required.
The Special Educational Needs Code of Practice 2002	The SEN Code has the following general principles: ● A child with special needs should have his or her needs met. ● The special needs of children will be met in mainstream schools – wherever possible. ● The views of children should be sought and taken into account. ● Parents have a vital role to play in supporting their child's education – and must be seen as partners with local education authorities (LEAs) and other agencies. ● Children with special educational needs should be offered full access to a broad, balanced and relevant education, including an appropriate curriculum for the Foundation Stage and the National Curriculum. ● All early years settings have a special educational needs policy and follow the integrated team approach of the EYFS profile. ● Early identification, Early Years Action, Early Years Action Plus and, for some children, statutory assessment.	Parents and children are more closely involved in decisions about their education. According to the Code, every school must appoint a member of staff who takes responsibility for special education needs: the special educational needs coordinator or SENCO.
The Children and Families Act 2014 / SEND Code of Practice 2014	● A clear and transparent 'local offer' of services across education, health and social care. Children, young people and parents will be involved in preparing and reviewing the offer. ● Joint commissioning of services across education, health and care. ● Education, Health and Care (EHC) plans will replace statements and Learning Difficulty Assessments (LDAs) with the option of a personal budget for families and young people who want one. ● New statutory rights for young people in further education. They have the right to request a particular institution to be named in their EHC plan and the right to appeal to the First-tier-Tribunal (SEN and Disability). ● A stronger focus on preparing for adulthood including better planning for transition into paid employment and independent living and between children's and adults' services.	The Children and Families Act 2014 introduces a range of new legislation regarding adoption and family justice. In Part 3 it includes a new Special Educational Needs and Disabilities (SEND) Code of Practice. This supersedes the Code of Practice from 2001 (but it does not replace the Special Educational Needs and Disability Act 2001). Under this code of practice local authorities will draw up education, health and care (EHC) plans for children identified as SEND. They are also required to publish a 'local offer' of services and offer a personal budget to meet the EHC plan.
United Nations Convention on the Rights of the Child (1989)	As an early years practitioner, you must know and understand the basic requirements of the United Nations Convention on the Rights of the Child. These rights are for children and young people (up to the age of 18 years). (The only two countries in the world that have not signed the Convention are the USA and Somalia.)	Children's views, wishes and opinions should be taken into account as much as possible. ➔

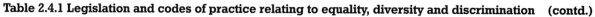

Table 2.4.1 Legislation and codes of practice relating to equality, diversity and discrimination (contd.)

Legislation and codes of practice	Relevant points	How it affects practice
	The rights embodied by the UN Convention which particularly relate to childcare and education are these: ● Children have the right to be with their family or with those who will care best for them. ● Children have the right to enough food and clean water for their needs. ● Children have the right to an adequate standard of living. ● Children have the right to healthcare. ● Children have the right to play. ● Children have the right to be kept safe and not hurt or neglected. ● Disabled children have the right to special care and training. ● Children must not be used as cheap workers or as soldiers. ● Children have the right to free education. ● All children should be listened to and their views taken seriously	

Figure 2.4.1 Children have special rights, including the right to play

The policy statement

Every employing organisation should set out a clear policy statement that can be made available to employees and service users. The statement should include:

● a recognition of past discrimination
● a commitment to redressing inequalities
● a commitment to positive action.

Training should be provided to explain to all staff the implications and practical consequences of the policy. The organisation must also provide information about the law on direct and indirect discrimination.

Any policy which attempts to promote equality is only effective if the individuals working in the organisation incorporate its principles into their individual practice.

Equal opportunities policy

An equal opportunities policy represents a commitment by an organisation to ensure that its activities do not lead to any individual receiving less favourable treatment on the grounds of:

● gender
● ethnic or national origin
● disability
● religious belief
● race or skin colour
● age
● marital status
● skin colour.

Having such a policy does not mean reverse discrimination, but equality for all. An effective policy will establish a fair system in relation to recruitment, training and promotion opportunities, as well as to the staff's treatment of children, parents and one another.

Special educational needs policy

All schools must have a special educational needs policy. This should include information about:

● how they identify and make provision for children with special educational needs
● the facilities they have, including those that increase access for pupils who are disabled, and access to the curriculum

- how resources are allocated to and among pupils with special educational needs
- how they enable pupils with special educational needs to engage in activities of the school together with pupils who do not have additional needs
- how the governing body evaluates the success of the school's work with pupils with special educational needs
- their arrangements for dealing with complaints from parents.

In addition to having up-to-date policies, it is also important to pause at regular intervals and examine what happens in every work setting. Does what the team members say they believe in match what they actually do? Identifying problems in the way adults work with children and in the way children and adults relate to each other is essential before positive action can be taken by the whole team. It helps to work as

a team when doing this because it is hard for individual team members to inspect their own thinking in isolation from other people. It helps to share and discuss things with colleagues. The team should devise a policy of equality of opportunity and a code of practice and then, as a team, review them regularly:

- The policy states the values of the team and the aims of its work.
- The code of practice sets out how the team will put the policy into practice.
- The review process covers all aspects of the team's work in relation to its policy and code of practice.

In practice

Identify the policies and procedures in your setting relating to equality, diversity and inclusive practice. How effective do you think these policies are?

Figure 2.4.2 All children should be made to feel welcome in the setting

Figure 2.4.3 Every adult in the setting has a duty to support individual children's development

AC 1.2 Roles and responsibilities of the early years practitioner in supporting equality, diversity and inclusive practice

The early years practitioner has a key role in ensuring that they support equality and diversity, both in the way in which they treat others and by giving every child full access to everything that happens in the setting. This is particularly important for key workers who get to know individual children and their families in more depth, but it is true of your relationships with all children. You can support equality and diversity by observing the following guidelines.

Working within the policies and procedures of the setting

You will need to show that you work within the setting's policies and procedures that have an impact on equality, diversity and inclusive practice.

→ The relevant policies and procedures were discussed in AC 1.1.

This means reading and being aware of the contents of the policies and procedures, but also showing that you know and understand your responsibilities, as outlined below.

Valuing the individual child

You should be able to show that you value each child as an individual through the way in which you interact with them and their families. As you get to know children, you will be well placed to ensure that you demonstrate this through your interactions with them – for example, in the ways in which you listen and respond to what they say.

Developing and sustaining a child-centred approach

You should always set children tasks that help them to make decisions and to exercise choice. It is important to let all children make choices and decisions so that they feel a sense of control in their lives. When people feel they have some control over what they do, they learn better as it gives them greater equality of opportunity.

Engaging actively with the family to appreciate the holistic needs of the child

As you get to know children and their families, and particularly if you are their key worker, you will become more aware of their individual needs. It is important to involve all families through having regular contact with them and making them feel welcome. As you work with children, you may find out, for example, about the kinds of things they like to do, or learn about a particular situation which has had an impact on them at home. This is important as you will then be able to take these needs into account when working with the child.

Providing an inclusive environment which actively welcomes diversity

One of the ways in which early years workers can ensure that that the setting actively welcomes diversity is through providing an inclusive learning environment: this can be done in different ways but should be evident through the use of displays and environmental print (for example, signs that say 'Welcome' in different languages), books that contain positive images of people with disabilities, or those from different cultures and of different genders or family types. However, an inclusive environment also means showing that you include and involve all children in all aspects of the setting.

→ There is more on this in LO3 on page 132.

Being a positive role model in promoting equality, diversity and inclusive practice

You will need to ensure that you are a positive role model for children and families at all times through your work with children and families, and show the kinds of values that are expected by the setting. You

should do this by ensuring that you think about the way in which you treat others and how this affects your work with them.

Tips on being a positive role model

- Try to think why people have different views and customs from your own. Keep thinking about (or reflecting upon) what you do.
- Think about issues of race, gender, sexual orientation, age, economics, background, disability, assertiveness, culture and special educational needs.
- Be aware of your own opinions and views and question them if necessary.
- Value the things you learn about equality of opportunity so that you can look forward with positive images about yourself and other people.
- Make a point of pronouncing and spelling names correctly, and understand the systems which different cultures have when choosing names.
- Learn about the types of clothes people wear in different cultures and what they are called.

Recognising discriminatory practice

As well as being responsible for your own interactions with others, you should make sure that you take a 'no tolerance' approach if you discover that others are being discriminatory.

Each individual worker needs to be committed and empowered to carry out the team's anti-discriminatory policy. You can have a great impact on the lives of the children and families you work with, and equally you can have an influence on combating discriminatory behaviour.

Knowing how, why and when to challenge discrimination

When challenging discrimination, it is important to be assertive but not aggressive. Being assertive means talking clearly and politely about how you feel, which is very different from being rude and angry. For example, you might say, 'I felt very uncomfortable when you asked me to give a drink to the girl with a hearing aid. I felt I needed to know her name, because I am worried that I might stop seeing her as a person if I just think of her as "the girl with a hearing aid".'

Challenging situations

If you see a child hurt or insult someone, explain that such behaviour is not acceptable. Never ignore or make excuses for a child's discriminatory behaviour towards another person. Explain to the child why such behaviour is unacceptable and encourage them to see how hurtful their comments or actions appear to the other child. Criticise the behaviour rather than the child.

Engaging in effective partnership working to enable the child

It is important to remember that you are part of a multi-professional team and that each member has something different to bring to early childhood work. You may also work alongside professionals outside the setting.

When you meet children, whether they are in a mainstream school, a special school or an early years setting, make sure that your expectations of what each child can do are high enough so that you can enable them further.

Case study

Sasha is working in a reception class with Tom, who has a severe visual impairment and very limited vision. He needs to sit at the front of the class and it has been adapted so that he can find the doorway and other key areas. The team works alongside the sensory support service, who come into the school regularly to review his progress. Sasha has assumed that Tom will not be able to participate in many of the activities alongside other children and does not encourage him in the same way. However, as time goes on, she is surprised to discover that he is very able and his impairment does not limit him at all.

1 Why is it important that Sasha encourages Tom just as much as she does the other children?

2 How can Sasha work with others to ensure that she supports Tom as much as she can?

In practice

Practical ways of supporting equality, diversity and inclusive practice

- Provide a range of activities which celebrate cultural differences. For example, make children aware of what is involved in celebrations of religious festivals such as Diwali and Chinese New Year, as well as Christmas and Easter, whether or not there are children in the setting who celebrate these occasions.
- Promote a multicultural approach to food provision. For example, parents could be invited into the setting to cook authentic national and regional dishes – Caribbean food, Yorkshire pudding as a dessert, Welsh bara brith, Irish stew or Asian sweets.
- Encourage self-expression in solo and in group activities – for example, by providing 'tools' for cooking and eating from other cultures, such as woks, chopsticks and griddles.
- Celebrate the diversity of language. Use body language, gesture, pictures and actions to convey messages to children and young people whose home language is not English.

Research it!

Find out about the legislation covering equality and inclusion and how it relates to your setting – for example, the setting's equal opportunities policy and/or inclusion policy.

LO2 Be able to use information, advice and support to promote equality, diversity and inclusion

First, you will need to understand the laws and codes of practice relating to equality, diversity and discrimination and how they apply to you and your work role. In each early years setting, you will meet people of many different backgrounds, cultures and beliefs – your colleagues as well as the children and their families. Make the most of this opportunity: be open with people, and listen and learn from others about their experiences.

AC 2.1 Accessing information, advice and support

Sources of information and support

As part of your ongoing personal and professional development, you should always be willing to improve your practice by seeking further information and support from a variety of sources. No one will expect you to know and understand everything, and you may come across situations that you find difficult or challenging. It is your responsibility to seek advice and support from your tutor or line manager, and to use your experience as a valuable learning opportunity.

Colleagues

In most settings, there is a special educational needs coordinator (SENCO), whom you can approach for information or support when working with a child with additional needs. It is important to get to know the strengths and personal expertise of individual members in your staff team; you will often find that they can offer useful support, having encountered a similar situation before.

Parents and families

Remember that parents, carers and family members can be a valuable resource if you need further information about an individual child's:

- disability or condition
- home language
- special dietary needs or allergies, and preferences
- cultural preferences.

Organisations specialising in equality issues

There are various useful sources of information relating to equality, diversity and discrimination:

- the relevant Acts of Parliament: www.gov.uk
- the Equality and Human Rights Commission (EHRC): EHRC has a statutory remit to promote and monitor human rights, and to protect, enforce and promote equality across the seven 'protected' grounds – age, disability, gender, race, religion and belief, sexual orientation and gender reassignment: www.equalityhumanrights.com.
- Early Education: the leading national voluntary organisation for early years practitioners and parents, Early Education promotes the right of all children to education of the highest quality: www.early-education.org.uk.
- National Children's Bureau (NCB): NCB is a charitable organisation dedicated to advancing the health and well-being of all children and young people across every aspect of their lives, and providing them with a powerful and authoritative voice: www.ncb.org.uk.
- Organisation Mondiale Education Pre-Scholaire (OMEP): OMEP is an international, non-governmental organisation founded in 1948 to benefit children under the age of eight years throughout the world. OMEP's aim is to promote the optimum conditions for all children, in order to ensure their well-being, development and happiness, both within their family unit and the wider communities in which they live: www.omepuk.org.uk.

> **Research it!**
>
> Research some of the organisations listed above and find out more about them. How do they provide advice and support? Can you find out about any other organisations that might be useful to early years practitioners?

AC 2.2 How information, advice and support about equality, diversity and inclusion informs practice

Using reflective practice will help you to review and evaluate your own practice. Having accessed information about equality, diversity and inclusion, practitioners should reflect on the ways in which the information could improve their own practice.

> **Reflect**
>
> - Do you believe your environment is welcoming to all children and their families?
> - Do you know how to challenge prejudice?
> - Do you record prejudice-related incidents?
> - Do you ensure that children's names are spelt and pronounced correctly?
> - Do you offer children a secure environment in which to explore their own culture and that of their peers?

Test yourself

Look at the relevant policy and code of practice on equal opportunities in your own setting and then answer the following questions, making brief notes on current practice:

- How do you show that you value differences between children, and ensure good communication and liaison with parents to ensure that the records for children and young people contain relevant information?
- How do you develop children's sense of identity and raise their self-esteem?
- How does the curriculum planning reflect equal opportunities within every activity and area of learning?
- What do you do to acknowledge the diversity of backgrounds and cater for the individual needs of the children and young people in your setting? (This should include dietary, medical and cultural needs.)

- To what extent do your resources reflect a full range of the diversity within society, avoid stereotypes and promote positive images?
- Who is responsible for planning resources, and how often are the resources reviewed?
- How do you value different spoken and written languages and other forms of communication encountered in your setting?
- To what extent do you take into account the requirements of those with special educational needs and disabilities?

For each question, identify any areas that could be improved, and suggest ways in which this could be achieved.

LO3 Be able to work in ways which support equality, diversity and inclusive practice

Early years practitioners should work in a fair, just and inclusive way, taking into account both the statutory legal framework in the UK and the policies and procedures in their setting. You need to value, and show respect to, all those you encounter in your setting as individuals. Examples of ways of working inclusively are given below.

Definitions of inclusion have developed from being primarily focused on integrating children with special educational needs into a much broader concept concerning social justice and equality for all. Inclusion is the process by which early years settings develop their ethos, policies and practices to include all learners with the aim of meeting their individual needs.

AC 3.1 Interacting with children and meeting their individual needs

As early years practitioners, we are responsible for ensuring inclusive practice and equal opportunities within our settings. There are many ways in which we can promote such practice, such as using the examples shown in Figure 2.4.4.

Promote a sense of belonging

As children grow up, they need to feel that they belong to the group, whether that group is their family, their culture, the community they live in and experience, or their early years setting. Belonging to a group is the result of either:

- being allocated to a group defined by someone else – for example, being British-born
- deciding to join a group – for example, choosing to be a vegetarian or joining a football club.

Until recently, people tended to be seen as belonging to a particular ethnic group if they shared a culture, language, physical features (such as skin colour) or religion. This way of grouping people is no longer thought to be useful. Increasingly, people *choose* the groups they want to be identified with. The early years setting is often the first group that the child joins outside the family and its friendship network. It is important when welcoming families to a setting that they feel a sense of belonging.

Standard English is the usual way of communicating in public, educational, professional and commercial aspects of life. However, young children need to be confident in talking, reading and writing in their home language and to be

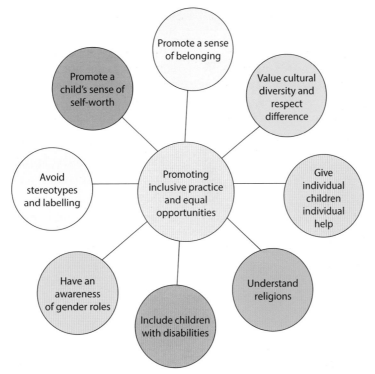

Figure 2.4.4 Promoting inclusive practice and equal opportunities

supported in this early years setting. This actually helps children to develop fluency and literacy in English. So, it is very important that the child's own language is valued and that efforts are made to develop balanced bilingualism.

Value cultural diversity and respect difference

In the UK, we live in a diverse and multicultural society. This means that it is important to appreciate, understand and respect different cultural and religious ideas. The whole environment of the early years setting needs to reflect a multicultural and multilingual approach. For example, the home area, like every other area of the environment, should include objects that are familiar to children and link with their homes and culture. These are often called cultural artefacts.

Using everyday activities to explore different cultures

It is particularly important to introduce children to different cultures through the activities of daily life, such as preparing food and cooking. This is because they can most easily relate to these events.

Figure 2.4.5 It is important to be warm towards children

Figure 2.4.6 Materials such as dough allow children to play in ways that reflect their home culture

For example, for those children who have not met Chinese people or who have not experienced Chinese food, it might be possible to invite someone to the nursery to demonstrate and introduce the children to another culture. Remember that it is important not to stereotype your visitor. For instance, not all people of Chinese background will use chopsticks at home: some families may be using knives and forks. Sets of cultural artefacts should not be mixed up in one home area, as this confuses everyone. It also makes it difficult for the children to value the area and take pride in keeping it looking attractive.

There are opportunities for mathematical learning in sorting out chopsticks from spoons, knives and forks, and Chinese soup spoons, or in knowing which sets of utensils relate to Chinese life, which to African, Indian or Asian cooking, and which to European cultures.

In practice

1 Be willing to find out about different religions and to respect them. Every religion has variety within it. For example, there are Orthodox and Reformed Jews, Roman Catholic Christians, Church of England Christians, Methodist Christians, Quaker Christians, Jehovah Witness Christians and Mormon Christians. Ask religious leaders and parents for information.

2 Find out about different disabilities. Ask parents and voluntary organisations (e.g. Scope, RNIB, RNID) to help you.

3 Do not be afraid to say that you do not know and that you want to find out and learn. Remember that minority groups of all kinds are as important as the majority groups and are included as part of the whole group.

4 Respect and value the child's home language. Think how you can make yourself understood using body language, gestures and facial expression; by pointing; by using pictures; by using actions with your words. Try asking children if they would like a drink using one of these strategies. You could use objects as props. It is important to be warm towards children. Remember to smile and to show that you enjoy interacting with them. Make sure that you are giving comprehensible language input.

5 Create opportunities for children to talk with other children and adults who are already fluent in English. Try to accompany a child's actions with language by describing what is happening. For example, talk with the child and describe what they are doing when they cook, or use clay.

6 When telling stories you could:
  • use puppets and props, flannel boards, magnet boards, etc.
  • invite children to act out pictures as you go through the story
  • use facial expressions, eye contact and body language to 'tell' a story and make it meaningful for the children.

7 Use books in different languages and tell stories in different languages. Remember that there can be problems with dual-language textbooks because, although a language like English reads from left to right, a language like Urdu reads from right to left.

8 Invite someone who speaks the child's language to come and tell stories. For example, ask a Hindi speaker to tell a story such as 'Where's Spot?' in Hindi, using the book in that language but in a session that is for all the children in a story group. Then tell the story and use the book in English at the next session, again with all the children in the story group. Remember that grandparents are often particularly concerned that children are losing their home language as they become more fluent in English (transitional bilingualism). They may enjoy coming into the group and helping in this way.

Encouraging children to use what they know

Children gain by using their own cultural experience and knowledge in an open way. For example, the advantage of play dough, rather than pre-structured plastic food, is that children can bring their own experiences to it. They can make it into roti, pancakes, pasties or pies, depending on their own past experiences. All experiences can be valued, not just those that a toy manufacturer has set in plastic.

Figure 2.4.7 Children need resources that reflect their culture and language

Introducing cultural artefacts

A home area needs to reflect familiar aspects of each child's home. It needs to build on all the children's prior experiences. This means that it should have crockery, cutlery and cooking utensils in the West European style. If, for example, there are children from Chinese backgrounds in the group, it would be particularly important also to have chopsticks, bowls, woks, etc. to reflect their home culture. These would need to be available all the time.

But many children will not know about Chinese woks because they do not meet anyone who cooks with one. These children will need extra help in understanding about cultures other than their own. It is very important to include activities that introduce them to the purpose and function of, for example, Chinese ways of cooking. So, it is important not only that Chinese children see their own culture reflected, but also that other children have the opportunity to learn about different cultures in ways that hold meaning for them and, therefore, are not tokenist (see below).

A child who has never seen a wok before will need to do real cookery with it, and be introduced to this by an adult. **Remember, children learn through real first-hand experiences**. It is no good simply putting a wok in the home area and hoping the children will then know about Chinese cooking. That would be tokenist.

Reflect

- How do you reflect and acknowledge an understanding of your local community in your setting? Are there cultural references that will mean something to all the children and their families?
- Do you include local cultural events and traditions as well as a range of world festivals and national celebrations?
- How would you support and challenge colleagues who make comments that reflect a limited cultural view such as, for example, 'It's not polite to eat with your fingers'?

Give individual children individual help

There may be children with special educational needs using the home area, for example, and they might need special arrangements to allow them access: a child in a wheelchair will need a lower table so that a mixing bowl can be stirred; it might be necessary to make a toy cooker of an appropriate height. Children love to construct their own play props; allowing them to do so makes for a much more culturally diverse selection because they can create what they need in order to make a play setting like their own homes.

Understand religions

In order that every child feels accepted beyond their home, those working with children and young people and their families need to learn about belief structures other than their own. It is also important to remember not to judge people or make assumptions about their values or behaviour based on whether or not they believe in a god or gods. Some children are brought up in families that follow more than one religion. For example, there might be a Roman Catholic Christian father and a Muslim mother, or a Hindu father and a Quaker Christian mother.

Include children with disabilities

Inclusion is about being able to support, encourage and provide for all with individual needs, whether they are temporary or permanent. Excluding children with disabilities from everyday experiences can lead to a lifetime of segregation. In addition, lack of contact with disabled people can lead to fear and ignorance of those who seem 'different'.

Have an awareness of gender roles

Creating an environment where girls and boys are respected and cared for equally in early childhood is the first step towards breaking cycles of discrimination and disadvantage, and promoting a child's sense of self-worth as it relates to their gender. It is important to remember that some children will have learnt narrow gender roles. Children need to see adults taking on broader gender roles and to learn about alternative ways for men and women to behave as themselves.

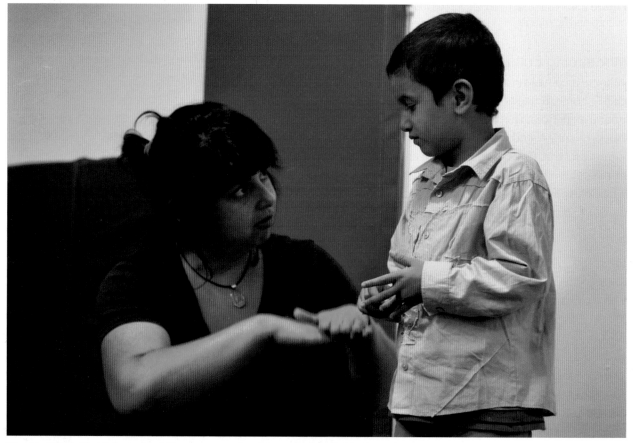

Figure 2.4.8 All children should be supported and have their individual needs met

Avoid stereotypes and labelling

When adults fill in forms, they decide whether to be described as Mr, Ms, Mrs or Miss, and whether or not they wish to describe themselves according to different ethnic categories. An adult with a hearing loss can also choose whether to be described as deaf, hearing impaired or aurally challenged. Children need to be given as much choice as possible about these aspects of their lives.

Promote a child's sense of self-worth

Children need to feel a sense of their own worth. This comes from:

- feeling that they matter to other people

- feeling able to take an active part in things
- feeling competent and skilled enough to do so.

Reflect

Promoting equality of opportunity

Think about different ways in which you have encouraged equality of opportunity in your work with children and young people.

- How can you ensure that your practice is not discriminatory?
- How can you promote equality of opportunity?

Write a short account of ways in which you can ensure that no child, young person or adult is treated unfavourably compared with others.

Tips for helping children to have a sense of their own worth

- Provide familiar objects for every child in the different areas of the room. These artefacts of their culture might be cooking utensils, clothes or fabrics.
- Positive images of different children in different cultures are important. Remember that the important thing about a child is not how they look or the extent of their learning difficulty, but that they are a person. The way you behave and talk will give messages about your mental image of each child.
- Make sure you tell stories, and make displays and interest tables with positive images of children with disabilities and children from different cultures. These stories should also be in the book area.
- Make sure that children meet adults with broad gender roles, to show them that men and women are not restricted respectively to a narrow range of activities.

- Encourage children to speak to other children and adults within the early years setting. Remember that children might feel powerless if they cannot speak to other people.
- Use stories from different cultures to introduce children to myths, legends and folk tales. The same themes crop up over and over again in different stories across the world. Find some of these universal themes in the stories you look at from different cultures – for example, the wicked stepmother, the greedy rich person, good deeds being rewarded after suffering.
- Make sure the indoor and outdoor areas offer full access to activities for children with disabilities.
- Do not forget that you need to have a sense of your own worth too. What did you do today that made you feel that you had a worthwhile day?

Case study

Read the following three scenarios and then discuss the questions below in a group:

1 Paul's mother arrives at the school open day. She is in a wheelchair, being pushed by Paul's father. The teacher welcomes the parents and then asks Paul's father if his wife would like a drink and a biscuit.
2 Patrick and Jo, both early years practitioners, are having a tea break and discussing a new child who has just started at their school. Patrick says, 'I can't stand the way these Travellers think they can just turn up at school whenever they feel like it – they don't pay taxes, you know, and they live practically on top of rubbish dumps … I feel sorry for the kids – they don't know any different.'

3 Rory, Jason, Lucy and Fatima are playing in the role-play area. The practitioner asks Rory and Jason to tidy away the train set and trucks, and asks Lucy and Fatima to put the dolls and cooking pots away, as it is nearly story time.

In both instances, certain assumptions have been made about other people.

- Why do you think these assumptions have been made?
- How would you explain to someone new to early years work why labelling and stereotyping people are wrong?
- Discuss ways in which you can interact with children in a way that values them and meets their needs

AC 3.2 The benefits of equality, diversity and inclusive practice

Under the EYFS, all settings must provide and implement an effective equality of opportunity policy. Good practice highlights how children, from a very young age, can learn to place a value on different races, cultures and disabilities. We have already considered the potential effects of discrimination on children and on adults.

The benefits of supporting equality, diversity and inclusive practice include the following:

- **Recognition of our own prejudices**: an awareness of our own bias and prejudices will help us to act to ensure they do not result in discrimination or bias towards others.
- **Welcoming diversity and working with it**: by presenting children with an environment which positively encourages diversity, we are helping children to develop a strong self-identity.
- **Helping young children to develop a sense of belonging**: the EYFS emphasises the importance of developing young children's own sense of identity and a positive sense of pride in their own family origins. By supporting diversity and inclusive practice in the setting, young children can develop a sense of belonging to the local community and begin to understand and respect less familiar cultures.

In your setting

It is everyone's responsibility to promote inclusion, but early years practitioners should actively seek to break down the barriers that prevent those from minority groups having their own voice in the way services are planned and delivered. Think about the following issues within your setting:

- Do you have opportunities within your setting to share ideas about equality issues?
- Do practitioners have a safe space where they can debate and discuss issues of equality, including gender, membership of a minority ethnic group and disability?

AC 3.3 Our own attitudes, values and behaviour and equality, diversity and inclusive practice

Inspecting our own attitudes and values

In the UK, there is now legislation on race, gender and disability discrimination, which helps teams of people working together to have an impact on racism, sexism and disablist attitudes and work practices, however unconscious these may be. In addition, it is important that each of us inspects what we do so that we become aware of our attitudes and values. Only then can we act on the unwittingly discriminatory behaviour that we will almost inevitably find. Discriminatory behaviour occurs when, usually without meaning it, we are sexist, racist or disablist. For example, an early childhood worker might ask for a strong boy to lift the chair. We need to look to see whether what we say we believe matches what we actually do. Sometimes it does not! So then we have to do something about it.

Each of us has to work at this all the time, right throughout our lives. It is not useful to feel guilty and dislike yourself if you find you are discriminating against someone. It is useful to do something about it.

The process of inspecting our basic thinking needs to be done on three levels:

1 within the legal framework
2 in the work setting as part of a team
3 as individuals.

Valuing cultural diversity and respecting difference

Much can be gained from respecting different ways of bringing up children. For example, the Indian tradition of massaging babies is now widely used in British clinics and family centres; so is the way that African mothers traditionally carry their babies in a sling on their backs. It is important to understand and respect what the child has been taught to do at home. For example, in some cultures, it is seen as disrespectful for a child to look an adult directly in the eye, whereas in others children are considered rude if they do not look at an adult directly.

In practice

Working together to promote equality of opportunity and inclusivity

The following list provides good opportunities for you to check your practice and ensure that you are:

- **observing** children
- **planning** to meet every child's needs
- **implementing** and **evaluating** the activities.

1 **Plan a multicultural cooking library**: make six cookery books with simple recipes from a variety of cultures. Find or draw pictures to illustrate the books. Write the text in English, and another language if possible. If you write in Urdu or Chinese, remember that you will need to make two separate books, as Urdu and Chinese text runs from right to left. Use the books with groups of children and run a series of cookery sessions. **Observe** the way the children use and respond to the cookery books. **Evaluate** the aim of your plan, the reason for the activity, how the activities were carried out and what you observed in the children's cooking activities.

2 **Storytelling**: plan a story that you can tell (rather than read from a book). Choose a story you enjoy and make or find suitable props. You could make puppets out of stuffed socks, finger puppets out of gloves, stick puppets or shadow puppets; or use dolls and dressing-up clothes and various other artefacts. **Observe** the children listening as you tell the story. Focus on their understanding and their language, especially children whose first language is not English. **Evaluate** your activity.

3 **Religious festivals**: plan how you can make the children you work with more aware of religious festivals in a variety of cultures – for example, how could you introduce the children to Diwali (a Hindu festival with lights, held in October and November) in a way that is not tokenist? Remember to offer children meaningful first-hand experiences. **Observe** the children and assess how much they understand. Look particularly at the reactions of children who are familiar with the festival you choose, and compare their behaviour to that of children for whom this is a new experience. **Evaluate** your plans and observations.

4 **Inclusion**: plan how you would include a child with disabilities in your early years setting. Remember that your plans will be different according to each child's needs. A child with a hearing impairment will need different help from a child who is a wheelchair user, for example. Carry out and **observe** your plan in action. Focus on how you meet the child's individual needs through your plan. **Evaluate** your plan.

5 **Equality of opportunity**: read your setting's policy on equality of opportunity, and look at actual practices in the daily routine – for example, meal times and books. Does what happens match the policy? **Evaluate** your observations.

6 **Musical development**: plan a series of activities which introduce children to the music of a variety of cultures. You will need to help children to listen to music and make music. Make musical instruments out of cardboard boxes, elastic bands, yoghurt pots, masking tape and other materials.

7 **Booklet**: plan a booklet that introduces different religious festivals and helps parents to understand different religious perspectives in your setting. Make the booklet and use it in your early years setting. **Evaluate** it.

8 **Display**: plan and make a display using a multicultural theme. **Evaluate** it. How did the adults use it? How did the children react?

9 **International book**: choose one picture, book, story or poem from each of the seven continents: Africa, North America, South America, Asia, Australia, Antarctica and Europe. Make the collection into a book that you can use with children of three to seven years of age. **Evaluate** the activity.

10 **Multicultural provision**: plan an area of provision that is multicultural in approach – for example, the home area. Perhaps you can add more ideas to those suggested in this section. Implement and **evaluate** your plan.

Helping children form positive images of people

- **Storytelling**: ask storytellers (for example, parents) from different ethnic groups to tell stories in their own languages, as well as in English. This helps children to hear different languages, so that the idea becomes familiar that there are many languages in the world.

- **Using arts, crafts and artefacts from different cultures** (fabrics, interest tables, books, posters, jigsaws, etc.): this helps children to realise, for example, that not everyone uses a knife, fork or spoon when eating; they might use fingers or chopsticks instead. Children are helped to learn that there are different ways of eating, something which might seem strange to them at first.

- **Including music and dances from different cultures**: listening to them, watching them, and perhaps joining in a bit. In every culture, children love to stand at the edge while people perform. Children often 'echo dance'. Watch out the next time you go to a fête. If there are Morris dancers or folk dancers, you are likely to see children watching them and echo dancing at the sides. Being introduced to different cultures in this way helps children not to reject unfamiliar music. For example, Chinese music has a pentatonic scale; African music sometimes has five beats in a bar; European music has two, three or four beats but not usually five. A child who has never seen ballet before or a child who has never seen an Indian dance before might find these strange at first.
- **Doing cookery from different cultures**: you might have multi-language, picture-based cookery books that families can borrow (you might need to make these). For example, there could be a copy of a recipe for roti in English, Urdu and French, or for bread in English, Greek and Swahili; the choice of languages would depend on which were used in the early childhood setting.

- **Planning the menu carefully**: make sure that the menu includes food that children will enjoy and which is in some way familiar. One of the things young children worry about when they are away from home is whether they will like the food. Food and eating with others is a very emotional experience.

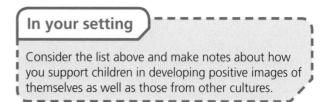

In your setting

Consider the list above and make notes about how you support children in developing positive images of themselves as well as those from other cultures.

Helping children feel that they belong

Ensure that children who look different, because they are from different cultures or because they have a disability, feel at ease and part of the group. In the early years setting, it is important not to have expensive outings or activities, and to be sure to invite all parents to take part in the life of the group. No parent or child should be left out because of their economic background. This is an important equality of opportunity issue.

Assessment

For this unit you will need to show that you have a good understanding of equality, diversity and inclusion and how this translates to your practice and also the practice in your work setting.

You will need to start by looking at the legislation that is in place and how this links to policies and procedures in your setting. To do this, you could look at the policies and procedures in your setting relating to admissions, special needs and also diversity and equality of opportunity. You could then link these to the overarching legislation that is in place. You will need to check that the legislation given in this unit is still current and you can do this by visiting the Equality and Human Rights Commission website (**www. equalityhumanrights.com**).

It will be worth keeping evidence that you have done this as you need to show your assessor for Learning Outcome 2 is that you can access information, support and advice about equality, diversity and inclusive

practice. For this second learning outcome you also have to show on how information, advice and support about equality can be used to inform your practice. It is therefore worth thinking about how through the course of studying this unit your practice has changed.

Finally, you need to show for assessment criteria in both Learning Outcome 1 and Learning Outcome 3 that you have a good understanding of why it is important to promote equality, diversity and inclusive practice, and that you understand the roles and responsibilities of early years practitioners in relation to this. Your practice will also be looked at. Your assessor is therefore likely to watch you work and may focus on aspects of your practice, such as how well you value children and to what extent you show that you value children. Your assessor also needs to see that you can evaluate the impact of your own attitudes, values and behaviour in relation to supporting equality, diversity and inclusive practice.

Useful resources

Book

Lindon, J. (2006) *Equality in Early Childhood: Linking Theory and Practice*, London: Hodder Arnold.

Organisations

The Alliance for Inclusive Education

This is a national campaigning organisation led by disabled people: **www.allfie.org.uk**.

Early Support

This organisation provides materials for families and professionals, including a service audit tool, a family pack and information for parents on certain disabilities and impairments: **www.ncb.org.uk/early-support**.

KIDS

KIDS works for disabled children, young people and their families: **www.kids.org.uk**.

Unit 2.5 WB Working in partnership

What do you think partnership working means? You might think it means working with parents, but actually partnership working in early years settings also covers working with colleagues and other professionals. In this unit, we look at the policies and procedures involved with partnership working, as well as the roles of those involved in partnership working. We look at the different family structures that children live in, as well as the times when parents may need additional support. We also look at some of the challenges of partnership working and the importance of keeping records.

Learning outcomes

By the end of this unit, you will:

1 Understand the principles of partnership working in relation to current frameworks when working with children.
2 Understand how to work in partnership.
3 Understand challenges to partnership working.
4 Be able to work with parents/carers in a way which encourages them to take an active role in their child's play, learning and development.
5 Be able to complete records.

LO1 Understand the principles of partnership working in relation to current frameworks when working with children

Have you noticed that sometimes other professionals visit your setting? Or perhaps children have appointments to see other professionals, such as physiotherapists? These are all examples of partnership working where children and their families gain additional support. Parents too are part of partnership working and in this section we look at the importance of partnership working and also the policies and procedures behind it.

AC 1.1 Why work in partnership

There are a range of people with whom early years practitioners work. These include parents, colleagues and other professionals. In this section, we look at the wide range of people with whom we may work and consider their role. People with whom we work in partnership will all in some way be involved with the child or their family. The key reason for working in partnership is to ensure children's overall needs are met.

Working with parents

All early years practitioners will work closely with parents. This is one of the most important partnerships that we will make. It is essential that we develop strong partnerships with parents because they know their children well and, by sharing information with them, we can find out more about their child's care and also their emotional needs. If partnership working is in place, we can exchange information with parents about their child's learning so that they can further support their learning at home.

Working with colleagues

Partnership working with colleagues allows a setting to run smoothly, which means that children's needs are more likely to be met. It means that activities and resources can be planned more easily to meet children's play needs as colleagues work together to provide a play and learning environment. Good partnership with colleagues also means that we can share ideas and reflect on our practice.

Reflect ?

Write a list of ways in which colleagues in your setting have helped you to improve your practice.

Working with other professionals

The main reason for strong partnership working with other professionals is to ensure that children's needs can be identified and met. It also allows for good communication to take place so, where there are concerns about a child, support can be put in place. Strong partnership working also means that we can learn skills from other professionals, which we can use to develop our practice further with children.

AC 1.2 Policy and procedural requirements for partnership working

There are requirements in the EYFS for early years settings to work with parents in a number of ways. As part of the EYFS, it is one of the roles of the key person to work with parents to understand and meet children's individual care and learning needs. In addition, the key person should also help parents to support their child's learning at home. All early years settings will have a key person system in place in the setting.

In addition, there is also a requirement for early years settings to work closely with other professionals where there are concerns about a child's welfare or where the child has additional needs that should be supported.

Policies and procedures

There is a range of factors that early years settings have to consider in partnership working and these are reflected in various policies.

Confidentiality

One of the most important aspects of partnership working is maintaining confidentiality. This is because one of the features of partnership working is the sharing of personal information about individual children and their families. To make sure that everyone working with children understands the importance of confidentiality, early years settings and other professionals will have policies in place. As a general principle, you should never pass on information that you have received about a child or a family with anyone else other than the child's key person or your manager. You should also not talk about colleagues' or other professionals' decisions or their personal information to others. If you are unsure of whether information is confidential, you should always check.

There will also be procedures about how much information can be disclosed. Usually, when working with other professionals, information should only be given that is relevant to their work.

In practice

Explain your setting's confidentiality policy.

The Data Protection Act 1998

As well as policies about confidentiality, there may also be procedures about data protection. This is because there are laws about how personal information can be stored and used. The Data Protection Act means that information about children and their families cannot be passed to other professionals without parents' consent. The only exception is where there are concerns about a child's welfare. This means that, before a child can be referred to another professional, such as a speech and language therapist, the child's parents would have to give consent.

In all early years settings, parents have a right to see their children's records – this is personal information and so, under the Data Protection Act, they are able to see it. It is also good practice to share records with parents as it helps us to work in partnership.

Research it!

Find out more about the Data Protection Act 1998 by visiting www.ico.org.uk.

What rights do you have over the personal information that your setting and other organisations, such as online shops, hold about you?

In your setting

What steps does your setting take to protect the personal information of children and their families?

Reporting lines

For partnership working to be effective, there have to be clear lines of reporting. This ensures that information is given to those who need it and that information does not go astray. It is usual, for example, for children's key persons in early years settings to share and exchange information on a day-to-day basis with parents. On the other hand, where there are safeguarding concerns about a child's welfare, information will be exchanged between the early years setting's designated person and other professionals.

LO2 Understand how to work in partnership

Have you noticed that parents and staff in your setting spend a lot of time talking? You may also have noticed that sometimes visitors, such as early years advisors, come to the setting too. These are both examples of partnership working. Partnership working is important for a range of reasons. In this section, we look at the wide range of people who support children and their families, and their roles. We also look at how partnership is essential in three key areas of working with children, including safeguarding. Finally, we look at the importance of working with parents and how family structures vary.

AC 2.1 The roles in partnership working when supporting children

There are a surprising number of professionals who may support children and their families. Table 2.5.1 on page 146 shows the range of professionals and what they do.

> ### In your setting
>
> Look at Table 2.5.1, the list of professionals who may work with a child or their family. Which of these professionals does your setting have links with?

AC 2.2 Evaluate partnership working

There are three areas where early years settings work closely with other professionals:

- meeting children's additional needs
- safeguarding children
- children's transitions.

Meeting children's additional needs

Where children have additional needs, such as speech and language delay or sensory impairment, other professionals will be involved in supporting them. It is important to work in partnership as they will be supporting and helping the child to make progress. In practice, partnership working may be exchanging information about the child's interests as well as their additional needs. Other professionals may give suggestions as to how early years settings can work to modify the environment or work in ways that will benefit the child. In addition, professionals such as speech and language therapists and physiotherapists will often want early years practitioners to implement some aspects of the programme that they have developed for the child. This might mean practising certain movements or encouraging a child to make certain sounds.

Safeguarding children

Safeguarding children, as we saw in Unit 2.2, requires a partnership approach as exchange of information is vital. In some cases, early years settings will flag up concerns about children to the relevant professionals so that the child can be protected from any potential harm. In other cases, it may be that a social worker who is involved in supporting a family will ask the setting to contact them if a child does not attend, or ask the setting to be particularly vigilant about children's state of health and well-being.

In addition, decisions about how best to protect children may require input from all professionals who are involved with the child and so attendance at a case conference might be needed. This helps those making decisions about the child's welfare gain an all-round view of the child and their family.

Children's transitions

When children move from one setting to another, they are making a transition. They may do this during the course of a day or a week or they may move onto school or another early years setting. As we saw in Unit 1.4, children need emotional security and so partnership working is essential for providing children with continuity. Early years practitioners will exchange information about the child's progress, interests and needs, always with a parent's permission. For a child who moves between a childminder and a pre-school, a notebook might be used to exchange information about what the child has done. In the case of children starting school, it is usual for children to visit the school with their early years practitioners and also for the new teachers to come to the early years settings. During transition, partnership working also means that records about children's learning and progress are transferred, provided parents have given consent. This allows for continuity and helps the next practitioner plan for children's needs and interests.

Table 2.5.1 Professionals who support children and their families

Social worker	Works to support families who are judged in need because of welfare concerns or because a child has a disability. Social workers also work with children who have been taken into local authority care and may be in foster homes or care homes.
Speech and language therapist	Works to maximise and support children's communication, speech and language. May provide information to settings on how to support an individual child's speech or language.
Physiotherapist	Works to maximise children's physical movements and may provide early years settings with advice about how best to support an individual child's progress through a programme of physical movements.
Police liaison officer	Works closely with social workers when there are concerns about a child's welfare or directly with families who have been victims of crimes.
Dietician	Works to provide advice about individual children's diets, including helping families who have children with food allergies and medical conditions, such as diabetes. Children will also be referred to a dietician when there are concerns about their weight.
Sensory impairment team	Works with children and their families who have sight and/or hearing problems. The sensory impairment team visits early years settings and provides advice and equipment so that children can be supported in the setting.
Family doctor (GP)	Works in the community treating illness and medical conditions. Family doctors also have a role in preventing diseases and so will provide advice as well as immunisations.
Paediatrician	A doctor who specialises in the medical care of young children and who is usually based in a hospital. Children with a medical problem will be referred to a paediatrician via their family doctor.
Health visitor	Supports the health and welfare of children by visiting families or being available at clinics. They provide information and advice about a range of health topics, such as weaning, sleeping and immunisation. Health visitors monitor children's development as well as health. Many health visitors work closely with family doctors.
Child psychiatrist	Works with children and their families when children show signs of having mental health difficulties, such as depression. Referral is usually made through the family GP. Child psychiatrists may liaise closely with play therapists.
Play therapist	Works with children to help them deal with traumas through the medium of play. Children may be referred via a family doctor, paediatrician, police liaison service or a child psychiatrist.
Educational psychologist	Works to advise and support parents and other professionals about how best to progress children's learning and behaviour. Individual children are often referred by a SENCO (see below) or family doctor (with parent's consent) when their learning or behaviour seems atypical.
SENCO	A member of staff in early years settings and schools with the responsibility of coordinating the support for children with additional needs.
Early years teacher	Trained as a teacher to work with children of nursery and reception age.
Family outreach worker	Works to support families who may need help with a range of issues, including parenting, life skills and child development. Family outreach workers are often based in Children's Centres.
Early years advisor	Works to support settings to improve and develop their practice. They are usually employed by the local authority, but day care chains and academies may have their own team in this role.

Figure 2.5.1 Communicating with other professionals can support children's transitions

AC 2.3 Different family structures

While there are some children who are brought up with a mother, father and siblings, this is not how all children are brought up today. This is because over the past few decades society has changed. There is now a range of different family structures and it is thought that, as long as children receive love, attention and security, the type of family structure which they are in makes no difference.

It is important to be aware of the many ways in which children may be brought up so all children and their families can be welcomed into our settings.

Nuclear families

The nuclear family was seen as the traditional family, where children live with a mother, father and any siblings. Until recently, parents would be married, but today many children in nuclear families have parents who are in stable cohabiting relationships.

In addition, some children live in a nuclear family where their parents are in a gay relationship, which means that they have two parents of the same gender.

Single parents

Some children are brought up in single-parent households. Single parents may be either fathers or mothers. Sometimes a single-parent household is the result of the death of partner, husband or wife. In some cases, single parenthood is a lifestyle choice.

Reconstituted families

Some children will grow up in families where they live with one of their natural parents and a step-parent. In reconstituted families, it is not unusual for children to have half brothers and sisters as well as stepbrothers and stepsisters.

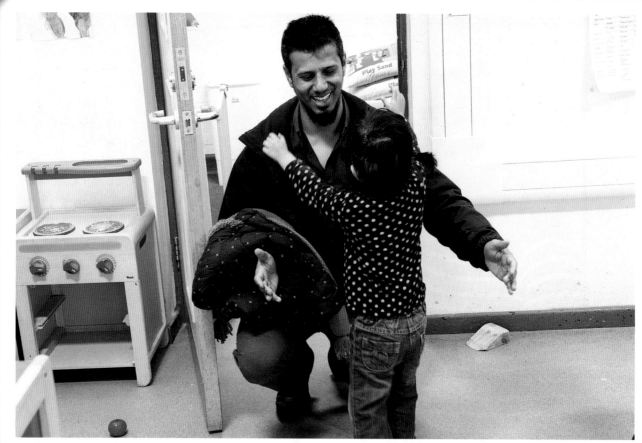

Figure 2.5.2 There are many different family structures that you might come across in the setting

More than one family

Some children who have reconstituted families will share their time between two families. They may spend half of the week with one of their natural parents and the other half with the other parent. This can mean that some children have two bedrooms, two sets of toys and two routines to follow.

Extended families

Some children are brought up in extended families where they live with their parents but also other family members. In some cultures, this is the traditional model of family life and so children may have their grandparents or other family members living with them.

Foster families

Some children live with foster parents who are looking after them because either their own parents are unable to do so or concerns have been raised about safeguarding. Foster families may include children's grandparents or other family members who

have care of the children as a temporary measure. Some children are with foster families because they are the responsibility of the local authority.

> ### In your setting
>
> Look at the different types of family structures. Does your setting have children from a wide range of family structures?
>
> How does your setting work to ensure that no assumptions are made about children's family structures when there are events such as Mother's Day?

AC 2.4 Benefits of working in partnership with parents/carers

We know that parents play an essential role in children's lives. They offer emotional security and stability as well as influencing children's values and attitudes. Unlike professionals who work with children, parents are there for the long term. They know about their child's personality, interests and also quirks. There are therefore many benefits of working in partnership with parents.

Transition

When children move from their home to an early years setting, we need to find ways of making this as smooth as possible. Where there are strong partnerships with parents, it is easier to help the child make the move.

Sharing of information

When there are strong partnerships with parents, information that can help in the care and education of children can be easily exchanged. This is important as what happens at home can affect children in the early years setting, but also what happens in the early years setting can influence the child at home.

Positive outcomes for children's learning

There has been research to show that, where there is strong partnership working and parents feel involved, children do better in their education. This is because parents and settings share ideas, and so parents can put these into practice at home.

In practice

Explain how your setting works with parents and the benefits of doing so.

AC 2.5 Identifying when parents/ carers need support

Being a parent is a responsible and emotionally charged task. While most parents love being with their children and cope with the demands of parenting well, there are times when families or parents can come under pressure and need more support. It is important for early years settings to pick up on when parents may need support so that they can suggest organisations or professionals who may be able to support them.

As people respond to stress differently, there are many ways in which parents may show that they need support. These include being unusually short tempered, anxious or indifferent with their children. Some parents may also become aggressive or frustrated with staff at the setting. We may also notice that parents who are usually chatty are suddenly quiet or distant. In some cases, parents may confide directly in us.

Where there are concerns that parents may need additional support, it is likely to be the manager's or leader's role to have a quiet word with parents and to ask them if they need any help.

Table 2.5.2 shows some of the common reasons why parents may need additional support.

Table 2.5.2 Reasons parents might need additional support

Parenting issues	
Sleep	Some parents need support because their children will not sleep through the night or won't go to bed alone.
Behaviour	Many behaviours that children show, such as tantrums, are linked to their stage of development. Parents can find it hard to deal with issues such as tantrums, attention seeking and biting.
Sibling rivalry	Some parents find sibling rivalry a problem after the birth of a baby or as part of the family dynamics.
Feeding	Some parents can find meal times stressful because their children are fussy eaters.
Transition – settling in	Many parents find it hard when their child first starts off in a setting or when their child changes setting. →

Table 2.5.2 Reasons parents might need additional support   (contd.)

Stresses	
Poverty	When parents are on a low income, it may place more stress on the family.
Relationship breakdown	Any difficulties where relationships break down or become strained between parents can cause additional stress.
Bereavement	The death of a close family member or friend can put pressure on a family.
Redundancy	When a parent is made redundant, this can cause financial hardship, but also stress.
Illness	The long-term illness of a child in the family, a family member or parent can cause stress in the family.
Medical issues	
Depression	Parents can become depressed, which means that they will find it harder to respond to their children. Depression can be caused by stress but also, in the case of new mothers, by hormonal imbalances.
Addiction	Parents who are addicted to alcohol or illegal drugs may not be able to support their children.
Mental illnesses	Parents who have a mental illness (which may be temporary) may need additional support.

AC 2.6 Support services for parents/carers

There is a range of services that are set up to support families who need additional support. Some of these are voluntary organisations while others are provided by the local authority or council. There is a system in place that helps families gain support. The system in England is called the Common Assessment Framework (CAF). The CAF process is done with parents' consent and starts off with an early years setting filling in a form with parents. This is passed on to a specific team within a local authority, who will begin the process of coordinating additional support.

Research it!

Find out more about the Common Assessment Framework.

Find out how the CAF process is implemented in your local area.

Table 2.5.3 shows the wide range of services and support that families might access.

Research it!

Visit three of the following websites to find out about the work of these organisations. For each organisation, summarise how they might support a parent:

- www.cruse.org.uk – support and advice for people coping with a bereavement
- www.macmillan.org.uk – support and advice for people affected by cancer, including families and friends
- www.depressionalliance.org – support and advice for people and their families with depression
- www.relate.org.uk – support and advice about relationships, including couples and parent–child relationships
- www.gingerbread.org.uk – support for single parents
- www.citizensadvice.org.uk – advice about a range of issues, particularly money and legal help.

LO3 Understand challenges to partnership working

In an ideal world, partnership working should be easy. The reality, though, is that it requires a lot of time, effort and good communication skills. In this section, we look at the potential difficulties

Table 2.5.3 Support that may be offered to parents

Parenting issues	
Sleep	• Key person or experienced member of the early years team who has the training and expertise
Behaviour	• Health visitors
Sibling rivalry	• Family outreach workers
Feeding	• Voluntary organisations such as Home-Start
Transition – settling in	
Stresses	
Poverty	• Signposting in setting for benefits and bursaries • Social services • Voluntary organisations such as local food banks and Citizens' Advice Bureau
Relationship breakdown	• Relationship counselling • Voluntary organisations such as Gingerbread or Relate
Bereavement	• Bereavement counselling • Voluntary organisations such as Cruse
Redundancy	• Job centre • Counselling • Citizens' Advice Bureau
Illness	• Counselling • Voluntary organisations linked to the type of illness
Medical issues	
Depression	• Family doctor
Addiction	• Organisations specialising in the specific medical issue, e.g. rehabilitation
Mental illnesses	• Social services where there are concerns about children's welfare

that might affect partnership working and how these can be overcome. We also think about the complex nature of partnership working.

AC 3.1 Barriers to partnership working

There is a range of barriers that can mean that partnership working is not as easy as it should be. These barriers and how they affect parents and professionals are explored in Table 2.5.4.

AC 3.2 Strategies to overcome barriers

There are some key strategies that are important when working in partnership. These can overcome the barriers presented in Table 2.5.4.

Communication style

The way that we communicate can make a huge impact on how well we work in partnership with others. By communicating well and also choosing appropriate methods and language, we are more likely to prevent misunderstandings. It is also a way in which we can share information and show respect.

Face-to-face communication

Some communication will be face to face. This means that we will be talking directly to the parent or the professional. It is the most commonly used method of communication when working with parents.

- Always greet and acknowledge parents and other professionals.
- Be friendly, but remember to act professionally.

Table 2.5.4 Barriers to partnership working

Barrier	Parents	Other professionals
Time	Parents may be working and so may not come into the setting at all. Some parents may also be in a rush to get other children to school or to go to work.	Other professionals may have set days on which they work. They may have many other diary commitments and may need plenty of advance notice.
Priorities	Parents may not share the same priorities as us. They may be more interested in getting their child to sleep through the night rather than on whether or not their child has gained hand preference!	Other professionals have different priorities based on their roles. A physiotherapist's focus may be on a child's hand movement, not on whether the child is finding it hard to make friends.
Knowledge	Parents will have different knowledge and experiences to us. They may not know about the importance of sharing books at home.	Other professionals will have knowledge that is linked to their role. A speech and language therapist may not know about the demands of the EYFS and National Curriculum and so will not consider these when creating a programme for the child for us to carry out.
Approach	Parents will have different approaches to how they parent their child. Some may not want their children to play outdoors in the rain.	Other professionals will have different ways of working which link to their role. In the case of some types of therapy or programmes, these may not always be as child-led or play-led as the way in which an early years setting works.
Communication	Communication is essential, but not all parents will have English as a first language or they may not find reading and writing easy. This can cause misunderstandings or prevent parents from sharing information.	Other professionals may have certain protocols to follow when communicating, which may make it harder for spontaneous calls or meetings.
Relationships, respect and trust	All partnership working is based on good relationships, respect and trust. Where any adult feels that they are not trusted or respected, it can be difficult to work in partnership. Previous experiences or misunderstandings can mean that it is harder to establish a relationship.	
Sharing information	We know that sharing information is important, but we may not realise that we have information that others do not know about. A parent whose child is stammering may not think to tell us that there is a family history of this, and we may not think to ask! In the same way, a health visitor may assume that we have been told by a child's parent about the outcome of the two year old health check.	

- Explain your role clearly.
- Listen carefully to what they are saying.
- Show that you are listening by looking at the person.
- Take notes where appropriate.
- Ask for clarification if you feel that you have not understood or that you will need more information.

In addition, there may be times when a conversation is confidential and so you may also need to suggest that you talk in a more private place. You may need to think about whether additional support is needed when a person has difficulties in speaking English. This might mean looking for someone to translate. Where a person has a hearing problem, you may also need to ask them what you need to do in order to make it easier to communicate. This might mean moving to a quieter place or talking and positioning yourself so that they can follow your lips.

Writing

Another way in which we might communicate is through writing. There are many ways in which to communicate through writing, including letters, diaries, reports and emails. Writing can be useful as it can prevent misunderstandings, but it is important that the tone of the writing is appropriate. When writing to parents, it is important that the tone is friendly, but still professional. It is also important to check that writing is legible and properly laid out and that there are no spelling mistakes. It can be worth practising different types of writing.

In practice

Practise the following types of writing:

- a note to a parent explaining why their child has paint on their jumper
- an email to a speech and language therapist asking if an appointment can be changed
- a letter to parents asking for permission to pass information about their child to their child's childminder.

Using the telephone

The telephone is another way in which communication takes place. It is important to speak clearly and also to remember to be friendly, but not unprofessional. It is usually a good idea to make a note of a telephone conversation so that information is not forgotten and a record can be kept.

Showing respect and understanding

We have seen that parents and other professionals may have different priorities and approaches from ours. It is important that all communications show respect for these. One way of overcoming barriers associated with different priorities is to have an open conversation to find out about them. This avoids potential misunderstandings and makes it easier to work in partnership.

Avoid making assumptions

It is important that we avoid making assumptions as this can cause misunderstandings but may also result in other people not feeling valued or respected. We saw in the previous section that family structures vary and so making any assumptions can get a relationship with a parent off to a bad start.

In the same way, it is important not to assume that everyone knows about how the early years setting works or what our role is within the early years setting. A parent or another professional may not know what the term 'key person' means or what 'free-flow play' is.

AC 3.3 The complexity of partnership working

We have seen that there are several barriers to partnership working. What can make partnership working more complex is when families and children require the input of many different professionals at once. Coordinating the different input can be difficult and it is easy for communication and information sharing to break down. This might happen for a variety of reasons.

Parental consent

It may be that parents do not give their consent for information to be shared between professionals and, unless it is a safeguarding matter, their wishes have to be respected.

Systems of keeping information

We have seen that sharing information about a child is important when more than one professional is involved. This is not always easy as each service will keep their own records. In many areas of England, these cannot be accessed by other services, although in London a shared database of information is being rolled out. This should allow a speech and language therapist to enter their notes about a visit to a school, which the child's social worker will then also be able to access.

Changes of professionals

Difficulties can also arise when there are changes of professionals. Parents and early years staff might have built up a good relationship with one professional and then a different person may come into the role. When a child or family has many different professionals working with them, this may cause a lack of continuity.

Coordination

Ideally, when a child or family has many different professionals working with them, it would be good for everyone involved to meet up. Unless there are safeguarding issues, this may not happen very often, or not at all. This is because it can be difficult to coordinate a meeting when everyone is free to attend. Ideally, in complex cases, a lead professional is appointed. A lead professional is responsible for coordinating and sharing information with the range of professionals involved with the family.

Case study

Greta is four years old. She was born prematurely. She has complex needs, which include sight problems and learning difficulties. Her mother is a single parent and has recently been diagnosed with cancer. The treatment that she is receiving makes it hard for her to meet her daughter's needs.

1 Why would a range of professionals need to be involved in the support of this family?
2 Why is it important that a named person has an overview of this family's needs?
3 Explain some of the potential barriers involved in partnership working in this case.

AC 3.4 Maintaining confidentiality and the need to disclose information

We saw in LO1 that maintaining confidentiality is important in partnership work in order for others to trust us. There are times, though, when you would be justified in breaking confidentiality. It is important for everyone working with children to understand the three situations in which you might break confidentiality:

● when poor practice is identified
● where a child is at risk
● when it is suspected that a crime has been/may be committed.

When poor practice is identified

It is usual for most settings to have codes of confidentiality that state that details of how the setting works with children and information about staff members are not to be discussed out of work. However, these restrictions on confidentiality can be broken if you have seen poor practice in your setting

and you have either raised it with your line manager and nothing has changed or you do not feel that you can tell anyone in the organisation. This situation is sometimes referred to as 'whistleblowing'. One of the best ways that you can report poor practice anonymously is by calling Ofsted, who take all complaints and information seriously.

Where a child is at risk

Where you have concerns about a child's welfare, you can break confidentiality even if a parent, colleague or a child has told you something 'in private'. Where you have concerns about a child, you should tell the person in your setting responsible for child protection and safeguarding or, if you still do not feel that the matter is being taken seriously, you could call the police or the NSPCC.

→ In Unit 2.2, we looked at child protection and safeguarding procedures.

When it is suspected that a crime has been/may be committed

The final situation where you may break the codes of confidentiality is if you think that a crime has been or is about to be committed. This might link back to concerns about a child's welfare, but it might also be where a parent is the subject of domestic abuse or where you think that a colleague is stealing money or equipment from the setting.

Test yourself

Make a list of situations in which you would be justified to break confidentiality.

LO4 Be able to work with parents/carers in a way which encourages them to take an active role in their child's play, learning and development

Have you noticed that your work setting talks to parents about their child's development? Perhaps you have seen noticeboards with information about play or local opportunities for family activities. In this section, we look at how early years settings work in ways that encourage parents to take an active role in their child's play and development at home.

AC 4.1 Encouraging parents/carers to take an active role in their child's play, learning and development

It is a requirement of the EYFS for key persons to work closely with parents with the aim of helping them to support their child's development at home. There is research to show that parents who do things such as share stories, chat to their children and play with them make a significant difference to children's outcomes.

The starting point for this work is to ensure that you have a good relationship with parents. This is important because if parents do not trust their child's key person or do not enjoy working with them, they are less likely to take on board their advice and suggestions. It is also important that you show a good understanding of parents' own strengths and interests and acknowledge what some parents already do at home. In addition, we also need to think about barriers that might make it difficult for parents, such as having several young children or working long hours. Recognising these barriers should help us to provide suggestions that are realistic.

There are many practical strategies that early years settings use to work with parents to help them take an active role with their child at home.

Research it!

Visit Ofsted's website and download an inspection report for an early years setting: www.ofsted.gov.uk. See how, during the inspection process, there is a focus on how well early years settings work with parents to encourage them to support their learning at home.

Story sacks

Many early years settings lend story sacks to parents. These have proven very popular with parents. Most story sacks contain a book, some props but also some suggested activities and questions that parents can use at home.

Learning journeys

Many early years settings use learning journeys to share with parents their children's achievements and interests. Parents often find these very interesting and many will go on to do activities with their children which they in turn will share with the setting.

Parent workshops

Some early years settings share information with parents by holding workshops looking at particular aspects of child development, such as play, or giving parents information about the early years curriculum.

Noticeboards and suggestions

Many settings will put out information for parents about the type of activities at home that can support children's development, such as playing together, sharing books and visiting local play parks. They may also put out leaflets about local events, such as a free story session at the library.

Lending resources

Many settings will lend toys and books to parents. This is useful for parents who may not know what to choose for their children or who may not have money to pay for resources.

In your setting

How does your setting encourage parents to take an active role in their child's play, learning and development?

In practice

Ask your placement supervisor if you can practise working with parents to help them take an active role in their children's development. Create a story sack and then show it to a parent and explain how it might be used.

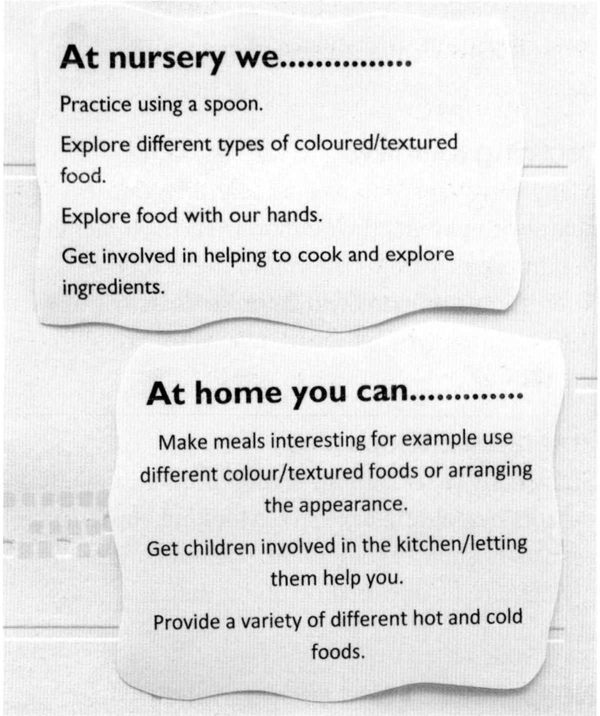

At nursery we...............

Practice using a spoon.

Explore different types of coloured/textured food.

Explore food with our hands.

Get involved in helping to cook and explore ingredients.

At home you can.............

Make meals interesting for example use different colour/textured foods or arranging the appearance.

Get children involved in the kitchen/letting them help you.

Provide a variety of different hot and cold foods.

Figure 2.5.3 Parents can be supported by providing information on how to help their child at home

LO5 Be able to complete records

Do you sometimes see staff completing records of children's progress? This is one of the many types of records that are kept in early years settings. In this section, we look at the importance of keeping records and also how to do so.

AC 5.1 Records that are accurate, legible, concise and meet organisational and legal requirements

There are many different types of records kept in early years settings. They all serve slightly different purposes, but they are all important. All record keeping is shared with parents in early years settings and, to ensure their accuracy, many records will also need the input of parents.

Contact details

It is a requirement of the EYFS for contact details to be kept and for these to be reviewed regularly to ensure that they are up to date. Contact details are used in the event of an emergency so that parents can be contacted or, if they are not available, another member of the family or close friend can be contacted.

Accident report forms

When there has been an accident, an accident report will need to be written. This will include details of what happened, the time and date of the accident and any treatment that was provided.

Administration of medicines

As we saw in Unit 1.5, every time a child is given medication, a record has to be kept.

➔For more on administration of medicines, see page 77.

Registers

It is a requirement of the EYFS that registers of children's attendance are kept for each session. This is in case of an emergency, such as a fire, but also for administrative reasons.

Records of children's care needs

As we saw in Units 1.1 and 1.2, it is essential that early years settings understand and meet children's dietary, medical and other care needs. This is also a requirement of the EYFS, and records of children's care needs have to be kept up to date.

Records of children's progress

It is a requirement of the EYFS that early years settings record and plan for children's learning and progress. Each child will therefore have their own record. In some settings, this is in the form of a 'learning journey'.

➔ See page 366.

For settings to be able to monitor and understand children's progress, it is good practice for parents to provide information about the child at home as they will see their children do different things.

Summative assessment

Most early years settings will also complete a summative assessment every few months as part of children's records. This is like a report that helps parents and practitioners understand children's overall development. When children are moving to other settings, such as a school or a nursery, a summative assessment is usually passed on, provided that parents have given consent.

Two year old progress check

It is a statutory requirement for early years settings to carry out a progress check when children are between the age of two and three years. The progress check looks at children's development in the three prime areas of the EYFS: 'personal, social and emotional development', 'communication and language development' and 'physical development'.

Reports for other professionals

Early years settings might also provide reports for other professionals. This might include written feedback on a child's development to help a physiotherapist or speech and language therapist understand more about a child's development. Where reports are provided for other professionals, parents need to give their consent and it is good practice for them to be able to read what is written. The only exception to this is where an early years setting is reporting concerns about a child's welfare or where a request has been made from

a social worker or case conference because there are existing safeguarding concerns.

The importance of completing records legibly, accurately and concisely

We have seen examples of the types of records that are kept. They are all important and so it is essential that others will be able to read what you have written. As information may affect decisions about the child or may be needed in the event of an emergency, it is also important that they are accurate and concise.

In practice

Ask your placement supervisor if you can practise filling in some forms and completing some records.

Tips on how to complete records

- Find out what exactly is required – for example, ask your manager or look at another completed form.
- If you are not sure about whether information is accurate, ask your line manager.
- Try writing out a draft first so that you can ask someone to check it for you.
- Remember that statements must be accurate about children's progress and, if you are not sure how children's progress relates to the early years framework or typical developmental patterns, do some further research.
- Do not write anything down in a style that you would not like to read yourself if you were a parent.
- Think about whether you need to find out information from parents before completing a record (e.g. contact details, care records).

Assessment

For this unit you will need to complete a variety of tasks. First, you need to revise the concept of partnership working and why it is important for the outcomes of children. You also need to be able to identify the partnerships that most early years settings develop and the roles and responsibilities of those involved, such as social workers, speech and language therapists and SENCOs. You should also revisit the potential barriers and tensions that exist in partnership working. You might like to talk to your placement supervisor about how these are managed in your settings.

Working with parents is an important component in the assessment of this unit and it is covered in several of the learning outcomes. Make sure that you know the different family structures that exist and also the different professionals that might work to support parents. You should also be able to explain why early years settings and other professionals work closely with parents and the benefits this brings. Your assessor will also need to watch you work with parents/carers in ways that encourage them to take an active role in their child's play, learning and development. As this requires practice and sensitivity, it will be a good idea to ask your placement supervisor to watch you do this and to give you feedback before your assessor observes you.

Finally, for this unit you need to be able to show that you can complete records such as observations, accident reports or assessments. This assessment criterion links to other units such as Unit 2.3 and Unit 3.14. To help you complete this assessment criterion, you will need to ask someone in your setting to show you how such records are completed in your setting. Take time to practise completing records before you show your assessor.

Useful resources

Organisation

National Parent Partnership Network and Parent Partnership Services (PPS)

These are statutory services offering information advice and support to parents and carers of children and young people with special educational needs (SEN): **www.parentpartnership.org.uk**.

THEME 3

Play, development and learning for school readiness

Unit 3.1 Understand the value of play in early years

Have you ever walked by a school at playtime or a play area and heard the sound of children playing? Play is an important part of childhood. In this unit, we look at what makes play so special and how it contributes to children's development. We will also look at children's right to play and how play opportunities need to be provided to all children.

Learning outcomes

By the end of this unit, you will:

1 Understand the role of play.
2 Understand children's rights in relation to play.
3 Understand play at different stages of children's development.
4 Understand different types of play for all children.
5 Understand inclusive play practice.

LO1 Understand the role of play

Do you ever find yourself wanting to ping a rubber band across a room or cupping and catching water in a shower? In this section, we look at why children seem to need to play and how play supports their overall development.

AC 1.1 Children's innate drive to play

Play is not something new. It would appear that for thousands of years children have played. It would also seem that children are born primed and ready to play and also to explore. Interestingly, they do this without needing any rewards from adults and will often play for hours at a time. There is some speculation that, as many young animals play as a way of practising skills, this is probably the basis for children's interest in play.

Watching children play is fascinating. Most children play and explore without wanting a reward or even encouragement from their parents. Indeed, in the history of play, children have often wanted to play when their parents and other adults in society have viewed it as unnecessary or a waste of time and children have even been punished for playing. This desire to play has led to the conclusion that play is a natural instinct for children. Happily today, play in the UK is valued and for some time has been fundamental to the early years curriculum.

AC 1.2 The necessity of play in the development of children

One of the reasons that play is included in the early years curriculum in the UK is that play is crucial for the overall development of children. From the child's point of view, play is enjoyable, pleasurable and something that they do for its own sake. From the practitioner's point of view, play is a valuable way of supporting development, and that is one of the reasons why a range of play opportunities are provided.

→ See also page 163.

Figure 3.1.1 Play is an important part of the early years curriculum

Table 3.1.1 on the next page shows how play supports different developmental areas.

Case study

Two children are playing outdoors. They spend a lot of time talking and even arguing, but eventually they decide to build a den. They find some cardboard boxes and fabric and move them over to a corner in the garden. They quickly work out that one of the cardboard boxes is too small and so it is put to one side. When the den is finished, one of the children decides that their den should have a cooker and so the small cardboard box becomes the cooker. The children gather up some leaves, put them in a tin and then go back to pretend to cook dinner.

- What physical skills have these children practised?
- How has this play supported children's cognitive and language development?
- Explain the emotional and social benefits to this play activity?

Table 3.1.1 How play supports development

Physical development	Play usually involves children making movements of some kind. Fine motor movements involving the use of the hands is developed through play as children explore objects and use toys and resources, such as sand and water. Locomotive movements and gross motor movements are developed as children move their bodies during play, throwing and also learning to coordinate their movements with equipment such as tricycles. Children's stamina and other skills such as balance are developed as they enjoy playing.
Cognitive development	Play helps children to explore their environment and to learn from it. They learn about the textures and properties of different objects by playing with them. They may, for example, learn that it is difficult to build a sandcastle with very wet sand. They also learn about size and shape of objects. Through play, children also learn to think about and solve problems.
Language development	As children develop language, they use it to organise their play and so it is common to hear children talking as they play by themselves. Children also use language as they play with others and may use it as part of the play itself (e.g. putting on voices) or to agree the direction of play with others.
Emotional development	Play is pleasurable for children and can give them a great sense of achievement. It is also a way in which they can explore and release emotions. They can, for example, be destructive by knocking down a tower of bricks in a safe way and without upsetting anyone. Children also act out things that they have seen adults do and this can help them understand them better.
Social development	Play is a great way for children to learn to be with other children. They learn through play to take turns, to recognise when others need help and also how to be part of a group. Some types of play also help children to explore roles.

In practice

Observe a play activity where a child or children are very engaged. Write down exactly what the children are doing as part of their play. Afterwards analyse the developmental benefits of this play.

LO2 Understand children's rights in relation to play

How would you feel if you were constantly told that you were not allowed to play when you were young? Children today have rights and these include the right to play.

AC 2.1 The rights of children to play in the UN Convention on the Rights of the Child

The Convention on the Rights of the Child is a list compiled by the United Nations of rights that all children in all countries should have. Individual countries can choose whether or not to sign up to

this convention and so far 193 countries have done so. The United Kingdom officially adopted the convention in 1991. There are many rights within the convention, including the right for children to be educated. Another of these rights is the right for leisure, play and culture. This right is in Article 31, which states that: 'Every child has the right to relax, play and join in a wide range of cultural and artistic activities.'

Research it!

You can read a summary of all the rights that are accorded to children under 18 by visiting: www.unicef.org.uk/Documents/Publication-pdfs/UNCRC_summary.pdf.

AC 2.2 How settings can meet the right of children to play

There are many ways in which early years settings meet the right of children to play. Firstly, children are given opportunities to choose how they want to play and what they want to play with as part of

Figure 3.1.2 Play is a right for all children

the daily routine or session. In schools, for example, children will have playtimes, but in nurseries, childminding settings and other early years settings, these opportunities will be built into the structure of the day or session. Early years settings not only provide time for children to play but also the resources and the environment. It is usual for settings to have a wide range of equipment and also to provide opportunities for children to play outdoors. Where an outdoor area is not available, early years settings will usually take children to a local play area or space so that they can enjoy play outdoors. Early years settings also spend time helping parents to understand the importance and value of play and may give parents ideas of how to help their child at home.

> **Reflect**
>
> Think about how your setting meets children's right to play.

Figure 3.1.3 Children should be provided with plenty of opportunities to play

LO3 Understand play at different stages of children's development

Do you know if you had a favourite toy or play activity when you were a toddler? Perhaps you knocked down stacking beakers or spent time hiding behind the sofa. But the chances are that, as you grew, what you enjoyed playing with changed. In this section, we look at the ways in which children's play changes with age.

AC 3.1 Child-initiated play and adult-led play

If you watch children play, you may notice that sometimes children play by themselves or choose what to play with. This is called child-initiated play. At other times, adults may organise a game or lead children in play. This is known as adult-led play. Both types of play have advantages and this is why early years settings will organise both types of play.

Child-initiated play

In child-initiated play, children make a lot of decisions. They decide what to play with and how to play. Children also choose where to play and who, if anyone, they wish to play with. There are many benefits of child-initiated play:

- **Confidence**: children gain in confidence as choice is a feature of child-initiated play.
- **Concentration**: children tend to show high levels of concentration during self-chosen play.
- **Creativity and imagination**: children often combine materials and can be very creative and imaginative as they play.
- **Perseverance**: children often stay at a play activity longer or persevere to achieve a goal.

In your setting

How often do children engage in child-initiated play in your setting?

Adult-led play

In adult-led play, the adult decides what skills, concepts or knowledge children might need and organises an activity for the children. They might, for example, teach children how to play a board game or they may set up a hospital in the role-play area. Adult-led play is important as it can help children to explore new materials, resources, ideas and concepts. It is also a way of developing

Figure 3.1.4 Child-initiated play is often highly creative and imaginative

children's speech and building new vocabulary as adults spend time interacting with children. Adult-led play is also used to help children practise skills in areas where they need more support – for example, learning to take turns. Adult-led play often influences child-initiated play as, once children have learnt a new skill or game, they are likely to incorporate it into their own play or choose to repeat it.

There are many benefits of adult-led play but they only apply if the adult-led play is interesting for the children and if it meets their developmental needs. To help adults choose adult-led activities, early years settings spend time observing children to assess their interest and also their stage of development. This:

- helps children to learn new skills, concepts and knowledge that they may not gain alone

Figure 3.1.5 This is an adult-led play activity

- allows children to learn new games and ways of playing that they may otherwise not know or choose to try
- gives children opportunities to explore materials and resources that they might not otherwise select
- provides children with opportunities to develop language – for example, through adult-led role play or through mathematical games.

AC 3.2 How children's stages of development change their play needs and preferences

Children's play changes as they grow and develop. It is important for adults working with children to recognise children's changing play needs and interests in order to provide them with sufficiently challenging activities.

0–1 year

In the first year of life, babies are reliant on adults as playmates. They enjoy being held by adults and shown things such as rattles, which at first they stare at but over time they learn to reach out and grasp. Babies are also learning to control their large movements and so enjoy swiping at things, such as baby gyms, both with their arms and with their legs legs. A key feature of play in this year is that babies take all objects to their mouth to explore and so it is important that toys such as rattles, balls and shakers are checked to ensure that they are not choking hazards.

> **Reflect**
>
> Observe a baby under 12 months playing with a range of toys and objects for more than 15 minutes. How many times in this period did the baby take an object to their mouth?

1–3 years

In these next couple of years, babies and toddlers enjoy being mobile. While this age range will enjoy playing with an adult, time will also be spent exploring and playing alone, provided that 'their' adult is within sight. From 18 months, you may also hear children making sounds or talking as they play. A feature of their play is the way that they are physically quite busy. They have greater coordination so they start to enjoy climbing and throwing things. Their play is characterised by repetitive movements so that once a child has found something that is fascinating, such as dropping a ball onto the floor, the child will repeat the action over and over again.

→ On page 181, we look at the theories behind this type of play.

While children are likely to enjoy watching other children and may fleetingly try to join in, it is not until children are close to three years that they start to play in fully cooperative ways.

3–5 years

In these years, children are starting to enjoy playing together as their social and language skills have developed. Imaginative play in which children do a lot of pretending is a particular feature and so you may see children play with farm animals and cars but also in the home corner. Children's play is also more complex and far less repetitive than in the earlier ages. They may talk about what they are going to do first and, from four or five years, children start to enjoy games that have rules.

Gender concept

In addition to changes in children's play needs, which are linked to development, from around three years children also start to show clear play preferences. Some of these are linked to their exploration of gender concept. In practical terms, this means that some girls will choose not to play with 'action' toys or with items that they consider to be masculine and will prefer to play with toys and activities that link to their emerging view of

Figure 3.1.6 From around three years of age, children start to engage in more social and imaginative play

femininity. The opposite is true with some boys. Recognising when gender concept is preventing children from taking up play and therefore learning opportunities is important so that alternative activities can be provided.

Friendships

Another influence on children's play is their friendships. From three years, children start to develop friendships, which become increasingly important for them. This means that they may choose to play games based on their friendship preference and may sometimes leave a play activity in order to follow a friend.

Test yourself

List three ways in which a two year old's play will be different from that of a five year old.

LO4 Understand different types of play for all children

Have you seen the range of different toys and resources available for children in early years settings? While most children simply enjoy playing with different things, the reason why different types of resources are provided is that all support different areas of development. In this section, we look at the different types of play.

AC 4.1 The benefits of the different types of play

Play is often divided into different types to help practitioners plan and also because each type of play has slightly different developmental benefits. There are many ways to define play types, but for the purpose of this unit, play is divided into types as shown in Figure 3.1.7.

Physical play

Physical play is often defined as play that involves physical skills and particularly large movements, such as climbing, running and throwing. For the purposes of this unit, play that involves construction, such as children playing with building blocks, is also included. We will look at the benefits of construction play separately.

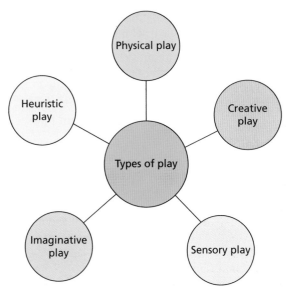

Figure 3.1.7 Types of play

Benefits of physical play: movement

There are health benefits as well as developmental benefits when children are engaged in physical play and are moving.

The health benefits of physical play are as follows:

● develops muscles and strengthens bones
● builds children's stamina and supports heart and lung function
● helps children to sleep and is good for building an appetite.

The developmental benefits of physical play are outlined in Table 3.1.2.

Table 3.1.2 Developmental benefits of physical play

Physical	● Helps children to master skills such as balance, steering and pedalling. ● Encourages children to make a range of movements, such as throwing and jumping.
Cognitive	● Helps children to explore and learn from the environment. ● Develops spatial awareness. ● Supports trial by learning.
Language	● Depending on the type of activity and age of children, language may be used to organise a play activity.
Emotional	● Gives children a sense of achievement as they master a skill. ● Gives children confidence as they increasingly become skilful. ● Provides an outlet for emotions.
Social	● Depending on the exact play opportunity, it may encourage children to play together cooperatively.

Benefits of construction play

Construction play, which in this unit is being linked to physical play, allows children to use their hands, but also has other benefits which are important to understand. While some of the benefits are similar to those in Table 3.1.2, there are some differences, as shown in Table 3.1.3 on the next page.

Creative play

Creative play is about children expressing themselves through a range of media, including musical instruments, painting, drawing and modelling. For babies and toddlers, creative play and sensory play are linked as they enjoy the sensory feel of paints and other materials.

Imaginative play

Imaginative play includes play in the home corner, playing with dressing-up clothes and pretending to take on roles, such as superhero play. Imaginative play also includes small-world play, which is when children play with miniature models of items, such as play people, cars and farm animals. Imaginative play tends to be seen more in children from around three years as it is reliant on language levels.

Sensory play

Sensory play is the term used to describe play with materials and resources such as sand, mud or dough. These types of resources give children a lot of sensory feedback as they touch them.

Table 3.1.4 Developmental benefits of creative play

Physical	• Helps develop fine motor skills and hand–eye coordination as children hold paintbrushes, use musical instruments or make things.
Cognitive	• Drawing and painting give children an opportunity to use symbols to represent what they have seen or done.
Language	• Children may use talk to organise their ideas as they are playing. They may also talk to adults and other children while playing.
Emotional	• Gives children a chance to express their emotions and feelings. • Provides children with a sense of achievement if they are happy with what they are doing.
Social	• Depending on whether children are working together in their play, children are able to cooperate with each other and discuss ideas.

Table 3.1.3 Developmental benefits of construction play

Physical	• Supports children's fine motor skills and hand–eye coordination.
Cognitive	• Provides opportunities for problem solving. • Allows children to plan and organise their play.
Language	• Depending on whether children are playing with others, children use language to organise their play, negotiate and talk about their ideas.
Emotional	• Provides children with a sense of achievement. • Encourages children to persevere. • Allows children to express their emotions.
Social	• Depending on whether children are playing with others, encourages children to share, take turns and also agree on ideas with others.

Table 3.1.5 Developmental benefits of imaginative play

Physical	• Encourages children's fine motor movements and hand–eye coordination as they manipulate resources such as dressing-up clothes or small-world toys.
Cognitive	• Helps children to think in the abstract. • Provides opportunities for problem solving and reasoning.
Language	• Encourages children to talk to each other, learn new vocabulary and practise different communication styles as they take on different roles.
Emotional	• Allows children to re-enact what they have seen adults do and so gain a greater understanding. • Helps children to express a range of emotions. • Is enjoyable for children and gives them feelings of powerfulness.
Social	• Encourages children to play together and to take turns and negotiate.

Table 3.1.6 Developmental benefits of sensory play

Physical	<ul><li>Encourages fine motor movements and hand–eye coordination as children scoop, fill and pour.</li><li>If provided in large quantities, encourages children's gross motor movements as they transport resources from one place to another.</li></ul>
Cognitive	<ul><li>Encourages children to learn about the textures and properties of different materials.</li></ul>
Language	<ul><li>Depending on whether children are playing with each other, sensory play allows children to talk to each other about what they are doing and to organise their play together.</li></ul>
Emotional	<ul><li>Provides children with opportunities to express emotions.</li><li>Can be relaxing for children.</li><li>Provides pleasurable sensations.</li></ul>
Social	<ul><li>Provides opportunities to take turns and share resources.</li></ul>

AC 4.2 Principles of heuristic play

The term 'heuristic' comes from a Greek word meaning to discover, and so heuristic play helps children to discover the properties of different types of objects. The main principles of heuristic play are that children are able to explore materials without adult direction. There are two types of heuristic play used in early years settings: treasure basket play and heuristic play.

Treasure basket play

Treasure basket play is for non-mobile babies. Between 30 and 50 objects, all made of natural materials such as wood, metal and cloth, are put in a basket and babies play and learn by touching and mouthing them. The key principles for treasure basket play are that, while adults are there to supervise and keep babies safe, they do not direct the play. This allows babies to reach into the basket and choose for themselves what to touch, feel and mouth.

Figure 3.1.8 Heuristic play allows children to explore different objects

Heuristic play

When babies start to be mobile, the type of heuristic play changes and children are presented with a wider range of materials, including objects made of plastic. The objects are also presented differently and are usually put in a pile. Common objects include containers such as biscuit tins, plastic bottles and cardboard tubes, along with plenty of smaller objects, such as corks, shells and wooden rings. An important principle for heuristic play is that no toys are provided and, as with treasure basket play, adults supervise for safety, but do not take the lead in the activity. Table 3.1.7 shows the benefits of heuristic play with children.

Key terms

vocalisations A range of sounds, including babbling, that are made before children are ready to make words.

self-talk Where young children use language to talk aloud.

Table 3.1.7 Developmental benefits of heuristic play

Physical	• Develops children's fine motor skills and hand–eye coordination.
Cognitive	• Allows children to explore properties of different materials. • Encourages problem solving. • Provides a practical opportunity to experience shape and size. • Allows for creativity as children bring items together and find out ways of making them connect.
Language	• **Vocalisations** or **self-talk** may take place as children explore items. • Older children may talk to each other about what they have found and its possibilities.
Emotional	• Allows opportunities to explore independently and make choices. • Gives children a sense of achievement as they discover properties of materials for themselves.
Social	• Babies and toddlers usually explore independently, but may want to show an adult what they have discovered. • Older children may use objects to work together to create play.

AC 4.3 Evaluating resources for the types of play

There is a range of resources that can be used to support the different types of play. Table 3.1.8 shows common resources that are used to support the different types of play at different ages.

In your setting

Look at Table 3.1.8 on the next page. What other resources does your setting use with children of different ages?

Factors to consider when evaluating resources

There is a range of factors to consider when choosing resources for children, which are discussed on the following pages.

Figure 3.1.9 An early years setting should offer plenty of creative resources

Table 3.1.8 Resources to support different types of play

	Physical play	Creative play	Imaginative play	Sensory play	Heuristic play
Non-mobile babies Note: All activities must be carefully risk assessed to check for choking hazards and also possible allergic reactions	• Rattles • Soft toys • Baby gyms • Baby bouncers For construction: • Stacking beakers	Not usually associated with this age	• Puppets used by adults	Activities for babies six months plus: • Water • Gloop • Yoghurt • Mashed potato	Treasure basket play – items made of natural materials, e.g.: • Metal spoon • Honey spoon • Lavender bag
1–3 years	• Small slides • Swings • Push-and-pull toys • Balls • Rockers • Sit-and-ride toys For construction: • Jigsaws • Simple train sets • Duplo	• Large markers • Paints • Sponges • Large crayons and chalks • Glue sticks	• Toy telephones • Pushchairs • Shopping bags • Toy kitchens	• Water • Dough • Gloop • Shredded paper	Heuristic play with containers and smaller objects of interest, e.g.: • Shells • Corks • Wooden rings
3–5 years	• Tricycles • Scooters • Skittles • Beams • Balls • Bats • Tunnels • Hoops • Wheelbarrows • Wheeled toys For construction: • Wooden blocks • Lego • Jigsaws	As above plus: • Small paintbrushes • Cardboard boxes • Glue • Staplers • Items of haberdashery • Masking tape • Scissors • String	Props for playing shops, e.g.: • Baskets • Cash tills Props for dressing up, e.g.: • Belts • Hats • Shoes • Cloaks Props for home corner, e.g.: • Sink • Washing machine • Cot • Cooker Props for small-world play, e.g.: • Farm animals • Cars • Dinosaurs • Play people	As above plus: • Buttons • Tea • Coffee grinds • Compost • Foam soap • Dry sand • Wet sand	Loose part play: children find a range of natural and manmade objects scattered outdoors so that they can incorporate them into their play

Are they safe?

As we have seen, babies and toddlers up until around 18 months will put objects into their mouths as a way of exploring them. Resources such as sand, for example, may not therefore be safe for younger children. In addition, some sensory play resources may also cause allergies and so settings have to check with parents about whether this could be problematic – for example, foam soap or dry pasta.

How much adult supervision is needed?

Babies and toddlers will always need constant adult supervision in order to engage with many play activities – for example, sitting on a swing or exploring paint and water. Other play activities may also need close adult supervision to prevent accidents (e.g. wheeled toys, climbing) and again how much will depend on the activity and also the age/stage of the children.

Are they age/stage appropriate?

Resources have to be right for children's age and stage. This is because how they play with resources does change.

➡ For more on how play changes with age, see page 181.

If resources are not sufficiently challenging, children may become bored with them or if children are given toys and games that they are not ready for, they may become frustrated and demotivated.

Are they of interest to children?

Resources need to be chosen on the basis of how interesting children will find them. In some settings, children's interests are observed and resources are selected according to what has been noted. It is also good practice to talk to children about what they would like to do.

Is there enough space?

Some resources require more space than others in order for children to play with them. Wheeled toys are an example of this

Is there sufficient quantity?

We have seen that younger children may find it hard to share resources as they are not yet cooperatively playing. A single pushchair for a group of two year olds will probably result in squabbles. Some types of resources, particularly ones for sensory play, need to be provided in great quantity so that children can scoop, pour, fill and generally enjoy using them. A tiny amount of dough or a small amount of sand can affect the quality of the play.

Is there a balance of resources?

We have seen that there are different types of play and that each type of play has its own benefits. It is therefore important to look overall at the resources to check that all types of play are available.

How cost effective are the resources?

Most resources have to be bought by early years settings. It is therefore important that resources are good value. Resources that are good value allow children to play with them time and time again. Poor-value resources tend to be of interest to children for short periods and so may spend more time in a cupboard than out!

In your setting

Talk to the staff team in your setting to find out how they choose the resources that are available for children. Do they have a rota system for resources or do they ask the children what they would like to be available? Or do they do a mixture of both?

In practice

With your setting's permission, make a list of resources that are available for each of the types of play. Evaluate to what extent the resources meet children's needs and also whether they provide sufficient challenge. Make recommendations as to what other resources could be used, if money was not an issue.

LO5 Understand inclusive play practice

Would it be fair if a girl was not allowed to play with the same toys as a boy? Would it be fair if some children were not allowed to play because they had a disability? In this section, we look at the concept of 'inclusive play' and how this allows all children to enjoy play.

AC 5.1 Current frameworks of inclusive play practice

Inclusive play means making sure that all children have equal opportunities to play and that no children are excluded on account of things such as their gender, race, religion or disability. Inclusive play is underpinned in law by, firstly, children's right to play, as we saw earlier, and also by the early years curriculum. In the case of the Early Years Foundation Stage, it is made clear that all children's needs must be met and these needs include play:

Practitioners must consider the individual needs, interests, and stage of development of each child in their care, and they must use this information to plan a challenging and enjoyable experience for each child in all of the areas of learning and development.

Source: Para 1.6 of the EYFS statutory framework

For children who have additional needs, such as a disability, they also have added protection under disability laws.

→ See page 124.

There are many ways in which early years settings provide inclusive practice:

- Firstly, they think about each child's developmental needs and interests. From this, they can make sure that resources are interesting and suitable. They may, for example, make sure that the home corner has resources in it that a child is familiar with so as to make role play there more meaningful.

Figure 3.1.10 Some children may need additional support during play

- Early years settings also spend time thinking about how to ensure that children who have additional needs can join others in play, assuming that this is developmentally appropriate. They may, for example, play alongside a child who needs support communicating to facilitate play with the other children, they may play with a child who needs physical support or they may adapt resources or games to make sure the child can join in.
- In addition, settings also have to create a culture whereby children are not excluded from play by other children. This requires sensitivity as children's social skills and social awareness are still developing and so they may not realise that they are rejecting another child because they are not of the right gender or that their language skills are not at the same level. Settings often achieve this by involving adults

in the play and also role modelling inclusive play. They also talk to children about why it is important to let others join in.

> **Research it!**
>
> Look at your setting's policy in relation to inclusive practice. How does the setting work to ensure that children can benefit from the play opportunities provided?

AC 5.2 How play supports the interests and abilities of children

It is good practice to observe individual children to make sure that the play opportunities and resources are sufficiently engaging and challenging. When observing children the following questions can be considered.

Figure 3.1.11 Children should be given opportunities to engage in play that they find interesting

How engaged is the child in their play?

This is important because children who do not focus on a play activity are less likely to be gaining from it.

How long does the child stay with an activity?

The length of time is important because children need to spend enough time in order to learn from it. Children sometimes give up on an activity because it is not interesting or they are finding it hard to join in.

Why did the child leave an activity?

We can sometimes pinpoint the reason why a child left an activity. Common reasons include because they wanted to play with a friend, because there were not enough resources or because they were rejected by others.

How much did the child seem to enjoy the activity?

Sometimes we can see that a child is happy through their body language – for example, smiling or showing a sense of achievement. If activities are not of interest, children may not show enjoyment.

Did the child play with others?

From three years, we would expect to see that most children are enjoying being with other children. If a child is not playing with others, it might mean that the child needs support or another adult needs to intervene.

Does the child show signs of frustration?

If activities are too challenging or a child does not have the skill to manage, children may show signs of frustration, which may include throwing things to the ground, walking off or disrupting others' play.

How much adult interaction and support do children need?

Young children and some children with additional needs require adult support to help them enjoy and benefit from an activity. If children are not getting support, they may leave an activity or not show pleasure.

In your setting

Ask a key person to explain how, through their planning, they ensure that play is meeting children's interests and needs. What do they look for when children are playing to check that it is meeting children's needs?

In practice

Observe two children of different ages in your setting. Using some of the questions above to help you, analyse whether the children's play is sufficiently interesting and meeting their developmental needs. If needed, make recommendations about other support, resources or help that could be given to make the play inclusive. Think also about what other play opportunities each child might enjoy and benefit from.

Assessment

This is a knowledge-based unit that will provide you with the underpinning knowledge to support your practice with children. To complete this unit you are likely to be given a variety of tasks from your assessor. The starting point is to revise the reasons why children are thought to need to play and how it supports their development. You should be able to identify the rights of children to play. You can read about this in this unit and also by visiting UNICEF's website and reading the webpages about children's rights (**www.unicef.org.uk**). You should also be able to explain how children's rights to play are provided in your own work setting.

As part of the assessment for this unit you also need to know about the difference between child-initiated and adult-led play, as well as how children's play needs change according to their age/stage. It is worth thinking about this in relation to what your setting does. You could talk to your placement supervisor about how they provide a balance of adult-led and child-initiated play.

You also need to show that you know about the different types of play that settings provide, their benefits and the resources that can be used to support these different plays. There are many different types of play that are used including heuristic play for babies as well as physical, sensory and creative play.

Finally, you should be able to explain how play supports the interests and abilities of children and why inclusive play practice is a requirement of current early years frameworks.

Useful resources

Organisation

Play England

Promotes free play opportunities for all children and young people, and works to ensure that the importance of play for children's development is recognised: **www.playengland.org.uk**

Unit 3.2 WB Plan, lead and review play opportunities which support children's learning and development

Have you noticed that there are always things out for children to play with in your setting? Have you ever thought about what is provided and why? Some settings choose only to use natural materials with children, while others spend hours outdoors. In this section, we look at different theories of play and approaches. We also look at how you might plan and support a range of different play opportunities linked to the different theories and approaches as well as the play types that we looked at in the previous unit.

Learning outcomes

By the end of this unit, you will:

1 Understand theoretical perspectives and philosophical approaches which support play.
2 Be able to apply theoretical perspectives and philosophical approaches in planning play opportunities.
3 Be able to lead and support play opportunities.
4 Be able to review how planned play opportunities contribute to own practice.

LO1 Understand theoretical perspectives and philosophical approaches which support play

What is the best way for children to play? Should they be given only natural resources and should adults guide them as they play? Over a number of years, different views about how and why children play have developed. There have also been different ideas about how play can be used to support children's development and the role of the adult. In this section, we look at the many different perspectives on play and how they shape practice in early years settings.

AC 1.1 Theories and philosophical approaches play

There are many theories and philosophical approaches about how children should play and what the role of the adult should be in supporting play. Interestingly, the debate about the value of play and what children should play with continues to this day.

What is play?

A good starting point when looking at different perspectives in play is to recognise that they reflect very different views of what play actually is. For some pioneers of early years, such as Montessori, play is not considered valuable unless an adult is involved. For others, play can only be defined as being play when it is not being directed by an adult.

Tina Bruce – features of play

Professor Tina Bruce is well known for her work looking at play and learning. She has defined play as having 12 features.

1 Play is an active process without a product.
2 Play is intrinsically motivated.
3 Play exerts no pressure to conform to rules, goals or tasks, or to take definite directions.
4 It is about possible, alternate worlds which involve the concepts 'supporting' and 'as if' and which lift the player to the highest levels of functioning. This involves being imaginative, creative, original and innovative.
5 Play is about participants wallowing in ideas, feelings and relationships, and becoming aware of what we know (metacognition).
6 It actively uses first-hand experiences.
7 It is sustained, and when in full flow, helps us to function in advance of what we can actually do in our real lives.
8 In play, we use technical prowess mastery and competence that we have previously developed. We are in control.
9 Children or adults can initiate play but each must be sensitive to each other's personal agenda.
10 Play can be solitary.
11 It can be with others, each of whom is sensitive to fellow players.
12 Play integrates everything we learn, know, feel, relate to and understand.

Free-flow play

Tina Bruce is also known for the term 'free-flow' play. She uses this term to mean that children are able to play freely and usually imaginatively. Activities such as cooking, exploring gloop or being taught a game such as snap are not, in this model, counted as being 'play'. This is not to say that they are not viewed as important, but that they are not play in themselves. Children, however, may use these experiences in their play and so help children develop further their thoughts.

Janet Moyles

Janet Moyles has looked at the way that adults can influence children's learning through play. She has suggested that play can be enriched using a spiral model. The starting point for this play comes from children's interests and child-initiated activity. From this starting point, the adult can enrich this play by directing it through the use of questions and adding in resources. This allows the child to learn further and so in turn helps them to enrich their child-initiated play. The process then carries on.

Philosophical approaches to play

Some of the key perspectives in play that we can see in early years settings have their origins in a philosophical debate about the nature of childhood and whether children were born good or evil. Other approaches developed as a result of a desire to improve conditions for poor children and their families.

Friedrich Froebel, 1782–1852

Froebel was born in what is now Germany. At the time of his work, there was much philosophical interest in the nature of childhood. Some believed that children were born evil and it was through harsh education and discipline that they would learn to be good. Froebel, on the other hand, believed that children were essentially born good but that adults need to provide the right care and environment to protect them from evil. He felt that adults could help children on their journey and that play was important in this. He suggested that adults might give children objects for them to explore and so learn from. These 'gifts' would help children to learn concepts – for example, a hard and a soft ball. Froebel also used rhymes and music as a way of helping children learn about concepts and he is thought to be responsible for rhymes such as 'Round and Round the Garden Walks the Teddy Bear'. Froebel is particularly noted for his idea that children should spend a lot of time outdoors and in nature. The term 'kindergarten' comes from German, meaning 'child's garden'. Froebel put his ideas into practice by setting up a kindergarten. Many of Froebel's ideas are still at the heart of German early years settings.

Margaret McMillan, 1860–1931, and Rachel McMillan

Margaret McMillan and her sister Rachel were social reformers who wanted to improve conditions for poor children and their families. They were involved in many activities and campaigns to improve social conditions, including a successful campaign to ensure that children from poor families were given free school meals.

One of their projects was to fund a nursery school in a poor area of London in 1914. While their primary concern was for the health of young children, they were also interested in early education. Margaret McMillan was influenced by the work of Maria Montessori (see below), but more by Froebel. The nursery that they funded was therefore an 'open air' nursery where the children spent much of their time outdoors. Imaginative play was also seen as important as a way of helping children to learn. Interestingly, the McMillan sisters were also keen that nursery should be seen as an extension of home and so tried to involve the parents in their work.

Maria Montessori, 1870–1952

Maria Montessori trained as a doctor and spent her first years working with children who had learning difficulties. Through her work with these children, she realised that, by using a very structured approach and using structured teaching materials, children were able to make progress. Later, in 1907, she was invited to Rome to oversee the education of a group of children in a poor neighbourhood. She implemented many of the techniques and methods that she had used earlier and very quickly the structured approach was hailed as a success. Maria Montessori continued to refine her method and ideas and, through scientific close observation of children, her ideas about early education were further developed. Today, there are Montessori nurseries and early years settings using her approach all over the world.

Key features of Montessori's approach

- **Absorbent mind**: Montessori believed that there was a period, up until they were around six years old, when children could learn effortlessly. She called this the period of the 'absorbent mind'.
- **Time should not be wasted**: Montessori felt that opportunities for children to learn should not be wasted while they were able to pick things up so quickly. She therefore viewed children simply playing for the sake of it as a waste of this precious time.
- **Active learners**: Montessori believed that children were active learners and were also more interested in practical objects rather than toys. She therefore created an environment that allowed children to help themselves to objects and also child-sized tools that would help them to gain practical skills, such as gardening, dressing or cooking.
- **Autonomous learners**: Montessori believed that young children were capable of great

concentration and independence, provided they were given the conditions to allow for this. A calm environment where children could get on by themselves was therefore important.

- **Role of the adult**: Montessori felt that the role of the adult was to guide children so that they did not waste any time on doing tasks that would not progress their learning. Adults should guide children on a one-to-one basis so as to ensure that the tasks or play were appropriate for the child's stage of development.

> **Research it!**
>
> Find out more about the equipment used in Montessori education today by visiting **www.montessorieducationuk.org**.

Susan Isaacs, 1885–1948

Susan Isaacs is known for promoting the importance of play in young children. She wrote many articles and put her ideas about child development and play into action. She is known for stressing the link between play and children's emotional and social well-being. She believed that through play children could release their feelings safely and also explore a range of emotions. She suggested that adults should not direct children's play but instead provide a supportive environment for it.

> **Research it!**
>
> Find out more about Susan Isaacs by visiting the Early Years Foundation Stage Forum website at **eyfs.info** and navigating to the Pedagogical section of the FSF Articles menu.

Rudolf Steiner, 1861–1925

Steiner education is based on the work of Rudolf Steiner, an academic with an interest in social reform and philosophy but also religion, architecture and science. His views on childhood and early education were developed in relation to his spiritual beliefs and a movement that he founded called the 'Anthroposophical Society'. His ideas on education

were first published in 1907 and as a result he was offered the chance to lead a school. The first school proved a success and further schools were created. Today, there are a number of schools in the UK which are known as Steiner Waldorf schools.

Key features of Steiner's approach

- **Link to spirituality**: According to Steiner, children are reincarnations and are in need of adult guides to give them protection and to help them find their way.
- **Natural materials rather than toys**: Steiner believed that children need space and time to discover themselves and that they could only do this if they were given opportunities to be imaginative and explore senses at their own pace. Toys and man-made materials would inhibit this process and so natural materials should be provided instead.
- **Practical skills**: Steiner believe that children needed practical skills involving the hands in order to develop, including knitting and crotchet.
- **Reading and writing**: Steiner was not an advocate of early reading and writing as this would impose a viewpoint on the child and so prevent the child from thinking for himself. Instead storytelling and making books based on stories originating from the child were considered to be essential.
- **Role of the adult**: Steiner believed that the role of the adult was to guide the child so that the child could discover himself and that this would happen through allowing the child to be imaginative.

> **Research it!**
>
> Find out more about the Steiner Waldorf approach to early education by visiting **www.steinerwaldorf.org**.

Theoretical approaches to play

As well as philosophical approaches to play, there are also theories of how and why children play.

→ These theories are also related to how children learn and there are some links to Unit 3.9.

Figure 3.2.1 Steiner believed that young children should play with natural materials

Piaget's stages of play

In Unit 3.9, we look at Piaget's theory of children's cognitive development. In this section, we look at how he viewed play in relation to his cognitive theory. Piaget believed that children's cognitive development is linked to their experiences and that they use their experiences to develop ideas and concepts. Piaget's theory of cognitive development and play was developed through his close observations of watching children develop and play. Through his observations, he noticed that children of similar ages tended to play in the same way (see Table 3.2.1). He came to the conclusion that the way they played reflected their cognitive development. He noticed, for example, that older children started to use more rules and that this was linked to the development of abstract concepts. Rules are of course something that you cannot see.

Table 3.2.1 Piaget's stages of play

Age	Type of play	Common features
0–2 years	Mastery play	Children's play is repetitive and also quite physical. Piaget suggested that this was because children are developing control of their bodies and by doing this are developing early concepts.
2–7 years	Symbolic play	Children use language in their play as a way of communicating their ideas. Children use symbols in their play – for example, a stick becomes a spoon.
7–11 years	Play with rules	Children enjoy playing with rules. These are abstract. They like making up rules and also telling others about them.

Lev Vygotsky

In Unit 3.9, we will look at Vygotsky's theory of how children learn. Vygotsky was very interested in imaginative play, which he suggested began when children were around three years old. Through imaginative play, Vygotsky believed that children could absorb and develop thoughts and concepts. He noted that at first children tend to recreate their first-hand experiences but with time they were able to play more imaginatively and thus use their abstract thinking. Vygotsky also recognised that play supported children's emotional and social development.

Chris Athey

Chris Athey was greatly influenced by Piaget's work on children's cognitive development. Piaget suggested that children were active learners who, through their experiences, reached conclusions about their world, which he called schemas. Athey, through observing children as they played, noticed recurring play patterns, which are referred to as play schemas. She suggested that these play schemas were linked to children's cognitive development.

Table 3.2.2 shows examples of play schemas.

Other approaches

As well as theories and philosophies of play, there are other approaches from other countries that have influenced the provision of play in the UK.

Forest School approach

For many years, Scandinavian countries have used forests and other outdoor locations as a tool for early education and play. This is partly linked with the geography and culture of countries such as Norway and Denmark where there are many schools in rural, wooded areas. The benefits of children being able to play out in natural environments are significant, which is why many practitioners in the UK have become interested in incorporating the approach and have been on Forest School training. Children can see nature, observe changes in the weather

Table 3.2.2 Examples of play schemas

Schema	Features
Transporting	Children who are interested in moving things from one place to another, e.g. putting objects in a pushchair and taking them across the room, pouring water from the water tray into a bucket.
Enveloping	Children who enjoy covering things or themselves, e.g. putting a blanket over the whole of a doll.
Enclosing/containing	Children who enjoy putting things in and out of containers or spaces, e.g. sitting in a tent.
Trajectory	Children who are interested in the way things move through the air, e.g. throwing and dropping.
Rotation	Children who are interested in circles and things that turn around, e.g. washing machines.
Transforming	Children who enjoy watching things change, e.g. mixing paint, dropping food colouring into water.
Connecting	Children who are interested in putting things together, e.g. lines of cars or tying string from a chair leg to a table leg.
Positioning	Children who take time to place objects and themselves in a particular order or position, e.g. laying a table with accuracy.
Orientating	Children who are interested in seeing things from different positions and viewpoints, e.g. trying to climb to be up high.

and also learn physical skills, including how to keep warm and dry, move safely and manage risk. Children also play differently and more creatively in large spaces where there are no toys. While few early years settings have day-to-day access to woodlands, many settings instead take children to a woodland space each week.

Reggio Emilia approach

Reggio Emilia is a small area in Northern Italy. It is known for its pre-school education for a variety of reasons. Firstly, the system of pre-school education is very collaborative, with parents and practitioners working together to meet children's interests and needs. Adults play an important role when working with children. They facilitate their play, photograph and record children's work and spend time with children reflecting on what they have learnt. The environment is set out so as to encourage children's creativity and there are zones where children can

experience a range of different resources. This approach to pre-school education is child-centred and views children as capable of directing their own learning. It also stresses the importance of adults listening to children and being partners in their play.

> **Research it!**
>
> Find out more about the Reggio Emilia approach by visiting http://web.ccsu.edu/italian/Conference/reggio_aprroach.pdf.

AC 1.2 How theoretical and philosophical approaches to play inform practice

The theoretical and philosophical approaches that we have looked at link to current practice in early years settings in a variety of ways. Table 3.2.3 shows how each perspective informs current practice in settings.

Figure 3.2.2 Children use play to explore different objects

Table 3.2.3 How different approaches to play inform practice

Bruce	Many settings provide free-flow play whereby children can access different resources and so play without interruption.
Froebel	Froebel stressed the importance of the outdoor area and also contact with nature. Early years settings are increasingly using the outdoor area and some early years settings regularly access natural environments in which children can play. Froebel used rhymes with children as a way of introducing concepts, and rhymes are still considered to be important for children. Froebel also suggested that children needed wooden blocks and materials to learn from and today many settings provide blocks of different shapes and sizes so that children can play and learn from them.
McMillan sisters	The McMillan sisters stressed the importance of involving parents and also ensuring that children's physical needs are met. The McMillans also stressed the importance of children playing outdoors and this is still considered to be good practice.
Montessori	Montessori stressed the importance of children being independent and the environment enabling children to access materials. In early years settings, children have access to materials to which they can help themselves. Montessori also suggested that the adult needs to plan for children's learning and today early years settings plan for individual children.
Steiner	Steiner suggested that natural materials were important for children and many settings try to use natural materials, although very few early years settings, apart from Steiner Waldorf schools, are toy free.
Piaget	Piaget suggested that children play in different ways according to their age/stage of development. Early years settings plan and provide different resources for different ages and stages of children.
Vygotsky	Vygotsky emphasised the importance of imaginative play. Most early years settings provide opportunities for role play. It is also recognised that play is important for children's emotional development and play therapy is used in specialist settings to help children come to terms with traumas or difficulties.
Athey	Athey's work on play schemas has proved very popular in many early years setting. Staff observe how children play, recognise potential schemas and then organise play opportunities accordingly.
Forest School	Many practitioners have completed Forest School training and organise for children to access outdoor spaces, including fields and woodlands. An interest in outdoor education has increased because of concerns that children are not spending sufficient time outdoors in natural environments.
Reggio Emilia	The Reggio Emilia approach has been influential as practitioners spend time engaging with children and following their interests through play. Areas for play and exploration are also used in most settings. The importance of working in partnership with parents and learning about the child together is also linked to the Reggio Emilia approach.

LO2 Be able to apply theoretical perspectives and philosophical approaches in planning play opportunities

Different theories and approaches to play can help early years settings plan play opportunities for children. In this section, we look at how you might create a plan for different ages of children based on different play perspectives.

When creating a plan, there are several steps to take. Below are five key steps that you should consider when planning play opportunities.

Step 1: Find out about planning in your setting

All early years settings vary in their approaches to planning. Your first step is therefore to find out how your early years setting organises its planning. It may, for example, plan for children on a weekly basis or over a month. You should also find out how your setting plans in relation to the Early Years Foundation Stage areas of learning.

Step 2: Find out if a particular approach is used in your setting

The next step is to find out whether your setting already uses one of the approaches that we looked at earlier. If not, you should talk to your placement supervisor about which they feel would most fit in with the ethos of the setting.

Step 3: Consider the age and stage of children

You need to consider the age and stage of the children that you are working with and start to think about activities that will be of interest to them and will also support their development. You might, for example, begin by observing how they play. You might also look at their stage of development in relation to the aspects and areas of learning and development within the EYFS

Step 4: Research play opportunities

Start researching play opportunities and think about the resources that will be needed for

each play opportunity. Think about how these play opportunities link to the aspects and areas of learning and development within the EYFS.

Step 5: Share your ideas

Show your placement supervisor your ideas for play opportunities and talk through how they might be implemented. Create your plan based on your setting's planning.

Research it!

Find out more about the areas of learning and development in the EYFS by reading Unit 1.2 and downloading the framework from **www.foundationyears.org.uk**.

AC 2.1 Planning and theoretical and philosophical perspectives

There are many ways in which plans for play opportunities can be linked to the different perspectives that we looked at earlier. Table 3.2.4 provides you with a few suggestions that might be helpful when creating plans for different age ranges.

Table 3.2.4 Suggestions for planning play opportunities

Age	Play opportunities	Perspective
0–1 year 11 months	Look out for opportunities to help children control their physical movements, e.g. baby gym, shakers, activity centre, pop-up toys.	Piaget
	Plan rhymes and songs.	Froebel
	Treasure basket play with natural materials.	Steiner
2–2 years 11 months	Observe children's movements and link them to a play schema. Plan further play opportunities based on the schemas.	Athey
	Take children for a walk in a wood and let them explore objects.	Froebel Forest School
	Observe children's stage of development and put out resources that, with adult support, they may learn from.	Vygotsky
3–5 years	Observe children's movements and link them to a play schema. Plan further play opportunities based on the schemas.	Athey
	Plan different role-play scenarios for children.	Vygotksy
	Talk to children about what play and activities they would like to explore, e.g. cooking or drawing, and create areas for them to do this with you.	Reggio Emilia

Figure 3.2.3 Throwing objects links to Chris Athey's trajectory schema

LO3 Be able to lead and support play opportunities

Does your setting plan a range of play opportunities for children? In this section, we look at how you might plan a balance of child-initiated and adult-led play opportunities for the different types of play that we looked in Unit 3.1. In this section, we also look at how to lead play opportunities and help parents to understand their importance.

AC 3.1 Planning a balance of child-initiated and adult-led play opportunities for all types of play

In the previous section, we looked at the stages involved in creating a plan linked to a theoretical or philosophical approach. In this section, we consider how plans might also be developed to create opportunities for different types of play opportunities for both adult-led and child-initiated play.

→ To help you with this learning outcome, it would be worth revising Unit 3.1, which looked at the different types of play and also the resources that could be used.

Creating a plan with adult-led and child-initiated play opportunities

The steps for creating a plan for different types of play are pretty much those that we looked at on pages 184–185. It might be a good idea to revisit these again. The focus, though, is to think about the needs and interests of an individual child or group of children and to link these to the aspects and areas of learning and development within the EYFS. It is therefore worth starting by observing what children currently do and what their play preferences are. If, for example, you spotted that a four year old was very interested in playing with dinosaurs, you might think about how you could incorporate the theme of dinosaurs into all of the different play types – for example, putting out shredded paper with dinosaurs for sensory play or creating a dinosaur cave for imaginative play. When creating a plan, you should also think about ensuring that play opportunities are available indoors and outdoors.

As your plan needs to incorporate adult-led and child-initiated play opportunities, you need to think about which play opportunities would benefit from an adult-led approach. It is also worth recognising that some play opportunities might start off being adult-led but then children might later choose to repeat them or, during the course of the activity, they might put their 'own stamp' on them by adapting them (e.g. making up additional rules).

→ In Unit 3.1, we looked at the difference between adult-led and child-initiated activities.

Planning for child-initiated play

When it comes to planning for child-initiated play, there is of course a bit of a dilemma. Child-initiated play occurs when children choose what to play with and how to use it in their play. If planning for child-initiated play is very structured – for example, coins hidden in the sand tray, with no other sand toys available – the question is whether it is still child-initiated as the child can only play in the way that has already been decided by the adult.

Good child-initiated planning is therefore about considering the range of resources that might be available for children and making sure that they are attractive and accessible. It is likely that children will use resources aimed at one play type and use them to support another (e.g. using dough in the role-play area). As settings are likely to have many resources, they may choose to rotate what is available over the week so that children are able to try out different things.

Child-initiated play for the under-twos

Safety and stage of development have to be a major consideration when planning for babies and toddlers. Some opportunities are therefore always adult-led, either for safety reasons or because the child is not yet able to access them independently. There is often therefore a blurring in some play types between adult-led and child-initiated play opportunities. Having said this, sensitive working with this age group means that you can see whether a baby wants more of an adult-led opportunity by observing, for example, if the child stops smiling or if the baby looks at you intently.

Table 3.2.5 shows examples of adult-led and child-initiated play opportunities for each type of play. The table is split into two age ranges because, in practice, adult-led and child-initiated play opportunities for children aged 2–3 years are similar to those for older children. The only difference is that the adult-led activities will need to be adapted or simplified.

⟶ Also see Unit 3.1.

Test yourself

Make a list of resources that you might use to set up a dough table.

Figure 3.2.4 Adults need to know when to let children take the lead

Table 3.2.5 Examples of adult-led and child-initiated play opportunities

Age	Adult-led play	Child-initiated play
Physical play		
0–2 years	<ul><li>Blowing bubbles</li><li>Action rhymes such as 'Row, row, row the boat'</li><li>Pushing them in a swing</li><li>Rolling a ball to the child</li><li>Encouraging the child to kick a ball</li><li>Going for a walk (mobile children)</li></ul>	<ul><li>Baby gym</li><li>Balls</li><li>Treasure basket play (non-mobile), heuristic play (mobile children)</li><li>Push-and-pull toys</li><li>Rockers</li></ul>
2–5 years	<ul><li>Parachute games</li><li>Obstacle courses</li><li>Games such as 'What's the time, Mr Wolf?'</li><li>Singing and dancing games, such as the 'Hokey Cokey'</li><li>Building a den</li><li>Making a castle for Teddy</li></ul>	<ul><li>Balls and bean bags</li><li>Play tunnels</li><li>Hoops</li><li>Wooden building blocks</li><li>Skipping ropes</li><li>Wheeled toys</li><li>Fabrics</li><li>Stilts</li><li>Cardboard tubes</li></ul>
Creative play		
0–2 years	After risk assessment, adults encourage children to explore:<ul><li>Paint</li><li>Large markers</li><li>Brushes</li><li>Sponges</li><li>Large crayons</li><li>Musical instruments, such as shakers and rattles, which can be left for children to explore alone as well as used with the adult</li></ul>	
2–5 years	<ul><li>'Join in with the beat' games</li><li>Creating a sound wall</li><li>Dance to the music</li><li>Mixing colours</li><li>Folding paper to make a card or envelope</li><li>Marble painting</li><li>Modelling with clay</li><li>Using tools such as scissors and staplers</li><li>Santa's workshop</li></ul>	<ul><li>Musical instruments, e.g. shakers, rattles, xylophones</li><li>Paints, different types and colours</li><li>Sponges, different types of brushes</li><li>Tools for mark-making, e.g. charcoal, chalk</li><li>Cardboard boxes</li><li>Glue, staplers</li><li>Items of haberdashery</li><li>Masking tape, scissors</li><li>String</li></ul>
Imaginative play		
0–2 years	<ul><li>Playing with a puppet</li><li>Playing with a jack in the box</li><li>Playing 'Peek a boo'</li><li>Playing with the children using small-world sets</li></ul>	<ul><li>Toy telephones</li><li>Large toy cars</li><li>Small-world play people designed for this age group</li><li>Teddy bears</li><li>Dolls</li></ul>

→

Table 3.2.5 Examples of adult-led and child-initiated play opportunities (contd.)

Age	Adult-led play	Child-initiated play
Imaginative play		

2–5 years	• Playing with children and showing them how to use the equipment in a role-play area
	• Playing shoe shops
		• Role play:
		  • Dressing-up clothes
		  • Props from role-play area, e.g. bags, pushchairs
		• Small-world play:
		  • Small-world toys, e.g. dinosaurs, cars, play people, farm animals

Sensory play		
0–2 years	Adult sitting with the child and encouraging them to explore: • Water • Gloop (cornflour and water) • Yoghurt • Mashed potato • Ice cubes	
2–5 years	• Making dough with an adult • Making gloop with an adult • Finding buried treasure in sensory materials • Making a boat to keep Teddy dry in the water tray • Making dough cakes for Teddy • Using dough to make matching shapes • Counting sandcastles	Examples of materials: • Water • Dough • Gloop • Shredded paper • Sawdust • Foam soap • Bark chippings • Compost A wide range of tools and resources to be available with sensory materials: • Spoons • Funnels • Bottles • Teapots • Biscuit tins • Buckets and spades • Cutters • Rolling pins • Scoops • Small-world toys

AC 3.2 Leading a planned play opportunity

Preparing for play

Many adult-led play opportunities do need some preparation. Begin by making sure that you have the necessary resources to hand. Check also that they are age/stage appropriate. You should also think about your relationships with children. Children who have a strong relationship with the adult and enjoy being with them are likely to be keen to join in adult-led play. Think about whether you still need to work on relationships with children, especially younger children, who may take time to get to know you. Below are some tips about how you might lead a play opportunity.

Initiating adult-led play

Some adult-led play opportunities are easy to initiate. The adult simply has to set up the play and start it off alone – for example, making a tower of bricks or beginning a jigsaw puzzle. For some types of play, particularly games, adults will need to invite children to join them. Look out for children whose play has come to an end or who are not yet engaged in play. Avoid approaching children who are already engaged in purposeful play.

Commencing the play

Children find it hard to stay still and listen to long explanations. Try to start play quickly and, wherever possible, show children the play

possibilities. Once they have started, you can always give some more direction if needed.

Observing children during a play opportunity

It is important during adult-led play to be very observant. Which children are enjoying the play and which children are less engaged? The adult also has to think about whether they should leave the play because the children can now take over or whether the play needs to come to an end because the children are no longer interested.

> **In practice**
>
> Write about how you have led a play opportunity in your own setting. Explain how you prepared for the play opportunity and how you ensured that children enjoyed it.

Figure 3.2.5 An example of adult-led play

AC 3.3 Supporting children's participation in planned play

Children are very good at playing if the play opportunity is sufficiently interesting and they are given sufficient time. Adults, though, can make a difference to play and so it is worth looking at the role of the adult.

The role of the adult in adult-led play

In adult-led play, the role of the adult is to help children learn skills or knowledge that otherwise they would not be able to access. The role of the adult is not to be a 'teacher', but instead to be a play partner who takes the lead at the start. To make sure that children can participate in the play, make sure that there are sufficient resources and that children do not have to spend a lot of time waiting around either before the play begins or during the game. Encourage children to talk, ask questions and aim to create a 'chatting' style as you play together. It is good practice to encourage children who want to develop variations to the play as this means that they are thinking and therefore learning more.

Figure 3.2.6 Adults should find ways to support children in their play without taking over

Case study

Mark has planned an adult-led game of animal pairs with two children aged four years. One of the children wants to put the cards into a circle rather than in straight lines. Mark says no. A few minutes later, the other child starts to make the sound of the animal that is on the card. Mark tells the child to stop. After 10 minutes, the children ask if they can leave the game and go and do some painting.

1 Explain why this is an adult-led game.
2 Why did the children want to leave the game?
3 Suggest how the adult could have improved his work.

The role of the adult in child-initiated play

Children need sensitive adults to join them when they are engaged in child-initiated play. The skill when joining children in child-initiated play is not to take over and turn it into an adult-led activity. This means carefully observing what children are doing and instead looking for ways to support their play. This might mean bringing over additional resources that could enrich the play, if the children choose to use them, or modelling ways of extending the play. A child, for example, who is building sandcastles might enjoy putting flags onto them and so an adult might start making some flags with the child. By joining children in their child-initiated play, adults are able to give children new options or draw their attention to features of their play – for example: 'Your sandcastles are larger than mine. How do I make one as large as yours?'

In practice

Write about how you have encouraged children's participation in child-initiated play and also in an adult-led play activity.

AC 3.4 Providing a balance between child-initiated and adult-led play

When looking at your plan, you need to consider whether there are sufficient opportunities for both adult-led and child-initiated play. There are no set rules about how much is needed in the Early Years Foundation Stage, but both types are considered to be valuable. We have already seen that, with babies and toddlers, there is often a blurring between the two because younger children need adult input in order for them to participate. When planning and leading adult-led play with older children, you should ideally try to set it up in ways that will allow children to be able to repeat the play by themselves. A good example of this is the way that you might show three year olds how to make a sandcastle, but then leave out the materials so that later on they can choose to return and repeat the play.

Case study

Cassie has created a vegetable shop for the pre-school children. She has put out real vegetables, including some that she thinks the children might not recognise. There is a cash till, a basket to put the shopping in and a roll of receipts. The children are interested in playing. Cassie takes the role of the shopkeeper and tells the children what is for sale today. She picks up a broccoli and says, 'Lovely, fresh broccoli, only 2p!' She plays with the children for 15 minutes. She leaves the activity, but the children carry on playing. A few minutes later, she hears one of the children saying, 'Lovely broccoli that princesses want to eat.'

1 Why was this adult-led play to begin with?
2 Why does this play support children's learning?
3 When did the play become child-initiated?

In practice

Write about how you have created play opportunities that moved from being adult-led to child-initiated play. Consider the benefits for the children in having access to both types of play. Think also about what allowed the play to move from being adult-led to being child-initiated.

In your setting

Ask your placement supervisor if you can observe adult-led play. Look to see afterwards if any elements of the play are being used by children in their child-initiated play.

Play opportunities in a session

Most early years settings working with groups of children try to provide a balance of adult-led and child-initiated play at the same time. Some children may be invited to join adult-led play, while others will be engaged in child-initiated play. This means that children have access to both types of play during the session. If you create a plan for a day, you might like to think about the balance between the different types of play opportunities.

In your setting

Look at the balance between adult-led and child-initiated play during a session or day. How much time do children spend in adult-led play?

In practice

Look at your plan. What is the balance of adult-led play to child-initiated play?

AC 3.5 Encourage parents/carers to take an active role in play

Parents play a significant part in children's development. It is for this reason that the EYFS requires practitioners to think about how they can help parents to support their children's learning. One of the ways in which settings can do this is by sharing with parents information about what type of play and resources their child is interested in. This should be part of a two-way exchange of information as quite often parents will also be able to tell us about how and what their child enjoys playing with at home. Many settings share information about play by showing photographs or film clips to parents of their child playing in the setting and explaining to parents how the play is helping their child's development. Some settings also lend out resources so that parents can use them to play with their child, such as puzzles, role-play items and dough. To help parents see how their children respond to play, many settings also encourage parents to drop in or come to sessions where they can join their child.

Figure 3.2.7 Some settings hold stay-and-play sessions where parents can join their child in play activities

As well as encouraging parents to play with their children, it is also good practice to help parents understand more about the early years curriculum and how different types of play support children's development. Some settings will put up displays that parents can look at or signs in the environment so that parents can find out more. With many early years settings having their own websites, these can also be used for giving information to parents about how they can support their child's play.

Whichever means is chosen, it is always important to be sensitive to parents and to get to know their circumstances as time, space or resources might be an issue. It is also important to make sure that any suggestions are safe and also achievable in a home environment.

In your setting

Find out how your setting shares information about supporting children's play with parents.

LO4 Be able to review how planned play opportunities contribute to own practice

Have you ever planned a play opportunity with children and found that they quickly lost interest? Or have you planned something and it was a great success? Being able to reflect on play opportunities and also thinking about how play supports children's development are important. In this section, we look at how you might evaluate a play opportunity, think about how it supports children's learning with the EYFS and also think about how you might support children's further learning through play.

AC 4.1 Evaluating a planned play opportunity

During and after a play activity, it is a good idea to carefully consider how it has supported play, learning and development. Evaluating carefully can help us plan further play opportunities that will build on children's skills or knowledge of concepts. It can also help us to improve the quality of activities that we provide. There are several things that you might consider about each child's experience during a play opportunity. Focusing on individual children is important as, while three children in a group may find a play opportunity interesting, it might not be as enjoyable for another child.

Children's motivation
Some children are quicker to try out new experiences than others. If you have planned a play opportunity that will require children to explore something new or to use a new material, notice which children are the quickest to try it out and which children would prefer to wait and let others go first.

Children's level of engagement
In order for children to learn from a play activity, the play needs to be sufficiently interesting so that children are able to concentrate. It is worth therefore observing children during play to see

how much concentration they are showing and noting what elements they find of particular interest. This is important for both adult-led and child-initiated play.

Children's level of activity

It is important to think about how involved children are during play, especially during adult-led play. In small groups, some children may let others do the talking or be more active. A child in the home corner may, for example, lead the play while another child takes on a minor role, such as that of a baby whose role is just to stay still.

In practice

Ask your placement supervisor if you can observe two children who are playing in the same area (e.g. water tray). Spend 10 minutes watching them. Consider whether they are both equally engaged in the activity. Think also if one is more active than the other.

Children's processing of information

When children are doing or listening to something for the first time, some children take longer than others to process this information. Thinking about this is important because sometimes it may be that, during an adult-led play opportunity, we have bombarded children with too much information or not allowed enough time for children to process it. Look out for children who seem to make connections between previous experiences and knowledge and what they are doing during play. A child may say, 'My granny has one like this,' in response to seeing a tea strainer in the sand tray. This shows that the child is processing the information well.

Research it!

The EYFS statutory framework refers to the characteristics of effective teaching and learning. There are three characteristics, which correspond very much to the first three sections in this assessment criterion. Find out about them by reading about it within the EYFS statutory framework, which can be downloaded at www.foundationyears.org.uk.

Children's level of communication and language

It is worth reflecting on how much language children use during their play and how easily they manage to communicate. With older children, you might also note whether they are able to answer questions or use the detailed vocabulary that has been introduced to them. It is also worth being aware of children who are very quiet. It may be that they are not as confident or that they need more time to absorb and process information.

In practice

Observe another member of the team working with a child. Watch how much communication and language the children are using.

Children's physical movements

During play, you should notice children's physical movements. How easily do they manage the physical skills that are involved in the task? It might be that they are using a tool, such as a dough cutter or a pair of scissors, or they are using larger movements, such as attempting to steer a bike.

Children's behavioural responses

The way children behave during a play opportunity can give us information about the suitability of the play opportunity, but also the developmental needs of a child. Look out for children who quickly lose interest. This might mean that the play opportunity was not sufficiently challenging, there were not enough opportunities for the child to participate or that it was too difficult. Think also about issues such as children finding it hard to share or to wait. This might tell us that we have not designed the play opportunity with the children's stage of development in mind or that the group size was too large and so children were becoming bored while waiting. On the positive side, look out for excitement, interest and concentration because these, as we saw earlier, are linked to motivation, engagement and processing.

AC 4.2 Planned play opportunities and current frameworks

All early years settings in England have to show how they are supporting children's progress in each of the seven areas of learning and development.

→ We look at these areas of learning and development in more detail on page 263 and it would be useful for you to read that section as well.

Many of the play opportunities that we looked at in LO3 will support children's progress within the areas of learning of the EYFS. Table 3.2.6 shows broadly how each play type links to the areas of learning and development. The relevant aspect of learning and development is given in brackets.

In addition, depending on the tools, resources and role of the adult, additional links to the EYFS might occur during your planned play opportunities. While being involved in a shoe shop role play, children may talk about money or about the size of different shoes and so, in this example, there would be a link to mathematics.

AC 4.3 The role of the practitioner in planned play opportunities

It is important during and after a play opportunity to reflect on your own practice. This helps you to learn from the experience and to improve your ability to plan further play opportunities.

Preparing the play opportunity

- To what extent was the play opportunity based on children's interests and stage of development?
- To what extent did you focus on the learning that individual children would gain from the play opportunity and link it to the EYFS?
- Did you carry out a risk assessment of the play opportunity?
- Were all the resources required available and were they suitable for the play opportunity and the stage of development of the children?

Encouraging children's participation

- How eager were children to join you in this play opportunity?
- Consider what allowed children to be eager – for example, their relationship with you.
- Were any children reluctant to join in?
- What could you have done differently that might have made them more interested?
- To what extent did you encourage children to be involved in the play opportunity?
- How did you do this and were the strategies you used effective?
- Were all children equally involved?
- What could you do to support those children who were less involved?

Developing children's communication and language

- To what extent did you encourage the children to talk and communicate?
- What strategies did you use and were these effective?
- To what extent did you listen to children and acknowledge their thoughts and ideas?
- How could you improve your communication skills with children further?

Supporting children's learning

- Did you extend children's thinking as they were playing?
- What strategies did you use to do this and were they effective?
- What do you think individual children gained from the play?
- What might you do to further support individual children?

Table 3.2.6 How different play types link to the EYFS areas of learning and development

Type of play	Links to the EYFS areas of learning and development
Physical play	**Personal, social and emotional development** (self-awareness and confidence) **Physical development** (moving and handling) Through physical play, children are learning to use tools, coordinate and make a range of movements.
Creative play	**Personal, social and emotional development** (managing feelings and behaviour; self-awareness and confidence) Creative play allows children to express themselves through music, modelling and mark-making. Children also feel pleased with themselves during the process, especially if they have done something that is new or different. **Physical development** (moving and handling) Children use hand movements and hand–eye coordination as part of this play. They also use tools. **Expressive arts and design** (exploring and using media and materials; imagination) By making music, painting and drawing, children are able to try out different media and material.
Imaginative play	**Personal, social and emotional development** (managing feelings and behaviour; making relationships) Through imaginative play, children can take on different roles and express their feelings in a positive way. Most imaginative play is done alongside other children, so they also learn about relationships. **Communication and language** (all aspects) Talk and listening to others are a key benefit of imaginative play. **Expressive arts and design** (imagination) Imaginative play is one way in which children are able to show imagination.
Sensory play	**Personal, social and emotional development** (managing feelings and behaviour) By exploring textures and using malleable materials, children can express their feelings. **Physical development** (moving and handling) Children use hand movements, such as pouring and hand–eye coordination, as part of this play. They also use tools, such as funnels and tongs. **Understanding the world** (the world) Children can compare differences between materials and textures.
Structuring of play	
Adult-led play	**Communication and language** (all aspects) Where play is adult-led, it is likely that there will be opportunities for children to pay attention and listen. Adults are also likely to draw children's attention to new vocabulary. **Personal, social and emotional development** (making relationships) Where children are enjoying the company of the adult during an adult-led activity, children are likely to be developing their relationships. **Mathematics** (number; shape, space and measures) During adult-led play, adults are more likely to draw children's attention to mathematics by counting out objects or by talking about the size and shape of objects.
Child-initiated play	**Personal, social and emotional development** (self-awareness and confidence; managing feelings and behaviour; making relationships) By choosing what to play with and how to play, children build their confidence. During child-initiated play, children also have to take on responsibility for their behaviour as they play with others. They also learn social skills by playing with others.

AC 4.4 Planned play opportunities and making recommendations for the next stage of children's learning and development

In Units 3.14 and 3.15, we look at the importance of observing and assessing children during play and activities. This is important when it comes to making recommendations for the next steps in children's learning and development.

→ Therefore, you may find it helpful to read from page 364 in addition to this section.

One of the ways that most early years settings work is to consider after each planned play opportunity what children might like to do next or what they might benefit from. For example, a child who found it difficult to pour water into a funnel might need play opportunities that support hand–eye coordination. Assuming that the child enjoyed the water play, the next step would be to think about how this movement could be practised there. It might be that the size of the containers could be changed or the adult might need to help the child to stabilise the funnel.

There are a couple of important tips on how best to make recommendations for children's next steps in their learning and development, as outlined below.

Children's interests

Wherever possible, you should build on children's interests and think about what aspects of a play opportunity seem to be particularly fascinating or enjoyable for a child. These can then be transferred into another play opportunity.

Children's stage of development

It is important to think about what skills and knowledge the child has already acquired. You should then think about what the child might be able to do next, if they were shown and supported or if they practised further. A common mistake with inexperienced adults who work with children is to assume that children's development will occur in huge jumps. This is rarely the case. Most development is very gradual, and quite often, in some areas such as mathematics, children need a lot of practice in order to master a concept. For example, it takes a while before children can recognise any four objects presented in any order. A good tip when looking at supporting children's progress is to make a gradual change to an existing activity – for example, putting out narrow bottles to encourage more skilful pouring of water or adding a 'stop and go' sign to the tricycle track.

Case study

Janey has introduced a simple dice game to a group of four year olds. She has altered the dice so that it only has the numbers 1–3. Janey notices that one of the children, Kyle, is quick to recognise the number and can also move his counter forward accurately. She decides that Kyle's next step is to move onto doing simple sums. She puts out a sheet of paper with some sums on and encourages Kyle to add up. The child soon becomes frustrated.

1 What did Janey learn about Kyle during the activity?
2 Why was Janey's next activity for Kyle not successful?
3 Suggest another play activity for Kyle.

Assessment

This unit is a combination of knowledge and practise. For Learning Outcome 1 you will need to start by showing that you can identify the range of theories and philosophical approaches that we looked at in this unit and link them to practice. Being able to create plans is a major focus for this unit so you will need to practise different ways of planning. Start by looking at the plans that your settings use before creating plans that link to the different theoretical and philosophical approaches that were looked at in Learning Outcome 1.

For Learning Outcome 3 you have to create plans for a range of different play opportunities. These were considered in Unit 3.1 so it will be useful to revisit that unit. Once you have completed your plans, you will need to show your assessor that you can lead one play opportunity. Your assessor will be looking to see whether you can encourage children to participate. As planning and implementing play opportunities is a skill that comes with experience, make sure that you practise these skills before your assessor's visit. Talk

to your placement supervisor to gain feedback. For Learning Outcome 3 you also have to show that you can help parents take an active role. It will therefore be worth thinking about this when you plan the play opportunities. It may be that you could offer to send home resources or you can take photographs and use these to talk about the child's progress with parents. Again, you may need to seek the support of your placement supervisor to learn how best to do this.

For Learning Outcome 4 your assessor will need to see that you can review play opportunities in terms of how they met children's needs and learning, and also how you might develop your own practice. You will also need to show that you can think about play opportunities in relation to planning for children's next steps. You can practise the skills needed for reviewing by writing a reflective diary and gaining feedback from your placement supervisor or more experienced colleagues.

Useful resources

Organisation

5x5x5creativity

This is an independent, arts-based action research organisation and has been influenced by theory in Reggio Emilia in Italy: **www.5x5x5creativity.org.uk**

Books and journals

Brooker, E. (2002), *Starting School: Young Children Learning Cultures*. Maidenhead: Open University Press.

Bruce, T. (1996), *Helping Young Children to Play*. London: Hodder & Stoughton.

Bruce, T. (2004), *Developing Learning in Early Childhood*. London: Paul Chapman Publishing.

Bruce, T. (2009), 'Learning through Play: Froebelian Principles and their Practice Today', *Early Childhood Practice: The Journal for Multi-professional Partnerships* 10(2): 58–73.

Bruce, T. (ed.) (2010), *Early Childhood: A Guide for Students* (2nd edn). London: Sage.

Kalliala, M. (2006), *Play Culture in a Changing World*. Oxford: Oxford University Press.

Langer, E. (1997), *The Power of Mindful Learning*. Harlow: Addison-Wesley.

Matthews, J. (2003), *Drawing and Painting: Children and Visual Representation* (2nd edn). London: Paul Chapman Publishing Ltd.

Ouvry, M. (2004), *Sounds like Playing: Music in the Early Years Curriculum*. London: BAECE/Early Education.

Sylva, K., Melhuish, E., Sammons, P., Siraj-Blatchford, I. and Taggart, B. (2004), *The Effective Provision of Pre-School Education (EPPE) Project: Final Report*. London: DfES/Institute of Education, University of London.

Unit 3.4 WB Promote enabling play environments

Do you remember enjoying playing outdoors? This is an example of a play environment. In this unit, we look at different types of play environments and how to create a play environment for different ages and stages of children. We also look at how to support children's socialisation and behaviour. The unit also looks at how to plan and lead opportunities that support two areas of learning and development within the EYFS: 'Understanding the world' and 'Expressive arts and design'.

Learning outcomes

By the end of this unit, you will:

1 Understand the play environment.
2 Understand how the early years practitioner supports children's behaviour and socialisation within play environments.
3 Be able to support children's behaviour and socialisation within play environments.
4 Understand how the characteristics of an enabling indoor and outdoor play environment meet the age, stage and needs of children.
5 Be able to provide enabling play environments.
6 Be able to plan and lead opportunities which support children's understanding of the world.
7 Be able to plan and lead opportunities which encourage children's engagement in expressive arts and design.

LO1 Understand the play environment

Do you remember as a child that some places were better than others to play in? In this section, we look at how environments can support play and also how collaborative working can support play.

AC 1.1 Types of environment

The term 'environment' is very broad. An environment is made up of several features, including the physical one.

Physical environment

The physical environment includes both indoors and outdoors. Early years settings will set up the physical environment so that it is attractive and so that children can access a range of play opportunities. Figure 3.4.1 shows some of the key features of the physical environment in early years settings.

In your setting

Make a list of how the physical environment in your setting is welcoming and attractive.

Social aspects

The term 'environment' also covers the social aspects. Children need to feel part of a group and to feel that they belong. This is important for their emotional well-being as well as their social development. In early years settings, the key person system helps children to settle in and to develop relationships with their key person, but also other children. The routines of the setting are also important as these provide opportunities for children to play with each other and also to enjoy snacks and meals together.

In your setting

How does your setting help children to socialise? Do staff share meals and snacks with children?

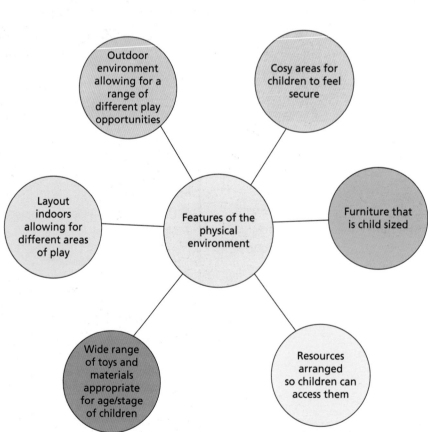

Figure 3.4.1 Features of the physical environment

Cultural aspects

The term environment also refers to the cultural aspects of an environment. In early years settings, the children's home cultures are reflected through the use of fabrics, props and resources. Posters, books and signs may also be written in children's home language.

Personal attributes

A key feature of any early years settings is the adults who work with the children. This means that the personal attributes of adults make a difference to the feel of the environment. Figure 3.4.2 shows the key personal attributes that adults working in early years settings need to have.

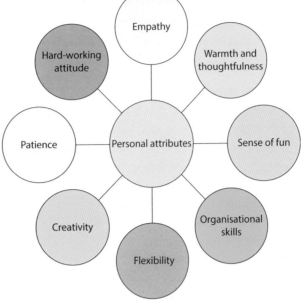

Figure 3.4.2 Personal attributes

In practice

Write a list of ways in which a setting may, through various aspects of its environment, create a warm, stimulating and attractive environment.

Figure 3.4.3 Some play environments need a cosy feel

AC 1.2 How environments support play

There is a range of ways in which the different features that create an environment come together to support play.

Physical environment

The physical environment is important for children as this has the resources and the layout that will motivate children to play. Ideally, each time children enter the physical environment, they should see something that interests them and that will prompt them to explore and play. This is why it is good practice for early years settings to set up play opportunities attractively and to vary what is on offer.

Social aspects

Children are interested in other children and this can be seen even between babies. From two to three years, children spend a lot of their time playing with each other. An environment that promotes social interaction helps children to play together. This in turn can enrich children's play as they copy and learn from each other.

Cultural aspects

Where children's home culture is reflected within the environment, they are more likely to feel comfortable and know what is expected of them. A good example of this is where children recognise props that they see at home, which allows them to replay experiences in the home corner.

> **In your setting**
>
> How does the play environment reflect children's cultures?

Personal attributes

We have seen that the personal attributes of adults working with children are important, but they are also important for play. Adults who are warm and empathetic will help children to feel confident about trying out new play opportunities. In the same way, children are more likely to respond to an adult during a play opportunity if the adult is fun to be with and is patient.

AC 1.3 Working collaboratively to provide enabling play environments in early years settings

It is important that everyone works together to provide a play environment that meets children's needs and interests. An enabling play environment is one in which children are able to physically access materials and resources and also one which takes account of their play interests and needs. There are many ways in which collaborative working may take place.

Parents

Parents will often be able to tell us about what their child enjoys doing at home. They may also share with us toys and resources that seem to hold their children's attention.

Colleagues

In order to create a play environment, in group settings it is important to work as a team. This is because a wide range of resources and play opportunities indoors and outdoors will need to be set up at the start of each session. Everyone needs to agree on what should be available and also who is going to take responsibility for each opportunity. In addition, early years settings will plan play opportunities to support children's individual needs and interests. These will usually be planned by the children's key persons. Collaboration is needed so that everyone in the team knows what will be available and how different adults will be working with children.

> **In your setting**
>
> Make a list of ways in which your team works together to create a play environment for children.

Other professionals

Collaboration is also needed where other professionals are working with children to meet their additional needs. A professional from the sensory impairment team may explain that a child with sight problems will find it easier if small-world toys are put out on a contrasting background or that additional space will be needed around an activity. Other professionals may also want certain activities incorporated with play opportunities. A physiotherapist may suggest that an individual child needs play opportunities that will encourage a pincer grip movement – for example, putting out tweezers with beads.

LO2 Understand how the early years practitioner supports children's behaviour and socialisation within play environments

Have you ever seen a two year old snatch a toy that another child is holding? This is quite common behaviour for two year olds and is linked to their stage of development. In this section, we look at the role of the early years practitioner in supporting children's socialisation and strategies that they use to help children manage their own behaviour. We also look at how the early years practitioner provides for group learning and socialisation.

→ This unit should be read alongside Unit 3.12, which looks at children's stages of social development.

AC 2.1 The early years practitioner and supporting children's socialisation in play environments

One of the skills that young children need to develop is the ability to play and learn alongside other children. This is a gradual process, with most children being three years old before they are able to engage in cooperative play. One of the roles of the early years practitioner is to help children develop the skills that they will need. There are several ways in which practitioners will do this depending on the developmental stage of the children.

Figure 3.4.4 Play can support children's social skills

Playing and modelling

Children can learn how to socialise with others when adults join them in play. This is a key way in which babies and toddlers learn about turn taking and also responding to others. Older children can learn to play games that require rules, such as picture lotto, by playing them with an adult. When adults play with children, they can also show children how to share materials and resources and also to cope when their idea is not accepted by others.

Acknowledgement

Early years practitioners can help children by acknowledging when they are being cooperative. This will help children recognise that this is a valued skill. They may notice children playing well together and ask them whether they are enjoying themselves.

Planning play opportunities

Some play opportunities will help children develop the skills of socialisation. One of the roles of the early years practitioner is to plan play opportunities that are stage appropriate but that will help children play alongside or with each other. With babies and toddlers, this might mean putting out resources which will help children to play near each other, while with older children this might mean adult-led activities where children play in teams – for example, obstacle races or making dens.

In practice

Write about a recent example when you have helped children to socialise. What skills did you use?

AC 2.2 Strategies to support children managing their own behaviour toward others

Children's behaviour, which is linked to their social development, depends on a variety of factors. These include children's age and stage of development, their tiredness and also their emotional security. Early years practitioners have to take these into consideration when thinking about fair expectations for behaviour and also when choosing which

strategies to use with children. This means that, if a young toddler takes an item from another toddler, an early years practitioner will not make the child say sorry, but instead may simply return the item to the other child. There is a range of strategies that early years practitioners can use to help children manage their own behaviour. These should reflect the behaviour policy of your setting. A behaviour policy is a requirement of the EYFS.

Research it!

Find out about the behaviour policy in your setting.

Explanation

In some situations where resources or materials need to be shared, early years practitioners will talk to children and explain that they will need to take turns. This works well with children who have good language development as they are able to understand this.

Reminders

It can be helpful for early years practitioners to remind children about turn taking or sharing during an activity. This can prevent arguments or situations of unwanted behaviour arising. As with explanation, it works best with children who have good language levels.

Distraction

With babies and toddlers, who do not have the social skills or language development, distraction is a common strategy that is used. Children are shown or given something that will change their focus from the unwanted behaviour.

Ignore

Some unwanted behaviour is the result of children wanting to gain adult attention. These behaviours tell us that a child needs more attention. The strategy for dealing with unwanted behaviours is to ignore what the child is doing unless there is a safety issue, but then to give children plenty of positive attention at other times. Where there is a safety issue and the behaviour cannot be ignored, the adult removes the child or the equipment, but says very little to the child.

Case study

Anna is working for the first time in the two year old room. She notices that one of the children is banging the radiator with a piece of jigsaw puzzle. She mentions this to the child's key person, who tells Anna not to look at the child. Anna is surprised. She thought that it would be better to tell the child to stop. Instead, the key person starts to sing a song and a couple of the children start joining in. The child who was banging the radiator stops what she is doing and comes and joins. Afterwards, the key person explains that, by giving the child attention, there would be more of a chance that the child would repeat the behaviour.

1. Why was the child's behaviour linked to their age/stage of development?
2. What two strategies did the key person use to help the child show positive behaviour?
3. Explain how these strategies work.

Explaining consequences and possible sanctions

With older children who have good language and cognitive skills, early years practitioners may help a child to modify his behaviour by explaining the consequences and sanctions that will take place if the behaviour continues.

Modelling positive behaviours

Some behaviours, such as turn taking and being considerate to others, can be modelled. This is a strategy that works well with all ages, although children will not copy all of the actions all of the time. They will, however, be able to try out an action if reminded and encouraged.

AC 2.3 How the early years practitioner provides group learning and socialisation

Group learning

Most early years settings start to plan some play opportunities for children in small groups from around three or four years. This is because, before this age, children's stage of development means that they find it hard to concentrate and engage. For group learning to be effective, early years practitioners have to ensure that the play opportunities are active and also suitable for children's stage of development. The type of group learning opportunities on offer usually include board games, story times and rhymes, as well as specific adult-led activities of the kind that we looked at in Unit 3.1. These might include planting bulbs, cooking, going on an outing or taking part in role play.

In your setting

Give examples of how your setting uses group learning. Why is it important that the activities carefully match children's age and stage of development?

How the early years practitioner provides for socialisation

Early years settings also support children's socialisation. This has to be done according to children's age and stage of development and is done mostly through providing play opportunities. While at first very young children do not play cooperatively, they do tend to enjoy playing in parallel and so some of the earliest opportunities involve children playing with the same materials, such as a tray of gloop or in a paddling pool. As children become older, early years practitioners continue to provide play opportunities that allow children to gather around and play together but they will increasingly expect that children will take turns and play more cooperatively. In addition, from around three years, most children start to enjoy role play. Early years practitioners can use this as an opportunity for socialisation by providing a wide range of role-play opportunities.

Test yourself

At what ages are most children able to share and play cooperatively?

Figure 3.4.5 Play opportunities should be provided that encourage turn taking

LO3 Be able to support children's behaviour and socialisation within play environments

Have you seen how adults sometimes distract younger children from difficult situations? In this section, we look at how, in practice, you can work to support children's behaviour through modelling, creating enabling environments and also using behaviour strategies.

AC 3.1 Modelling positive behaviour

We saw earlier that it is essential to model positive behaviour as this is one way in which children can learn. There are many situations in which it is useful to model positive behaviour.

Snack and meal times

Children can learn from adults the social codes that are usual at meal times – for example, serving, turn taking and using cutlery. Children can also learn from adults how meal times can be social occasions where, as well as eating, we can talk.

During play

When adults join in with play, they can model positive behaviour, such as offering resources to a child who is just joining or tidying things away when play is finished. Adults can also show children how to take turns and share resources.

Caring for the play environment

Adults can show children how to care for toys and resources by, for example, tidying items away where necessary or picking up items that have fallen down.

> **In practice**
>
> Explain how you help children to care for the play environment. What other skills do children gain when they help to care for the environment?

Figure 3.4.6 Children learn from adults who model positive behaviour

AC 3.2 Planning an enabling environment

The way that we set up an environment can make a difference to how children behave and their ability to socialise and get involved in group learning. As we have already seen, the starting point is to be aware of children's age and stage of development and so this should always be reflected in the environments that we create.

Sufficient materials and resources

An enabling environment must contain sufficient resources and materials so that children can join an activity easily. A good example of this is a dough table where three or four children may want to play with dough at the same time. If there is sufficient dough, children are able to play and explore the dough together. Having sufficient resources and materials is particularly important when working with two year olds, who tend to want to copy each other's actions. This means that, when they see another two year old with a pushchair, for example, they will want one exactly the same and, if this is provided, the children will play in parallel.

Defined areas

Older children seem to enjoy playing in defined areas, such as the role-play area or mark-making area. This seems to help children understand the expectations of what type of play and behaviour is needed. It also helps children to remain engaged and can prevent distraction.

Cosy areas

Children seem to socialise well together when they are in cosy areas, such as a role-play area or an area which feels snug. Creating environments that have a cosy area can therefore support children's socialisation. Such areas can also work well for group learning experiences, such as small story groups.

Routines

Some routines in a setting can help children's socialisation and group learning. Meal times and snack times are good examples of these. It is good practice for children to sit with each other in small groups and to serve themselves. This helps children to take turns and also to enjoy being part of a group. These routines can also be opportunities for group learning if an adult draws their attention to, for example, the food on their plates or leads a discussion about favourite foods.

> **In practice**
>
> Write about the principles of planning an environment that allows children to play and socialise. Give examples of how you have tried to put these principles into practice in your setting.

AC 3.3 Using strategies to support children managing their own behaviour

While we have already looked at the strategies that can be used to help children manage their behaviour, there are some things that have to be considered when using these strategies.

Following the policy of the setting

As part of the EYFS, all early years settings will have policies relating to supporting children's positive behaviour. A member of the team in a group care setting will be responsible for this. This means that an important part of promoting children's positive behaviour is to do so in line with your setting's policy. Most policies will cover the importance of adults having fair expectations that are carefully linked to children's age and stage of development. Following policies is important because we know that children respond well to consistency, as the following case study shows.

Case study

In Little Angels nursery, the children are encouraged to tidy up before leaving an activity. A new member of staff does not think that this is important and so does not remind the children. The children are starting not to tidy up automatically and look surprised when another member of staff tells them to go back and tidy.

1 Why are the children no longer tidying up automatically?
2 Why might other staff become irritated with the new member of staff?
3 Why is it important for staff to follow the agreed policies and procedures?

Age and stage of the children

The strategies that we looked at in the previous section are not all suitable for children who are very young or who have language delay. It is therefore important to be very aware of what is typical behaviour for the age and stage of children and to choose a strategy and your expectations of their behaviour accordingly. In general terms, young children are impulsive and also have limited understanding. This means that too much talk and reminding may not work well. It is also important to think about how tired children are as this tends to affect their behaviour. Older children who are tired may find it much harder to share and take turns and so we may need to change the environment to suit them.

Organisation

Children tend to show more unwanted behaviour when they are bored. This means that we have to be organised when working with all ages of children. In practice it means ensuring that children have plenty of different play opportunities and also that at meal times and other points in the routine they are not left with nothing to do. Being organised also means recognising when children are becoming bored and planning ahead so that new opportunities or activities can quickly be implemented.

LO4 Understand how the characteristics of an enabling indoor and outdoor play environment meet the age, stage and needs of children

Are you in a setting where children can help themselves to toys and resources? This is important for children as it gives them a chance to take ownership of their play. In this section, we look at what makes an enabling environment and how this helps support children's developmental needs and interests.

AC 4.1 The characteristics of an enabling indoor play environment

There are several characteristics which make an indoor environment enabling for children. Here are some of the key characteristics that early years settings will try to provide.

Opportunities for children to socialise and communicate

Children need opportunities to be with other children as well as adults and to communicate according to their age and stage of development. In indoor spaces, this might mean cosy corners and areas where children can play together or with an adult.

Opportunities for children to make choices

Children need opportunities to choose what resources to play with. In indoor environments, this will mean that resources are put out at child height on low shelves or in baskets. For non-mobile babies, this will mean that a range of resources might be put within reach and an adult will follow their gaze and support them.

Opportunities to show independence

Children need opportunities to be as independent as is possible. In indoor settings, this means labelling items with print or with photographs so that children can find what they are looking for. It also means making sure that furniture and storage are child sized and that areas for keeping coats, bags and shoes allow children to be independent. Enabling environments that support independence indoors also encourage children to self-serve at meal and snack times or in the case of babies to self-feed where possible. With babies, it also means that members of staff work in ways that recognise what babies are trying to communicate – for example, not continuing to feed when babies turn their heads.

Figure 3.4.7 Photographs or labels on drawers encourage children to be independent

In your setting

Explain how your setting helps children to show independence in the play environment.

Opportunities to play in a range of ways and have a range of experiences

Within the indoor environment, children of all ages will need a wide range of play opportunities and experiences. The indoor environment should have plenty of resources that children can access which develop a range of skills. For babies, this might mean treasure baskets for fine motor and exploratory play, as well as sensory materials. For older children, it may mean a wide range of different play types, including imaginative, construction and sensory play, as well as having opportunities to cook or join in musical activities.

Opportunities for children to have challenge

An indoor enabling environment also recognises when children need more challenges and provides for this in their play. Resources may be put out that

are new for children or an adult may engage with children so as to give them new experiences – for example, showing them how to use a computer program or singing a new rhyme to a baby.

Opportunities for children to rest

Many children will need opportunities to rest, especially if they are very young or in settings for most of the day. An enabling environment should have comfy cosy areas where children can relax.

In your setting

How does your setting help children to rest during the day?

An enabling outdoor play environment

Many of the characteristics of an indoor enabling environment that we have looked at are needed outdoors as well. It is a requirement of the EYFS that children should go out every day and that the outdoor environment reflects the seven areas of the EYFS.

Opportunities for children to socialise and communicate

Children need opportunities to socialise and play together outdoors. This might be achieved through the use of cosy areas where children can talk together, pathways where children can follow each other and also areas such as large sandpits where children can play alongside each other.

Opportunities to play in a range of ways and have a range of experiences

The outdoor environment is not just about encouraging physical development. An enabling environment allows children to play in a range of ways, including sensory play, mark-making and role play. This means that, while the outdoor environment should include areas to support physical activity, there should also be resources that allow children to continue to play in a range of ways. Children also need adults to help with certain experiences, such as taking them for walks to take photographs of mini beasts or helping them to create a den.

Figure 3.4.8 An enabling outdoor environment has plenty of rich opportunities for children to choose from

Opportunities for children to be independent and make choices

The outdoor environment should be one where children can be as independent as possible. This means making sure that the environment is secure and safe so that children can freely move around. It also means that careful assessment has to be made of the equipment that is provided, especially when the outdoor environment is used by different ages of children – for example, a climbing frame suitable for a four year old may not be safe for a two year old without adjustment or supervision.

Opportunities for children to have challenge

An outdoor enabling environment gives children a range of challenges that allow them to build on their level of development. This is achieved firstly through careful observation by adults

as to how children are using the environment and then changing the environment to provide greater challenge. This might mean putting out new resources or grouping existing resources differently.

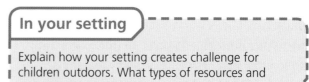

In your setting

Explain how your setting creates challenge for children outdoors. What types of resources and activities are on offer?

Opportunities for children to experience the natural world

Outdoors, children need opportunities to experience the natural world. This might be achieved by taking babies outdoors for a walk in different weathers or, with older children, allowing them to experience playing in puddles.

AC 4.2 How enabling environments meet the age, stage and play needs of children

When indoor and outdoor environments are enabling, they can meet children's age and stage of development, but also their play needs. There is a range of ways in which this happens.

Role of the adult

While the physical environment is important, an enabling environment also includes adults who carefully observe children and are ready to use their observations to support children. In an indoor environment, an adult may see that a baby is looking at a window and so carries the baby over so that they can look out together. In an outdoor environment, an adult may see that a toddler is becoming frustrated with a large tricycle and so will offer help or the choice of a tricycle that is lower in height.

Equipment and resources

Enabling environments, as we have seen, contain equipment and resources that are suited to children's developmental ages and needs. This helps children to build on their existing physical skills but also to master new ones. A range of equipment and resources also helps children's cognitive development as, through different types of play, they learn new concepts and explore shapes and textures. Equipment and resources that are carefully selected also mean that children can find challenge in them but do not become frustrated. This supports their confidence.

Choice and independence

As we have seen, choice and independence are key features of enabling environments. They are important because they support children's emotional development. They provide children with opportunities to be competent and so help children to gain in confidence.

> **In practice**
>
> Choose one area of your setting's provision. Explain how it meets the age, stage and interests of the children that use it.

LO5 Be able to provide enabling play environments

Do you find yourself often putting out a range of equipment and resources before a session starts? This is one of the ways in which we create an enabling play environment for children to come into. In this section, we look at how to plan an enabling play environment and how to ensure that it happens in practice.

AC 5.1 Planning an enabling play environment indoors

The starting point for planning environments is to think about children's age and stage of development. This is important as an enabling environment for a baby will not be suitable for a three year old.

Babies: 0–1 year

Babies need an environment that feels homely and relaxed. They need plenty of opportunities to interact with their key person and so the layout of the room should enable this. This often means that early years settings will have a rocking chair or sofa where the adult and the baby can cuddle up together. Babies also need plenty of opportunities to explore resources with their mouths and hands. Therefore, the environment needs treasure baskets and other resources that the baby can easily access. Once babies are starting to crawl or otherwise become mobile, they need floor space that allows them to move freely. They also need opportunities to pull themselves to standing and so the arrangement of furniture has to allow for this, although in some early years settings hand rails are provided. Babies will sleep during the session and so a sleeping area that allows babies to be safe, but also to feel emotionally secure, is important. As with all ages of children, babies can become bored and so new play opportunities, such as sensory play, need to be regularly provided.

Toddlers: 1–3 years

Once children start to walk, their needs change again. The usual pattern of development is that they are very active. Most children in this age range spend a lot of time moving and a lot of their play involves carrying objects or pushing items, such as pushchairs.

This needs to be taken into account when planning an environment and most early years settings set up their indoor environment in ways that allow this movement. Children in this age group, as we have already seen, are usually not developmentally ready to share and be cooperative. This needs to be considered when planning environments as you should provide enough resources so that children can engage in parallel play.

Children in this age range enjoy playing in a range of different ways. While role play is not fully established, they enjoy using props, such as phones, and putting on simple dressing-up clothes, such as hats and shoes. They also enjoy making marks, sensory play and, with some adult help, using construction toys, such as bricks. One of the features from around 18 months is that children are often trying to be independent. There should be opportunities for them to access their coats, shoes and also at snack and meal times for them to be as independent as possible.

Children in this age group find it hard to wait. This means that resources that are suitable for them should be easily available. As children are also impulsive, with little awareness of danger, safety is another key factor when planning an enabling environment, and the layout should allow adults to easily see what children are doing.

In your setting

Observe two toddlers as they play for 20 minutes. How much movement is involved in their play?

Children from three years

For children from three years, an enabling environment is one in which they are able to operate fairly independently. The environment should also reflect all areas of the EYFS and provide opportunities for children to access these. This means that most early years settings will create areas within the indoor environment where toys and resources are grouped together to support a wide range of play opportunities – for example, mark-making areas, creative areas, sensory play areas and

construction or block play areas. Toys and resources should be presented in ways that allow children to access them easily – for example, in baskets, in storage boxes or on shelves. Children will also need opportunities to develop their interest in reading and so a story area where books are easily accessible should be provided, as well as props which might support stories. Role play is a key way in which children of this age learn and play, so it is worth planning more than one area where role play can take place – for example, a shop alongside a home corner. The routines of the setting also have to be planned to allow children to be as independent as possible. This might include a snack bar where children can choose when to have their mid-session snack. It is also good practice for children to be involved in the preparation of the snacks.

In practice

Create one area indoors for children aged 3–5 years to play in. Choose which type of play opportunities you feel will be of interest to them. Write about how you planned this play environment and how the children responded to it.

Plan an enabling play environment outdoors

As with planning an enabling environment indoors, it is important when planning an enabling environment outdoors to think about the needs of children according to their age and stage of development.

Babies: 0–1 year

Babies need plenty of opportunities to be outdoors. This might be the provision of a safe area where they can crawl or move without being 'run over' by older, mobile children. As most babies like to pull themselves to standing towards the end of their first year, it is important to plan opportunities for them to do this safely – for example, by putting a circle of logs out or putting up a low hand rail on a wall. Babies also need to experience motion and so it is worth looking out for equipment such as swings or seesaws, which the adult can hold and rock the baby.

In your setting

How does your setting create an enabling environment for babies? What play opportunities and resources are provided? What are the barriers to creating an enabling play environment for this age group?

Toddlers: 1–3 years

Once children can walk, they are keen to move and explore. An enabling environment needs to have plenty of opportunities for children to practise their new-found walking skills. Equipment includes items that are sturdy for them to push, such as brick trolleys and wooden pushchairs. Once children are walking well, they then like to experience sit-and-ride toys where they can propel themselves with their feet. Toddlers also enjoy kicking balls, by walking into them, and also throwing balls. From around two years old, toddlers also love climbing and so opportunities for children to move up onto climbing frames or to walk on low walls or crates work well. Toddlers will also enjoy making marks outdoors by squirting water, using chalks and using paintbrushes and water. An enabling environment will also provide some adult-led activities where children can play alongside adults or join them in activities such as planting.

Reflect

Think about where toddlers in your setting most enjoy being independent.

Children from three years

From three years, an enabling outdoor environment provides children with a large range of experiences, including digging, planting and looking at nature. Children will still want to engage in physical play and it is worth planning an environment that builds on children's developing skills. Obstacle courses are, for example, very popular. It is also good practice for many elements of what is available indoors to be available outdoors, such as mark-making boards, role-play and even story areas.

In your setting

Observe a group of children aged three and over in the outdoor environment. Consider how they use the space and monitor their activity.

In practice

Using the information gained form observing children aged three and over in the outdoor environment, write down and, if possible, implement changes to enrich it.

AC 5.2 Creating an enabling play environment

Very few early years practitioners have the opportunity to create an enabling play environment from scratch. Mostly, it is about reviewing what is already available and considering how to improve it further. It can be useful to consider the questions in the following box when reviewing and creating an enabling play environment both indoors and outdoors.

Tips: questions to consider when planning an enabling play environment

- What aspects of the current environment allow children to be independent?
- Which aspects of the current environment prevent children from being independent and why?
- How do the furniture, layout or routine need to be changed in order to allow children to become more independent?
- How does the environment meet children's age and stage of development as well as their play interests?
- Are there any aspects of children's development or the current early years framework that are not being promoted?
- How engaged are children as they play?
- Are resources arranged in ways that are stimulating for children?
- How are new challenges created?
- What choices are available for children?

LO6 Be able to plan and lead opportunities which support children's understanding of the world

Have you seen children enjoy looking at things through magnifying glasses? Or playing with gadgets? 'Understanding the world' is an area of learning within the EYFS. It covers a wide range of different skills for children to gain. In this section, we look at how to plan and implement opportunities for children that will support this area of learning developing within the EYFS.

AC 6.1 Planning opportunities to support children's understanding of the world

The area of learning and development known as 'Understanding the world' is a specific area. This means that it is not the focus of work with babies and very young children, although it is expected that links should be made to it. In order to plan opportunities for different ages of children, it is important to understand that there are three aspects within the EYFS area of learning called 'Understanding the world'. Early years settings have to plan for each of the following different aspects:

- **People and communities**: this aspect helps children to understand more about their family and community. It also helps children become aware of the differences and similarities between themselves and others.
- **The world**: this aspect helps children find out about the similarities and differences in relation to places, materials and objects. Children are helped to notice features of their own environment and how some environments change or may be different. This aspect also helps children to notice animals and plants and to learn about why things happen and change.
- **Technology**: this aspect helps children learn why technology is used and also helps them learn to use different types of technology, such as robots, remote-controlled toys and simple computer programs.

People and communities

When planning opportunities for this aspect, it is important to start by basing opportunities on children's own knowledge and experiences. This acts as a good starting point. There is a range of opportunities that can work well with children, as shown in Table 3.4.1.

The world

This aspect of learning is very wide and children need many different opportunities to cover it. It is an aspect of learning that should be active and lends itself to many first-hand experiences. For examples, see Table 3.4.2.

Technology

There are plenty of opportunities to help children learn about and also use technology. It is important to plan opportunities that are age and stage appropriate so that children can be active. For examples, see Table 3.4.3.

Table 3.4.1 Planning opportunities around 'People and communities'

Opportunity	Benefits
Preparing and tasting different foods	It is interesting for children to try out new foods and tastes. Through this, they can learn that other people may like different foods. They may find that the child next to them loves something that they are not sure of. It can also help children talk about what they eat at home.
Planning a party	Children love parties and celebrations. By talking about parties and planning a party, children can tell us about what their family celebrates. This can be an opportunity for children to find out that other families have different ways of celebrating.
Visitors	Children enjoy learning about the roles that different adults have. A visit from a police officer or from an optician can help children learn about others.
Sharing stories	Some stories can help children to think about other families and other children's lives. When choosing stories, think about the quality of the story and illustrations as well as the plot.
'My family' book	It can be useful to make books for children so that they can talk about their families. Look out for photographs of children as babies and also as toddlers with their families and friends. Encourage children to look at their 'family' book and also, once children are around three years, encourage them to look at each other's books.

Table 3.4.2 Planning opportunities around 'The world'

Opportunity	Benefits
Visit to the shops or local play park	Walking in the local area helps children to think about the area around the setting. It is worth repeating these types of outings at different times of the year and in different weathers so that children can talk about the changes. Photographs can also help children to make comparisons.
Collections of objects, e.g. old and new, mechanical, magnetic	Putting out a range of objects for children to explore can help them to explore new materials, but also help them to notice textures and differences. A collection of objects that are old or new, such as keys and locks, will help children talk about how things have changed.
Making birdseed cake	Children can learn to observe birds and also enjoy making and putting out birdseed cake. This can help them understand nature.
Planting seeds and bulbs	Planting seeds and bulbs can help children learn about how things grow. If different types of bulbs or seeds are planted at the same time, it also means that children can see the differences in the shape and size of leaves.
Mini beast hunt	With magnifying glasses, children can look for mini beasts, such as spiders, caterpillars and earwigs. They can talk about the different places in which they find them.

Table 3.4.3 Planning opportunities around 'Technology'

Opportunity	Benefits
Books and toys that make sounds or light up	Some toys have chips in them which help children to learn about the cause-and-effect nature of technology. These types of toys are useful for very young children, who enjoy pushing buttons.
Remote-controlled toys	Remote-controlled toys are popular with children who enjoy making them move using a control.
Appropriate computer programs	Children can also enjoy learning about technology by using programs on tablets, computers and laptops. It is important that software encourages children to be active and that the learning is appropriate.
Technology walk	Children can learn about technology by going on a 'technology walk'. The walk could be indoors or outdoors and could show children pelican crossings, sensors on car keys and remote-controlled gadgets, such as televisions.

In your setting

What opportunities are there for children to explore technology in your setting?

AC 6.2 Leading opportunities which support children's understanding of the world

As well as planning opportunities to support children's understanding of the world, we also have to work in ways that will help children to learn and explore. What we need to do when leading an opportunity will depend on the aspect of learning. Let's look at how you might lead opportunities for each of the different aspects within this area of learning and development.

People and communities

This aspect is one which takes time for children to fully understand. This is because, developmentally, children find it hard to understand that others have different lives from them. One of the ways in which we need to lead opportunities relating to this aspect is to spend time talking with children and encouraging them to reflect and make connections. A child may say that she likes visiting her nan, while another child might chip in that his grandmother lives in his house. There is therefore a strong link between this aspect and communication and language.

Role model

One of the ways that children learn to respect others, who may have different dress, culture or food from theirs, is by seeing adults' reactions. If adults talk about things being 'strange' or 'odd', children are more likely to reflect this in their talk and behaviour. It is, therefore, important to show children that we are interested in differences and that we are respectful of others.

In your setting

Write about how your setting plans play opportunities that will help children learn about 'People and communities'.

The world

Interestingly, this aspect has many links with communication and language. This is because children need time to talk about what they are seeing and doing. Adults will need to use many of the same skills that we looked at in Unit 3.5.

→ You should look at Unit 3.5 when leading opportunities for 'The world'.

Following children's interests

We know that children learn more when they are interested in what they are doing and seeing. It is, therefore, important that we notice what children are fascinated in when they are outdoors or going for a walk. We should then use this to draw children's attention to details and to encourage children to talk about what they are seeing.

Drawing children's attention to details

One of the most important ways in which we can help children learn about their environment is by drawing their attention to specific features of it and then accurately naming it – for example, 'Look at the spider's web! Shall we see if we can see the spider now?'.

Using technology

While technology is a separate aspect, it is sometimes worth combining the two aspects by taking a camera out so that children can take photographs of things that have fascinated them.

Health and safety

Children enjoy looking at and touching things outdoors. While this is an important part of their learning, we must be vigilant at all times. A child may find some fungi growing by a tree and want to pick it or another child might want to touch a wasp on the ground. Therefore, it is important that children are carefully supervised and also that a risk assessment is completed before taking children to new areas.

Technology

It is important to give children plenty of time to explore technology. Younger children will want to repeat actions several times – for example, turning a robot on and off. It is important that older children also start to have opportunities to talk about what they are doing and that they are allowed to try out new things. They may, for example, want to see if they can make a remote-controlled car move up a ramp. As using technology with children is quite intensive, you should work with small groups of children or ideally pairs. It is also important that sufficient equipment is available so that all children can join in. This prevents children from becoming frustrated or bored.

> ### In practice
>
> Choose one aspect from the EYFS area of development 'Understanding the world' and explain how you planned and led an activity to support it. Explain why you feel that this activity was suitable for the age and stage of children involved.

LO7 Be able to plan and lead opportunities which encourage children's engagement in expressive arts and design

Have you ever seen children scooping and playing with gloop? It is one of the many activities that are common in early years settings and that help children to express themselves. In this section, we look at the EYFS area of learning and development called 'Expressive arts and design' and how we may plan and lead opportunities that will support children's development.

AC 7.1 Planning opportunities for children's expressive arts and design

Expressive arts and design is a specific area of development within the EYFS. It covers all aspects of children's creativity, including moving to music, painting, modelling and imaginative play. Interestingly, it links closely to 'Physical development' as children will often be moving or using their gross and fine motor skills. There are two closely related aspects within this area of learning:

- Exploring and using media and materials
- Being imaginative.

Exploring and using media and materials

This aspect is about giving children plenty of opportunities to try out a range of different materials and also different types of activities – for example, dancing, painting and modelling.

Being imaginative

This aspect is about children being able to choose how they express themselves as a result of the skills that they have learnt from exploring and using different media and materials.

> ### Research it!
>
> Read the Early Learning Goals relating to this curriculum area of learning and development within the EYFS by downloading a copy of the statutory framework from **www.foundationyears.org.uk**.

Planning opportunities for supporting expressive arts and design

The two aspects of this area of learning are so connected that it is possible to plan opportunities for them jointly. This area of learning and development also covers a wide range of possible activities and experiences for children and so early years settings have to reflect this in their planning.

Factors to consider when planning for this area of learning and development

There are a few factors to think about when planning for this area of learning and development.

Health and safety

To prevent any accidents, it is essential to consider children's age and stage of development when planning opportunities. Children who are under three years, for example, are unlikely to be able to use scissors or tools such as staplers without supervision, while children under two years may still be putting objects in their mouths.

Choice and open-ended opportunities

This area of learning and development is about children exploring and also making choices. It is important that opportunities are chosen that will give children plenty of options and choice.

Stage of physical development

When planning opportunities, you also should think about children's stage of physical development as many activities will require children to use hand–eye coordination and locomotive movements.

Types of opportunities

Table 3.4.4 shows the types of opportunities that can be planned to support children's learning.

AC 7.2 Leading opportunities for children's expressive arts and design

There are some important principles to think about when leading opportunities for children's expressive arts and design.

Table 3.4.4 Planning opportunities around 'Expressive arts and design'

Opportunity	Example	Explanation
Sensory play	• Sand • Water • Gloop • Runny jelly • Cold, cooked spaghetti	These opportunities help children to explore different media. They can make a range of movements and use a variety of props and other resources to enrich their play and learning.
Malleable materials	• Dough • Clay • Play snow	These opportunities help children to squeeze and pound but also to shape and model. Children will need a range of tools to support these opportunities. Children can also use these materials to support their role play, e.g. making a tray of cakes for their home corner play.
Mark-making	• Painting • Drawing • Making marks in sensory materials, e.g. sticks in sand	From an early age, children enjoy making marks using a range of materials. To help children explore media and materials, they need a wide range of colours and implements, such as small and wide brushes, different sizes of markers and different types of paint. Children can use their mark-making to create stories, to do drawings and to add into role-play areas.
Musical instruments	• Shakers • Keyboards, chime bars • Range of percussion instruments	Children enjoy making sounds and listening to music from an early age. They need plenty of opportunities to explore making different sounds using different instruments. Children can combine making simple shakers with using them.
Moving to music	• Different types of music • Different props to go with music, e.g. masks, hats, scarves	Children love moving to music. Even babies like to be held while an adult dances to music. Children can also combine using instruments with moving to music, e.g. rattling a shaker while dancing.
Modelling and making things	• Junk modelling • Clay modelling • Cards	Older children enjoy making things as they have the hand–eye coordination to do this. It is important that children have a wide range of objects and materials as well as tools such as scissors, staplers and sticky tape. Children will often need adults to help them to join materials.
Role play	• Shops, e.g. shoe shops • Places, e.g. train station, garden centre • Fantasy, e.g. under the sea	Role play tends to work well for children from around three years. At first they play out their own direct experiences, but as they become older, they are able to use their imagination to take part in fantasy play. Adults need to provide sufficient props and think about choosing the right role-play opportunity for the age/stage as well as interest of the children.

Creative process

It is important when leading an activity to focus on children's enjoyment and exploration of the process. This is why it is not considered good practice for adults to create templates or set projects for children where there are no options for children to show their own creativity.

Time

When leading play opportunities, it is important to ensure that children have the time that they need. In some cases, older children often want to return to projects that they have started earlier. They may make a Lego model that the next day they want to add to or they may make some dough cakes that afterwards they want to use in a cake shop.

Facilitating

One of the key ways in which we can help children is to act as a facilitator. This means supporting children when they need some help or come across problems, such as not being able to join two tubes together. In some cases, where appropriate, we may also facilitate children by teaching them some skills, such as how to use a stapler or how to mix colours, so that they can do this independently.

In practice

Write a reflective account about how you have planned and facilitated a play opportunity relating to 'Expressive arts and design'. In your account, explain why you planned the activity and how the children responded.

Assessment

This unit is a large with seven learning outcomes. You might like to start by looking at Learning Outcomes 1, 4 and 5 as they relate to 'play environment'. Make sure that you have a good understanding of the concept of 'play environments', their characteristics and how both indoor and outdoor play environments support children's development. You should also think about how play environments are the result of collaborative working. To do this you might think about how in your setting the play environment is a result of the work of many people. You will also need to show that you can plan and create play environments both indoors and outdoors. You will need to talk to your placement supervisor and work together on how and when you might do this.

Learning Outcomes 2 and 3 look at how early years practitioners can support children to socialise and to promote positive behaviour. You should start by revisiting the different strategies practitioners can use and think about how they relate to your setting. You might also like to look at Unit 3.12 where we look at children's social development so that you can link this knowledge to your practice. This is important as you will need to show your assessor that you can model positive behaviour and create an environment that supports children's socialisation and group learning. Before your assessor visits you, it will be worth asking your placement supervisor to give you feedback about these aspects of you work. You may also think about which situations lend themselves to supporting group socialisation.

The last two learning outcomes relate to two different areas of learning and development within the EYFS. Your starting point for these learning outcomes is to look carefully at the requirements of the statutory framework for the Early Years Foundation Stage. In addition, you should talk to your placement supervisor or experienced colleagues about these areas of learning and development. This is important because you will need to plan and lead play opportunities for each of these areas of learning and development. You could base your play opportunities on the ideas given in the unit or choose ones suggested by your placement supervisor.

Useful resources

Organisations

Anna Freud Centre

The centre was established in 1947 by Anna Freud to support the emotional well-being of children through direct work with children and their families, research and the development of practice, and training mental health practitioners: **www.annafreud.org**.

High/Scope

High/Scope is an American approach to early education and care, with several decades of research into its effectiveness. The website includes books, DVDs and news of training events and conferences in the UK: **www.high-scope.org.uk**.

Kate Greenaway Nursery School and Children's Centre

This website includes news and policies for a centre based in central London: **www.kategreenaway. ik.org**.

Kidscape

This charity was established specifically to prevent bullying and child sexual abuse. The website includes resources for parents, children and professionals, and details of campaigns and training events: **www.kidscape.org.uk**.

The National Strategies (Early Years)

The government's programme for developing practice in the early years, including statutory requirements, advice on best practice, and research findings: **www.education.gov.uk** and search for early years.

Books

Axline, V. (1971), Dibs, *In Search of Self: Personality Development in Play Therapy*. London: Penguin.

Dowling, M. (2010), *Young Children's Personal, Social and Emotional Development* (3rd edn). London: Sage Publications.

Paley, V.G. (1981), *Wally's Stories*. Cambridge, Mass.: Harvard University Press.

Sylva, K. and Lunt, I. (1982), *Child Development: A First Course*. Oxford: Blackwell.

Tovey, H. (2007), *Playing Outdoors: Spaces and Places, Risk and Challenge*. Oxford: Oxford University Press.

Unit 3.5 WB Developing children's emergent literacy skills

Do you remember learning to read or write? Do you remember how you were taught? You probably learnt to read and write while you were at school. In this unit, we look at how early years settings develop skills in children so that when they start school they are ready to read and write. The term 'emergent' is used to describe these developing literacy skills. In this unit, we look at the importance of communication and language as well as strategies and activities used to support children's emergent literacy.

Learning outcomes

By the end of this unit, you will:

1 Understand the language and communication needs of children.
2 Be able to support children's language and communication needs.
3 Understand strategies which support emergent literacy.
4 Be able to use strategies to plan and lead activities which support emergent literacy.
5 Be able to review how planned activities support emergent literacy.
6 Be able to work with parents/carers in a way which encourages them to take an active role in their child's play, learning and development.

LO1 Understand the language and communication needs of children

Do you ever find yourself speaking as you are writing or hearing a voice as you are reading? It may seem strange, but the first step in learning to read or write is to be able to talk. This is because what you read on a page or write on a page will be words. Children's speech is very important for literacy, which is one of the reasons why it is a prime area of learning and development within the EYFS. In this section, we look at the usual sequences and stages by which children learn to talk. We also consider some of the factors that might affect children's language and also the importance of working with others.

AC 1.1 The development stages of language and communication from birth to seven years

Learning to talk and communicate is an important skill for children to master and overall it takes around four years before most children are fluent speakers. It takes, though, a further three years before most children are able to produce all of the sounds needed in English and also for them to be grammatically sound. However, throughout our lives we are likely to keep on learning and using new words.

The process of learning how to talk is at first quite slow and most babies in their first year, while being able to understand a few words, are not yet able to talk. This first phase of learning speech is known as the pre-linguistic phase. Children then go on to a linguistic phase, whereby they start to use words. Table 3.5.1 shows the usual pattern of children's language development.

AC 1.2 Factors that affect language and communication needs

There are many factors that affect children's language and communication. It is important to recognise these because, if they are not identified early, it can mean that children will not be able to learn to read, as learning to talk is the first step in learning to read.

Figure 3.5.1 From an early age, babies are interested in listening to people talk

Table 3.5.1 Pattern of language development

Stage	Age	Features	Comments
Pre-linguistic stage			
Cooing	6 weeks–6 months	Cooing – soft sounds in response to being cuddled or during feeding	While babies use crying to express their needs, they start to make cooing sounds at around six weeks to show pleasure.
Babbling (phonemic expansion)	6–9 months	Babies blend vowels and consonants together to make tuneful sounds e.g.ba, ma, da	Babbling seems to be a way for babies to practise sounds. Over time, babies increase the number of sounds or phonemes. This is sometimes called phonemic expansion. All babies, even deaf babies, produce a wide range of sounds during this period. As well as developing speech sounds, babies have developed many important communication skills, including the ability to recognise emotion in others, tune into particular voices and also attract attention by smiling or making sounds.
Babbling (phonemic contraction)	9–12 months	Babies babble but the range of sounds is limited Echolalia: babies seem to repeat the same sounds in long strings, e.g. 'babababab'	From around 10 months, babies start to crack the code of language and show this by responding to around 15 words, such as 'bye-bye'. In terms of speech production, the range of sounds or phonemes that babies produce becomes more limited. This reflects the speech sounds used in the language that they are hearing. Babies' communication skills have also developed further. They now know how to attract an adult's attention by pointing and raising their voices.
Linguistic stage			
First words	Around 12 months	Babies repeatedly use one or more sounds which have meaning for them	Most first words are very unclear and they may be mixed up with babbling. They are often one sound, but are used regularly in similar situations – for example, 'ba' to mean drink and cuddle. Babies are now able to understand a lot of what is being said directly to them.
Holophrases	12–18 months	Toddlers start to use one word in a variety of ways	The number of words that babies have increases slowly, but they make full use of the words that they have. The term holophrases is used to describe the way that toddlers will use one word in a range of situations but will adjust the tone of their voice and body language to help the adult understand its meaning. Most toddlers have 10–15 words by 18 months. By this time, toddlers have often learnt how to get an adult's attention and how to make them laugh.
Two-word utterances – telegraphic speech	18–24 months	Two words are put together to make a mini sentence	In this period, toddlers start to put two words together to create mini sentences. They seem to have grasped which are the key words in a sentence. - 'dada gone' or 'dada come'. At two years, most children will have around 50 words.

→

Table 3.5.1 Pattern of language development   (contd.)

Stage	Age	Features	Comments
Language explosion	24–36 months	A large increase in children's vocabulary combined with increasing use of sentences	Children's language develops rapidly, with children using new words each month. They move from having 50 words or so at two years to having 300–400 words at three years. At the same time, the child uses more complicated structures in their speech. Plurals and negatives begin to be used, e.g. dogs and sheep.
	3–4 years	Sentences become longer and vocabulary continues to increase	Children use language in a more complete way. Mistakes in grammar show that they are still absorbing the rules and sometimes misapplying them! Mistakes such as 'I wented' show that they have learnt that 'ed' makes a past tense. These types of mistakes are known as 'virtuous errors'. By this time, children are able to use their communication skills in order to socialise with others in simple ways. They may, for example, repeat a question if they think that they have not been understood.
Fluency	4–6 years	Mastered the basic skills of the language	Children have mastered the basic rules of English grammar and are fluent, although they will still be making some 'virtuous errors'. They may still struggle with pronouncing some letter sounds, particularly 'th' and 'r'.
Speech maturity	6–8 years	Mastered the reproduction of most sounds	During this period, children's language becomes clearer as their tongue, teeth and jaw develop. Children begin to use language to get their point of view across to others.

Relationships

The quality of relationships between adult and child can have a very significant impact on children's speech and language. When children have a strong relationship with an adult, they are more likely to want to communicate and talk. Where adults have strong relationships with children, they appear to be better at understanding babies and toddlers. They also seem to adjust their style of talking and body language so as to make it easier for children to understand. The link between relationships and language is one reason why most parents are very good at encouraging their children's speech. It is also why it is important that children spend sufficient time with their key person as, in theory, their key person will be good at working with them.

Quality and sufficient adult interaction

While we have seen that relationships play an important role in children's communication and language development, children also need sufficient time with those adults with whom they have a strong relationship. Babies in particular need plenty of adult interaction as they need to tune into the sounds of the language and also be encouraged to vocalise. While toddlers and older children do not need constant interaction with adults, they do need sufficient time as it is through adult interaction that their language continues to develop. In addition to the quantity of time, adults also have to be skilful in the way that they work.

→ We look at the skills needed in the next section on page 226.

Background noise

Background noise can impact on children's speech and language. In the first year of life, babies need to tune into the sounds of those who are directly talking to them. Music, radio or television can impact on this process. For children who are starting to talk, too much background noise seems to inhibit their desire to talk and so it is suggested that, wherever possible, noise should be reduced.

Figure 3.5.2 Adult interaction plays an important part in supporting children's language development

Screen time

While some time spent in front of a computer or television is unlikely to be harmful, when children spend more than two hours doing so, it seems to have an impact on their language. This is because learning to use language and communicate is an active two-way process. Spending time watching a DVD or following a computer program does not provide the type of interaction that young children need. This means that children who spend a lot of time engaged in screen activities are more likely to have a speech and language delay.

Hearing loss

Children need to be able to fully hear so that they can pick up the speech sounds and intonation that are used. Where children do not hear, they may also find it hard to reproduce speech sounds and therefore their speech is likely to be unclear, which prevents others from understanding them. There are two types of hearing loss: senso-neural and conductive.

Senso-neural hearing loss

Senso-neural hearing loss is a permanent hearing loss and is usually identified in the first months of a baby's life. It may result in a child wearing a hearing aid or having a cochlear implant.

Conductive hearing loss

While senso-neural hearing loss is fairly rare, conductive hearing loss is very common, especially glue ear. Glue ear is caused by fluid building up in the Eustachian tube, which runs from the outer ear to the inner ear. This prevents sounds from being heard distinctly. Children are more likely to have this type of hearing loss in the winter, especially after a cold. It is sometimes difficult to spot because it tends to come and go. It is important that it is recognised, though, because it does affect children's speech and understanding. There are many signs of conductive hearing loss, but you should be aware of the following:

- muffled speech
- intent staring at adults' lips
- varying levels of responsiveness
- slowness to react to instructions
- lack of interest in watching television
- being withdrawn
- aggression due to frustration.

AC 1.3 Working with others to support children's emergent literacy

Children's emergent literacy can be supported more effectively when early years settings work with others.

Parents

Parents play a huge role in the development of children's speech and language. It is parent's voices that children first hear and children's interest in learning to talk begins with this. Interestingly, parents are often good at tuning in accurately to their child's level of language and, in turn, children are very responsive to the attention of their parents. This means that, when parents spend time talking and chatting to their children, children's progress in communication and language is often smooth. In addition, when parents share books with their children, it seems to have a significant impact on children's interest and progress in reading. Parents play such an important role in children's emergent literacy, so it is essential to recognise this and to exchange information with them. Early years settings do this in a variety of ways, including lending books, creating story sacks and also sharing with parents books that their child has enjoyed in the setting.

Speech and language therapists

As speech and language are so important to literacy, children who are not making expected progress in their language or who may have difficulties in pronouncing or hearing certain letter sounds may need additional support. Speech and language therapists assess children's needs and offer advice or work directly with children to enable them to make progress.

Figure 3.5.3 Early years practitioners can support children's literacy by sharing with the parents books that the children have enjoyed

Occupational therapists

Some children may need additional support in order to cope with the physical process of literacy as they may have difficulties in coordinating or using the fine or gross motor skills associated with writing or holding a book. Occupational therapists who are involved with children will aim to maximise their movements and to find ways of helping children to access literacy.

LO2 Be able to support children's language and communication needs

When was the last time that someone really listened to you and gave you their full attention? For babies and young children, this is one of the most important things that adults can do. In this section, we look at how adults can support children's language and communication needs.

➔ You may wish to read this section alongside Unit 3.10, where we also look at children's communication and language.

AC 2.1 Develop a language-rich environment for children

A language-rich environment is one that prompts children to talk and communicate.

➔ We look at this in Unit 3.10 on pages 301–03 and you should read these pages alongside this section.

In the context of emergent literacy, a language-rich environment is one that prompts children to notice and to explore print. Early years settings do this in a variety of ways. They may provide an attractive book corner for children to look at books with adults or independently. They may also put up signs to help children become familiar with print. You are also likely to find that many early years settings help children to learn to recognise their name by having name cards and by writing children's names on paintings or drawings. As well as providing plenty of opportunities for children to see print, a language-rich environment also encourages children to explore mark-making and early writing. Most early years settings will create a writing area with paper, envelopes and pens and other prompts to encourage children to write. In other areas, they may also provide white boards, chalk or notepads so that children can enjoy writing.

AC 2.2 Interaction and children's language and communication needs

The way that we interact can have a significant influence on children's language and communication. The starting point, as we have already seen, is our relationships with children, but there are other skills that are important too.

Figure 3.5.4 How adults interact with children has a significant effect on children's language development

Figure 3.5.5 Adults should show interest in children and give them their full attention

Mirroring

One of the ways that we can interact with children is by mirroring their facial expressions and gestures. This means that if a child is looking slightly unsure, we could mirror this look back to them. If a child is making an action for a choo-choo train, we could copy them.

Tone of voice

The tone of voice that adults use makes a difference to children. The tone will of course depend on the situation, but we should aim for tuneful and soft tones. Tuneful voices help imitate the beat and rhythm of language and so help babies and children break into the sounds of the language. On the other hand, harsh, loud tones distort sounds and so can be a barrier to communication. Monotone voices do not provide any cues for children and so children's interest often wanes.

Interest

Quality interactions also require interest. Adults can show interest by smiling, making eye contact and listening carefully to children. It is therefore important to get down to children's eye level and to give children your full attention.

Recasting

Recasting is a skill that allows children to hear a correct version of what they have said. It also allows children to feel that they have been listened to. To recast a phrase, simply repeat back to the child what they have said but using the correct words. For example, the child says, 'My dad goed' and the adult recasts back, 'Yes, your dad went.'

Expansion

Another skill to use when interacting with children of all ages is expansion. It helps children to hear a longer and more sophisticated version of what they have said. Expansion also acts as a way of recognising what children have said. An example of expansion would be if a child says, 'Me not like dat' and the adult repeats back, 'No, you don't like broccoli, do you?'

Figure 3.5.6 It is important to listen to children and give them plenty of time to respond

Questioning

While questions can be helpful, it is not a good idea to overuse them as it can prevent natural conversations. Questions should be used to clarify rather than to check children's knowledge.

Response time

Children need plenty of response time, especially babies and children who have language delay. It is important to give children sufficient response time to allow them the time to understand what has been said and also to form their thoughts and words in response.

LO3 Understand strategies which support emergent literacy

Have you ever seen a child who is 'reading' a book that he is holding upside down? As well as being amusing, it is a good sign as it

means that the child is beginning to enjoy books. In this section, we look at the range of strategies that are used to support children's emergent literacy.

AC 3.1 Current frameworks and strategies to support the development of emergent literacy

The EYFS does not give any specific strategies for developing emergent literacy, but there is a range of strategies that can be used to support children's emergent literacy in early years settings. The strategies outlined in Table 3.5.2 on the next page focus on giving children the skills they need so that they will be ready for the literacy programmes in reception and Year 1.

AC 3.2 Systematic synthetic phonics in teaching reading

The current approach used to teach children to read in England is known as phonics. Children learn to associate a letter or group of letters with a sound – for example, c-a-t. There are different types of phonic teaching, but the one currently used in most schools is known as synthetic phonics. Synthetic phonics teaches children to look at each letter or group of letters separately and to blend or 'synthesise' them together. While there are different synthetic programmes being used in schools, every programme has a clear structure so that children learn 'sounds' in a particular order – that is, systematically. Most phonics teaching begins in the reception year and carries on into Year 1. Usually, phonics is taught each day for around 15 minutes and taught separately from other curriculum activities. This is thought to be the most effective way of teaching phonics. If you are working in a reception class, it will be important to find out more about the programme that the school is using as there are slight variations between them. It is also helpful to understand some of the terms used in the teaching of phonics as these will be used by teaching staff and also in the programme – see Table 3.5.3 on the next page.

Table 3.5.2 Strategies for developing emergent literacy

Modelling of writing	Adults often write words or label displays and photographs in front of children.
Scribing	Adults write down what children want to say about a picture or something that they have done.
Mark-making opportunities	A variety of different opportunities for children to make marks are provided, including paintbrushes and water, dried rice, make-up brushes and shaving foam on a tray with sticks.
Writing tables	Adults set up opportunities for writing with markers, pens and a variety of pads and paper. This can be part of role play, e.g. an office or a card-making workshop.
Hand movements	Adults put out a range of equipment that will help children to develop the hand movements needed to hold a pencil, e.g. pincer grasp. Activities might include threading and picking up small items such as sequins from a bowl of chickpeas using tweezers or finger and thumb.
Sound games	Adults plan sound games as a strategy to promote children's auditory discrimination. They may play 'I spy' or ask children to find an object in a basket that begins or ends with a particular speech sound.
Nursery rhymes	Adults plan nursery rhymes to promote auditory discrimination. They look for particular sounds in rhymes and, as they say them with the children, draw children's attention to the sound.
Story sacks	Adults encourage children's interest in books by creating story sacks that have a book and some props inside.
Sharing books	Adults encourage children's knowledge of print by sharing books with them. They may choose books that focus on particular sounds or words. They may encourage children to point at specific words.

Table 3.5.3 Terms used in the teaching of phonics

Term	Explanation
grapheme	The sound made by a letter or group of letters, e.g. '-tion' sounds likes 'shun'
phoneme	The smallest unit of sound, e.g. 'fl' can be broken down into the phonemes 'f' and 'l'
digraph	Two letters that come together to create a new sound, e.g. 'ch'
blend	Draw phonemes together to create a word, e.g. s-n-i-p are blended together to create 'snip'
segment	Split up words into separate phonemes – this skill is needed for spelling
CVC	This an abbreviation for words made up of consonant-vowel-consonant, e.g. c-a-t or p-a-t. These are the first words that children learn to read and also segment for spelling.

Figure 3.5.7 A synthetic phonics helps children make links between sounds and letters

Research it!

Find out from your local reception class how they teach synthetic phonics.

AC 3.3 How the early years practitioner provides opportunities for sustained shared thinking

Sustained shared thinking is the process by which, through talk, we explore a topic or problem with a child. In terms of emergent literacy, early years settings will do this when adults share a book with a child and also when supporting children's mark-making. Sustained shared thinking is also used when listening to children read once they are in school.

Sharing books with children

Shared sustained thinking when sharing books means talking to children about the pictures and the story together and interpreting what is happening. Interestingly, children often notice small details or have their own ideas about what is happening and why. It is important to listen carefully to children and allow them to take their time when they are formulating their thoughts. It is also helpful, when appropriate, to link what is in the book to children's own lives. For example: 'I think that Stephen brought in one of those the other day. Do you think it is the same?'

Supporting mark-making

It is good practice for early years settings to provide plenty of opportunities for children to explore mark-making. It is also an opportunity for shared sustained thinking as adults can talk to children about the marks they have made. They also help children to make connections between what they want to write and the letter sounds and shapes needed.

Supporting children's reading

When children first start to read, they need a lot of adult input. This is a time when sustained shared thinking can be used to help children solve some of the problems they encounter as they read. An adult might ask a child to look back at the same word that he has already read or talk about the possible meaning of a word.

Figure 3.5.8 Books without words can help children to think about what they are seeing

LO4 Be able to use strategies to plan and lead activities which support emergent literacy

AC 4.1 Strategies to plan activities

There is a range of ways in which we can use different strategies to plan activities that will promote children's emergent writing.

AC 4.2 Leading activities to support and extend emergent literacy

In order to lead an activity, it is important to think carefully about the age/stage of the child or children that you are working with. Young children who are not writing, for example, will need mark-making activities, while children who are just starting to write sounds will need some extension activities. You should also remember that all activities need to be of interest to children and

Table 3.5.4 Examples of activities that will promote children's emergent writing

Area of emergent literacy	Activities
Speaking and listening	• Singing nursery rhymes with props such as 'Ten green bottles', 'Ten currant buns' and 'Pop goes the weasel!' • Playing sound games such as 'Hunt the thimble', 'I spy' and 'Find the matching sounds'
Reading	• Setting up a role-play library for children to borrow books and share them with adults • Hiding letter shapes or words in the sand for children to find • Using story
Sustained shared thinking	• Setting up treasure hunts with written clues for children to use to find 'treasure' • Making recipe books with children following a cooking activity
Writing	• Posting letters to Teddy • Writing invitations to a party • Mark-making activities, such as paintbrushes and water, make-up brushes with dried rice
Digital literacy	• Creating a talking book for children about an outing that they have been on • Using computer games to help children match letters and sounds • Looking at letter sounds using a smart board • Using a smart board to drag names to match children's photographs

Figure 3.5.9 Making marks with sponges and soapy water is a popular activity

so this is why role play, treasure hunts or games with props tend to be used. As well as thinking about the age/stage and interest of children, there are other factors to think about when leading an activity:

Response time

How quickly children respond to questions or remember a shape or letter sounds depends partly on their age and familiarity with what you are doing. It is important when working with groups of children to remember that even children of the same age will have different response times. This means that you should not create situations when children who are lucky to be responding quickly are always chosen. You should also not assume that a child has not understood if they do not respond straight away because some children will take more time than others to process information.

Adapting activities

As we have seen in other chapters, it is important to be ready to adapt activities if children are not enjoying them. It is also beneficial to allow children to come up with their own ways of doing activities as this usually allows them to absorb a concept more easily.

AC 4.3 The benefits to children's holistic learning and development

There are many benefits to children's overall learning and development when we support children's emergent literacy.

Personal, social and emotional development

There are many benefits to children's personal, social and emotional development when supporting children's emergent literacy. Firstly, children will

Figure 3.5.10 Mark making is the first step toward children learning to write

have plenty of opportunities to spend time with an adult as many activities, such as sharing a book, require adult input. Activities such as mark-making also allow children to express emotions as well as improve their confidence.

Physical development

The mark-making activities that are used to support children's early writing skills, such as using sensory materials, will also help children's fine motor movements.

Communication and language

As we have seen earlier in this unit, communication and language are the starting points for emergent literacy. This means that by sharing books, singing rhymes and also providing opportunities for early writing and mark-making, children's communication and language are also supported.

Cognitive development

Children's cognitive development is supported through emergent literacy. This is because writing is an abstract concept as sounds are translated into marks. The abstract nature of print therefore extends children's thinking. Through sharing books, children can also learn about a range of things, including animals, colours, shapes and places.

Reflect

Make a list of ways in which literacy supports your day-to-day life.

LO5 Be able to review how planned activities support emergent literacy

Have you ever carried out an activity that went brilliantly? It can be tricky to know why some activities work well, while others fall flat. This section looks at how you might review your planned activities and reflect on them.

AC 5.1 Current frameworks and evaluating how planned activities support emergent literacy

As part of the planning process, it is good practice to work out how the activity links to the different areas of learning and development within the EYFS or the National Curriculum. During and after an activity, you should think about the extent to which children benefited from it. To help you evaluate a planned activity, here are some tips.

Think about each child

When evaluating planned activities that several children participated in, think about each child's level of interest and learning. This is needed later on in order to plan future activities for individual children.

→ See page 253.

Think about what children learnt from the activity

This can sometimes be tricky to evaluate because some learning is not immediately seen and it may not be until afterwards that we see the impact of an activity. A good example of this is when you share a book with a child. While the child might appear to be interested at the time, we may not be able to tell just how much information she has taken in. However, if later on we see the same child with the book pointing aloud to the words and pictures, we can gain a clearer idea of what they have learnt. Table 3.5.5 shows some examples of the skills that you might notice.

AC 5.2 The practitioner's role in planned activities

During and after an activity, it is good practice to reflect on your role. You may, for example, have recognised that the activity was interesting and enjoyable for children, but by reflecting on your role, you may be able to work out what you did that made it so. In the same way, if an activity did not work out in the way that you had

Table 3.5.5 Observing children's literacy skills

Speaking and listening	• Able to listen to a story and understand its meaning • Able to retell a story or event • Able to follow two-part instructions, e.g. put your coat on and then stand by the door • Able to repeat a nursery rhyme • Able to hear rhyming words • Able to complete a rhyme • Able to identify particular sounds in words
Reading	• Able to recognise own name • Able to recognise other words in environment • Able to match words, e.g. pairs • Able to turn pages in a book • Able to follow print from left to right • Able to recognise some letter shapes and say their sounds • Able to read some simple CVC words
Writing	• Able to make rotational anti-clockwise marks • Able to make vertical lines going downwards • Able to make shapes that go from left to right • Able to create some letter shapes • Able to write own name • Able to attempt writing using sound knowledge

Table 3.5.6 Analysing your role

Planning	• Did you know exactly what the activity involved? • Did you have all the resources to hand? • Did you plan for the right group size? • Did you choose the right children for this activity?
During the activity	• How did you introduce children to the activity? • Did you respond warmly to the children? • How did you encourage interaction and participation? • How did you ensure that the activity was enjoyable for each child? • Did you focus children on the aspects of emergent literacy that you planned for?
After the activity	• Did you ensure that the area of the activity was left in an appropriate state? • Did you ensure that information gained about individual children's learning was recorded? • Did you feed back to others about individual children's learning?

hoped, you might be able to identify why that was and so be able to improve your practice for another time. Table 3.5.6 shows some questions that might help you to reflect on and analyse your role.

AC 5.3 Recommendations to meet children's individual literacy needs

Young children have a lot of skills to learn in order to read and write. It is important when carrying out activities to think about what the next steps might be for each child. Sometimes, the recommendations for a child would be to repeat an activity, provided that they enjoyed it, to allow them to become more confident. The recommendations for each child will, of course,

depend on the type of activity that was planned, but here are some points to think about:

• Which aspects of the activity did the child seem to enjoy? This is important because, if you know what the child enjoyed, you can then tailor another activity to incorporate the same aspects.
• Which aspects of the activity did the child find easy? Thinking about the aspects that a child has mastered will help you to recognise that a child may be ready for an additional challenge.
• Which aspects of the activity was the child able to complete with support? Learning the skills involved in literacy does require practice. Some children may need to repeat the same or a similar activity a few times in order that they can become secure with the concepts and skills.
• Which aspects of the activity did the child find difficult? This may mean either that the child was not ready for this element within the activity or that they need further practice.

LO6 Be able to work with parents/carers in a way which encourages them to take an active role in their child's play, learning and development

AC 6.1 Encouraging parents/carers to take an active role in their child's play, learning and development

In Unit 2.5, we looked at ways in which early years settings might help parents take an active role in their children's play, learning and development. We also saw that it is a requirement of the EYFS for the key person to do this so that parents can support their children at home. In terms of emergent literacy, there are many ways in which we can work with parents.

Sharing stories

There is research to show that parents who spend time sharing books with their children will help make a difference to children's literacy. We can help parents by suggesting books that we know that their child will enjoy. Some early years settings will also lend books to parents or will let parents know about the local library so that they can borrow books from there.

Rhymes

We know that rhymes are great for helping children's auditory discrimination. In some settings, parents are sent the words of the rhymes that the children will be learning. This means that parents can practise rhymes with their child at home

Mark-making

Many early years settings will carry out information sessions so that parents know about the importance of mark-making and how best to help their child with their handwriting.

Day-to-day discussions

Many early years settings will talk to parents about their child's development. As part of these ongoing discussions, the key person can talk about how the setting approaches literacy and give parents ideas for home. In some settings, learning journeys are used as a starting point for these discussions as parents can look at observations or notes about their child's interest in books, rhymes or mark-making. The key person can then suggest ways of supporting this further at home.

Assessment

To complete this unit you are likely to be given a variety of tasks. Learning Outcomes 1 and 2 link closely to Unit 3.10 so you may find it useful to read it alongside this unit. For Learning Outcomes 1 and 2 you will need to have a good understanding of the stages of children's communication and language, including the factors that affect children's language and communication. You also need to be able to explain how working with others will support children's early literacy skills. You could start off by rereading about that in this unit. It is also important to revise how best to create language-rich environment and interact with children as your assessor will need to see that you can do this.

For Learning Outcomes 3, 4 and 5 you need to know about the many ways settings promote early literacy and the role of synthetic phonics in the teaching of reading. As well as reading information provided in this unit, you can also find out more by visiting the website of the Literacy Trust (**www.literacytrust.org.uk**).

For Learning Outcome 4 you will need to show your assessor that you can plan a range of activities to support different aspects of emergent literacy. It will be worth talking to your placement supervisor about suitable activities and also to agree on one that your assessor could watch you carrying out. As practise makes perfect, think about trying out different activities and reflecting on your performance with your placement supervisor or an experienced colleague.

For Learning Outcome 5 you will also need to show that you can review planned activities. Get into the habit of planning in conjunction with the EYFS and, as a result of carrying out activities, thinking about what the next steps might be for individual children. Finally, you need to show that you can support parents taking an active role in their child's development in relation to emergent writing. Talk to your placement supervisor about the ways in which your work setting currently does this and see if you can practice doing this, too.

Useful resources

Books and journals

Conteh, J. (ed.) (2006), *Promoting Learning for Bilingual Pupils 3–11: Opening Doors to Success*. London: Sage.

Nyland, B., Ferris, J. and Dunn, L. (2008), 'Mindful hands, gestures as language: Listening to children', *Early Years* 28(1): 73–80.

Palmer, S. and Bayley, R. (2004), *Foundations of Literacy: A Balanced Approach to Language, Listening and Literacy Skills in the Early Years*. Edinburgh: Network Educational Press.

Siraj-Blatchford, I. Sylva, K., Melhuish, E.C., Sammons,P. and Taggart, B. (2004),*The Effective Provision of Pre-School Education (EPPE)*. London: DfES/Institute of Education, University of London.

Trevarthen, C. (2004), *Learning about Ourselves from Children: Why a Growing Human Brain needs Interesting Companions*. Perception-in-Action Laboratories, University of Edinburgh.

Whitehead, M. (2010), *Language and Literacy in the Early Years 0–7* (4th edn). London: Sage.

Unit 3.6 WB Developing children's emergent mathematical skills

How can young children effectively develop mathematical skills and what does this look like? In this unit, we will look at the way in which mathematics relates to the everyday lives of children. We will then explore the different ways in which skills develop and consider how early years practitioners can support early mathematical learning.

Learning outcomes

By the end of this unit, you will:

1 Understand how mathematics relates to children's everyday lives.
2 Understand how working with others supports children's emergent mathematical development.
3 Understand how to create an environment which supports children's emergent mathematical development.
4 Understand the role of the early years practitioner in relation to supporting children's emergent mathematical development.
5 Understand how opportunities support children's emergent mathematical development.
6 Be able to implement activities to support children's emergent mathematical development.
7 Be able to review how planned activities support children's emergent mathematical development.
8 Be able to work with parents/carers in a way which encourages them to take an active role in their child's play, learning and development.

LO1 Understand how mathematics relates to children's everyday lives

How can mathematics relate to the everyday lives of very young children? This section explores how different areas of mathematics tie in to many aspects of their lives, as well as exploring factors which will affect their learning.

AC 1.1 How mathematics is evident in children's everyday lives

From an early age, children are surrounded by mathematics and mathematical language: 'Haven't you grown!' 'It's time for bed,'

'You must be full by now!' Although we may not think of some of the areas listed in Table 3.6.1 as mathematical, they are all related to and form the basis of mathematical development in children. You will need to be able to recognise opportunities to engage children in mathematical thinking so that you can develop their ideas and support their understanding.

> **Reflect**
>
> Think about how many mathematical skills you use in a typical day and list them. This should also include the use of mathematical language – for example, filling up your car with petrol or looking at the alarm clock and realising you may be late!
>
> Feed back to your group.

Table 3.6.1 Areas of mathematics in everyday life

Mathematical area	Where it may be evident
Number	Numbers are all around us in the environment – from road signs, shop windows, clocks, bus numbers, television remote controls and phones, to street numbers and calendars.
Pattern	Patterns can be seen in different places – in wallpapers or fabrics, in tiles and paving stones, on keyboards, in plants. They are also evident in numbers, and the ability to see patterns and sequences is crucial to mathematical thinking.
Matching and sorting	Matching and sorting skills are used when washing, laying the table, arranging shoes or putting on clothing in pairs. Items can be matched and sorted according to colour, size or shape.
Shape and space	Shapes are all around us and can be seen both indoors and outdoors. Children also need to develop spatial awareness through activities such as jigsaw puzzles.
Measuring	Children will need to know, use and understand the language of bigger and smaller, lighter or heavier, longer or shorter, empty and full.
Problem solving	We often need to work things out – if my bag isn't big enough, is there another way of getting my shopping home? Children should be given problem-solving activities in order to develop their mathematical skills.
Time	Children will need to understand basic concepts of time – we often say 'Just a minute', but what does this mean to them? They will hear about days, weeks and months and will need this to be put into context.
Estimating	We often need to estimate different things – for example, how long something will take, whether something will fit or how much money we might need for a particular item.
Mathematical language	Mathematical language can be heard in many contexts – in any kind of comparison of quantities, e.g. in 'Measuring' above, or when describing position, e.g. on top of, next to, inside, around, as well as specific vocabulary when describing mathematical concepts such as shape, e.g. corners, edges, sides and so on.

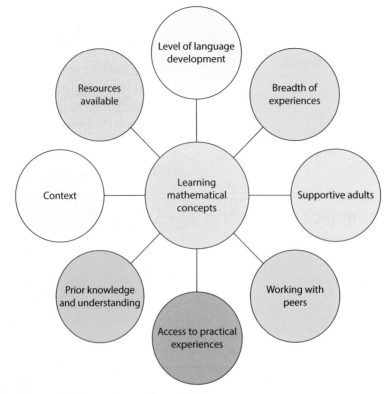

Figure 3.6.1 Learning mathematical concepts

AC 1.2 Factors that affect children learning mathematical concepts

Prior knowledge and understanding

Children who are learning mathematical concepts will need to have some prior knowledge in order to understand new ideas and have something to base these ideas on. For example, a child who is starting to learn about coins will need to have some knowledge of number to know what the coins represent; a child who is learning about shapes will need to have the vocabulary with which to describe them.

Context

Another key factor is that learning a new mathematical concept must make sense to the child. It will be difficult to understand the meaning of what they are being told without anything to relate it to. Adults will need to ensure that concepts are taught in familiar environments so that children are able to relate them to their experiences. An example might be learning about weight in the context of cooking, or learning about money in the context of shopping.

Resources available

If children have a variety of resources to support their learning, they will be able to consolidate what they have learnt in different ways. For example, they may be able to use computers to reinforce what they have learned about number, or carry out practical activities, such as those in 'Access to practical experiences' below.

Access to practical experiences

As mathematics is often talked about in an abstract way, children will need to have experienced practical activities before moving on to the abstract. An example for very young children might be sorting socks into pairs, creating patterns using peg boards or playing hopscotch to help them remember their numbers. These types of early practical experiences will also build children's confidence with using mathematics before they move on to more abstract ideas.

Level of language development

Children will find it difficult to learn mathematical concepts if they have not been exposed to the

Figure 3.6.2 This child is counting out the cakes

appropriate vocabulary. They will need to be able to talk about what they are doing and describe features of their work. A further challenge of mathematics is that it may use some familiar words in an unfamiliar context – for example, a table, a set, a pattern or a star.

Supportive adults

One of the key factors that will affect children's learning of mathematical concepts is the teaching, encouragement and support given to them by adults. It is vital that parents and carers as well as early years practitioners talk to children and support the development of their mathematical vocabulary in the early years so that they have a basis on which to form mathematical ideas. Supportive adults will engage with children about what is happening on a day-to-day basis so that they are able to make sense of what is happening in their world.

> **In your setting**
>
> Look at and list the kinds of practical mathematical experiences that are available to children in your setting. Are they adult-supported or child-initiated? How do you think they support children's learning of mathematical concepts?

Breadth of experiences

We know that children will thrive best in a stimulating environment and will need to have a broad range of experiences on which to base their understanding. Children who have had more experiences of everyday activities such as shopping (using money) or tidying up (sorting) will be able to relate to mathematical ideas more easily.

Working with peers

Children should have the opportunity to play with children of their own age so that they can reinforce their learning and language. Learning through play is one of the most important things that children can do as they are building up their mathematical skills in a non-threatening environment.

Children will need to learn mathematical topics in order, which means that they should be exposed to practical activities and language before the introduction of concepts and abstract ideas. In this way, they will have a better basis for building connections and supporting imagery.

→ There is more information about this in LO2.

Reflect

You have been asked to work with a group of four and five year olds on the subject of weighing. The learning objective is to find out and talk about heavier and lighter. You have a set of balance scales and need to tie your activity in to the current topic, which is 'Food around the world'. The children have not had any school experience of the subject of weighing before. How might you introduce the activity?

LO2 Understand how working with others supports children's emergent mathematical development

Why is it important for early years professionals to work with **others** to support children's emergent mathematical development? This section looks at the different ways in which adults can work with others to help young children to understand and develop mathematical concepts.

Key term

others Relates to parents, carers and other professionals.

AC 2.1 Working with others and children's mathematical development

Working with others means that you are able to collaborate with them to ensure that children achieve the best possible outcomes in all subject areas.

Early years workers will need to be able to work effectively with others so that they can support children's development in all areas, not just mathematics. The term 'others' relates to:

- colleagues and other professionals
- parents.

Colleagues

Effective communication is clearly the most important aspect of working with colleagues and other professionals. In a busy environment, there should be routines and systems in place to ensure that time is set aside to discuss planning, assessment and discussion of children's progress in all areas. Meeting times should be set as part of the weekly cycle so that it does not need to be found as 'additional time'.

Figure 3.6.3 Regular meetings should be set up to discuss planning and assessment of mathematics

You should be able to meet with others to plan the way in which mathematical concepts are taught and to consider resourcing. Such meetings can also be used to evaluate the way in which children have responded to the activities after they have been carried out.

➡ For more on planning and evaluating mathematics activities, see LO6 and LO7.

When planning work on early mathematical concepts, early years professionals will need to discuss with colleagues the progression which should take place in any given topic so that all members of staff are working together. For example, if you are planning activities to do with length, you should start by considering the vocabulary and the introductory activities associated with length.

Early progression of ideas: length

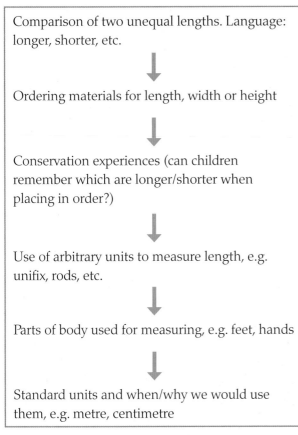

Comparison of two unequal lengths. Language: longer, shorter, etc.

⬇

Ordering materials for length, width or height

⬇

Conservation experiences (can children remember which are longer/shorter when placing in order?)

⬇

Use of arbitrary units to measure length, e.g. unifix, rods, etc.

⬇

Parts of body used for measuring, e.g. feet, hands

⬇

Standard units and when/why we would use them, e.g. metre, centimetre

Source: Lines of Development in Primary Mathematics, Mary Deboys and Eunice Pitt (Blackstaff Press, 1980)

All staff will need to know the progression of ideas and why these are important in mathematics – it is very important for children's understanding that ideas are approached in a particular order. At each stage in the example above, the children will be using the language of length and consolidating what they know through practical experiences. This is true of each mathematical topic.

➡ This will be looked at in more detail in LO5.

Parents and carers

You will need to ensure that you have clear lines of communication with parents and carers in your setting so that they are aware of the mathematical skills that are being delivered to their children. This should include communication about all areas of the curriculum and what children are learning at a particular time. In this way, parents and carers will be able to talk to children at home about what they are doing and share their learning. Settings may have different ways of doing this. For example, some may send home newsletters or have noticeboards, while others may upload topic outlines on their websites so that parents and carers are able to look at them. The Early Years Foundation Stage document emphasises the importance of sharing information in all curriculum areas: 'the range and type of activities and experiences provided for children, the daily routines of the setting, and how parents and carers can share learning at home'.

Reflect

- How does your setting communicate curriculum plans to parents and carers?
- Are there channels of communication so that parents and carers can feed back to the setting about children's development at home?
- What form does this take?

LO3 Understand how to create an environment which supports children's emergent mathematical development

How can early years workers create a supportive environment for the emergence of mathematical skills? This section explores ways in which adults can influence children's learning through the learning environment and the opportunities which they provide.

AC 3.1 Creating an environment in relation to current frameworks for children from birth to seven years

You will need to know how to create an environment in which children's early mathematical development is supported. This means that it should reflect the ideas and concepts which are being explored and allow children to explore them independently as well as through their work with adults. A supportive environment is one which prompts children to think about and explore mathematical concepts, and one which values their contributions and ideas. In a classroom or early years environment, this may take the form of a specific area of the setting which is dedicated to maths activities and resources. It should relate to current frameworks, which means that it should reflect the concepts explored in the Foundation Stage and Key Stage 1 curriculum.

Early Years Foundation Stage – the two areas of mathematics studied are number, and shape, space and measure.

The National Curriculum 2014 – the areas explored in Years 1 and 2 are number, geometry and measurement; in Year 2, statistics (the interpretation of charts and diagrams) is also studied.

In a typical maths area of the learning environment, there might be resources for different maths topics – for example, time, weight, shape, capacity, length, pattern and sequencing, as well as number. Children should be able to access the resources and they should be clearly labelled. Depending on the topic, displays might focus on a particular area – for example, if telling stories to do with maths, you may choose to have a wall display for *Goldilocks and the Three Bears*, including bowls, chairs and beds of different sizes and also the specific vocabulary. In Years 1 and 2, there may be topic vocabulary on the wall to support the area of study that children are exploring. An early years environment may also have a maths area in the outdoor classroom, giving children opportunities to work on open-ended practical activities outdoors.

Figure 3.6.4 The environment in which children learn should support mathematical development

In your setting

Look around your setting – is there a specific area dedicated to maths? How does the environment support children's emergent maths skills and allow them to explore mathematical concepts independently?

LO4 Understand the role of the early years practitioner in relation to supporting children's emergent mathematical development

What is the role of the early years practitioner in relation to supporting children's mathematical development? This section examines the ways in which early years practitioners enable children to explore mathematical concepts in a supportive environment.

AC 4.1 Scaffolding children's mathematical development

Key term

scaffolding Setting opportunities that are relevant, meaningful and purposeful for the children with varying adult intervention.

Can you remember learning mathematical ideas in school? Unfortunately, it is common for adults to have lasting negative ideas about mathematics due to the way in which concepts were presented to us as children. It is therefore very important that we are able to **scaffold** children's learning in such a way that they do not feel confused or lose their enthusiasm for mathematics. Children who are learning mathematical skills will need supportive adults who recognise the importance of this and are able to foster feelings of interest and achievement in the subject.

There are three key reasons that early years practitioners should scaffold children's early mathematical development:

- to build their confidence
- to make maths meaningful to them
- to encourage them to talk about mathematics and develop and extend their ideas.

To build their confidence

Adults should build children's confidence in mathematics at every opportunity as it is easy for children to feel discouraged or feel that they are unable to do it. Unfortunately, mathematics is a subject in which we may quickly feel that we are 'unable' to work on ideas if we are not supported sensitively. We can help to build children's confidence in a number of ways:

- Listen to children when they are talking to you about maths. Engage with them and respond to what they are saying with interest.
- Make sure you talk through ideas with them and support their learning so that you can reassure them about what they are doing.
- Take time to get to know children and find out about any specific interests so that you can help them to extend their thinking.

To make maths meaningful to them

Adults will need to ensure that mathematics is presented in a way which is meaningful to them and their experiences. This means that they should be put in context as much as possible so that children can see when they would use the mathematical skill they are developing. As children grow older and learn more complex and abstract mathematical ideas, this becomes more difficult, but at the earliest stages we should always ensure that we give children tasks that make sense to them.

To encourage them to talk about mathematics and develop and extend their ideas

Young children need to develop their ideas through talking about what they are doing to broaden and develop their mathematical vocabulary. Early years practitioners should extend their ideas wherever possible – in other words, take them to the next level or stage.

In all of these examples, early years practitioners should intervene where necessary, and not as a matter of course. This is because children will benefit from working independently as well as talking things through with their peers.

Case study

Rania, aged four, is working in the sand tray and exploring the dry sand using containers of different sizes. She is working on her own and is pouring from one container to another. She turns to Michael, an adult at the next table who is working with a group of children, and says, 'Look, I can put much more sand in this jug than this one!' Michael turns to her and says, 'Rania, be careful! You are getting sand all over the floor!'

- Why shouldn't Michael react in this way?
- What could Michael have said to extend Rania's learning?

In practice

Think about the ways in which you scaffold children's mathematical development through the way in which you talk to and question them. Do you use all of the methods described above?

AC 4.2 Valuing individual interests when supporting children's emergent mathematical development

Children will come to the setting with their own individual interests and ideas, some of which will be related to maths. This starting point is a very powerful one for providing opportunities for mathematical activities. You should always value what children have to say, whatever their interests, and encourage them through talking or allowing them to talk to their peers about them, for the following reasons:

- **To retain their enthusiasm** – children who have a particular interest in maths will usually be enthusiastic and want to talk about it. You should always listen to and support their enthusiasm so that it does not become lost.
- **To develop their curiosity** – adults can question children about their interests and encourage them to be more curious about aspects of their learning.
- **To increase their confidence** – whatever children practise, they will become good at. It is very important that we support the development of children's confidence as it can diminish if adults do not respond appropriately.
- **To give them opportunities to extend their learning** – we can help children to extend their learning by encouraging them to think about what might happen next or to find patterns in what they are learning.

Case study

Luis has started in the reception class and clearly enjoys working on mathematical ideas. He is very able in maths – he can count past 50 and write many of the numbers without help. He is also very interested in shape and knows the names of many 2D and 3D shapes. Luis often enjoys working with construction materials and regularly comes to you with models, telling you all about them.

- How can you value Luis' interests and achievements in the early years environment?
- Why is it important that early years practitioners do this?

AC 4.3 How the early years practitioner provides opportunities for sustained shared thinking

Key term

sustained shared thinking Supporting children to solve problems and to apply new learning to their mathematical development.

Early years practitioners will also need to provide children with opportunities for **sustained shared thinking**. This means that children should have the chance to carry out problem-solving activities and to use their mathematical skills in different ways. Adults can use this as a way of finding out how methodical children are in their working and look at the different ways in which children approach these kinds of tasks.

Examples of sustained shared thinking are activities in which children work together on real-life problems and use what they know to solve them. These can be carried out both indoors and outdoors and children should be encouraged to ask questions and talk about the problem as a group. Examples of problem-solving activities are as follows:

- Bring in a tray of assorted animals, five of each type, with one animal missing. Ask the children how they will find the missing animal.
- Share food between two soft toy animals – for example, six dog biscuits between two dogs. Then add a third dog. Ask the children what happens now.
- Tell the children that, for example, Sarah has two sisters. Ask them how many children her parents have. Give different scenarios for the children to work out.

Often the best problem-solving activities occur as part of the day-to-day running of the setting:

- Our soft toy/football is stuck in a tree/on a roof. What is the best way to get it down?
- I have 25 bananas and 30 children and everyone wants a banana. What should I do?

Figure 3.6.5 Outdoor activities can be set up to support children's mathematical learning

In practice

Plan and carry out a problem-solving activity with a group of children in your setting and feed this back to your group. How did the activity support the development of children's mathematical skills?

Research it!

For more ideas for problem-solving activities in the early years, investigate the NRICH website: **www.nrich.maths.org/early-years**.

LO5 Understand how opportunities support children's emergent mathematical development

Early years practitioners will need to use different strategies to support the development of mathematical concepts in young children. You will need to be aware of different strategies that can be used as well as opportunities available to you to support the development of their ideas.

AC 5.1 Current frameworks for children from birth to seven years and strategies to support emergent mathematical development

Key term

strategies Recognised approaches which can be applied to mathematical learning.

Early years practitioners will need to be able to use a range of **strategies** to support children's emergent mathematical development. These will be through a range of planned activities and also through opportunities which arise on a daily basis.

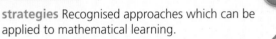 For more on opportunities that arise on a daily basis, see AC 5.2.

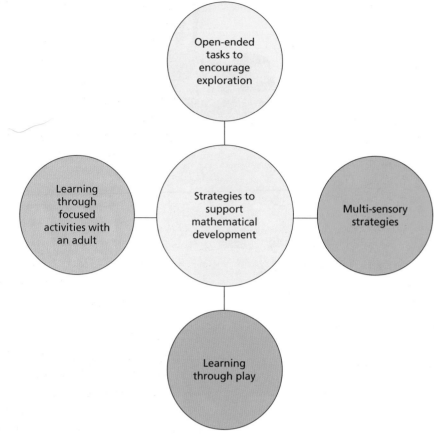

Figure 3.6.6 Strategies to support mathematical development

The kinds of strategies that adults might use in the Early Years Foundation Stage and Key Stage 1 to support the EYFS framework and the mathematics area of the 2014 National Curriculum are shown in Figure 3.6.6.

Learning through play

Children should be given plenty of opportunities to learn through play in the early years. There should be a range of high-quality activities for children to choose from so that they can develop their mathematical skills. It is also vital that children should have a chance to play with and explore new equipment and resources before being asked to use them in a particular way.

Learning through focused activities with an adult

Working with adults is the best way for us to be sure which children have understood a particular mathematical skill. We are able to talk things through with children to ensure that they are clear on any concepts which have been introduced and also extend their learning by taking them further if they pick them up easily. As well as checking their learning while they are working with children, early years practitioners can also support children by explaining and reinforcing the correct use of mathematical vocabulary.

Case study

Danny and Sheniz are playing in the role-play area. It has been set up as a pet shop for children to use and includes a till, a variety of different soft animals, pet carriers, clipboards and writing materials, balance scales, receipts, pet foods and so on.

- What kinds of opportunities to use mathematical skills do you think would be available in this context?
- Apart from role play, can you think of other ways in which children can use play to develop mathematical skills?

Open-ended tasks to encourage exploration

These kinds of tasks are those which encourage children to use mathematical skills but which do not have an obvious outcome – for example, leaving counters and other mathematical equipment as well as tweezers and numbered pots for children to play with, or putting out different items and egg boxes so that children can sort using their own criteria.

Multi-sensory strategies

Early years practitioners need to ensure that they provide multi-sensory activities in order to improve other areas of children's development as well as maths – for example, cutting up play dough into different lengths is also beneficial for children's fine motor skills, and counting how many skips they can do also develops their gross motor skills.

AC 5.2 Supporting children's understanding of mathematical concepts and vocabulary

Early years practitioners should take advantage of different opportunities throughout their work with children to support and reinforce children's understanding of mathematical concepts as well as the vocabulary used. Depending on the kinds of topics they are working on with children, there will be many opportunities for them to include different mathematical concepts during their daily practice.

Number

There are a large number of opportunities in which children's understanding of number can be supported on a daily basis, as they are so prevalent in all aspects of their day. From the start of the day in the setting, early years practitioners can use counting activities: 'How many children are here today?' 'How many children will be having lunch/a snack/going outside?' They should also be exposed to counting and number songs on a daily basis to reinforce their knowledge of number.

Shape, size and pattern

Early years practitioners should give children opportunities to handle and play with different shapes and to create patterns using different resources, such as peg boards, two-dimensional shapes and other mathematical equipment, through open-ended activities that are undirected. They should also point out patterns which can be found in the natural environment, such as looking in detail at leaves and flowers. Patterns should also be pointed out to children when working in other areas such as music, art or dance so that they are able to recognise them in different contexts.

Weight, volume and capacity

Children should have opportunities to experiment and play with different containers and objects as part of their free play in sand and water, as well as through structured activities that enable them to explore different concepts.

Space and time

Early years practitioners should talk to children about events in time, where possible, in order to develop their vocabulary, as learning the different words to do with time is the first step in learning about the concept of time. For example, when greeting the children in the morning or afternoon, practitioners can ask what day it is and put this in context for the rest of the week – 'What day was it yesterday?', 'What day will it be tomorrow?', 'How long until the weekend?'. Routines are also a good way for children to develop an understanding of time as it is through these that time develops meaning. Practitioners can develop an idea of time through talking with children about how long something will take. For example, 'How many jumps can you do before the egg timer runs through?' or 'How many skips before it is time to go in from lunch?'

Matching and sorting

Children should be able to sort items using different criteria, and early years practitioners can also find ways in which to talk about things which go together.

Data representation

As part of topic work, children may be able to collect data and organise them into charts and graphs. For example, 'How many children in our class have blue eyes?' or 'How many children like eating apples?' **However, there is no statutory requirement under the 2014 National Curriculum for children to gather data and represent them using graphs and diagrams until Year 2**.

Problem solving

Children will often respond enthusiastically to problem-solving activities, and they are a good opportunity to extend children's learning and encourage them to think differently. The advantage of problem-solving activities is that there is often no 'right' or 'wrong' answer, and children can be encouraged to find different ways of arriving at an answer without feeling that they have approached it in the wrong way.

→ For more on problem-solving activities, see page 246.

> **Test yourself** ✓
>
> Outline six strategies and examples of activities you could use to support the development of mathematics in relation to current frameworks.

LO6 Be able to implement activities to support children's emergent mathematical development

Where can we start when implementing activities which support children's emerging mathematical development? As an early years practitioner, you will need to know about different forms of planning and how to use it. This section explores the ways in which we can plan and lead mathematical activities with children.

AC 6.1 Planning activities to support children's emergent mathematical development

Planning is usually divided into long-term, medium-term and short-term planning: long term for the year, medium term for termly or half-termly, and short term, which is divided into topics or weeks. Finally, you will need to have a daily plan. When planning an activity, you should also try to link it to your topic or medium-term plan so that it is put into context for the children. For example, if

Table 3.6.2 Activities that support children's emergent mathematical development

Area of mathematics	Activity
Number	• Counting songs and nursery rhymes, such as 'Five little speckled frogs', 'Alice the camel', '1, 2, 3, 4, 5, Once I caught a fish alive' • Opportunities to count using a variety of resources, such as natural materials • Board games that use numbers • Displays showing numbers, which children can use in their play
Pattern	• Children should look for patterns in the environment and around the setting or school – they can do this using a digital camera and then display them • Looking for patterns and repetition in wallpaper/wrapping paper • Making patterns using beads and peg boards or painting/printing
Matching and sorting	• Different receptacles for sorting, e.g. fairy cake baking trays, egg boxes, plastic bowls or baskets • A variety of items which can be sorted by different criteria, e.g. colour, shape or size • Clearly labelled trays or baskets so that children can pick their own resources
Shape and space	• Printing using different shapes • Making shape pictures using coloured paper • Looking for shapes in the environment and photographing them →

Table 3.6.2 Activities that support children's emergent mathematical development (contd.)

Area of mathematics	Activity
Measuring	• Finding different things to measure and ways to measure them. Start with the children themselves. Have a permanent display so that they can see how much they are growing • Measuring beans/other plants they may be growing • Measuring areas of the classroom
Problem solving	See activities on page 246.
Time	• Using a countdown timer at tidy-up time • Using tidy-up music – when it goes on, children need to finish tidying up before it finishes • How many hops/skips can you do in one minute?
Estimating	• How many of these yoghurt pots will it take to fill this container? • How much do you think you will grow while you are in reception?
Mathematical language	Mathematical language should be used in all activities with children and you should be clear on the kind of vocabulary you will be using before you start.
Technology	• Using computer programs that encourage mathematical skills • Using giant calculators to promote number recognition • Using a smart board to reinforce mathematical learning

your topic is 'Animals', you might plan to carry out different activities that involve animals.

If you are planning to carry out a mathematical activity with young children, you will need to be clear about what you are hoping the children will get out of it before you start. You should think carefully about the age and stage of development of the children that you are working with and also where the activity links to areas of learning and development in the EYFS or the National Curriculum.

In your setting

How would you go about starting to plan an activity to support children's mathematical development? Do you have access to long-term and medium-term plans to help you?

AC 6.2 Leading activities to support children's emergent mathematical development

If you are leading the activity, you should be clear that any adults who are working on the activity with children know exactly what their role is and have

a copy of your plan. The kinds of headings to think about should include:

• what you want children to learn
• the role of adults
• resources needed
• next steps for learning.

While working on the activity, you should also be able to adapt or change activities if children are not responding as you would hope, or if they are not enjoying them. This may mean simplifying them if they do not understand, or just allowing them more time to play before taking them to the next stage.

Case study

Leanne is working with two children on a problem-solving activity in which they have to use positional language to put toys on different shelves – for example, 'The car is above the doll,' 'The doll is in between the car and the skipping rope,' and so on. She has found that one of the children is struggling with the activity and is starting to be distracted away from the task.

• What could you do in this situation to adapt the activity for the child?
• How could you do this while encouraging the other child with what they are doing?

Table 3.6.3 Example of a planning document for EYFS

Foundation Class B	
Date: 23 January 2014	**Time:** 9.30–10.30

Focus areas of learning: For children to start to use everyday language relating to weight and have the opportunity to use balance scales.

What do I want the children to learn?

To be able to use the terms 'lighter than' and 'heavier than'.

Why do we need to weigh things? When would we weigh them?

Prior learning: No previous school experience of weighing but start by gauging prior experience.

Activity:

Choose a volunteer to stand at front with arms out to hold two shopping bags – one with heavy items and one with light items inside. Ask children about the result and why it happens. See if anyone comes up with the terms heavier and lighter.

Introduction:

Discuss objective with children: Today we are learning about things that are heavy and light. We are going to look at different things in the classroom and outside and say which is heavier and which is lighter.

Show interactive whiteboard activity so that they see balance scales in action. Ask them to talk to their partner and discuss which animal will be heavier and which will be lighter in each case.

Show our balance scales and explain the activities which we will be carrying out in class.

Activities:

Teacher activity: with small groups of children. Allow children time to play with balance scales as they have not used them before/talk about what they are doing. Then continue by predicting outcome and using balance scales to find heavier and lighter items. Give them the opportunity to record what they have found out.

DH: Water tray – selection of heavy and light objects – predicting what will happen and why and allowing children to explore. See intervention sheet/record outcomes.

Independent activities:

- Two boxes at front of classroom labelled 'Heavy' and 'Light' – ask children to put items in during the lesson to investigate and check at end of session
- Builder's tray – diggers and gravel/sawdust
- Small world – dolls' house
- Construction – bricks
- Writing corner – variety of paper and pens
- Leave interactive activity on board for children to use if sensible

Outside – adult support:

RM outside with groups of six children at a time (working with two on focused activity using see-saw) – see recording sheet.

Also look for heavier and lighter items outside and bring in to put in boxes.

Role of adults: Encouraging correct use of vocabulary, keeping on task, extending children's learning where appropriate.

Key questions and vocabulary:

- How do you think we can do this task? How can you test out your ideas? Is there another way you could…?
- Which one do you think is heavier/lighter? Why? Are you surprised? Why/why not?
- What's different/what's the same?
- Do you think this will fit/be big enough?
- Can you weigh the box? What could we use to help us?
- Can you put them in order of weight? How can we do this?
- Which is heavier/ lighter/ bigger/ smaller? Could we arrange them in a different way?

Resources:

Balance scales, parcels and foods of varying sizes and weights, also feathers, logs, leaves, multilink

LO7 Be able to review how planned activities support children's emergent mathematical development

As a follow-up to planned mathematical activities, early years practitioners will need to show how they review the way in which they have supported children's emergent mathematical development. This section explores ways in which we can evaluate our work with children and plan their next steps for learning.

AC 7.1 Current frameworks and how planned activities support children's emergent mathematical development

It is always useful following an activity to think about how the children have benefited and the ways in which their learning has been adapted or extended. You will need to think about each child and what they have gained from an activity, based on their level of engagement and interest as well as skills that they have developed. Table 3.6.4 shows the kinds of skills that you might have worked on with children.

Table 3.6.4 Observing children's mathematical skills

Number	• Able to count reliably with numbers from 1 to 20 • Able to place numbers in order • Able to use some number names accurately in play • Able to say which number is one more or one less than a given number to 10, then 20 • Able to add and subtract two single-digit numbers • Able to solve problems including halving, doubling and sharing
Shape and space	• Able to use everyday language to talk about shape • Begin to use mathematical names for 2D and 3D shapes • Able to see shapes in the environment • Able to create shapes using different media • Able to describe relative position such as 'behind' or 'next to' • Able to engage in sustained construction activity
Patterns	• Able to recognise and describe patterns • Able to create patterns using different media
Matching and sorting	• Able to sort items using different criteria • Able to devise own criteria for sorting • Able to match different items and describe why they are together

Measuring	• Able to recognise and use the language of measuring for:
	  • lengths and heights
	  • mass and weight
	  • capacity and volume
	  • time

Time	• Able to order and sequence familiar events • Able to recognise and use language relating to dates and days
Problem solving	• Able to use what they know to solve problems

Figure 3.6.7 After an activity, such as cooking, you should evaluate how it benefited the child and what mathematical skills it helped them develop – in this case, weighing

AC 7.2 The practitioner's role in planned activities supporting children's emergent mathematical development

Following your work with children, you should reflect on your role and how the activity went. This should include whether you felt that children met the objectives and enjoyed the activity. If they did and it went to plan, you may be able to work out ways in which you contributed to this through your role. If it did not go well, you may be able to work out why this happened and amend your plan for next time. Table 3.6.5 has some questions which may support your reflection on the activity.

Table 3.6.5 Analysing your role

Planning	• Did the activity have a clear plan? • Did it fit in with other aspects of your topic? • Did you have all the resources you needed for the activity? • Was the activity for all children or a differentiated few?
During the activity	• Did you encourage the participation of all children? • Did you use questioning effectively? • Did you ensure that the children were focused on the learning objective? • Did you adapt the activity if necessary?
After the activity	• Did you ensure that you recorded information about children's learning? • Did you talk to children about how they felt about the activity? • Did you feed back information on children's learning and next steps?

AC 7.3 Recommendations to meet children's emergent mathematical needs

Children's mathematical needs are developing all the time and, as you carry out activities with them, you will need to have a clear idea about their next steps for learning. Your evaluation and analysis of mathematical activities should always include recommendations for next steps for each child and whether they need more work on specific concepts or whether they are ready to move on. You should think about their learning in relation to the following:

- **Whether the child enjoyed the activity**: if activities are based around the child's interests, they are far more likely to be engaged in it. You may find that you can tie in the child's interests to make the activity more enjoyable for them and focus their concentration more effectively.

- **Whether the child found the activity easy**: if the task was easy for the child, you should ensure that their next steps include a further challenge as they develop their mathematical skills in this area.

- **Whether the child needed support**: the child may have needed some help to complete the activity and this means that they may need to repeat it or a similar type of activity in order to consolidate what they have learned.

- **Whether the child found aspects of the activity difficult**: if this is the case, the child may not have been ready for this aspect of learning or they may need to practise further.

Case study

You have been working on an ordering activity with Jamaal, who is particularly interested in trains. As part of the activity, he needs to put different items in length order. However, he is not enjoying the activity and is losing interest.

- How could you make the activity more enjoyable for Jamaal?
- Why is it important to adapt the activity in this case?

LO8 Be able to work with parents/carers in a way which encourages them to take an active role in their child's play, learning and development

→ See also AC 2.1 on working with others on page 242.

When working with children on mathematical ideas and concepts, parents will often comment that they would like to have more information or know more about maths as it is an area in which they lack confidence. It is important to involve parents as much as possible in their children's learning as this can only be beneficial to them and provides a link between home and the setting. In this section, we will look at ways in which we can encourage parents and carers to take more of an active role in their child's play, learning and development.

AC 8.1 Encouraging parents/carers to take an active role in their child's play, learning and development

Settings may well provide curriculum information to parents and carers, as discussed in LO2, and encourage them to feed back to us about children's achievements at home on an ongoing basis. However, your setting may also provide further opportunities to communicate with parents and carers about the teaching of mathematics which is helpful to parents.

These kinds of opportunities are helpful as they enable parents and carers to discuss their ideas about mathematics and to move away from the concept that it always needs to have a written 'sum' in order to be a worthwhile activity. Parents should also be told about the kinds of strategies that we may use with children in order to arrive at an answer, and the importance of mathematical vocabulary, particularly in the early stages of mathematics.

Table 3.6.6 Opportunities to encourage parents to take an active role in their child's play, learning and development

Type of activity	How the activity supports parents
Maths evening or workshop for parents	Teachers and early years workers talk to parents about the way in which mathematics is taught, and the different areas which exist in the current curriculum. This is also a good opportunity for parents and carers to talk with others about the way in which they approach mathematics.
Parents' evening	This gives early years workers an opportunity to discuss the teaching of mathematics with parents alongside other areas of the curriculum.
Parent volunteers	Inviting parents into the setting to volunteer is an ideal opportunity to show them different approaches to mathematics and encourage them to work alongside children to try out the approaches.
Resource library/suggestions	A resource library or list of suggested activities is a good way of showing parents the kinds of activities that are beneficial for children to use at home. These may be very simple, practical activities but may give parents more confidence and reassurance about the kinds of activities that are helpful – for example, simple board games or cooking activities.
Recommending websites for use at home	Schools and settings will often work alongside parents to use websites such as 'Mathletics', which enables children to progress at their own rate at home and school.

Assessment

This unit has many learning outcomes and so you are likely to need to complete a variety of tasks. You should begin by revising the reasons why mathematics is important in children's everyday lives and the factors that might affect their learning of mathematical concepts. You should also explain how working with others supports children's emergent mathematical development. You could reflect on how in your setting a range of people, including parents and practitioners, help children gain mathematical concepts.

For Learning Outcomes 3, 4 and 5 you will need to know about how mathematical environments can be created and you may like to reflect on how your own setting does this. In addition you will need to know how adults can work with children to help them acquire mathematical concepts by building on their interests, and also use an approach known as scaffolding. This has been covered in this unit so you may need to reread it and check that you fully understand. You should also reread about the strategies that can be used to support emergent mathematics and the opportunities that build children's understanding of a range of concepts including shape, weight and data representation.

Learning Outcomes 6 and 7 require you to show that you can put your knowledge into practice. Your assessor will need to see that you can plan, lead and review an activity that supports children's emergent mathematical development. As part of Learning Outcome 7, you will also need to explain how you further individual children's mathematical development as well as reflect on your own practice.

Finally, you need to show that you can support parents in taking an active role in their child's development in relation to mathematical development. Talk to your placement supervisor about the ways in which your work setting currently does this and see if you can practise doing this too.

Useful resources

Books

Boaler, Jo (2009) *The Elephant in the Classroom – Helping Children Learn and Love Maths*, London: Souvenir Press.

Deboys, Mary and Pitt, Eunice (1980) *Lines of Development in Primary Mathematics*, Belfast: Blackstaff Press.

Haylock, D. and Cockburn, A. (2013) *Understanding Mathematics for Young Children*, London: Sage Publications.

There are a number of publications for parents available to help with mathematics but one of the best is:

Eastaway, Rob and Askew, Mike (2010) *Maths for Mums and Dads*, London: Square Peg.

Documents

The Early Years Foundation Stage documents: **https://education.gov.uk/schools/teachingandlearning/assessment/eyfs**

National Curriculum 2014: **www.education.gov.uk/schools/teachingandlearning/curriculum/nationalcurriculum2014/**

Websites

NRICH: **www.nrich.maths.org/early-years** – you can find problem-solving activities here.

Pinterest: **www.pinterest.com** – this site has a wealth of ideas for early years maths activities.

Mathletics: **www.mathletics.co.uk**

Unit 3.7 WB Support children's transition to school

Have you ever wondered why some children are more able to adapt to school than others? The transition into a school setting has long been viewed as a rite of passage, but how can children be supported in this often major change? In this unit, we explore what school readiness means and how early years practitioners can be proactive in ensuring the process is as smooth as possible for children.

Learning outcomes

By the end of this unit, you will:

1 Understand 'school readiness' in relation to the role of the early years practitioner.
2 Understand 'school readiness' in relation to the current framework.
3 Be able to work in partnership with others to support children's readiness for school.

LO1 Understand 'school readiness' in relation to the role of the early years practitioner

What is 'school readiness' and how does it relate to your role? This section explores the kinds of factors that will impact on children's readiness for school as well as looking at how early years practitioners can support children through careful planning and preparation.

AC 1.1 The characteristics of 'school readiness'

In the same way that adults respond and react to things in different ways, you will find that it is similar with children. A child who is ready for school will find the transition straightforward and adapt quickly to the changes in their environment and to the adults who support their learning. However, in most cases children will find some aspects easier or more difficult than others depending on their own experiences before starting school, and on their personality and maturity. The characteristics of school readiness give some indication of the skills which are useful to children when starting school (see Table 3.7.1).

In your setting

Look at a child with whom you work and identify whether they have some of the characteristics of school readiness which are described in Table 3.7.1. Outline what you are doing currently in order to support them in developing these characteristics.

AC 1.2 Factors affecting children's readiness for school

Home factors and background

Children will often react to events and circumstances in the same way as the adults around them and this is an important consideration when looking at the kinds of factors which will affect their readiness for school.

Table 3.7.1 Characteristics of school readiness

Communication skills	Children who have good communication skills may find the transition to school easier as they will be more able to express themselves and talk about their needs and interests. They will also be more used to listening to and giving their attention to others, and be able to follow instructions or wait until it is their turn to speak.
Self-confidence	Children who are more confident in themselves may be more willing to try new activities or to tell adults when they need help. This will affect their experiences and how they work with others.
Independence	Children who rely heavily on adults to carry out basic activities may find starting school more challenging. Seemingly simple things such as putting on and doing up their own coat or remembering to go to the toilet without being reminded are important, as well as being able to get themselves changed for PE, or use a knife and fork. Children will increasingly need to be able to think for themselves and act independently – for example, remembering to put their lunch box or book bag in a particular place in the morning.
Co-operation	Children who cooperate with others and can take turns when playing will be sensitive to the needs of their peers and will form more positive relationships with them.
Able to manage feelings and behaviour	This refers to children who are able to manage their feelings and talk about what is happening. Children who understand the need for appropriate behaviour and who follow the rules will find it easier to settle in to school routines.
Adaptable to change	Children who have had limited pre-school experiences may find it difficult to adapt to their new routines. Starting school may be daunting and they may be reluctant to leave parents and carers.

Attitudes and expectations – some parents and carers will view starting school as exciting and will instil this in their children; others may have had negative experiences as children and in turn pass this on. This will influence the way in which children react when starting school.

> ### Reflect
>
> Sami has been brought to school by her mum and as her key worker you notice during the first few days that Sami is very tearful in the mornings and constantly asks when it will be time to go home. As soon as she comes out of school, her mother asks her anxiously how she is and if she is all right. You notice that Sami's mum looks very worried and seeks reassurance from the teacher about Sami.
>
> - How do you think Sami's mother is affecting Sami's behaviour?
> - What would you do in this situation?

Cultural differences – if parents and carers are from other cultures, the school experience may be very different for them. In many countries, children start school much later, and parents may not feel that their child is ready. In addition, parents and children may speak English as an additional language and may not have had access to much information prior to their child starting school.

Family structures – children will come from a range of different families and backgrounds; some may be from very large extended families, while others may be only children or from single-parent families. There may also be social issues within their family which have affected the child and influenced their school readiness.

Pre-school experiences

Although most children will have had some kind of pre-school experience, some children may, for different reasons, not have been able to attend a nursery or pre-school. This means that they may not have had the social experiences to give them confidence in a school situation. Children who

Figure 3.7.1 Children should feel prepared for their entry to school

Case study

Ciara is from a single-parent family and lives with her mother and grandmother. Her mum is disabled and needs full-time care, which is provided by her grandmother, and Ciara has had to do many things for herself. She has had limited pre-school experience with children her own age as her grandmother is unable to leave her mother, but she attends your nursery on two mornings each week.

Michelle is from a small family, and speaks Tamil at home. She is always very quiet in the nursery setting, although she attends every day. She tends to play alongside others quietly.

Kia is an only child and her mother has told you that it took a long time for them to conceive and that she and her husband are unable to have any more children. Kia attends the pre-school on four days a week and is also taken to swimming, French and music classes.

- How might the girls' backgrounds affect them when starting school?
- Why is it important for early years workers to have some information about children's family backgrounds when supporting children's transition into school?

Figure 3.7.2 When they start school, children need to be able to do simple tasks independently

have limited pre-school experiences may also find the expectations of school challenging – for example, sitting and listening quietly with others, or being able to manage themselves when putting on a coat or going to the toilet.

Pre-school experiences will also relate to the different things which parents and carers have been able to do with their children depending on time and resources. Some parents will have taken children to the farm or the beach, or been able to spend more time sharing activities, such as playing games, cooking or talking to them. These kinds of activities are all important as they will develop children's vocabulary and knowledge, as well as their ability to understand their place in the world.

School and pre-school involvement

The amount of support and preparation which the school and pre-school provides will also have an impact on how well children are prepared for

school. A supportive school will prepare parents and children through giving as much information as they can and also being available for parents and carers to ask questions. (See also AC 1.3 for more information on how schools and early years practitioners can do this.) In some cases, however, parents may have chosen not to take advantage of this, and this will affect their child's readiness.

Age and maturity of the child

In England, children start school during the year in which they turn five. This has an impact on the child's readiness as children who are older when they start school will have had more experiences to draw on. They may also be more mature in different aspects of their development and, although there will always be exceptions to this, you should be aware of children's birthdays.

Case study

Isaac turned four on 29 August. He will be starting school in your class alongside Lauren, who will be five on 3 September. When you look at the class list, you notice that many of the children have birthdays towards the end of the year.

- Why is it important that early years practitioners are aware of the birth ages of children in their class?
- How might this impact on the children's school readiness?

In your setting

Look at a class list showing birthdays for your children. What do you notice about particular children? Does their age have any bearing on this?

Special educational needs

If children have a special educational need, one or more aspects of their development will be affected. This may be in the areas of physical, sensory, communication, learning, or emotional and behavioural development. When they are preparing to start school, it is possible that this may not yet have been picked up by other professionals, particularly if it affects their learning or behaviour. You should always be on the look-out for signs that a child's development is affected.

Case study

Ryan has been in your setting for a year and has always been one of the quieter children. He is due to start school the following term. Lately you have noticed that he is becoming even more withdrawn and does not communicate very often with other children or adults.

Bhumika is talking to you one day and, when you point to something outside, she does not appear to be able to see it. You do not ask her again, but monitor her in the setting and notice that she is not always aware of things in the middle distance.

- Should you have any concerns in either of the above situations?
- What would you do in these situations?

AC 1.3 How the early years practitioner supports children preparing for school

As an early years practitioner, you will need to be able to support children in their transition to primary school. Your team will have plans and procedures in place, but you should also be aware of the kinds of things you can do as an individual with children to prepare and reassure them, particularly if you are their key worker.

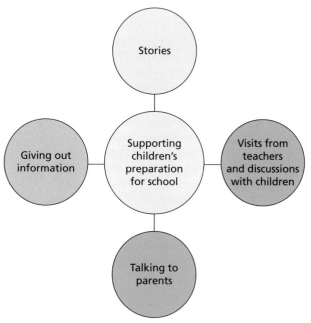

Figure 3.7.3 Supporting children's preparation for school

Stories – stories are always a good way to dispel any anxieties which children have and there are a number of books available for children on the subject of starting school. They are a good way of introducing the subject and children may be more confident in talking about it in this context.

Visits from teachers and discussions with children – sometimes teachers may visit nurseries and pre-schools to see individual children, and this can be a good introduction to children to talk about what is going to happen.

Prior to children starting school, you should also talk to them about what it means, and answer any questions which they may have so that they are reassured about the kinds of things that will happen.

Talking to parents – parents may feel more confident about approaching you than about speaking to the school as you are familiar to them. You should always be available to talk to parents about the practicalities of starting school and reassure them if necessary.

Giving out information – you should be aware of any information which is available so that you are able to pass this on to parents and carers if you are asked. Often pre-schools and nurseries will be provided with leaflets and information for parents and, as well as passing such leaflets on, you should be sure that you have read them.

> ### Reflect
> What sort of information is available in your setting for parents and carers of children who are starting school? Is it displayed prominently or handed out to them? How does your setting ensure that children are effectively supported when starting school?
>
> → See also 'Work with others to prepare children for school' – AC 3.1 on page 268.

LO2 Understand 'school readiness' in relation to the current framework

How does school readiness relate to what happens when children start school? This section looks at the Early Years Foundation Stage framework and what is expected of children in this context.

AC 2.1 Areas of learning and development in the current framework related to school readiness

The Early Years Foundation Stage (EYFS) is divided into seven areas of learning and development for use by all early years providers to the end of the academic year in which children

are five. This means that it is used by nurseries and pre-schools as well as reception classes in mainstream schools.

The areas of learning and development are split into two parts:

- Three prime areas – these are particularly important for firing children's curiosity and enthusiasm for learning, as well as their capacity to form relationships and thrive (see Table 3.7.2).
- Four specific areas – these blend together some of the more 'traditional' subjects and build on the basis of the prime areas (see Table 3.7.3).

Table 3.7.2 Prime areas

Personal, social and emotional development	Key points: • The development of children's confidence • How children manage their feelings • How children make friends and take turns
Physical development	Key points: • How children move and use **fine and gross motor skills** • How children learn about healthy living • Children's management of their self-care
Communication and language	Key points: • How children listen and pay attention • How children understand what is being said • The way in which children communicate with others and develop their vocabulary

> ### Key term
> **fine and gross motor skills** These relate to the way in which we move. Gross motor skills are large movements, such as running, skipping and hopping, or throwing and catching, and fine motor skills are small movements, such as using scissors, a pencil or a knife and fork.

Table 3.7.3 Specific areas

Literacy	Key points:
	• How children start to enjoy reading books
	• How children start to make marks and learn to write
	• The way in which children start to explore phonics and ways to write letters to match their spoken sounds
Mathematics	Key points:
	• How children learn about numbers and counting
	• How children use mathematical language
	• How children explore measures, including capacity, space, shapes, time and money during play
Understanding the world	Key points:
	• The way in which children find out about nature and the world around them
	• How children find out about their local communities
	• The way in which children develop their confidence when using ICT equipment
Expressive arts and design	Key points:
	• The development of children's creativity and imagination through art, dance and music
	• How children use play to develop these skills

The three prime areas of learning and development are those which relate most to school readiness, due to the fact that children need to be physically and emotionally ready as well as have the communication skills to be able to learn effectively in a school setting:

Personal, social and emotional development

This area of learning and development relates to how children manage their behaviour and develop relationships with others. Children who are immature in this area or who have had limited experiences of playing and sharing with others will find it difficult being part of a large group.

→ See also case study in AC 1.2 on page 261.

Physical development

This area of learning and development relates to the way in which children manage their own physical needs, such as self-care and healthy living. It also relates to their physical control and coordination in both large and small movements. Children will need to have a good level of physical development in order to negotiate space effectively as well as having the control needed to start to use tools such as pencils for writing or scissors for cutting.

Figure 3.7.4 Children need to develop physical skills to be able to use tools such as pencils and scissors

Communication and language

This area of learning and development clearly relates to how children communicate with others but is also about their ability to listen and understand, as well as developing their vocabulary. Children who can listen, understand and follow instructions and express themselves effectively will be better placed when starting school.

Reflect

What kinds of opportunities are given to children in your setting on a daily basis to support the development of both large and small motor skills?

In your setting

How does your setting plan for and deliver activities and experiences which will develop children's skills in the three prime areas of learning? How will this then support their school readiness?

Reflect

The EYFS framework also requires early years practitioners to look at the way in which children learn, known as the characteristics of effective learning. All early years settings need to report to parents on these at the end of the reception year. They are set out in the following way:

Playing and exploring or engagement

a finding out and exploring
b using what they know in their play
c being willing to have a go

Active learning or motivation

a being involved and concentrating
b keeping on trying
c enjoying achieving what they set out to do

Creating and thinking critically or thinking

a having their own ideas
b using what they already know to learn new things
c choosing ways to do things and finding new ways

Why are these aspects of learning important? Have a discussion about whether you think early years practitioners should also report on the way in which children learn before they start school.

AC 2.2 Assessment strategies and the current framework

Early years practitioners in pre-schools and reception classes will need to use different assessment strategies to monitor children's learning in relation to the current EYFS framework. Ongoing or formative assessment of the seven areas of learning is an essential part of the teaching and learning process, as it helps practitioners to understand children's achievements, as well as look at the ways in which they learn, and helps them to plan next steps. Settings may keep their assessment records for different children electronically or they may be paper based, depending on ease of access for staff.

Observation

Observation is the primary assessment strategy that practitioners use as it allows practitioners to note down children's responses in different ways. There are different kinds of observation but you are most likely to use those outlined in Table 3.7.4.

Observations from parents and carers

As part of the EYFS framework, parents and carers should also be encouraged to share their observations with settings so that early years professionals are able to gain a more rounded picture of all aspects of the child's development. Settings may choose to do this in different ways, and parents and carers will need to be aware of the importance of their contribution.

In your setting

How do you encourage parents and carers to contribute their observations on children's development? Discuss this with others in the group and compare the ways in which settings might do this.

Questioning

Questioning is a useful form of assessment as adults can ask children directly about their understanding. It can be done at any time and adults may wish to note down children's responses in different formats.

Outside Jimmy was playing with his friends. They had taken the play cars out of the shed. Jimmy said to one of the other children, 'We need to get a bucket of water so that we can wash it because it's so dirty.'

He then asked an adult to help him to get a bucket of soapy water and two sponges for himself and Oscar, one of his friends. They moved one of the cars onto the grass as Oscar has said that it would be easier.

Jimmy helped the adult bring over the bucket and said, 'This is so heavy!'

He said to Oscar 'We need to clean the outside and the inside!' as the two of them started to clean the car.

Jimmy realised as they were washing it that it was easier to move the car than the bucket and so this is what they did as they went on.

He encouraged Oscar to keep cleaning it, 'Come on, we have nearly finished.' but Oscar lost interest towards the end and Jimmy finished the job himself.

Figure 3.7.5 Example of a free description observation

Table 3.7.4 Types of observations

Type of observation	What it means
Checklist	A checklist might be used to record whether children can use a particular skill – for example, catching a ball – or whether they have completed a specific activity. The focus will not be on how they do it but whether or not they are able to.
Simple note-taking	This type of observation is usually very short and may be written on a post-it note or sticker, so that early years practitioners remember an idea or comment that a child has made.
Free description	This type of observation is sometimes used where children are carrying out an activity and the observer wishes to write everything down. This includes how the participants interact with one another, both verbally and non-verbally, and includes a lot of detail. Free description observations are usually written in the present tense.
Event sample	This method of observation is used to note down how often a pupil shows a particular type of behaviour or goes to an activity over a period of time. Event samples should be carried out simply by watching the child and noting down the frequency of the focused behaviour. For an event sample, the observer should not be participating in the activity, only observing what is happening.
Informal observation	This kind of observation may be used if you have been asked to keep an eye on a child for a specific reason, in particular if adults have concerns about them. The format is not important, although you will need to be careful about confidentiality if you use notebooks.

Discussion

Both when children are sitting on the carpet and having topic-based discussions, stories or news and when they are speaking to children individually, adults can note down when children demonstrate their knowledge in a particular area, or use vocabulary or ideas which are significant. This form of assessment gives a snapshot of children's speaking and listening skills and is also a useful way of assessing their understanding.

Checking children's understanding

Early years practitioners may choose to check individual children's understanding of facts and concepts by going through key points with them and noting down their responses. For example, if they have been working on shapes as part of a topic, children may be questioned individually so that adults know how much of the vocabulary and shape recognition they have understood. This can then be added to their records.

Reflect

How does your setting keep assessment records of children's progress in relation to the EYFS framework? Is this available to all staff at all times? Think about how you contribute to the assessment process. Would you change anything about the way in which assessment is carried out in your setting?

AC 2.3 The current framework's assessment process to support children's school preparation

Although children's assessment is ongoing, the EYFS requires practitioners to review children's progress at two key points: the two year old development check and the Early Years Foundation Stage Profile at the end of the reception year. In most cases, they will also give parents an up-to-date assessment prior to children starting school, although this is not statutory.

Progress check at age two

Under statutory requirements, early years practitioners need to report to parents about their child's progress and development in the prime areas. This may take the form of a short summary designed to show the child's strengths as well as identify any areas in which they are not progressing as expected. Early years practitioners need to work alongside other professionals, such as the early years SENCO, if there are concerns about any aspect of the child's development.

In practice

Although the two year development check is statutory, at the time of writing, schools will not have access to this information for children starting school as the updated EYFS was introduced in September 2012. Does your setting have any other information which it passes on to schools?

On school entry

Although this is not a requirement, nurseries and pre-school settings should provide information to schools about children's learning and development. Before children start school, early years practitioners should report to schools on the children's progress to date in each area as well as passing on any concerns and what has been implemented to date. This will usually take the form of a report – for example, in the form that it has been sent to parents at the end of the pre-school year. It is not a requirement of the EYFS to do this; however, it is good practice and is carried out by most early years settings.

In your setting

Look at the way in which your setting assesses pupil progress and how it reports to schools. What do you think about the process? How does it support pupils' preparation for school?

Assessment at the end of the EYFS

The EYFS Profile. This is completed during the final term of the reception year. Teachers need to report to the local authority about each child's progress towards the 17 Early Learning Goals and indicate whether children are Emerging, Expected or Exceeding in each

case. This gives a picture of the child's knowledge, understanding and abilities, their progress against expected levels and their readiness for Year 1. The Profile will reflect the observations and records which have been made on each child as well as discussions between early years practitioners and parents. The results of the Profile will then be shared with parents and carers, usually as part of their child's end-of-year report. Results should also be discussed with Year 1 teachers, as well as the characteristics of effective learning (see page 265), so that they can effectively plan for children as they move into Key Stage 1.

Research it!

Look at page 10 of the EYFS framework document at the requirements for assessment. What does it say about what assessment should entail? Why is this important?

LO3 Be able to work in partnership with others to support children's readiness for school

What is meant by working in partnership with others? You may have limited experience of working with others apart from parents and carers, as well as colleagues in your setting. However, there is also a range of other professionals with whom you may need to work in order to support children's readiness for school. You should remember that you will always need to act professionally with others and that you are there to support the interests of the children.

AC 3.1 Working with others to prepare children for school

As part of your role as an early years practitioner and key worker, you will constantly need to share information with others so that you are able to effectively monitor and assess children's progress. Those with whom you need to work when preparing children for school are likely to come from a range of backgrounds, from both inside and outside the setting. During the course of your career and depending on your role, it is likely that you will come into contact with a number of these professionals for different reasons.

Sharing information in line with current frameworks

Apart from parents and colleagues, it is likely that the first time you will share information with others will be at the age two progress check, if you are working with children of this age. The check must be completed when the child is aged between 24 and 36 months and will be dependent on timings, such as when the child started nursery and parental preferences. Early years practitioners, and other professionals if applicable, will be required to review the progress of each child in each of the three prime areas of learning by providing a short written report to parents. Its main aims are to ensure that parents have a clear picture and understanding of their child's development so that, if there are any areas in which the child is not progressing, this can be addressed at an early stage. The check also ensures that practitioners are able to understand and plan for the needs of each child and identify priorities where needed. There is no standardised format for the two-year check as professionals and early years settings or childminders can use their own discretion.

You should ensure that you have read and taken account of the two-year development check if you are working with older children in your setting so that you are aware of what has taken place, and in particular if you are passing on information on your key children to schools.

Reflect

Are you aware of the way in which your setting reports to parents at the two year old check? Where will records of the check be kept in your setting?

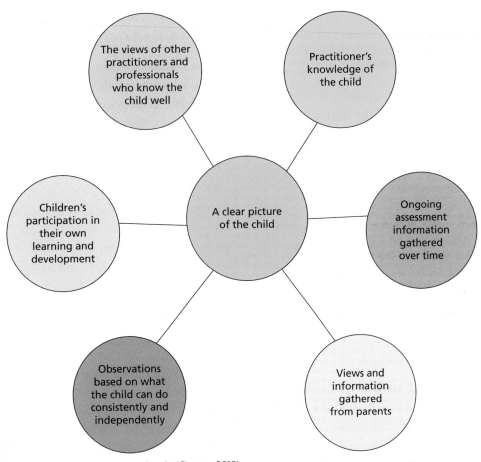

Figure 3.7.6 Principles for the progress check (Crown 2012)

Prior to completion of the check, all of those who know the child and have worked with them should reflect on what they know about the child and their development. The voice of the child should also be heard, which means that children can themselves talk about what they have enjoyed doing and what they have found difficult. Parents and carers should then be invited to the setting to talk through these and discuss the child's progress with professionals, so that next steps can be planned for the child both at home and in the setting. In this way, shared knowledge and understanding of the child should lead to improved outcomes for children.

Some parents and carers may find this easier than others and early years workers may need to support them through the process, encouraging them to engage with the setting in different ways.

In your setting

Find out about how your setting involves parents and carers in the two year old check. Consider the importance of building effective parent partnerships with this in mind and how your setting does this.

Following this meeting, practitioners will need to reassess what they know about the child and then provide a summary to parents. If there are any causes for concern, parental permission may need to be sought so that information about the child can be shared with other outside agencies.

For further information about the two year old progress check and examples of different formats as well as suggestions for engaging with parents, see the publication. 'A know how guide: the EYFS progress check at age two', available at **www.gov. uk**. Your local authority may also provide support and additional materials.

Supporting individual needs of children during transition

Each child is unique and will have different needs, and early years workers should ensure that they are supported as effectively as possible through their transition to school. Your setting is likely to have some procedures in place, which may include:

Nursery and pre-school visits – although some schools are attached to a nursery, which can make the transition into school easier for children, the majority of reception classes will take children from a number of different pre-school settings. This means that school staff will often visit nurseries and pre-schools to meet individual children and to talk to early years staff about the children who will be coming to school. You may be asked about the backgrounds or needs of specific children when school staff come into your setting.

School-based events, such as parents' evenings or open days – schools will often have parent information evenings or open days prior to their children starting school. This allows both sides to meet before school starts and gives children the chance to look at their new environment with their parents or carers. As an early years worker, you should ask parents and children about these events and encourage them to attend.

Home visits – sometimes in smaller schools, reception teachers will visit individual children at home prior to their starting school and speak to parents and children about the process. In this way, the engagement with parents and carers about their child can be initiated by the school and positive relationships formed.

Specialist support for speakers of other languages – if the school is in an area with a high proportion of speakers of English as a second language, they or the local authority may provide information on starting school that has been translated so that all parents have access to it. You may need to support parents by providing access to the different information available to them.

Making sure records are up to date – you will need to be prepared so that your setting can pass on information to schools about children's development and achievements. As a key worker, you should ensure that all records on your individual children are up to date and passed on to schools.

be ready to talk to other professionals about the child and how their individual needs will need to be supported when they move into reception.

Key term

SENCO Special educational needs coordinator.

Key workers and colleagues from your setting – the child's key worker as well as everyone who has had contact with them in the setting should be involved in the meeting in some way. If they cannot be there in person, their opinion should be sought and included in the discussion.

Parents and carers – parents should always be involved in meetings concerning their child.

Your early years SENCO – the early years SENCO should instigate and participate in the meeting so that they can ensure that all professionals have been able to participate.

In addition to this, if you have a child or children with additional needs in your setting who will be transferring to school, your early years **SENCO** will need to set up a meeting between all of those professionals who have had contact with the child up to this point. This is known as a transition meeting and takes place so that information can be exchanged as to the child's needs and any adaptations or considerations that will need to be taken before they transfer from the setting. These may be set up by the school or local authority and will include all those professionals who have been involved with the child up to this point. Your early years SENCO may ask you to prepare a report, or

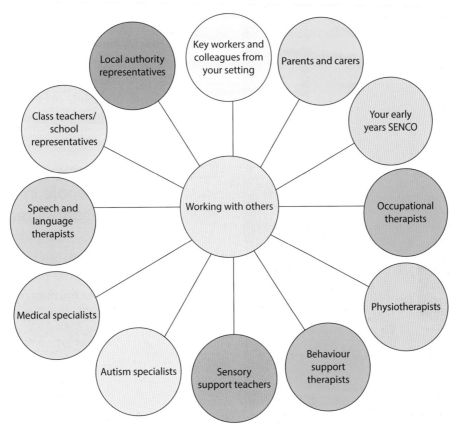

Figure 3.7.7 Working with others

Occupational therapists – the occupational therapist will be involved if the child has a special need in relation to their fine motor skills and will provide information and specialist equipment if needed.

Physiotherapists – a physiotherapist will be involved if the child has a special need in relation to their gross motor skills and if the school environment needs to be adapted in any way.

Behaviour support therapists – behaviour therapists will support the needs of children who have behaviour and emotional problems. They will need to be involved so that they can work with the child throughout the transition process.

Sensory support teachers – these teachers will have a specialism in the area of sensory support; in other words, they will work with children who have visual or hearing problems. They may advise on the kinds of adaptations or equipment that children need and should provide ongoing support when children start school.

Autism specialists – autism specialists support the needs of children who have an autistic spectrum disorder (ASD). They will need to be involved so that they can work with the child throughout the transition process and beyond.

Medical specialists – healthcare professionals may be involved if the child has medical needs, and in particular if they will need additional support in school.

Speech and language therapists – the speech and language therapist will be involved if the child has communication issues. These may be due to difficulties in articulating words or in processing language.

Class teachers/school representatives – reception class teachers and the school SENCO will need to be involved in the meeting so that they are able to plan for the provision which is needed.

Local authority representatives – representatives from the local authority may or may not be present depending on the involvement of the early years SENCO. They will provide information about any funding which is available to support the child's transition to school.

AC 3.2 Encouraging parents/carers to take an active role in their child's preparation for school readiness

As well as involving parents through ensuring that information is passed between the setting and school during this important transition, you will also need to ensure that you encourage them to take an active role in their child's learning and development when preparing for school. Early years settings should always have close links with parents and this should be a natural progression.

The EYFS document states that 'providers … must work in partnership with parents and/or carers to promote the learning and development of all

Figure 3.7.8 Professionals need to work together to meet the needs of individual children

Table 3.7.5 Encouraging parents to take an active role in their child's play, learning and development

Method of communication	Encouraging parents' role
Verbal	Parents may catch early years workers at the start or end of the session to tell them about their child's achievements. A disadvantage of this is that it is easy to forget to pass the imformation on and settings will need to have a system to ensure all staff can access the information.
Written format	Early years settings may have a pro-forma which is easily accessible to parents through their website or as a handout with other information in the setting. Parents can then note down any of their child's achievements.
Displays	Some early years settings will have displays in entrance halls which parents can add to so that everyone can see what children have been doing at home.

children in their care, and to ensure they are ready for school'. This means that at all times parents should be encouraged to contribute to observations and assessments made by early years practitioners so that a more rounded picture can be gathered of individual children.

→ In AC 2.2, we looked at parents contributing observations about their children's learning – this should also continue when children start primary school.

Different early years settings may encourage parents in a variety of ways, as shown in Table 3.7.5.

Early years settings may hold meetings for parents (as discussed in AC 1.3), so that they can discuss the ways in which they can help their child to prepare for school. Key workers should also work closely with families as they will have a greater knowledge and understanding of individual children's needs.

RFS (Ready for School) is an app which can be downloaded from the Bright Horizons nursery's website (www.brighthorizons.co.uk). It is useful to give to parents and shows a series of activities which can be carried out with young children prior to starting school.

Research it!

Look at the roles on the previous pages and research one that you would like to know more about.

Test yourself

Can you outline the role of each of the professionals listed on the previous pages? Why might you need to know what these are?

How can you find out about which of these professionals are involved with children in your setting?

Case study

Anya is about to move into reception. She has a disability which means that she is mainly wheelchair bound, although she can use a walking frame and should be encouraged to do this some of the time. Her disability does not affect her learning. A meeting has been set up between your setting and Anya's new school and you have been asked to write a report to present at the meeting.

- What do you think that the school will need to know about?
- Apart from Anya's new reception teacher, what other professionals do you think will need to be present at the meeting?

Assessment

To complete this unit you will need to complete a variety of tasks. Your starting point should be to understand the concept of school readiness, its characteristics and the factors that might affect children's readiness for schools. This has been covered in this unit and so you could revise this ready for a task. You also need to explain the role of the early years practitioner in supporting children to prepare for school. This links closely with Unit 1.4 so you should revisit that unit along with the information in this chapter.

For Learning Outcome 2, you will need to look at the current version of the statutory framework for the early years foundation stage in order to consider the areas of learning and development that will help children prepare for school. You also have to find out the current ways in which children are assessed at the end of the reception year, as well as between moving from nursery or pre-school into school. In addition to the information in this unit, you can talk to your placement supervisor, who will be able to give you their perspective as well as information on current arrangements.

For the final outcome, you will need to show that you can put the knowledge gained from this unit into practice. You will need to show your assessor that you can work with others including parents to prepare children for school. You could provide evidence in a range of ways including through activities, displays and the completion of observations, assessment and reports. It will be important to talk to your assessor and placement supervisor about how best to provide evidence for this in the setting in which you work.

Useful resources

The Early Years Foundation Stage documents
**https://education.gov.uk/schools/
teachingandlearning/assessment/eyfs**

The EYFS progress check at age two
**www.gov.uk/government/publications/a-know-
how-guide-the-eyfs-progress-check-at-age-two**

EYFS exemplification materials
**www.gov.uk/government/publications/eyfs-
profile-exemplication-materials**

Unit 3.9 WB Develop children's cognitive skills

Have you ever seen a baby or a toddler stare at something that they have not seen before? Have you been asked a question by a child that has made you laugh, even though the child was quite serious? What you might not know is that you have seen a child engaged in thinking and learning. In this unit, we look at how children's **cognitive skills** develop. These are the skills involved in learning and the thinking process. We also consider explanations that might account for how children think and learn, before considering how we might support their cognitive development.

Learning outcomes

By the end of this unit, you will:

1 Understand about cognitive development in children.
2 Understand theory underpinning cognitive development.
3 Be able to implement a learning experience which supports the development of sustained shared thinking in children.
4 Be able to evaluate the provision for supporting cognitive development in own setting.

LO1 Understand about cognitive development in children

What can you remember from your childhood? The chances are that your earliest memories are very vague and quite fragmented. This is because your brain was still developing. In this section, we look at how children's **cognition** develops.

AC 1.1 Sensory development in the first year of life

The first year of a baby's life is packed full of learning. The baby learns to use its five senses to begin to make sense of its world. At first, some of the senses are linked to survival, such as the sense of smell or grasping onto a finger. Over the first few months, many of the reflexes start to disappear and the baby starts instead to actively use their senses to learn. Table 3.9.1 shows the progress of children's **sensory development** over the first year.

Key terms

cognition The processing and interpreting of information which supports the learning of concepts and the development of ideas and thoughts.

cognitive skills Skills associated with cognition, such as the ability to understand number.

sensory development The process by which the body learns to process information gained from touch, taste, sight, sound and smell.

binocular vision Single vision, although each eye is seeing a slightly different view.

pincer grasp Using the thumb and index finger to make a squeezing movement.

pointing Using index finger to touch or to show something.

mouthing Exploring an object by putting it in the mouth to touch and taste.

In practice

Ask your placement supervisor if you can observe a child under one year. Using Table 3.9.1 as a reference, write down what you observe the child doing and how this relates to their sensory development.

Test yourself

Write down three cognitive skills that a nine-month-old baby may have mastered.

Figure 3.9.1 This baby is six months old. He can now focus and reach for objects

Table 3.9.1 Babies' sensory development over the first year

Newborn	<ul><li>Extremely sensitive to light</li><li>Brain is not yet coordinating vision from each eye so babies can only follow objects that are very close to them</li><li>Reflex sucking movements</li><li>Reflex grasp movement if an object is put into the hand</li></ul>
One month	<ul><li>Startles in response to sudden noises</li><li>Starts to move head in direction of a human voice</li><li>Turns head towards light</li><li>Follows movements of toys or faces if held near to them, especially if they are contrasting colours</li><li>It is thought that babies do not yet perceive colours; instead they see objects as either light or dark</li><li>Stops crying when held and spoken to</li><li>Feeds well and will attempt to suck other items</li></ul>
Three months	<ul><li>Stares at human faces</li><li>Moves head to follow an object at 15–25 cm</li><li>Watches movement of own hands</li><li>Enjoys touch of water at bath time</li><li>Holds rattle and make movements with it but cannot coordinate eye contact with it</li><li>Is able to differentiate between colours</li><li>Moves head to source of sounds</li><li>Coos in response to a familiar adult</li><li>Becomes excited at sound of preparation of feed</li></ul>
Six months	<ul><li>Perception of depth allowing the child to reach out and grasp a toy can be seen as a result of **binocular vision**</li><li>Can pass a toy from one hand to the other</li><li>Recognises familiar voices across the room</li><li>Seeks the source of a sound</li><li>Takes everything to mouth to explore</li><li>Touches bottle or breast when feeding</li><li>During weaning process, may reject certain tastes and textures</li></ul>
Nine months	<ul><li>Pokes at objects with index finger</li><li>Uses **pincer grasp** to pick up small object or food</li><li>Can reach object if accessible</li><li>Can drop an object</li><li>Watches people or objects across a room</li><li>Listens out for everyday sounds and starts to recognise their significance</li><li>Takes everything to mouth to explore</li><li>During weaning process, explores lumpy foods and new tastes; some may be rejected</li></ul>
12 months	<ul><li>Uses pincer grasp easily to pick up objects</li><li>Can drop and throw objects at will</li><li>Explores primarily through vision and touch, although still **mouthing** objects</li><li>Enjoys musical toys and songs</li><li>Has food preferences, although still developing taste for foods and textures</li></ul>

AC 1.2 Stages of cognitive development from birth to seven years

Cognitive development is the ability of children to process and interpret information that in turn allows them to learn and develop an understanding of concepts such as number, time, colour, as well as cognitive skills such as logic and reasoning. Children's cognitive development is linked to many factors, including the amount of stimulation they receive, as well as the development of language. This means that individual children's cognitive development can be variable. Table 3.9.2 shows some of the typical skills linked to memory and concepts that you might expect to see at different ages.

AC 1.3 Current scientific research on neurological and brain development in early years

Many of the theories of how children learn and think that we will look at in the next section were developed in a period when brain imaging was not available. Over the past ten or so years, scientific advances have allowed researchers to look at images of the brain, which has enabled them to see how children's brains develop, but also how the brain functions. The science is new and it will be some time before we have a complete understanding of how the brain works and how it responds to new situations.

In practice

With the permission of your placement supervisor, observe two children of different ages over a couple sessions. For each child, write down the cognitive skills that they have mastered.

How does their development compare to that shown in Table 3.9.2?

Figure 3.9.2 Simple games such as pairs help children to practise their matching skills

Table 3.9.2 Cognitive skills at different ages

0–1 year	From three months: • Recognises familiar faces and voices From eight months: • Looks for an object that has been removed • Places an object in a container when asked • Finds an object that has been seen and then hidden
1–2 years	• Understands simple instructions, such as 'come' • Points to parts of the body • Points to a named picture
2–3 years	• Completes a three-piece puzzle • Copies a circle • Matches textures • Is able to point to little and big, e.g. 'Which is the big spoon?' • Matches three colours • Stacks beakers in order • Can find the odd one out in a group of objects, e.g. a large bead in a group of shells
3–4 years	• Tells if an object is light or heavy • Is able to repeat a simple story • Matches objects one to one, e.g. putting one plate on each placemat at table • Points to long and short objects • Is able to sort objects by shape and size • Knows the name of primary colours • Names three shapes • Counts 10 objects with support
4–5 years	• Recognises and writes own name • Picks up a number of objects, e.g. 'Find me four large beads' • Names eight or more colours • Is able to decide which object is the heavier by comparing them • Is able to complete a 20-piece jigsaw
5–6 years	• Counts accurately to 20 or more • Can manage simple calculations using objects • Can play a board game involving simple rules • Can point to half and whole objects • Enjoys simple jokes • Is able to make connections between different experiences and articulate these easily
6–7 years	• Can read and write • Can play a board game that requires some logic • Can manage simple calculations without the use of concrete objects • Predicts what might happen next in a story • Understands and can make simple jokes • Can argue using some logic

Early development

Brain development is a long process. The structure of the brain keeps changing until early adulthood. It is thought that babies are born with 100 billion neurons. These are brain cells which are shaped to allow them to form connections and which pass electrical pulses between one another and so allow the brain to respond and function. These connections are often referred to as neural pathways. Some neural pathways have already been formed during pregnancy, allowing the baby to survive by, for example, breathing and feeding, but in early childhood the number of neural pathways increases. It is thought that neural pathways are

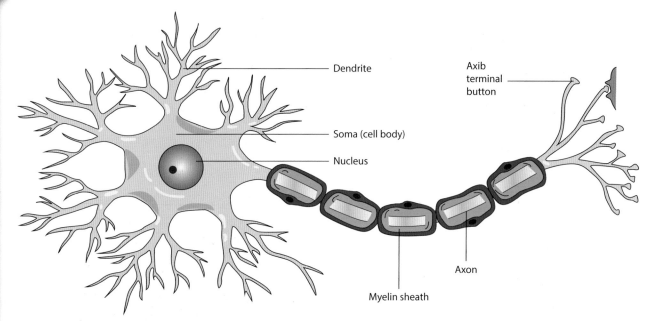

Figure 3.9.3 Neural connections are made when a dendrite of one neuron touches the axon of another

formed in response to experiences, stimulation, love and attachment. Interestingly, while early childhood is significant in brain development, the process by which new connections is formed continues throughout our life in response to new tastes, sounds or movements. This means that our brains are being continually shaped.

Neural pruning

From around 18 months, neural pathways that are no longer being used are 'pruned' by the brain. This may sound bad news, but in a healthy brain that has been stimulated, it allows the remaining connections to pass electrical pulses faster. This results in young children being able to respond faster or being more coordinated. Neural pruning is thought to be why adults cannot learn a new language as easily as a young child.

Myelinisation

Myelin is a coating that covers the neural pathways and helps the electrical pulses to move quickly along. Throughout childhood, a process of coating the pathways takes place, known as myelinisation. This results in better coordination and speed of connections. Sadly, in adulthood, some brain diseases, such as multiple sclerosis, are caused by the deterioration of this coating.

In practice

Neural pruning and myelinisation help children's physical coordination. Ask your placement supervisor if you can observe a child of 13–16 months and a child of 22–24 months.

Show each child an object and encourage them to come and collect it from you. Note the differences in speed and coordination between the different children.

Brain growth

As well as connections forming in early childhood, parts of the brain also develop. An area of the brain known as the frontal lobe, associated with logic and reasoning, is one such area. The increase in neural pathways in this area seems to allow children to acquire concepts such as number and also to solve problems.

Research it!

There are a lot of myths about brain development. You can read more about brain development and also some of the things that are said but are not true by visiting: www.tlrp.org/pub/documents/Neuroscience Commentary FINAL.pdf.

Figure 3.9.4 Neural pruning allows children to respond faster during tasks

AC 1.4 How current scientific research influences practice in early years settings

The understanding that children's brains are shaped according to their experiences, including early relationships, has influenced early years settings in a variety of ways.

Importance of the key person role
The finding that strong relationships and attachment matter to the healthy development of brains has meant that all early years settings have a key person system.

→ See also Unit 1.4.

Stimulation
The recognition that children's brains respond to different experiences and stimulation has meant that early years settings need to provide a wide range of play opportunities and sensory resources.

Work with babies and toddlers
As a result of neuroscience showing that early stimulation is essential for babies and toddlers, the Early Years Foundation Stage in England includes a curriculum from birth. Early years settings spend time planning a wide range of experiences, such as going on outings and providing sensory play. Time spent interacting with babies and toddlers is also prioritised, along with providing plenty of sensory resources, such as treasure basket and heuristic play.

LO2 Understand theory underpinning cognitive development

Were you ever asked as a child whether a kilo of feathers was heavier than a kilo of gold? Young children tend to reply 'gold' because they know that feathers are light. They do not seem to spot that the weight given is the same. In this section, we look at

Figure 3.9.5 Plenty of sensory resources should be provided to aid brain development

theories of how children learn and also how these theories influence current practice in early years.

AC 2.1 Theoretical perspectives cognitive development

There is a range of theories that attempt to explain how children learn and/or the stages of their cognitive development. These theories have, over the years, influenced education practice, as we will go on to see on pages 286–287.

Behaviourist approach

The behaviourist approach to learning suggests that we learn as a result of what happens after an event. A child looking at a book may associate books with pleasure if an adult praises them or reads it to them. A child might learn their times tables because a reward is offered if all of the answers are correct. Children who enjoy an activity are more likely to choose to do it again. The theorist who spent time training animals to learn new skills and who developed this approach

was B.F. Skinner (1904–90). There are many criticisms of the behaviourist approach to children's learning. It is thought to be too passive as the approach considers the adult to be the one who decides what the child is meant to learn. It also does not give an account of how children's logic changes over time.

→ We look again at Skinner's theory on page 286 in relation to behaviour.

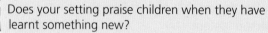

In your setting

Does your setting praise children when they have learnt something new?

Constructivist approach

The constructivist approach to learning emphasises the child as an active learner. The child learns from doing and creates thoughts based on their experiences. There are several theorists who approach children's cognitive development and learning from this viewpoint.

Jean Piaget (1896–1980)

Jean Piaget was originally a zoologist but became involved in intelligence testing of children. He soon became fascinated by the way that young children seemed to have their own logic and that quite often groups of the same age children gave the same incorrect answers. Having observed his own children closely and also having carried out experiments with different age groups of children, he created a theory that explains how children learn, but also how their cognitive development changes over time.

Children's thinking

Piaget came to the conclusion that children develop patterns of actions and also thinking that provide them with conclusions about the world. He called these 'schemas'. A child might, for example, come to the conclusion that all trousers are blue given that his trousers are blue. Piaget suggested that there come times when children are forced to adapt their conclusions. The child might be given a pair of dark red trousers. Piaget used specific terms for the process by which young children would need to develop or adapt new schemas:

Assimilation: the child constructs a theory (or schema).

↓

Equilibrium: his experiences to date seem to fit the schema (everything balances).

↓

Disequilibrium: an experience occurs that casts doubt on the effectiveness of the schema (things don't add up any more!).

↓

Accommodation: the child changes the original schema to fit the new piece of experience or information.

Unlike the behaviourist approach, Piaget's theory of cognitive development suggests that the child is very active in their learning.

Research it!

The concept of the child as an active learner is reflected in the Early Years Foundation Stage. Download a copy of the EYFS by visiting **www.education.gov.uk**. Read the section relating to the characteristics of learning.

How does this relate to Piaget's view that children learn using their experiences?

Piaget's stages of cognitive development

Piaget also suggested that, as children develop and they have more experiences, this is reflected in their thinking. He grouped children's cognitive development into four broad stages. Each stage has certain features. Table 3.9.3 outlines these four stages.

In practice

Conservation

It is interesting to repeat one of Piaget's tests with children. Ask your placement supervisor if you can observe a child in your setting aged four years. Set out eight buttons in a row. Count the buttons with the child. Agree that there are eight buttons there. Move the buttons around to form a close group. Ask the child if there is still the same number.

Research it!

There have been criticisms of Piaget's work. It is thought that he underestimated children. Find out more about the reasons for this criticism by searching for 'Piaget criticism' on the internet.

Figure 3.9.6 This baby is in the sensorimotor stage of Piaget's stages of cognitive development – they realise that an object hasn't disappeared just because it has dropped out of view

Table 3.9.3 Piaget's stages of cognitive development

Stage	Features	Description
Sensorimotor (0–2 years)		Babies' first schemas are physical ones. They learn to repeat movements and control them.
	Development of object permanence	By 8–9 months, babies gain the concept of object permanence. They search for objects that have been hidden rather than accept that they have 'disappeared'.
	Child begins to use symbols, e.g. language	Babies start to understand that words have meanings – thus they are starting to use symbols.
Pre-operational (2–7 years)	Child uses symbols in play and thought	Children become active users of symbols, especially in their play, e.g. a cardboard box is used as an oven.
	Egocentrism	Children assume that their experiences and preferences are shared by everyone else. Piaget called this 'egocentrism'.
	Animism	Children talk or draw objects as if they have feelings too, e.g. a sun with a happy face. Piaget called this animism.
	Inability to conserve	Children have not understood conservation (see below).
Concrete operational (7–11 years)	Ability to conserve	Children understand that just because objects may have been reordered, the quantity remains the same. Ten counters in a circle is the same as 10 counters in a straight line. Piaget called this 'conservation.' Children understand the importance of rules and enjoy games that have rules. They also impose rules on others, e.g. you can't put that there!
	Children begin to solve mental problems using practical supports such as counters and objects	Children use everyday objects and their own experiences to help them solve and think about problems, e.g. a child makes a bridge that looks like one that she has seen.

Lev Vygotsky (1896–1934)

Lev Vygotsky, a Russian psychologist who was working at around the same time as Piaget, came also to the view that children were more active in their learning. However, he suggested that the role of interaction between adults (or older children) and the child was of great significance. Young children were in effect apprentices learning from watching, interacting and being coached by adults or older children.

His theory is therefore sometimes referred to as a social constructivist model, in which value is placed on the social dimension of learning. For Vygotsky, children developed more sophisticated thinking and reasoning through interactions, which he referred to as higher-level thinking.

Zone of proximal development

The zone of proximal development is a term that Vygotsky used to describe the benefits and ways in which, through adult interaction, children's cognition develops. The zone of proximal development describes the potential difference between a child's current abilities and what they might be able to achieve given adult encouragement and interaction. To understand this, it is worth looking at an example of what this means in practice.

In Figure 3.9.7a, the child can count, but has not seen or discovered how to count in pairs. With the adult's help (Figure 3.9.7b), the child's development has been extended and he learns to count in pairs on his own (Figure 3.9.7c).

Jerome Bruner (b. 1915)

Jerome Bruner was influenced by Piaget but especially by Vygotsky's work. His work has several aspects. Firstly, he suggested that there are different modes of thinking. As adults, we are able to access all of those modes, but children acquire them over time.

Table 3.9.4 Bruner's modes of representation

Enactive	Learning and thought take place because of physical movements.
Iconic	Thoughts are developed as mental images, e.g. a child thinks about milk and sees in their head a picture of it.
Symbolic	Symbols, including language, are used for thought.

Adult's role in children's learning

Like Vygotsky, Bruner believed that adults play a vital role in children's development. He suggested that children could learn anything provided that the information was sufficiently simplified and presented to them in a way that they could access. He proposed that a **spiral curriculum** would be an effective way of teaching children. Children would learn something at a simplified level, then it would be repeatedly covered in increasing depth.

Key term

spiral curriculum The concept that a subject may be repeatedly taught but in increasing depth.

Bruner also valued play as a tool for children's learning, but suggested through his research that adults are able to enrich and develop learning if they join children in play. He showed, through observing children in a range of different play settings, that when children played without any adult input, their play and ideas were less sophisticated than when adults were involved.

Figure 3.9.7a The adult observes the child can count one by one

Figure 3.9.7b The adult shows how to count in pairs

Figure 3.9.7c The child learns how to do this alone

In your setting

Are there topics, such as autumn, that children will do more than once while they attend your setting?

Social cognitive theory

Social cognitive theory was put forward by Albert Bandura (b. 1925). The theory does not explain changes in children's cognitive development but is more a theory of how children learn. Originally called social learning theory, the idea is quite simple – children learn by observing adults and others and then incorporate what they have seen into their actions and learning. This process is known as modelling. The original experiment that showed modelling is known as the Bobo doll experiment. Groups of children saw an adult in a room with a Bobo doll (an inflatable doll). When the group who saw an adult being aggressive with the doll were later put into the room with the doll, they tended to repeat what they had seen.

Since the original theory was proposed, more thought has been given as to the conditions needed in order for children to learn this way. Four key conditions are thought to be important:

- attention
- encoding and retrieving information
- opportunity to reproduce actions
- motivation.

Attention

Children need to be sufficiently attentive to the actions or skills that the adult is modelling. They also need to notice the important elements of what is being modelled. If a child saw an adult sweeping the floor but also singing at the same time, the child might focus on the singing rather than the actions involved in sweeping.

Encoding and retrieving information

The skills and actions also have to be remembered by children. Complex tasks will be difficult for children to master as their memories are still developing.

Opportunity to reproduce actions

Children also need to be able to copy fairly immediately what they have seen. If the adult uses a dustpan and brush, they will need one as well. Delay in being able to reproduce the actions can interfere with the modelling.

Motivation

What is being modelled and who is doing the modelling also seem to be important. Children may also model an action because they have seen that there is a reward or positive consequence for the action.

In practice

Observe children during role play. Can you hear any phrases or see any actions that have clearly been learnt from listening to or watching adults?

AC 2.2 How theoretical perspectives on cognitive development impact on current practice

The work of these theorists has influenced educational practice in a variety of ways.

Behaviourist approach: Skinner

The behaviourist approach is primarily used to motivate children. By praising a child who has persevered with a task, the idea is that this reinforcement will help the child persevere in future. The behaviourist approach can be used when thinking about the quality of activities themselves. We know that when children enjoy an activity, they are more likely to want to try it again. Thus a child who had a great time using markers on a whiteboard is likely to want to repeat the activity. While, on the other hand, a child who has not enjoyed an activity might try and avoid it.

Social constructivist approach: Piaget

Piaget's work has influenced current practice in a variety of ways. It is recognised that children need to have a range of opportunities in order to master concepts. There is also an understanding that children will think in different ways according to their age/stage of development. Piaget's suggestion that there are stages of cognitive development also link in with the way that the curriculum is organised at different ages – for example, Key Stage 2 begins at seven years, while Key Stage 3 begins at 11.

Social constructivist approach: Vygotsky

Vygotsky's work has been very influential in current practice. There is now a great of emphasis on carefully observing and assessing children in order to plan their next steps. The role of the adult in talking to children sensitively and drawing their attention to concepts to help them develop further is seen as important. The quality of interaction and the relationship with the adult are therefore seen as important. The emphasis on children learning by being alongside adults has meant that early years settings provide opportunities for adult-led activities as well as child-initiated ones.

Social constructivist approach: Bruner

Bruner's work on the role of the adult in scaffolding and supporting children as they learn is reflected in the importance of adult-led activities as well as the way that children in Key Stage 1 are given feedback on their activities. Bruner's belief that language is central to cognitive development as it allows children to think more symbolically is also reflected in the current frameworks. The Early Years Foundation Stage has communication and language as a prime area as it is seen as being crucial to the development of other areas of learning.

Social cognitive theory: Bandura

Bandura's social cognitive theory emphasises the role of children learning through observing others. In early years settings, adults will often initiate an activity such as writing, digging in the sand or reading a storybook. Children will often then want to join them and copy their actions. In addition, younger children in a nursery will often learn from older children by watching what they do. They may, for example, go and put on an apron before painting because they have seen that this is what the older children do.

In practice

Choose one theoretical perspective. Consider how it links to one aspect of practice in your setting.

LO3 Be able to implement a learning experience which supports the development of sustained shared thinking in children

Do you remember trying to build or make something with the support of an adult? Or perhaps you did some cooking with an adult and explored together textures or tastes. Experiences and activities with adults can help children to gain further knowledge and understanding. This way of working is sometimes called sustained shared thinking. In this section, we will look at how you might plan and implement a learning experience that will support children's sustained shared thinking.

AC 3.1 Planning a learning experience to support the development of sustained shared thinking

Key term

sustained shared thinking An interaction between adult and child that allows for the development of ideas.

Sustained shared thinking is about creating opportunities to explore ideas and concepts which allow children to learn from an activity or something that they have seen. Opportunities for sustained shared thinking can be spontaneous and based on something that children have noticed or an unplanned event, such as the arrival of snow or a child finding a spider. As well as taking up opportunities for spontaneous shared thinking, early years settings also support children's cognitive development by planning activities that might develop children's learning further.

→ In Unit 3.2, pages 184–89, we looked at planning play opportunities. As many of the same principles apply, it is worth revisiting that section alongside this one.

0–1 year 11 months

When thinking about activities in this age range, it is important to recognise that 'talk only' activities will not be appropriate. At 18 months, most children have around 15 or so words and so expecting them to give a commentary is not realistic. Instead activities have to be based on physical actions and helping them to explore their world through what they mouth, touch and can do with objects. This means that it is important to think about their current stage of development, especially their physical development.

Table 3.9.5 shows activities that could be used for this age group.

2–2 years 11 months

With children aged 2–3, it is a good idea to give them new experiences as through new experiences children can learn new vocabulary and be exposed to new concepts. As this stage of development is thought to be very active, it is important to choose activities that will allow them to be active. As their language is not yet fluent, the focus on the activity should be the 'doing'.

Table 3.9.6 shows activities that could be used for this age group.

3–5 years

From three years onwards, activities need to be sufficiently challenging and open ended so that there is a lot for the adult and the child to talk about! While the focus is still on the child being active, a good activity for this age group should generate plenty of questions or problems for the adult and child to explore together.

Table 3.9.7 shows activities that could be used for this age group.

Table 3.9.5 Activities to support sustained shared thinking for children aged 0–1 year 11 months

Activity	How it promotes sustained share thinking
Shakers and rattles	Babies and toddlers can explore different sounds. They can learn that, through their movements, they can make different sounds.
Books	Through picture books that show objects that are familiar to them, babies and toddlers can connect the objects that they see in the pictures to what they have experienced. They may, for example, point to the same item that they can see in the picture.
Knock-down play	Babies and toddlers enjoy knocking down towers of bricks. They can learn that a swiping movement causes the bricks to fall. They can also see that the taller the tower, the more bricks fall.
Pop-up toys	Working with an adult, children can learn that certain movements can cause a toy to 'pop up'. They can also learn that items that are hidden are still there.
Mirrors	It takes a while for children to learn that the reflection in the mirror is themselves. Mirrors are interesting to children and can be used as a way of helping children to look more closely at the human face and body. Adults can help the child by naming parts of the body.

Table 3.9.6 Activities to support sustained shared thinking for children aged 2–2 years 11 months

Activity	How it promotes sustained share thinking
Gloop (a mixture of cornflour and water)	Exploring the mixture of cornflour and water is pleasurable for children. Cornflour changes from solid to liquid depending on whether it is being squeezed or poured.
Outing	An outing to a local shop or play park helps children's cognitive development as the adult and the child can focus on what they see. This can provide opportunities for talk.
Books	Books that reflect children's own experiences are useful, e.g. a book about pets or a book about being messy. By looking at books, children can think about their own experiences and make connections between what they have done and what they see. Homemade books can be used for this.
Where's teddy?	Activities that encourage children to hunt for things can promote thinking. Children can think about where to look and adults can help to guide them by asking them questions.
Making shakers	An activity such as making shakers helps children's problem solving but also helps them to explore the link between sounds and materials.

Figure 3.9.8 Activities for 3–5 year olds need to be challenging but fun

Table 3.9.7 Activities to support sustained shared thinking for children aged 3–5 years

Activity	How it promotes sustained shared thinking
Sorting, e.g. button box	Sorting activities can help children to group objects together, and find matches and pairs. Sorting activities work best when the materials are sensory and varied. Button boxes are ideal for this as children may also make connections about where buttons come from.
Nature walk with magnifying glasses	Taking children outdoors to look closely at what there is in the garden or outdoor area can support shared thinking. Children can talk to each other about what they find and adults can encourage children to make connections about what they have found.
Cooking	Children can learn about size, shape and also how, through heating or mixing, ingredients can change. Children can also make connections between the cooking activity, home and also their own food preferences.
Activities linked to the weather, e.g. making windmills	Activities that link to the weather can help children's thinking. If they make windmills, they can make connections between the speed at which the windmill turns and the strength of the wind. If they look at puddles after it has rained, they may make the connection between the speed at which the puddles disappear and the sun shining.
Making models	Through making models using, for example, junk modelling or materials such as clay, children are able to express ideas based on their experiences. Adults can use this as an opportunity to explore the children's ideas further. Modelling also requires problem solving and so this helps children's thinking.

AC 3.2 Leading a learning experience to support the development of sustained shared thinking

The style we use when leading an activity that has a focus on sustained shared thinking is important. The focus is on encouraging children to reach and explore their own conclusions and so a chatty conversational style works better than a string of questions. In some ways, the role of the adult is to draw children's attention to what is happening rather than to teach the child. This style of working takes time and experience to perfect. A key factor in sustained shared thinking is time. Experiences and activities that work well are not rushed. Children need time to think and ideally the conversation with children should last until such time as the topic or feature has reached its natural conclusion.

0–1 year 11 months

When working with children aged 0–2 years, adults have to be patient and allow babies and toddlers time to touch and explore. Babies and toddlers tend not to be able to process language while being busy and so a good strategy is to wait until the child wants to involve you rather than keep interrupting them. Toddlers may, for example, pick up some shakers one by one and try them out. When they find one that is interesting, they may then make eye contact with the adult. This is a signal that the toddler is ready to explore this with the adult. As well as eye contact, babies and toddlers may also bring you things or point to objects that are of interest to them. Once this happens, you should aim to talk about what they are seeing. By naming the object or the action, they can make the connection between the word and what they are seeing.

Figure 3.9.9 The baby is learning from playing peek a boo

2–2 years 11 months

With activities for 2–3 year olds, the adult's role is again to follow the child's lead and interests. A chatty style that acknowledges that the child has found something of interest and also draws their attention to certain features can be used. For example, 'Look what you have found! A large bead. It is quite shiny, isn't it?' As two year olds are quite active, you shouldn't expect them to respond or answer straightaway; instead, they might 'do' something, such as find another shiny bead. It is also important when leading activities with this age range to recognise that their stage of language development means that it takes time for them to process information and talk back in answer to a question.

3–5 years

Children aged 3–5 years are very curious and show this by asking questions. Their language level also allows them to understand replies

> **Reflect**
>
> Have you ever seen a baby pointing at something and expecting you to look there as well?

and they increasingly enjoy solving problems with adults or doing tasks with them. It is important to follow children's interests, but increasingly we can ask questions that encourage children to speculate or explain. For example, 'Why do you think that the windmill is turning faster now?'

Reflect

Write a reflective account of how you have planned and led an activity that has allowed for sustained shared thinking.

LO4 Be able to evaluate the provision for supporting cognitive development in own setting

AC 4.1 Supporting cognitive development in your own setting

Cognitive development is an important area of development for children. Early years settings need to provide opportunities for stimulation, including sustained shared thinking. It is good practice for early years settings to review their provision to include resources, activities and also how adults work with children.

Table 3.9.8 Evaluating the provision for supporting cognitive development in own setting

Range of objects for treasure baskets	• Are there sufficient objects so that babies have plenty of different textures, shapes and sizes to explore? • Are different combinations of objects used so that babies have new exploration opportunities?
Range of objects for heuristic play	• Is there a range of different-sized containers and interesting smaller objects for toddlers to explore?
Sensory materials, e.g. gloop, sand, water	• Is there a range of different sensory materials that will encourage children to explore their properties as well as texture and capacity?
Books	• Is there a range of books for babies and toddlers to help them make connections between the pictures and their experiences? • Is there a range of books that explore colour, counting and shapes?
Building blocks	• Are there blocks or Duplo available for children to create shapes and structures?
Jigsaw puzzles	• Is there a range of jigsaw puzzles that are suitable for different ages/stages of development?
Sorting resources	• Is there a range of interesting objects available for children to count, sort and group?
Modelling	• Is there a range of resources that will allow children to create their own models and structures as this helps with problem solving?
Painting and drawing	• Is there a range of resources that will allow children to experience making colours and expressing their vision of the world?
Games, e.g. picture lotto, pairs	• Is there a range of games that will encourage children's problem solving, logic and number skills?
Mathematical resources	• Is there a range of mathematical resources that will encourage children to recognise number, count and measure, e.g. number line, measuring scales, measuring beakers and dice?
Outings	• Do children go on a variety of outings to extend their knowledge and to help talk about what they see?

Figure 3.9.10 Does your setting have blocks that help children engage in problem solving?

Resources and experiences

There needs to be a range of resources in order to give children of different ages a range of opportunities to explore different concepts.

> **In your setting**
>
> Look at the resources and range of experiences available for children. For each age range, give five examples and explain how they benefit children's cognitive development.

Planning

As well as looking at resources, early years settings also have to reflect on their planning in relation to cognitive development. It might be worth noting that cognitive development links in particular to the following EYFS areas of learning and development:

- Communication and language
- Understanding the world
- Mathematics.

You should consider the following questions when evaluating planning in your setting:

- Is children's cognitive development accurately assessed?
- How are children's interests extended?
- How are resources and activities planned to ensure that children of all ages have sufficient stimulation?
- How are adults deployed to ensure that sustained shared conversations can take place?

Role of the adult

While resources and planning are important, the style that adults use is also worth reflecting on:

- Do adults listen to children and follow up their comments and questions?
- Do adults hold worthwhile conversations with children that extend children's learning?
- Do adults work in a style that allows children to put forward their ideas?
- Do adults look out for opportunities to draw children's attention to concepts in a way that does not detract from the activity or experience?

> **In practice**
>
> Think about how your work in the setting supports children's cognitive development. Consider the resources, planning and also your style of working with children.

Assessment

For this unit you will need to complete a variety of tasks. To start with you will need to revise the stages of sensory and cognitive development that are in this unit. (You need to be secure in this knowledge as it links also to the mandatory task that also has to be completed.) You will also need to look at the scientific research in relation to neuroscience. In addition to the information in this unit you could also visit the website for the centre for Neuroscience in Education run by the University of Cambridge, which provides a range of resources and links to latest research: **www.cne.psychol.cam.ac.uk**.

In addition, for Learning Outcome 2, you need to be able to describe the different theoretical perspectives that we have looked at and be able to link these to current practice.

For Learning Outcome 3, you will need to put your knowledge into practice by planning several learning experiences that cover the three age ranges given in the assessment practice. You could consider using the ideas given in the setting or talk through possible experiences with your placements supervisor. It will be a good idea to practice the learning experiences and to gain feedback from your placement supervisor.

The final learning outcome looks at how your setting promotes cognitive development. You could use the checklist in this chapter as well as talking to experienced colleagues and other learners with whom you could compare experiences. This will help you evaluate your work setting's provision more easily.

Useful resources

Books and journals

Bruer, J.T. (1999), *The Myth of the First Three Years: A new understanding of early brain development and lifelong learning*. New York: Free Press.

Siraj-Blatchford, I. (2009), 'Conceptualising Progression in the Pedagogy of Play and Sustained Shared Thinking in Early Childhood Education: A Vygotskian Perspective', *Education and Child Psychology* 26 (2).

Websites

BBC CBeebies
www.bbc.co.uk/cbeebies

BBC Games
www.bbc.co.uk/cbbc/games/index.shtml

Berit's Best Sites
www.beritsbest.com

Enchanted Learning Online
www.enchantedlearning.com/categories/preschool.shtml

Kids @ National Geographic
www.nationalgeographic.com/kids

Kids Domain
www.kidsdomain.com

Kid's Wave:
www.safesurf.com/safesurfing

Microsoft Kids Website
www.kids.msn.com

Peter Rabbit
www.peterrabbit.com

PBS Kids
http://pbskids.org

Thomas the Tank Engine
www.hitentertainment.com/thomasandfriends/uk

Unit 3.10 WB Promote children's speech, language and communication

How often today have you used language and communication? You may have listened to the radio, said hello to someone or moaned to a friend. Being able to talk and communicate is a skill that children need to develop. It takes around four years before children are fluent talkers, but to become fluent, they need the support of adults. In this unit, we look at the theories behind how children learn language and how they link to the current early years framework. We also look at how early years practitioners can support speech and language in a variety of ways, including providing a rich environment and through the planning and implementing of activities.

Learning outcomes

By the end of this unit, you will:

1 Understand theory and current frameworks which underpin children's speech, language and communication development.
2 Understand how the early years practitioner supports the development of speech, language and communication of children.
3 Be able to create a language-rich environment to develop the speech, language and communication of children in own setting.
4 Be able to lead activities which support the development of speech, language and communication of children.

LO1 Understand theory and current frameworks which underpin children's speech, language and communication development

Have you ever heard the babbling of a baby? Interestingly, all babies babble in similar ways at first. So why do they babble and how do children learn language? There are many theories that explain this, which we will look at in this section. We also look at how these theories are reflected in the current frameworks.

AC 1.1 Speech, language and communication

The terms speech, language and communication are often used together because they are related, but they do have specific meanings. Figure 3.10.1 shows the relationship between them.

Speech

This term is often used to mean spoken language as opposed to written language or sign language. This is how it is used in this unit. For speech and language therapists, the term speech is used to refer to the sounds that children make as they talk.

Language

There are many different types of language, including sign language, reading and writing, and spoken languages. Language is a set of abstract symbols. A symbol is something that stands for something else. In a spoken language, words that we say stand for objects, people or ideas. When we say the word 'elephant', for example, we are referring to something grey and large with a trunk and flappy ears. It might not even be in the room, but we still know what that word stands for. Every language also has its own set of rules or grammar and is, in effect, a code. To use and understand a language, you have to know the symbols and the rules. The following 'sentence' is an example where the symbols and code of English are not being used consistently:

Banana a keeps fridge the□■◆ي

Communication

Communication is an umbrella term covering all ways in which information can be exchanged between people. It includes facial expression, body language and gestures, as well as spoken, signed and written language.

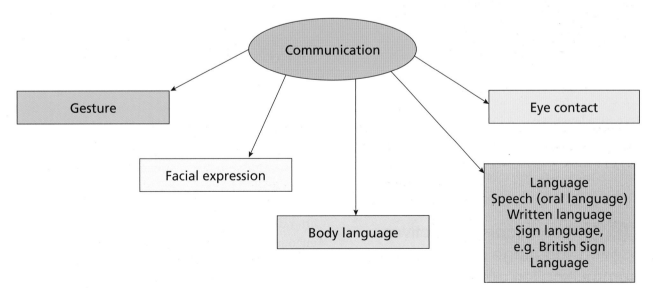

Figure 3.10.1 Communication is an umbrella term that includes a number of different communication methods

Figure 3.10.2 Facial expression is one of several forms of communication

Receptive and expressive language

There are two other terms that are frequently used when referring to children's speech: receptive and expressive. Receptive language is the ability to understand what is being said. Expressive language is about being able to use talk to communicate. As we saw in Unit 3.5, the usual pattern is that babies' receptive language develops before they start to express words. This means that by nine or ten months old, most babies understand a few words, but it is not until a few months later that they will start to use them.

AC 1.2 Theoretical perspectives speech, language and communication development

How and why children learn to speak are an area of ongoing research, although over the years four different theoretical perspectives have emerged:

- **innateness** perspective
- **behaviourist** perspective
- **constructivist** perspective
- **sociological** perspective.

Key terms

innateness Behaviours, skills or characteristics that are instinctive.

behaviourist Behaviours, skills or characteristics that are learnt as a result of reinforcement.

constructivist Behaviours, skills or knowledge that are learnt as a result of cognitive processing.

sociological Behaviours, skills or characteristics that are learnt as a result of being with others.

Innateness perspective

A key theoretical perspective is that language is natural and instinctive. There is much evidence in favour of the innateness theories, given that all humans learn language and that all babies follow similar patterns of learning language in their first year. The leading theory is that of Noam Chomsky, who suggests that children come primed not only ready to learn language, but also to pick up the rules of grammar. According to Chomsky, this ability comes from a 'language acquisition device' which children from birth use to work out the grammar or linguistic rules of the language that they are exposed to. As babies can pick up any language at first, Chomsky suggests that there must be some structures and rules that are the same in all languages. He refers to this as 'Universal Grammar'.

Behaviourist perspective

Behaviourism is a theoretical approach that believes children learn language because they are rewarded for it in some way. The behaviourist approach would suggest that, when babies gain attention and smiles when they babble, this encourages them to do more. The behaviourist model would suggest that parents respond to their children's speech more positively when they use correct grammar and so this helps children to work out the grammatical constructions. There are a few flaws with this approach, though.

Firstly, it does not explain why children's speech is different from adults'. For example, two year olds use abbreviated speech patterns, such as 'Me want book now', but if they were simply copying, they would use a more correct format because adults do not speak like that. Another flaw in this proposition is that babies and children will often talk to themselves, during which they are not getting any attention or reward.

Figure 3.10.3 The behaviourist approach to language development believes that children learn language through rewards such as attention and smiles

Constructivist perspective

The constructivist perspective argues that children work out the rules of language and the meanings of words because of cognitive processes. They draw conclusions from what they see and experience. For example, a baby notices that every time he is given a bottle, his parent mentions the word 'milk'. He therefore comes to the conclusion that 'milk' is the word used for what he is drinking. The key

theorist associated with the cognitive perspective of language is Jean Piaget.

➡We also looked at Piaget's cognitive theory on page 283.

Sociological perspective

Sociological perspectives focus on language acquisition as a tool to communicate with others rather than an area of development for its own sake. The child learns language as part of his social development. Social perspectives of language development stress the way in which adult–child interactions are different from adult–adult interactions. The term 'motherese' is used, for example, to describe the style of talking that parents use to encourage their child to vocalise and communicate.

AC 1.3 How theoretical perspectives inform current frameworks

The Early Years Foundation Stage and the National Curriculum reflect the theoretical perspectives in a range of ways.

Innateness perspective

One of the features of innateness as a perspective is that children learn language in a certain sequence. This is reflected in the way that the Early Years Framework and the National Curriculum set targets for what might be expected of children according to their age band. In the Early Years Foundation Stage, these are the Early Learning Goals. In addition to the early years goals, there is a non-statutory guidance document issued by the Department of Education, 'Early outcomes', which breaks down expected communication and language development into smaller age-related steps.

Behaviourist perspective

The behaviourist perspective is reflected in the frameworks because there is a focus on children enjoying speaking and gaining positive feedback from early years practitioners and teachers. The theory means that, if children are enjoying language activities, this in turn will help them to learn.

Figure 3.10.4 Children enjoy positive feedback from adults

Constructivist perspective

The current frameworks suggest that children's language can be supported through a range of activities, including the reading of books. The constructivist perspective on language would suggest that children learn the meanings of words and the structure of language by drawing conclusions from these experiences.

Sociological perspective

The sociological perspective would suggest that the role of the adult in building a relationship with the child and talking to them would be important in learning language. Role modelling would also be important in language, as would children talking and communicating with each other. The Early Years Foundation Stage and the National Curriculum both stress the role of the adult in supporting children's language and identify that children should have opportunities to talk and communicate with each other.

LO2 Understand how the early years practitioner supports the development of speech, language and communication of children

Do you remember learning to talk? Probably not, but you may remember adults talking to you when you were playing or sharing a story. The role of the adult seems to be important in promoting children's language. In this section, we look at ways in which language is important to children's overall development and how we can use technology to promote children's language.

→ This section links closely with LO3.

AC 2.1 The benefits to children's holistic learning and development

Language plays an important role in children's holistic learning and development in a variety of ways. This is why it is a prime area in the Early Years Foundation Stage and why settings will spend time assessing and monitoring children's progress within this area. Figure 3.10.5 shows the role of language in children's holistic development.

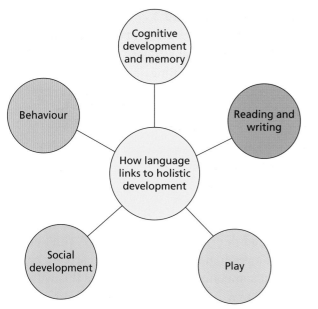

Figure 3.10.5 How language links to holistic development

Cognitive development and memory

Cognitive development and language are linked. We seem to use language to help us process information and store it. A good example of this is the way that, when we hear a phrase such as 'wellington boot', a picture is likely to come to mind. The picture is a memory, but the word itself has triggered the memory. Children also need good language levels to understand explanations and so to acquire new concepts. They may, for example, see that wood does not sink. Without knowing that wood fits into a category of materials that 'submerge' in water and hear the word 'submerge', they may carry on thinking that it 'floats'.

Children also learn by asking questions or drawing an adult's attention to what they have seen. One of the earliest questions that children ask is 'What's dat?' This in turn helps children's cognitive development as they learn what things are, how they work and also how to think about them.

Reading and writing

Language is also linked to reading and writing. A word on the page means nothing unless you have a memory of what it means, and similarly you cannot write a sentence if you do not have any words in your mind. As reading and writing allow children to develop their thoughts and ideas further, as well

as learn about others, children who are not given opportunities to develop their language lose out.

Behaviour

Children's behaviour is linked to many factors, including their stage of development, but also their language level. Language seems to help children to be less impulsive and to think through their actions. Some unwanted behaviours are also linked to children's frustration because they cannot make themselves understood. Supporting children's language can therefore make a significant difference to their behaviour.

Social development

One of the many skills that children have to learn is to socialise with other children. To do this well, children need to learn to 'read' others' faces and body language, and also to know how to express themselves. By supporting children's speech, communication and language skills, it means that we are also helping their social development.

Figure 3.10.6 Communication is an important tool in children's social development

Play

Play is important for children. As we saw in Unit 3.1, it gives them pleasure, as well as helping them to learn and socialise. As children's language develops, so too does the way that they play. Play becomes more cooperative, complex and imaginative. Communication also plays a large part in playing with others, so again supporting children's communication and language helps their play.

AC 2.2 How using technology supports speech, language and communication development

Over the past few years, technology has developed and so many settings use technology to support children's speech, language and communication. Table 3.10.1 shows how technology can be used.

In your setting

What types of technology are used in your setting to support children's speech and language?

The role of the adult

Technology by itself does not benefit children's language development. Indeed, research shows that too much screen time, including time in front of the television or computer, may have a negative impact on children's language. In addition, television, radio and music as background noise can also interfere with babies' and toddlers' interest in tuning into the sounds of words or interest in talking. For technology to be positive in terms of children's speech and language, it is important that it is a shared experience either with an adult or with other children. A child might look at a photograph of himself on a screen, but without someone to talk to and share this with, the child may not say anything. On the other hand, if an adult sits with the child, the child is likely to talk about the photo.

In practice

Ask your workplace supervisor if you can observe an adult working with technology to support a child's language. Write an account that includes the type of technology, how it was used and how you feel that it promoted the child's language.

Table 3.10.1 How technology supports the development of speech, language and communication

Computer programs	Software designed for young children can stimulate children to talk with adults as they complete a game.
Mobile phone apps	There are some mobile phone and tablet apps that allow parents to further their child's language and communication development by sharing interactive experiences. This includes apps that build the child's vocabulary, and prompt discussion. Apps also have the benefit of being relatively cheap (or free in many cases) and can be used on the go!
Recording devices	There is a range of devices that can be used by children to record their own voices. Children can talk to themselves and then play it back to an adult. In addition, recording devices can also be used by adults to help them assess the progress of children's speech and language.
Digital photographs and film recordings	Children love looking at images of themselves on a laptop, phone or smart board. Images in the form of photographs or films can be used to help children talk about events in the past. It is also possible to gain resources such as film clips to help children learn more about their world, e.g. 'people who help us' or different places, such as the seaside.
Digital books	Digital books can provide adults and children with the opportunity to share a book together.

Figure 3.10.7 Technology can be used in a variety of forms to support children's development

LO3 Be able to create a language-rich environment to develop the speech, language and communication of children in own setting

Have you ever been at a crowded party when there are so many people it is hard to hear what they are saying? Perhaps you have also found it hard to concentrate because the person you are talking to is distracted. Fortunately, early years settings know that this type of environment is not suited to the development of children's speech, language and communication! In this section, we will look at how early years settings promote children's language through the environment that they create.

AC 3.1 Creating a language-rich environment in your own setting

> ### Key term
>
> **language-rich environment** A term used to describe a way of working with children that provides them with plenty of opportunities to hear and use language and also to gain new vocabulary.

A **language-rich environment** is one where children have plenty of opportunities to interact with adults and also, for children who are speaking well, with each other. A language-rich environment also encourages interaction as there are interesting things to talk about and places where interaction can take place without interruption. There are several factors to consider when creating a language-rich environment.

Quality interaction with adults

Quality interaction is time spent listening, responding and talking. There are several features which make interactions high quality. Firstly, the interactions have to be enjoyable for both the child and the adult. They also have to be relaxed and unhurried. There needs to be enough time for the child to respond, even with babies, who may respond by smiling or babbling. One of the major factors in promoting children's language is how much interaction time is spent with adults. Babies and toddlers need a significant amount of time engaged in quality interaction. A language-rich environment allows adults to spend time interacting with children easily.

A cosy environment

Background noise can hinder children's language development at all ages. For babies who are just starting to work out the sounds used in language, they need a calm and quiet environment. Loud voices, constant music or voices on the radio or television can interfere with their ability to tune into 'their adult's' voice. Once children are talking, they need to be able to hear themselves talk and

Figure 3.10.8 Interesting resources should be available for children to talk about

also hear what others say. In terms of creating a language-rich environment, this means monitoring the amount of background noise, but also arranging furniture so that spaces are not too large. Many settings also create tents or cosy areas as these seem to prompt children to vocalise and talk more. Interestingly, many settings also create these cosy areas outdoors too.

> **In your setting**
>
> Do you have cosy areas where children can spend time talking?

Interesting resources and displays

Babies, toddlers and children of all ages are more likely to vocalise/talk when something catches their interest. A baby may point at an object or a toddler might pick something up to show their adult. In terms of creating a language-rich environment, this means making sure that there are resources and displays that are sufficiently interesting to prompt children into vocalising and talking. A pre-school might put out a nature table of objects for three and four year olds to touch, while a childminder might put out a treasure basket on the floor so that babies can handle and explore interesting objects. In a day care nursery, the table might be laid for lunch in different ways. Sometimes there are placemats on the table; at other times a tablecloth is put out and sometimes a table decoration is put out. In some settings, laptops and smart boards are used so that children can look at and talk about photographs or film clips, while in others, display boards are regularly changed to encourage talk.

Interesting resources for children to talk about also need to be available in the outdoor area.

Some settings keep pets so that children are able to go and look at them and feed them. This prompts children into a lot of interesting conversations. Other settings might have a bird table, a wind chime or some fabric windmills. It is also possible to put out objects that children 'find' – for example, a pair of shoes dangling from a tree or a suitcase. These unexpected objects are likely to be a source of interest to children and so encourage children to talk.

Opportunities for sharing books and rhymes

Looking at books with adults seems to promote children's language. This is why most settings will create areas where children can look at books independently and also share books with adults. Areas for sharing books need to be cosy and comfortable and so most settings will use a corner and put out cushions and sofas. The way that books are displayed is also important. The books need to be attractive and suitable for the age and stage of the children. The books also have to be accessible for children and so may be put into baskets for babies and low shelves so that toddlers can reach them. As well as sharing books, language-rich environments also provide opportunities for children to learn and use new rhymes and songs. Rhymes and songs seem to encourage babies and toddlers to vocalise. They are also helpful in encouraging older children to hear rhymes in words and particular sounds. This skill is called **auditory discrimination** and is needed when learning to read.

Figure 3.10.9 Sharing books with children supports their communication and language development

Opportunities for role play

Role play is a type of imaginative play.

→ See also page 339 for more on role play.

Most children start enjoying role play when they are around three years old. Role play encourages children to talk and communicate as they dress up or pretend to be someone else. Creating varied role-play opportunities is therefore a key way of creating a language-rich environment. Early years settings will often vary the props and the layout of the role-play area so that children can pretend to be in a wide range of situations, both indoors and outdoors. This in turn prompts children to learn and use a range of vocabulary. It is good practice when creating a new role-play situation for adults to model the language involved as, in some cases, children may not have been in the real-life situation and so will not know what to do – for example, at a train station or at the hospital.

> ### Key term
>
> **auditory discrimination** The ability to pick out particular sounds in words or music.

> ### Research it!
>
> Find out more about how sharing books with babies and young children can promote language. Visit the National Literacy Trust's website: **www. literacytrust.org.uk**.

In practice

Consider how you might develop a language-rich environment in your setting. Ask your placement supervisor if you could do any, some or all of the following:

- spend more time interacting with children
- find ways to cut down background noise
- put up a new display
- create an interest table
- organise a cosy area, e.g. outdoors
- organise a new theme for the role-play area
- put together a new treasure basket for babies
- choose new objects for the outdoor area for children to find and talk about
- create a different look for the story area.

After you have changed the environment, note the reactions of the children. Consider the impact of your changes on the children's level of interaction.

Case study

Jolly Tots nursery has decided to focus in the coming months on communication and language as this was one area that was highlighted in a recent Ofsted report. The team are aware that not all children are making sufficient progress. They begin by auditing the environment and then look at the resources. Finally, they observe each other working with children. As a result of their work, they realise that some children were not getting much interaction during the sessions. They also noted that there was a lot of background noise and that there were probably not sufficient cosy areas where adults and children could talk together. They also evaluated their book corner and decided that many books were not attractive.

A few weeks later, the environment and the way in which the staff worked had changed. Staff spent longer interacting with children and made sure that they were at eye level. Cosy spaces were created and staff made displays to encourage children to talk. While the team are pleased with the results, they have decided to look next at role-play opportunities.

1 Why would background noise affect children's communication and language?
2 How will the changes made so far support children's communication and language?
3 Why is role play important in supporting children's communication and language?

LO4 Be able to lead activities which support the development of speech, language and communication of children

Do you remember playing games when you were young or perhaps looking at books? You might remember learning nursery rhymes or joining in songs, such as the 'Hokey Cokey'. These adult-led activities are all important in developing children's speech and language. In this section, we look at how you might plan and implement activities for different ages of children. We will also think about how you can reflect on your language practice with children.

AC 4.1 Planning activities to support speech, language and communication development

There are many wonderful activities that adults can do to support children's speech and language. The starting point when choosing activities is to consider children's stage of development, especially their level of language. It is also important to think about children's interests and particularly how they play.

→ You might like to revisit pages 165–66, which look at how children's play needs change over time.

0–1 year 11 months

In this age range, babies and toddlers need adults who they are familiar with to work with them. They also like adults to be close to them during interaction. They tend not to like sudden noises or abrupt movements. So when planning activities for this age range, this needs to be taken into account. Babies and toddlers also like repetition, and activities that can be done several times tend to work well. This is because it often takes babies a while to work out what is happening and so, by repeating the activity, they start to anticipate what is due to happen. The repetition also helps babies and toddlers learn to associate particular words and phrases with the activity. From this repetition, toddlers are more likely to use the words and phrases that they have heard.

Table 3.10.2 Activities to support babies' and toddlers' language development

Activity	How they support language development
Pop-up puppets/jack in the box	Babies and toddlers are fascinated with things appearing and disappearing. Babies and toddlers start to recognise phrases associated with the activity, such as 'It's gone!' 'Ready, here it comes!' and 'Down he goes.' Toddlers will start to say these expressions.
Bubbles	Babies and toddlers enjoy watching bubbles and may reach out to find them. They can start to recognise words and phrases such as 'Pop' and 'Look, there's a big one.'
Books	Babies and toddlers like simple picture books that have a single illustration on each page. They especially like books that have animals in them and also objects that they can recognise, such as a beaker or teddy. Once a baby or toddler gets to recognise a book or picture, they will start to become excited and may point or vocalise. With toddlers, think about using flap books with very simple storylines.
Finger and action rhymes	Finger and action rhymes encourage vocalisation as well as help babies and toddlers to learn the meanings of words. Repeating rhymes such as 'Pat a cake' or 'Round and round the garden like a teddy bear' helps babies to anticipate the words and to link the words to the action. Toddlers are likely to start joining in.
Peek a boo	From around seven months, babies start to like playing peek a boo. Peek a boo, when an adult hides their face behind a scarf and then appears, is a source of great enjoyment for babies and it encourages communication. Once babies understand the game, they start first to be more active in pulling away the scarf and then use it to hide themselves. Toddlers like playing peek a boo by pulling a piece of fabric or scarf over themselves and will want you to 'find' them.

There is a range of different activities that can support babies' and toddlers' language. Table 3.10.2 shows some examples of activities that can be planned.

2–2 years 11 months

In this year, children's speech should be developing so that they progress from two-word sentences to longer sentences. They will also start to ask questions. Activities that work well allow plenty of opportunities for talk. As children in this age group are known to be active, activities need to be planned carefully so that there is not too much sitting involved.

3–5 years

Children who are in the 3–5-year age range need opportunities to develop their vocabulary and language further. They are starting to take turns, enjoy being together and love activities involving new experiences. While they can understand a lot of what is being said, they are likely to talk when they are listening. This is because when they hear something that links to another experience of theirs,

they make a connection and so talk about it. This is a good sign and shows that they are listening! This means that activities that work well allow children to talk a lot.

AC 4.2 Activities to support the development of speech, language and communication

Implementing an activity, especially if you are being observed as part of an assessment, can be daunting. The following box contains some tips to consider when implementing speech, language and communication activities.

Implementing activities for babies aged 0–1 year 11 months

The key when implementing activities with babies (see page 308) is to gain their attention and to use strong facial expression. Do not talk loudly, but instead use soft, warm tones. It is also important to understand that babies from seven or so months need to get to know an adult well before being ready

Table 3.10.3 Activities to support language development in children aged 2–2 years 11 months

Activity	How they support language development
Books	Two year olds enjoy sharing books with adults. They particularly like simple books that have a repetitive or rhyming narrative. They enjoy studying the pictures. Books helps children to hear grammatically correct sentences and new vocabulary, as well as giving two year olds opportunities to talk.
Short outings, e.g. to the park, to the shop	Two year olds are active and so enjoy short outings to local places, such as to the shops or to the park. The outing gives opportunities for children to notice new objects and features in their environment and learn the vocabulary associated with them. Outings also provide plenty of opportunities for language interaction as two year olds often stop and look at things and adults can follow up their interests.
Action rhymes	Two year olds love moving and also joining in rhymes. Action rhymes such as 'Head, shoulders, knees and toes' work well with this age range. They allow children to learn and use new vocabulary. Rhymes are also good for helping two year olds to develop their speech sounds as they repeat words clearly.
What's in the bag/box?	Two year olds enjoy exploring new objects. Putting out objects into bags or boxes for children to touch and explore is a popular activity. The items in the bag or box can be familiar or new to the child. This activity helps children to learn new words, but also helps them to ask questions and talk about what they are seeing and touching.
Helping adults, e.g. sorting washing, washing up, sweeping, laying the table	Many two year olds are interested in helping adults with tasks such as sorting out, washing, laying the table or sweeping up. These tasks help children learn to follow simple instructions and also learn new phrases and expressions. Some of the best activities have an element of repetition so that the child can copy what the adult has said, e.g. 'Another fork here', 'Another baby sock!'

Figure 3.10.10 Children enjoy watching puppets and they can be used to support their language development too

to join in. Babies can lose interest in activities quickly so be ready to end the activity once they no longer are interested.

Implementing activities for children aged 2–2 years 11 months

This age range is known for being active and restless. It is not uncommon for them to stand up or make actions while they are sharing a book with an adult or to leave an activity and then come back to it. It is important for adults to recognise that this is a characteristic of their stage of development and to work with it rather than to force the child to stay still. Most two year olds are not developmentally at an age when they can take turns or share and so pairs or individual work tends to be more effective. Children in this age range also need time to respond to questions and they may sometimes appear not to have understood or be willing to respond when in

Table 3.10.4 Activities to support language development in children aged 3–5 years

Activity	How they support language development
Role play	Creating a new role-play area and equipping it with plenty of authentic props can encourage speech and language. Children can also help in the creation of a role-play area.
Picture lotto	Simple games can be introduced to this age range that help children to learn vocabulary, take turns and also match sounds or words. It is important when planning games such as picture lotto to observe children's stage of development to make sure that the game will be suitable.
Books	Books are an important way of developing children's vocabulary and also encouraging them to talk about what is happening and what might happen next. Children in this age range enjoy stories with a plot, although they do need to be able to look at the pictures. If children have enjoyed a book, they are likely to want to hear it again and may choose to look at the book independently.
Cooking	Most children in this age range enjoy cooking. Through cooking, children gain vocabulary associated with measuring and counting. They also learn to follow simple instructions. Cooking also encourages children to talk.
Kim's game	Kim's game is a memory game. Objects are placed on a tray. Children look at the objects and name them The tray is covered and one object is taken away. The children have to work out what has been taken. This game can help children learn new words and the game can also be tailored so that all the objects begin with the same sound to extend older children's sound knowledge, e.g. bell, bag, ball, belt.

reality they still need time to get their thoughts together. Their speech is also likely to be unclear and so it is important that they spend time with the same adult, who slowly will start to understand their speech. See Table 3.10.6 on page 308.

Reflect

We know that nursery rhymes are important for children's speech. How many nursery rhymes do you know?

Tips for speech, language and communication activities

1 Make sure the activity is safe, especially if you do not know the child well or it is the first time that you have used the resource or material.

2 Be ready to practise the activity by yourself so that you know it well and are confident. For example, read a book first so that you know what is in it.

3 Consider whether the activity will be enjoyable and will interest the children. A good tip is to base activities on things that you have seen children enjoy.

4 Work out the best time to carry out the activity. Activities that require high levels of concentration are best done when babies or toddlers are not tired, while older children who are busy playing may be reluctant to stop what they are doing to join you.

5 Think about the best place to carry out the activity. In general, speech, language and communication activities need to be in quiet places so that children can easily hear and speak.

6 Consider the optimum group size. With babies and toddlers, activities with individual children are the most effective as they need high levels of adult attention. With older children, activities in groups of more than four can mean that children are not sufficiently active and so become bored.

7 Think about how you will present the activity. Long introductions usually mean that children lose attention and so think about how quickly you can start off the actual activity.

8 Remember that babies and toddlers need a lot of facial expressions, gestures and time to respond and so do not rush the activity.

9 With older children, it is worth remembering that listening for this age range is an active skill and so they will need to talk in order to process the information.

10 Monitor children's reactions during the activity. Be ready to adapt the activity, following children's interests, or if necessary end the activity.

Table 3.10.5 Implementing activities for 0–1 year 11 month olds

Activity	Implementation
Pop-up puppets/jack in the box	Sit close to the baby or toddler. Show the baby or toddler the toy and slowly show how it works. Allow the toddler to touch and use the puppet or jack in the box. Make eye contact with the baby or toddler and show 'mock surprise' when the puppet appears or the jack in the box pops up. Repeat the activity using the same phrases. Allow time for the toddler to join in with the phrase. End the activity promptly once the baby or toddler starts to lose interest.
Bubbles	Blow the bubbles gently, avoiding the baby's or toddler's eyes. Point to the bubbles and name them. Repeat the activity and pop a couple of bubbles. Encourage the baby or toddler to reach out and pop the bubbles. Use a similar phrase each time a bubble has been popped, e.g. ''it's gone.' Talk to the toddler about what size of bubble you should blow.
Books	Choose a book that has simple pictures and is robust as babies try to take books into their mouths, while toddlers like to turn the pages but may unintentionally rip them. Point to the pictures and talk about them. If it is an animal, make the animal sound. Do not worry if a baby or toddler wants to look at a picture for a long time or wants to look back at the preceding page. End the activity promptly once the baby or toddler starts to lose interest.
Finger rhymes	Sit the baby on your lap and let the toddler either sit near you or stand. Say the finger rhyme or action rhyme and make the movements. Speak softly and tunefully. If it is a new rhyme for the baby or toddler, do not expect much reaction the first time round. Repeat the activity and see if the baby or toddler starts to anticipate the movements and the words.
Peek a boo	Sit the baby on your lap. When you have his attention, pull a light piece of fabric or scarf over your head slowly. After a moment, pull the fabric away slowly and say 'peek a boo' with a smile. Allow the baby plenty of time to respond and then repeat. You may need to repeat four or five times to gain a response. If the baby seems upset, stop immediately. If the baby has done this activity before, you might find that the baby will pull the fabric away from your head. With toddlers, start by putting the fabric on your head, but expect that they will either want to drape the fabric over your head or over their own.

Table 3.10.6 Implementing activities for 2–2 years 11 month olds

Activity	Implementation
Books	Choose books with a rhyme or a pattern to it that will allow the two year old to anticipate what is going to happen. Practise reading it first so that you can get the intonation right. Expect that two year olds will also want to touch the book and spend time poring over the pictures. They may also want to go back and look at preceding pages. This is a good sign as it means that they are interested. Be ready to draw the activity to a close if the child loses interest.
Short outings, e.g. to the park, to the shop	A short outing will always require written permission from the parent and also a risk assessment. You should also study and know your setting's procedures for outings and, unless you are qualified, you will need to be accompanied by another staff member. When you are on an outing with two year olds, expect to walk slowly. Go at their pace and recognise that the journey is as important in talking terms as the actual destination. Stop and talk about what they are interested in and also draw their attention to things in the environment, such as trees, cats and even traffic. Take photographs of your destination so that afterwards you can make a display or book.
Action rhymes	Action rhymes such as 'Head, shoulders, knees and toes' or the 'Hokey Cokey' work well with this age range, as they like being active. Expect at first that children will just watch rather than join in. This is usual until they have heard the rhyme several times. Do not say the rhyme too fast to ensure that children have time to process the words.

→

Table 3.10.6 Implementing activities for 2–2 year 11 month olds (contd.)

Activity	Implementation
What's in the bag/box?	Look out for a bag or a box and choose some objects that are safe and interesting for a two year old to find. If you decide to do this with more than one child, think about having a bag or box for each child. Let them take out the object and talk to them about what they have found. Expect that they might walk around with it or stand as you talk to them.
Helping adults, e.g. sorting washing, washing up, sweeping, laying the table	Think about simple tasks where it would be safe for a two year old to help you. Risk assess where necessary. Start by simply doing the task in front of the child, rather than telling them what to do, as two year olds are quick to copy actions. Make sure that they have the same equipment as you so that they can follow exactly. Talk to the child as you are engaged in the task and, where you can, repeat phrases such as 'another one' or 'one more'.

Implementing activities for 3–5 year olds

Good preparation is the key to language activities with this age range. (See Table 3.10.7.) Make sure that you have your resources to hand and, with activities such as reading a book or cooking, practise first. You should also be aware during an activity that children should be given a lot of opportunities for speech and keep an eye on the balance between how much you talk and how much children talk. Children in this age range often make interesting connections between

Table 3.10.7 Implementing activities for 3–5 year olds

Activity	Implementation
Role play	Collect a range of props that will support the new role-play area. Check that they are safe for children to handle and use. Set up the role play and then introduce the children to it. Begin by playing a part in the role play so that children can learn the words, dialogue and actions associated with the type of situation on which the role play is based.
Picture lotto	Find out whether children have played picture lotto before. If it is a new game for them, start by choosing a set of picture lotto cards with fairly familiar images. Explain the game and allow children to look at the images on the cards. Take time during the game to talk about the pictures and avoid focusing just on the game itself. With children who have played this game before, make a picture lotto set with images that might give children more detailed vocabulary, e.g. instead of an image of a 'bird', look out for cards with specific birds, such as a robin. Monitor children's reactions carefully during the game and if necessary bring the game to a speedy end or allow children to use the cards to create their own version of the game.
Books	Sharing books remains important for this age range. Depending on the language level of children, books can be read to small groups, although wherever possible group size should be kept as small as possible. Practise reading the story first and make sure that the size of the book will allow children to be able to see the illustrations. Read the story, taking your time to ask questions. Expect that children will talk in response to a question and may not be able to take turns. Encourage children to talk to each other to discuss things, such as what will happen next. Monitor children's reactions and enjoyment carefully. Be ready to end the activity early if necessary.
Cooking	Choose a recipe which will allow children to be very active and where there is little waiting around. Try to make sure that each child can do their own cooking. Write out simple instructions using pictures so that children can learn the link between language and writing. Talk to children and use detailed language to explain the cooking process.
Kim's game	Prepare a range of objects that could be put onto the tray. Make sure that they are safe for children to handle. Put 10–20 objects onto the tray and explain the game to the children. Quickly start the game so that the children understand how it is played. Repeat the game with other objects, but this time encourage the children to talk about the objects. Repeat the game, but allow children to take turns to remove an object. Keep an eye on children's interest and adapt or end the activity if their interest is waning.

what they are doing and other experiences they have had. It is a good idea to follow these up and so do not worry if the direction of the activity changes – for example, you read a book about a lighthouse but children start to talk about a visit to the sea.

AC 4.3 The early years practitioner's role in supporting speech, language and communication development in their own setting

A major way in which we can help children's speech, language and communication is by reflecting on our role. There are many skills involved in supporting children's speech and language and so thinking about our practice can help improve our work with children. One of the best ways of finding out about your practice is to ask someone for feedback or to ask for someone to record you working with children. There are several things to consider when reflecting on your practice.

What do your voice tone and pitch sound like?

Young children respond better to soft, tuneful tones and a sing-song pitch.

How clearly do you speak?

Babies and young children need to hear clear speech that is not too fast or rushed in order that they can pick up the sounds in the words.

How warm are your facial expression and eye contact?

Babies and young children pick up language through quality interactions with adults. They are more likely to concentrate and learn if they are looking at a warm, interested face. When they vocalise or talk, they also need the adult to look at them as this shows that the adult is listening.

Do you recast and expand sentences?

When babies and young children vocalise or talk, they need adults to acknowledge their attempts at communication. Adults do this by repeating what the child has said and also expanding it – for example, a child says 'da' and points. The adult says 'Yes, Daddy's there!'

Do you allow for sufficient response time?

Babies and young children take time to respond to questions, activities or what they are seeing. If you ask a question, do you give them plenty of time to respond or do you repeat the question or answer it for them?

Test yourself

Why do young children need a longer time to respond than older children or adults?

Do you follow children's interests during interaction?

Babies and children who have seen something or want to say something need an adult to acknowledge what they have said and will adapt the conversation accordingly. Some adults decide on the topic of conversation or questions and, even when children are interested in talking about something else, will not follow the child's interest.

Do you choose books carefully according to children's language level and interest?

Books, as we have seen, are an important tool for children's speech and language. Adults need to make sure that there is a good selection of books available and that, when they share a book with a child, it is at the right level and is likely to be enjoyable.

Do you know your rhymes?

Finger and action rhymes help children's speech production and auditory discrimination. It is important to learn some rhymes by heart so that you can say them well rather than just read them. You should make sure that you know a range of rhymes suitable for different ages of children.

Research it!

Learn some rhymes for different ages of children by visiting the Words for Life website from the National Literacy Trust: www.wordsforlife.org.uk/songs.

Assessment

To complete this unit, you will need to complete a variety of tasks. As there is some overlap between Unit 3.5, it will be worth revisiting. Your starting point for this unit is to revise the meaning of the terms that are being used in relation to speech, language and communication. You have to show that you can describe the different theoretical perspectives and consider how they relate to the early years foundation stage. You could use the information in this unit to help you with this. (You need to be secure in this knowledge as it links also to the mandatory task that also has to be completed.)

For Learning Outcome 2, you need to show that you understand the importance of speech, communication and language to children's overall development as well as how technology can be used to promote children's development in this area. Information about these topics can be found in this unit.

For Learning Outcome 3, you will need to show that you can create a language-rich environment. To do

this you will need to work closely with your placement supervisor. It might be worth writing down some of the suggestions that you would like to try and gain some feedback before implementing them. You can also use the information within the unit to help you decide how you might attempt this.

For Learning Outcome 4, you will need to put your knowledge into practice by planning several learning experiences that cover the three age ranges given in the assessment practice. You could consider using the ideas given in this book or talk through possible experiences with your placements supervisor. It will be a good idea to practise the learning experiences and to gain feedback from your placement supervisor. You also need to reflect on your role in promoting speech, language and communication. To help you do this, you could gain feedback on your work from experienced colleagues and also your placement supervisor. You could also use the questions in the unit to help you with this.

Useful resources

Books and articles

Lindon, J. (2002), Child Care and Early Education: Good Practice to Support Young Children and Their Families. London: Thomson Learning.

'Statutory Framework for the Early Years Foundation Stage' (March 2012). DfE.

Whitehead, M. (1997), *The Development of Language and Literacy*. London: Hodder and Stoughton.

Unit 3.11 WB Promoting children's physical development

Do you remember enjoying running and climbing as a child? Perhaps you had a bicycle, scooter or skateboard. Physical development plays an important in children's lives and learning. In this unit, we look at the typical stages of children's physical development, the theories behind it and also how you plan opportunities to promote children's physical development.

Learning outcomes

By the end of this unit, you will:

1 Understand physical development of children.
2 Understand theory and current frameworks in relation to children's physical development.
3 Be able to implement opportunities which promote the physical development of children.

LO1 Understand physical development of children

Have you ever seen a baby trying to crawl? At first they tend to go backwards! In this section, we look at the usual pattern by which children's physical skills develop. We also look at the importance of physical development in relation to children's overall development.

AC 1.1 Physical development stages from birth to seven years

A good starting point when looking at physical development is to consider the terms that are used. Physical development is a broad area and covers children's ability to ride a bike through to how well they can hold a pencil!

Figure 3.11.1 shows how the many aspects of physical development come together.

Many tasks that we take for granted require more than one physical skill. Eating a bowl of cereal, for example, requires you to stand or sit, grasp the spoon and use hand–eye coordination to put cereal onto it and then move it towards your mouth! That requires a surprising amount of skill and so, as you can imagine, it takes a while before children can do this.

In your setting

Observe children in your setting and identify the different physical skills involved with each of the following everyday tasks:

- dressing
- feeding
- playing with sensory materials
- playing outdoors.

Stages of physical development

Physical development is something that occurs in a set sequence. It starts off with babies being born

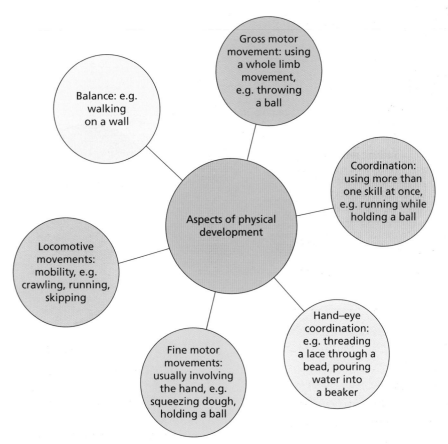

Figure 3.11.1 Aspects of physical development

Figure 3.11.2 A seemingly simple task requires a great deal of skill

fairly helpless, with only a set of reflexes for survival. Figure 3.11.3 shows some of the reflexes that are associated with newborns.

Over the following months, many reflexes disappear and instead are replaced by increasingly controlled movements. The speed of children's physical development is quite astonishing. It means that, by the age of four years, most children are able to move in a coordinated way and do quite a few tasks involving small hand movements. In this section, we look at the stages involved in learning to walk, use hands and develop grasps.

→ On page 316, we look at how children develop these skills further and start to apply them to a range of different situations.

Learning to walk

Being able to walk is an important skill. Most children learn to walk by the age of 18 months, although the majority will be walking between the ages of 12 and 15 months. There are distinct stages in children's learning to walk. Table 3.11.1 shows

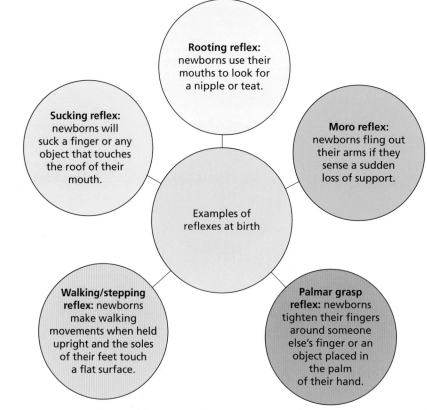

Figure 3.11.3 Reflexes at birth

the typical sequence of how children learn to walk, along with an indication of at what age this may happen. As the speed at which children learn to walk is variable, with some walking as early as nine months, these ages should only be seen as a guide.

Table 3.11.1 Typical sequence for children learning to walk

Age	Skill
Around six months	• Able to roll from back to front.
Around nine months	• Likely to be mobile, e.g. crawling, bottom shuffling or rolling. • Can sit up unsupported. • Starts to pull to standing using furniture.
At around 12 months	• Starting to stand without support, briefly at first and then with more confidence. • Walks along holding onto furniture, e.g. moving along the sofa. • Can move from standing to sitting.
At around 15 months	• Walking independently but often falling over.

Learning to use hands

Being able to use your hands is essential for survival as they are needed in order to feed but also in order to move things. Touch is also a key way by which we learn about the properties of objects. At first, babies are unable to coordinate their hands. In the first few months, they even hit themselves. The typical sequence for children learning to use their hands is shown in Table 3.11.2.

Learning to hold a pencil

Handwriting is still the first way in which children experience writing. Joined handwriting requires a flexible but firm grasp. The recommended grasp for children to acquire is known as the dynamic tripod grasp. Following are the stages by which children develop this grasp.

Pincer grasp

This grasp is used to pick up small objects between the thumb and the finger. It is usually first seen at around nine months. Young toddlers

Table 3.11.2 Typical sequence for children learning to use their hands

Age	Skill
Birth	• Palmar grasp reflex – babies grasp anything that touches their palm as a reflex action. This reflex continues for a few months but over time disappears and is replaced by conscious movements.
Three months	• Starting to become aware of their hands and interested in clasping and unclasping movements. • Can hold onto a rattle if put in the hand momentarily before dropping it.
Six months	• Can reach for a toy. • Can transfer an object from one hand to another. • Can put objects into mouth.
Nine months	• Can choose to release an object by dropping it. • Starts to point to objects with index finger.
12 months	• Can pick up small objects between index finger and thumb easily. • Can feed self with finger foods easily, although messily!

may try to make marks using this grasp holding a crayon at the top, for example.

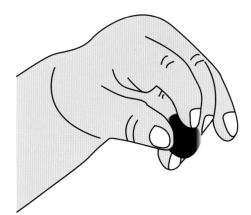

Figure 3.11.4 The pincer grasp is usually seen at around nine months

Palmar grasp

This is a whole-hand grasp which babies use to hold rattles and which toddlers, from around 18 months, use to make marks.

Figure 3.11.5 The palmar grasp is usually seen from around 12 months

Digital pronate grasp

Children will hold the pencil between two fingers and the thumb but in a very stiff way. Writing movements come from the elbow rather than from the wrist or fingers. This is the grasp that you are likely to see with most two year olds.

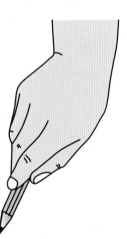

Figure 3.11.6 The digital pronate grasp is often used by two year olds

Static tripod grasp

Between three and four years, children will start to use a static tripod grasp. The thumb is separated from the fingers. Movements come from the wrist rather than the fingers.

Dynamic tripod grasp

This grasp allows for flexible movement because, instead of the wrist being used to manipulate the

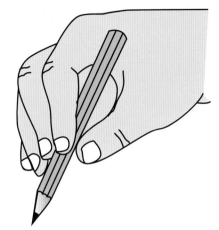

Figure 3.11.7 The static tripod grasp is usually seen with children aged 3–4 years

pencil, the fingers move flexibly. Most children develop this grasp from around four years onwards.

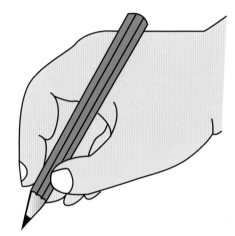

Figure 3.11.8 The dynamic tripod grasp allows the fingers to flex

AC 1.2 The development of children's physical skills

Earlier in this unit, we looked at the stages involved in learning to walk, use hands and hold a pencil. It is worth noting that learning a single movement is not in itself very useful. It is the combination and coordination of movements together that allows children to become skilful.

In this section, we look at how children continue to develop physically and how they may gain further skills. Table 3.11.3 shows what you might expect at different ages from the age of 12 months onwards,

Table 3.11.3 Development of children's physical skills

Age	Fine motor movements involving coordination	Gross motor movements involving coordination
15 months	• Can reach out and pick up small objects easily	• Walking with hesitations • May fall and also bump into furniture • Crawls up stairs
18 months	• Can use a spoon • Enjoys scribbling • Can build a tower of 2–3 bricks when shown how	• Walks unaided and is starting to run • Walks upstairs with help (two feet to a stair) • Climbs up onto a sit-and-ride toy • Squats to pick up a toy • Enjoys climbing
2 years	• Can draw circles and dots. Makes vertical marks • Uses spoon competently • Can turn pages in a book one by one • Can put on some items of clothing, e.g. hat and shoes (shoes might be on wrong feet)	• Pushes and pulls toys easily • Can open doors • Can throw small ball • Kicks by walking into a ball • Can use tricycle using feet rather than pedals
2 years 6 months	• Can manipulate simple jigsaw puzzles • Can pour sand and water into cups • Can pull down trousers • Shows hand preference, e.g. right- or left-handed	• Walks up and down stairs holding onto rail • Runs easily and avoids obstacles • Can jump with two feet together • Kicks ball with one foot, but with little power
3 years	• Can wash and dry hands with help • Can draw a circle and vertical lines • Can cut using toy scissors • Eats using spoon and fork	• Can steer and pedal tricycle • Can throw large ball overarm with some power • Starts to aim when throwing
4 years	• Can copy simple letters • Eats skilfully using spoon and fork • Can dress and undress well • Can draw a simple person • Can cut with scissors on a straight line	• Walks up and down stairs putting one foot on each stair at a time • Hops on one foot • Increased skill in throwing and kicking and is starting to hit a ball with a bat • Confident rider of tricycles • May be using a bicycle with stabilisers
5–7 years	• Increasing control of fine motor movements • Forming letters more easily, although letter shapes will be large • Cuts out shapes • Produces detailed drawings • Can colour within a boundary	• Walks easily on narrow line • Can hop and skip • Enjoys chasing games • Can throw and catch ball • Can use wheeled toys easily and may be progressing onto bicycle without stabilisers

but it is important to recognise that there are often variations between children and the skills that they develop. This can be partly down to opportunity as a child who has never been given a bicycle, for example, will not be able to develop the skills needed to ride one.

→ For more information on grasps, look back at the information in AC 1.1.

In your setting

Ask your placement supervisor if you can observe two children of different ages. Watch them as they play in a range of situations. Make a note of the skills that they are showing. For each child, describe their stage of physical development.

Figure 3.11.9 By three years, most children are able to draw circles and vertical lines

Test yourself

- Make a list of gross motor skills that a four year old is likely to have.
- Make a list of fine motor movements that a two year old is likely to have.

AC 1.3 The benefits of physical development to children's holistic learning and development

Physical development affects many other areas of development and, consequently, children's learning. This is because, as we have already seen in earlier units, development is interconnected. Where children's physical development is being promoted through a range of different opportunities and also encouraged by the adult, children are likely to benefit. Promoting children's physical development includes being aware of children who are not showing typical development. This is important too because, if a child has a developmental delay or medical condition which affects their physical development, other areas of learning are likely to be affected. This is one reason why, in the early months and years of a child's life, there are screening programmes designed to pick up on any areas of potential difficulty.

Figure 3.11.10 Physical development affects other areas of children's development, including playing with others

Physical development and children's holistic development and learning

Most adults working with children notice a significant change when babies become mobile. This is a good example of how physical development affects other areas of development and learning. Once babies are mobile, they start to explore more, are pleased with themselves and also start to want to communicate what they have found. Being mobile allows babies to learn from their environment as, while they crawl, they start to feel the difference between hard and soft surfaces or learn that objects such as sofas are solid!

Figure 3.11.11 shows how physical development links to other areas of learning and also has an impact on children's learning.

> **Key term**
>
> **holistic learning and development** Children's overall development and learning rather than a single aspect.

LO2 Understand theory and current frameworks in relation to children's physical development

Do you think that footballers or tennis players are born talented or that their skills are the result of the opportunities that they have had? In this section, we look at the theories of physical development and how they are reflected in the current early years frameworks.

AC 2.1 Theoretical perspectives in relation to physical development

There are two key perspectives when it comes to physical development: nature or nurture. There is plenty of evidence to support both perspectives.

Nativist perspective

The nature or 'nativist' perspective suggests that physical development is predetermined by nature. There is some evidence to support this perspective as, for example, all babies are born with the same set of reflexes and children usually follow the same sequence of development. Arnold Gesell is very much linked with this approach. Arnold Gesell was an American paediatrician who, from observing children, noted that there are three principles of physical development:

1 **Development follows a definite sequence**
Gesell suggested that all physical development follows a predetermined sequence. A good example of this is the way that children cannot run before they can walk or that they cannot crawl until they can sit.

2 **Development begins with the control of head movements and proceeds downwards**
Gesell noted that the first part of the body that babies learn to control is their head. This is thought to be important for survival as, if babies are able to lift and turn, they will find it easier to

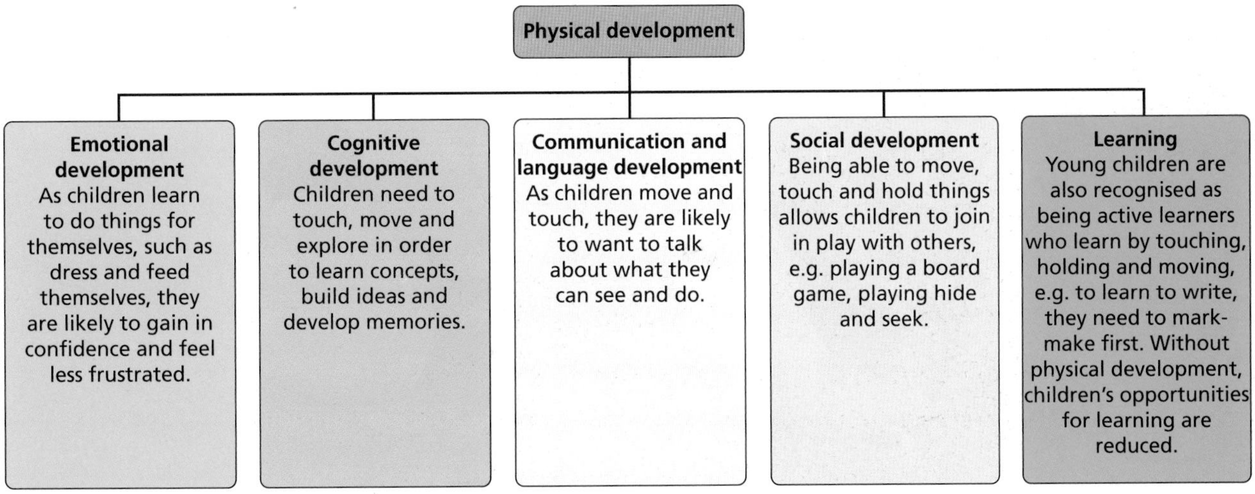

Physical development

Emotional development
As children learn to do things for themselves, such as dress and feed themselves, they are likely to gain in confidence and feel less frustrated.

Cognitive development
Children need to touch, move and explore in order to learn concepts, build ideas and develop memories.

Communication and language development
As children move and touch, they are likely to want to talk about what they can see and do.

Social development
Being able to move, touch and hold things allows children to join in play with others, e.g. playing a board game, playing hide and seek.

Learning
Young children are also recognised as being active learners who learn by touching, holding and moving, e.g. to learn to write, they need to mark-make first. Without physical development, children's opportunities for learning are reduced.

Figure 3.11.11 How physical development links to other areas of learning

feed and also attract attention. Once control has been gained over the head, babies gain control over their arms before, for example, gaining control over their legs.

3 **Development begins with uncontrolled gross motor movements before becoming precise and refined**

Gesell suggested that, before children would be able to make small fine movements, they would first have to master whole arm movements. You might have experienced this feeling when trying to do something requiring precision, such as sewing. At first, large stitches are easier than small ones.

In practice

Observe four children who are different ages or at different stages of development. Watch them throw a ball or object. Note the differences in how they do this.

Nativist explanation of individual differences

When it comes to explaining the differences between individual children's rate of physical development, the nativist explanation would link this to differences in children's genetic make-up. Interestingly, there are some families where there is a trend towards later walking or where most family members are very athletic.

Environmental perspective

While most people agree that nature does play a significant part in physical development, the **environmental perspective** would suggest that opportunities and stimulation are important too. Those families who are sporty, perhaps their children are sporty because their parents encourage them to throw a ball or swim from an early age. The environmental perspective would always stress the importance of children's experiences and opportunities for stimulation. This perspective

Figure 3.11.12 Babies may learn to crawl by at first rocking on all fours

accounts neatly for the differences that we might see between children of the same age. This perspective also links neatly to neuroscience, which suggests that neural pathways or connections are formed as a result of stimulation and experiences.

→ See also page 280.

Key term

environmental perspective Theories of development that suggest that what happens to children outweighs nature's impact.

Reflect

Were you given the opportunity to learn any of the following physical skills?

- Sewing
- Knitting
- Swimming
- Unicycling
- Rugby
- Juggling

Do you think that you might have mastered them if you had been given the opportunity?

Case study

Joel is two years old. He lives with his twin sister and his baby brother in a bed and breakfast. They are waiting to be rehoused by their local authority. There is little space indoors and going out is difficult as there is no lift and Joel's mother finds it hard to manage the pushchair and keep an eye on the children at the same time. Joel spends a lot of time watching television, doing jigsaws and also drawing. His mother also encourages him and his sister to tidy up and fold their clothes. Joel and his sister are due to start nursery next week.

1. How do you think Joel's living conditions might affect his fine motor skills?
2. Explain how Joel's living conditions might affect his gross motor skills?
3. What type of activities might he benefit from when he is at nursery?

Neuroscience and brain development

→ In Unit 3.9, we looked at brain development. You will need to look at pages 276–80 alongside this section.

Since the arrival of MRI scans and brain imaging, neuroscientists are learning more about the brain in relation to physical development.

Primary motor cortex

To make movements, a range of areas of the brain are involved, although the primary motor cortex could in some ways be seen as the control centre.

Stimulation

Stimulation would appear to be important as the brain makes new neural pathways in response to what babies and children are doing. This fits nicely with the environmental perspective of physical development.

Myelinisation

Myelin is a substance that coats neurons and myelinisation plays an important role in physical development. The process of myelinisation of neurons begins at birth and takes around 12 years to complete. It insulates the neural connections and so allows electrical pulses to pass more quickly across the brain. By the age of six, myelinisation of the neurons responsible for gross motor movements is usually complete. This is why children from this age are able to run faster and engage in more coordinated movements.

AC 2.2 Theoretical perspectives on physical development and current frameworks

The nativist and environmental approaches to physical development are reflected in the Early Years Foundation Stage. Physical development is an area of development and learning within the EYFS. It is one of the three priority areas, known as prime areas, within the EYFS. Along with 'Personal, social and emotional development' and 'Communication and Language', it is thought to be essential for later development.

Physical development within the EYFS is divided into two aspects: 'Moving and handling' and 'Health and self-care'. The aspect 'Moving and handling' considers all types of physical movements and also children's ability to use tools, including pencils. The aspect 'Health and self-care' includes dressing skills, although there is also a focus on helping children to learn about leading a healthy lifestyle.

Links to the nativist approach

The nativist approach is reflected in the EYFS as there are expectations that children will reach a certain level of physical development by the end of their reception year. These expectations are the Early Learning Goals. Adults working with children are also meant to check that children are showing expected development. There is also a two-year-old progress check and, as part of this check, early years settings have to assess how children are developing in the three prime areas. The idea of this check is to make sure, where children are not showing typical development, that they might gain further support.

> ### Research it!
>
> Look at the physical development area of learning and development in the EYFS. Read the Early Learning Goals for each aspect: 'Moving and handling' and 'Health and self-care'.

Links to the environmental perspective

The current framework also links to the environmental perspective as adults working with children are expected to provide a range of different opportunities to promote children's development. This is reflected in the wide range of resources to promote fine and gross motor movements. Early years settings are also expected to make sure that children have time outdoors.

> ### In your setting
>
> Make a list of ways in which your setting provides regular opportunities for children to gain the skills that they will need to work towards the Early Learning Goals for 'Moving and handling' and 'Health and self-care'.

LO3 Be able to implement opportunities which promote the physical development of children

Did you ever get to the top of a climbing frame or tree and suddenly feel scared? In early years settings, adults try to make sure that children's physical needs are linked to their stage of development. They also try to recognise which children may need support. In this section, we look at how to plan different play opportunities for physical development that link to children's age and stage of development and how adults might support children's physical development.

AC 3.1 Planning opportunities for physical development

The starting point for planning is, as we have already seen in other units, such as Units 3.10 and 3.11, that we consider children's stage of development and also their interests. When planning for children's physical development, there are also other factors to consider:

- **Identify the skill to be developed**: it is important to identify the skill that you are hoping to support. Physical development, as we saw in LO1, is a wide area and includes a range of skills and so you will need to think about what individual children or groups of children need. It may be that we plan an activity to help a baby to grasp a rattle and so support the baby's hand–eye coordination, as opposed to putting out a baby gym to encourage gross motor movements.
- **Resources**: there is a range of resources that can be used to support children's physical development. It is important to choose resources that are safe for the age of the child and also are within the capability of the child. You might, for example, start with sit-and-ride toys for toddlers before providing them with a simple push-along tricycle so that they can learn to steer. If resources are not developmentally suitable, there is a danger that the child will become frustrated.

- **Level of adult support**: when planning for children's physical development, you should also think about the role of the adult and how much support children might need. Some children will need encouragement in order to build their confidence, while for some activities, such as learning to use a needle and thread, the adult will need to show the child what to do. There are also some activities where the adult will have to play directly with the child. A good example of this is throwing and catching activities where children need an adult to work with them.
- **Space**: It is important for some physical activities to consider the space that is needed. Throwing balls, organising an obstacle course or using a climbing frame are all activities that are valuable but that require space in order to keep children safe.

0–1 year 11 months

This age range includes babies who might not be mobile through to toddlers who can climb and run. Table 3.11.4 below gives some examples of physical opportunities that an adult could provide for different ages of children. When deciding on activities for this age range, it is important to make sure that resources are safe and that the activities are carefully matched to children's developmental level.

Figure 3.11.13 You should plan activities based on the skill that you would like to support

Table 3.11.4 Physical opportunities for babies and toddlers

	Fine motor movements	Gross motor movements
Non-mobile babies	• Passing rattles and shakers for the baby to hold • Treasure basket play with a range of objects (see Unit 3.1) • Water play at bath time, e.g. splashing and kicking	• Putting out a baby gym and encouraging the baby to move their limbs • Putting out stacking beakers for the baby to swipe at
Mobile babies who are not walking	• Putting out pop-up toys • Heuristic play (see Unit 3.1) • Encouraging self-feeding • Sensory play with gloop	• Rolling a ball to the baby • Putting the baby on a swing • Going for short walks
Walking toddlers	• Introducing a spoon at meal times • Encouraging simple dressing skills, such as pulling off a hat • Hand and sponge painting	• Putting out a brick trolley and some objects for the toddler to push around • Encouraging the toddler to climb upstairs • Simple rockers

2–2 years 11 months

Children between two and three years are starting to enjoy making a range of movements. They are at an age when they are easily frustrated and so it is important to make sure that opportunities are developmentally appropriate and based on children's interests.

Table 3.11.5 Physical opportunities for developing fine and gross movements in 2–3 year olds

Fine movements	Gross movements
<ul><li>Encouraging children to use jigsaws</li><li>Helping children to use simple construction blocks, e.g. Duplo</li><li>Sensory materials, including dough or water with tools</li><li>Look out for activities that require two hands to do separate activities, e.g. dustpan and brush or fastening a buckle</li></ul>	<ul><li>Providing a swing or see-saw</li><li>Encouraging children to practise climbing stairs</li><li>Playing with a large ball to encourage the child to kick and throw</li><li>Putting out sit-and-ride toys and simple tricycles</li><li>Moving to music</li><li>Going for a walk</li><li>Walking along a wall with an adult holding the hand</li></ul>

3–5 years

This age range is likely to enjoy activities that allow them to combine skills – for example, treasure hunts. They also need increasingly complex opportunities for developing hand–eye coordination.

In practice

Ask your placement supervisor if you can plan an opportunity that will promote a child's physical development. Write down the benefits of the activity and why you think that it will be appropriate for the child. Show your proposed activity to your placement supervisor.

AC 3.2 Providing opportunities that promote physical development

As well as planning opportunities to promote physical development, it is of course important to organise them. Many of the principles for how best to implement opportunities are the same as we have previously considered in Unit 3.2. In terms of promoting physical development there are some additional things to consider too.

0–1 year 11 months

With this age range, you need to make sure that you consider children's level of tiredness. Babies and toddlers who are tired will find it hard to control their movements and so may lack motivation or the energy to engage with an activity. It is also worth remembering that they also need plenty of time to absorb and become familiar with a new resource or activity. It is important therefore not to rush or do too much too quickly. This age range can lose interest or become tired and so it is important to be ready to stop before they lose enjoyment.

Table 3.11.6 Physical opportunities for developing fine and gross movements in 3–5 year olds

Fine motor movements	Gross motor movements
<ul><li>Showing children how to do some simple sewing</li><li>Providing tools such as tweezers or tongs and encouraging children to use them to pick out specific objects hidden in sensory materials, such as picking out confetti in a bowl of chickpeas</li><li>Games such as fishing games and pick-up sticks</li><li>Jigsaw puzzles</li><li>Putting out dough and scissors so children can practise snipping skills</li></ul>	<ul><li>Creating treasure hunts</li><li>Playing games such as 'What's the time, Mr Wolf?'</li><li>Organising an obstacle course</li><li>Putting out bottles filled with water to use for target practice and bean bags for throwing</li><li>Organising parachute games</li><li>Putting out a range of wheeled toys</li><li>Playing throwing and catching games</li></ul>

Figure 3.11.14 Babies should be given time to enjoy planned activities

2–2 years 11 months

Children in this age range are known for trying to be very independent and also active. They may sometimes refuse an offer of help, even though they clearly need assistance. It is important for adults therefore to be on 'stand by'. Children of this age also have little awareness of danger and so need constant supervision. For opportunities involving wheeled toys, it is important to recognise that their steering skills are still in development and so they may not notice that they are about to crash.

3–5 years

Children in this age range enjoy playing together. They may be keen to try out things that they can see others do but become disheartened if they are not as competent. Some skills such as throwing and catching need a lot of practice and they will need a patient adult to support their development. It is also useful to

talk to children in this age range about possible risks when they are playing outdoors or with wheeled toys so that they can start to become aware of them and moderate their behaviour when necessary.

In practice

Ask your supervisor if you can plan and implement an opportunity that will support children's physical development in each of the following age ranges:

● 0–1 year 11 months
● 2–2 years 11 months
● 3–5 years

Write about the opportunities that you planned for each of the age groups. For each child, consider the benefits of the opportunity. Evaluate to what extent the opportunities promoted the children's physical development and include any suggestions for how you might adapt or improve the opportunities in future.

Figure 3.11.15 Catching a ball can be a tricky skill to master

AC 3.3 The early years practitioner's role in promoting physical development in their own setting

Adults can play a significant role in promoting children's physical development. There is a range of ways in which they may do this. You will need to think about how you support children's physical development. Below are some questions that might help you to do this.

Are you a good role model?

It is important that children see adults looking keen to take exercise – for example, spending time outdoors or going for a walk. Being positive towards exercise helps children to develop healthy attitudes

> **Reflect**
>
> How often do you go for a walk? When did you last swim, cycle or play a sport?

Do you accurately observe and assess children's stages of development?

We have seen when thinking about how to plan an activity that it is essential to be aware of children's stages of development. It is also important when watching children during a range of activities to recognise the skills that they have mastered as well as those that are still emerging. By doing this, you can plan other activities more effectively.

Do you provide a wide range of resources and activities?

We have seen that physical development covers many skills. Children therefore need a range of resources and activities to help them build skills and practise movements. Children also like to try out new activities and so it is important to read different articles or go on training courses so that you can extend your knowledge of ways of promoting children's physical development

Do you support children sensitively?

Some children like to be very independent. Others will need reassurance and encouragement. It is important that adults are able to respond and support all the children sensitively.

Assessment

This unit looks at physical development and it links closely to Unit 1.2, which you should read alongside this unit. In order to complete the assessment for this unit, you will need to start by revisiting the stages of children's physical development and their acquisition of skills. You will also need to describe the benefits and links between children's overall development and their physical development. The information needed to do this is within the unit and so you might like to re-visit it and take some notes. (You need to be secure in this knowledge as it links also to the mandatory task that also has to be completed.)

For Learning Outcome 2, you also need to consider the theoretical perspectives that relate to physical development and how they link to the current early years framework. While this information has been given in this unit, it will be worth referring to the current early years framework as well. You can do this by visiting **www.foundationyears.org.uk**.

For Learning Outcome 3, you will need to put your knowledge into practice by planning several opportunities that cover the three age ranges given in the assessment practice. You could consider using the ideas given in this book or talk through possible opportunities with your placement supervisor. It will be a good idea to practise the opportunities and to gain feedback from your placement supervisor. Finally, you need to reflect on your own role in relation to promoting physical development. To do this, you could gain feedback from experienced colleagues as well as look at the checklist provided at the end of the chapter.

Useful resources

Books

Blythe, S.G. (2006), *The Well-Balanced Child: Movement and Early Learning*. Stroud: Hawthorn Press.

Greenland, P. (2000), *Hopping Home Backwards*. Leeds: Jabadao, **www.jabadao.org**.

Unit 3.12 WB Promoting children's personal, social and emotional development

Do you ever remember not having anyone to play with? Or the realisation that a classmate was better than you at reading, drawing or sport? Friendships, relationships and self-awareness are all part of personal, social and emotional development, which is a very wide, but important, area of development. In this section, we look at the stages of personal, social and emotional development and the theories that explain this development. We also look at how adults can create an environment that will promote personal, social and emotional development. Finally, we look at some of the activities and opportunities that we might plan and implement with children of different ages.

→ As this area of development is underpinned by the development of early relationships with parents and carers, it would be a good idea to read this unit alongside Unit 1.4.

Learning outcomes

By the end of this unit, you will:

1 Understand personal, social and emotional development of children.
2 Understand theory and current frameworks underpinning personal, social and emotional development of children.
3 Be able to promote the personal, social and emotional development of children.
4 Be able to implement an opportunity which promotes the personal, social and emotional development of children.

LO1 Understand personal, social and emotional development of children

AC 1.1 The personal, social and emotional development stages from birth to seven years

There are many aspects to children's personal, social and emotional development, as Figure 3.12.1 shows.

Managing feelings and behaviours

Children's ability to manage feelings and behaviours is developmental to a large extent. This is because it is linked to children's language and cognitive development. Table 3.12.1 shows what you might expect at different ages and stages.

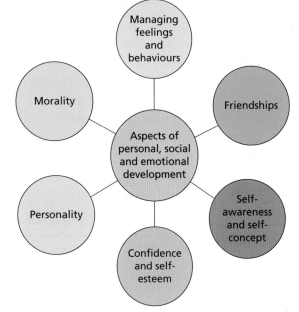

Figure 3.12.1 Aspects of personal, social and emotional development

> ### In your setting
>
> Ask your placement supervisor if you can observe a child of four years and a child of two years. Notice their behaviours and how they cope in situations where they may need to wait. Can you see the difference between the different age groups?

> ### Test yourself
>
> From what age might you expect to see children playing cooperatively?

Table 3.12.1 Managing feelings and behaviours at different ages

0–1 year	• Cries to have physical needs met • Cries for attention, although may over time babble or call out
1–2 years	• Has no concept of ownership and will try to take anything in sight • Easily distracted • Alternates between clinginess and independence • Impulsive • Shows signs of anger
2–3 years	• No concept of ownership • May have tantrums if wishes thwarted and difficult to distract • Impulsive and no sense of danger • Shows affection towards younger children • Shows emotions, e.g. jealousy by pushing away another child, anger by throwing objects to the ground • Alternates quickly between emotions
3–4 years	• Starts to understand the need to take turns • Able to wait for short periods • Able to play cooperatively, although still squabbles • Finds it hard to control emotions, such as anger and jealousy, and needs support
4–7 years	• Plays with other children cooperatively • Is able to wait for longer periods • Shows caring and concern for others • Is able increasingly to talk about their feelings

Friendships

Friendships are very important for children. By around three years, most children prefer children that they enjoy playing with. This is sometimes linked to the type of activity that the child enjoys doing, so that children who love imaginative play will tend to spend a lot of time together. Interestingly, you may also see children of the same sex starting to play together. By the age of five years, children usually have strong friendships and not having a friend is a cause of sadness.

In your setting

Can you see friendships emerging amongst different pairs or groups of children? How much time are they choosing to spend together?

Morality

Morality is a set of beliefs about what is wrong and right. These in turn determine our behaviours. Young children tend not to have a belief system of their own. Instead, between birth and around four years, it is thought that they work out what is right and wrong according to the reactions of adults around them in a very primitive way. So children might learn that adults get cross when they bounce on the sofa. They may also learn that adults get cross when they push their younger sibling over. But children will not understand the difference between these actions. From around four years, children's understanding of what is right or wrong is linked to what they guess adults will think. They may, for example, tell another child who has spilt a drink on the floor that he is in trouble on the basis that they think that an adult might not be pleased. In this phase, children are often able to say what they should or should not do, but this will not stop them from doing it. They may, for example, say that it is wrong to steal, but if they are left alone in a room with some sweets that do not belong to them, they are likely to still take one.

Self-awareness and self-concept

At first, babies do not know that they are separate and unique humans. It is thought that self-awareness develops in babies at around one year. The classic

Case study

Kemel is three years old. He is playing with some felt tips and enjoying making marks. He stands up and starts to make marks on the wall. His mother is very cross and tells him to stop. She takes his pens away. The following week at nursery he is doing some drawing and marking at the writing table. His pen slips and he makes a mark on the tablecloth. He is very frightened and starts to cry. He is surprised when an adult is kind and tells him that it doesn't matter because it was an accident.

1 Why did Kemel think he was going to be punished at nursery?
2 Why was Kemel surprised that at nursery his accidental markings were not a problem?
3 Does Kemel have an understanding of 'right and wrong' in respect of using felt tips?

test of self-awareness is to see whether or not a baby can recognise himself in a mirror rather than assuming that the reflection is another baby. Most babies manage this at around 18 months. Self-awareness is important because it is the first step in the development of children's self-concept. Your self-concept is about how you view yourself. Your name, your physical size and also your gender are all part of your self-concept. Over time, children may view themselves as being strong, loveable or clever. On the other hand, they may come to view themselves as being helpless, unpopular or difficult. As you might guess, self-concept is formed by children's experiences and also the reactions of others towards them. From the age of five, though, children also start to notice how they are doing in comparison to other children.

Sex concept

As a part of self-concept, knowing your sex and also what this means in terms of how you should behave seems to be important. Children develop their sex concept on the basis of what they see and how others react. Table 3.12.2 shows some of the stages in children's development of sex concept.

Confidence and self-esteem

Confidence and self-esteem are not quite the same. Someone can be confident in a situation because they are familiar or competent with it, while still having low

Figure 3.12.2 One of the first steps in the development of self-concept is when a child recognises the face in the mirror as his own

Table 3.12.2 Children's development of sex concept

9–12 months	Babies react differently to male and female faces.
18–24 months	Toddlers are starting to be interested in gender-stereotyped toys.
By 2 years	Children can recognise a photo of a same-sex child.
2 years 6 months to 3 years	Children are identifying the differences between genders by using clues such as hair length and style of dress.
3–4 years	Children are beginning to link tasks and objects with the gender of the person doing them. Many children still associate men with power tools.
5–6 years	Children have acquired the concept of gender stability. They know that gender is not dependent on type of clothes or haircut.

self-esteem. Self-esteem is thought to be an internal judgement of how much you like yourself and accept yourself. Self-esteem is linked to self-concept but it is thought that it is not until children are around 10 or 11 years old that it is fully established.

→ We look at the theory behind self-esteem on page 332.

Personality

The development of personality is of great interest to both parents and researchers.

→ We look at theories of personality on page 336.

The current opinion on personality is that it is not a single entity, but rather a collection of traits. There are thought to be five traits involved. These are known as the 'Big Five'.

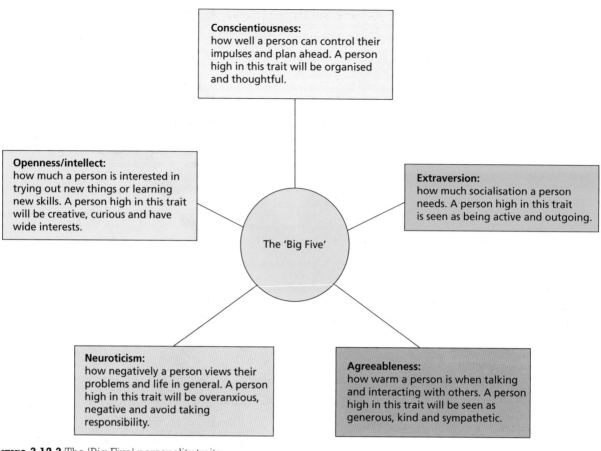

Figure 3.12.3 The 'Big Five' personality traits

Factors affecting children's personal, social and emotional development

While we have looked at some of the stages in children's personal, social and emotional development, it is important to understand that many factors will affect it. Some of these factors are shown in Table 3.12.3.

LO2 Understand theory and current frameworks underpinning personal, social and emotional development of children

If you are outgoing or, on the other hand, shy, do you think that you were born this way? How much influence do you think parents have on children's development? These are the types of questions that for years have been studied by researchers, theorists and psychologists. In this section, we look at the

different theoretical perspectives related to this area of development as well as how these in turn influence current practice.

AC 2.1 Theoretical perspectives of personal, social and emotional development

There are many theories which explain different aspects of children's personal, social and emotional development. Many of the perspectives take the view that children's development is heavily influenced by their environment and experiences, especially their relationships with parents and carers.

Theory of mind

In order to interact successfully with others, to make friends and to understand other people, you have to be able to imagine what they are feeling or thinking. The ability to do this is called 'theory of mind'. It is

Table 3.12.3 Factors affecting children's personal, social and emotional development

Quality of attachment with parents/carers	Where children have strong bonds with their parents and carers, this helps them to develop strong friendships and also a strong self-concept.
Opportunities to socialise with others	Some social skills are linked to having opportunities to play and be with other children.
Adults' responses	Children learn a lot by watching adults' reactions to them and also what they do. Children who are lucky to have usually positive reactions, such as smiles, are likely to develop a strong self-concept. The way in which adults provide guidance to children when they make mistakes or do something inappropriate is also important.
Language development	Levels of language development can affect what children are able to understand and how they express themselves. Lower levels of language are linked to levels of impulsivity, e.g. tantrums. Levels of language also influence how children play, with strong language levels being needed for cooperative imaginative play.
Experiences	What children see and do affects several aspects of their development. If they see men and women doing similar tasks around the home and in the environment, their view of sex roles will be shaped by this. In terms of morality, if they see that adults hit out when they are angry, they are likely not to see this as wrong.

thought that, until children reach the age of four or so, they may not be fully able to do this.

A classic experiment to test theory of mind is called the Sally–Anne test. Children are shown two dolls, which the tester uses. One is named Sally and the other is named Anne. Sally puts some marbles in her basket and then goes out to play. 'Naughty' Anne takes Sally's marbles out from the basket and puts them in a box. Sally comes back. The child is asked where she will go to find her marbles. Children who are starting to acquire theory of mind will point to the basket as Sally does not know that the marbles have been moved to the box.

Research it!

Try out the Sally–Anne test with children of two different ages in your setting.

Theory of mind is not recognised by all researchers, but for many it provides an explanation as to why younger children find it hard to play cooperatively or to understand the consequences of their actions. It explains why sometimes children may bring a toy over to another child and do not seem to understand why the other child will not play with it.

Mildred Parten's social stages of play

In the 1930s, a researcher called Mildred Parten looked at how children of different ages played together. She realised that that there were stages by which most children learn to develop the skills to play with each other. Table 3.12.4 on the next page shows these stages, although it is important to note that, while some children are able to play cooperatively with other children, they may still have times when they prefer to play alone.

In your setting

Ask your placement supervisor if you can observe two children of very different ages during child-initiated play. Look to see how they play with other children. Compare the way they play to the stages in Table 3.12.4 on the next page.

Erik Erikson's life stages

Erik Erikson (1902–94) looked at personal, social and emotional development from the point of view of personality, although his theory would also explain levels of self-esteem and ability to form relationships. He came to the conclusion that we are shaped throughout life. Interestingly, this view

Table 3.12.4 Social stages of play

Age	Stage of play	Characteristics
0–2 years	Onlooker	Babies are highly interested in what others are doing, although they will not be engaged in the play. Note: Onlooker play is often a first step for older children when they join a group for the first time. They may start off by watching others before joining in.
0–2 years	Solitary	Babies play alone, although they may notice that others are around them.
2–3 years	Parallel	Children are very aware of other children. They play side by side. At times they may notice what each other is doing and copy each other's actions.
3–4 years and onwards	Cooperative	Children can play without an adult being there. They are cooperative in their play and 'work' together as they play. From around four or five years old onwards, they increasingly plan their play together and negotiate roles.

concurs with what neuroscientists know about how the brain changes over the years. He saw early childhood as critical, with the role of parents and carers shaping children's early personality and confidence. In each of his life stages, children have to reach a conclusion about how they will deal with the world. Table 3.12.5 shows his life stages up until the end of childhood.

Albert Bandura's work on self-efficacy

Self-efficacy is the belief that you have the ability to succeed. Bandura's work on self-efficacy is part

Figure 3.12.4 Toddlers do not base their play choices on traditional gender stereotypes

Table 3.12.5 Erikson's life stages

Age	Stage	Description	Outcome
0–1 year	Basic trust versus mistrust	Babies need to reach a conclusion about whether the world is a safe place, where their needs are met with love, or a hostile one.	If babies do not have their emotional and physical needs met, they may come to the conclusion that the world is a negative place. This might affect later relationships.
2–3 years	Autonomy versus shame	Children are exploring their environment and doing new things for themselves, such as learning to dress. They are also moving out of nappies.	From the reactions of adults, children will either gain in confidence or be made to feel guilty about making mistakes. This may cause them to be more or less independent and so more or less confident in the future.
4–5 years	Initiative versus guilt	Children are increasingly able to plan and carry out activities. They also need to learn about their gender role.	Children need to feel independent, but also have boundaries on their behaviour. Too much control of the child can result in a fearful and dependent child, while no limits or boundaries can leave the child without any guilt or conscience.
6–12 years	Industry versus inferiority	Most children are in school at this point. They start to notice how well they are doing in comparison to others. Parents may also comment about their progress.	Children who experience failure may lose confidence and feel inferior, especially if they have not lived up to the expectations of their parents. Children who only meet with success during this phase may become overconfident and lack empathy.
13–18 years	Identity versus role confusion	Adolescents need to create their own identity and belief system in order to be different from their parents.	The need for adolescents to set themselves apart may lead to some young people feeling lost or having an identity crisis. Ideally, at the end of this stage, adolescents have a firm idea of who they are and what they want to go on to do.

Research it!

You might like to look at Erik Erikson's life stages in relation to adulthood and compare these to your current situation.

of his social cognitive theory, which suggests that we learn by being with others. People who have high levels of self-efficacy are likely to do well as they view themselves as being capable. They are also likely to accurately assess and deal with factors that might cause them problems (see case study below). According to Bandura, self-efficacy begins in the first year of life. If the baby is not given opportunities to try to do things for themselves or is prevented from exerting their will – for example, being forced to eat more when they have already turned their head – this may affect their sense of self-efficacy. Bandura's work on self-efficacy is important as it in turn will shape self-concept and self-esteem.

Charles Cooley's 'the Looking Glass Self'

How do you know what you are like? If you think about it, we learn a lot about ourselves from the reactions of others. This is the basis of Cooley's 'the Looking Glass Self'. Charles Cooley (1864–1929) suggested in 1902 that our self-concept was the direct result of our interactions with others and that these were highly subjective. For example, if a child does something that makes others laugh, the child is more likely to think of herself as being good at being funny. Adults and others might also tell the child that she is funny or she may overhear this in a conversation. We also know that children learn about themselves as a result of comparing themselves. The child might also reach the conclusion that she is funny because she makes other children laugh the most.

Susan Harter's model of self-esteem

Susan Harter, a psychologist, provided a model of self-esteem which has been widely accepted. Her model of self-esteem suggests that high or low levels of self-esteem are a result of how closely our self-concept matches our 'ideal self'. The ideal self is what we want to be like and this of course is very individual and will depend on what we and society values. Someone living in a place where money is valued is likely to have an ideal self that includes being rich. If someone wants desperately to be rich, but does not achieve this, the chances are that they are more likely to have a lower self-esteem because they have not measured up to their 'ideal'. While the ideal self is not developed

until later childhood, it is helpful to develop a strong and positive self-concept.

Figure 3.12.5 shows the link between the ideal self and self-concept.

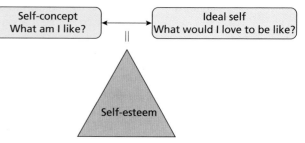

Figure 3.12.5 The discrepancy between the ideal self and the self-concept creates either positive or negative self-esteem

AC 2.2 Theoretical perspectives on personal, social and emotional development and current frameworks

Within the current Early Years Foundation Stage (EYFS), this area of development is seen as essential. It is one of the three prime areas thought to be building blocks for children's later academic development.

There are three different aspects within this area of learning and development within the EYFS:

- self-confidence and self-awareness
- managing feelings and behaviour
- making relationships.

Theory of mind

While theory of mind cannot be fast-tracked as it seems to be developmental, it is considered to be good practice to explain to children what others might be feeling and thinking. For example, 'Stephen does not have any friends. Should we go and play with him?' Once children have developed theory of mind, it should help them to meet the Early Learning Goal for the aspect 'Managing feelings and behaviour'. Understanding that it takes a while before children start to be able to imagine or guess what another person is feeling also affects how early years practitioners deal with unwanted behaviour.

→ See also Unit 1.4.

Mildred Parten's social stages of play

The Early Learning Goal for the 'Making relationships' aspect is that children will be able to play cooperatively. This links to Parten's work suggesting that most children are doing this by around four years or so. Early years settings will set up play environments that will allow children to socialise and begin to play with others.

Erik Erikson's life stages

Erik Erikson's life stage theory of personality has many implications for the way that adults work with children, and this is reflected in current practice. Adults need to make sure that babies have a warm nurturing environment so that they learn to trust. The EYFS has the key person system to ensure that babies' emotional needs are met and also focuses practitioners on the importance of meeting babies' other needs promptly. In terms of toddlers, it is good practice to provide plenty of encouragement for they as they try to do things for themselves. You may, for example, see that adults allow time at meals for two and three years olds to feed themselves and encourage them to explore materials through

Figure 3.12.6 Mildred Parten's work suggests that children are able to play cooperatively from around four years of age

open-ended activities such as heuristic and block play. When children are between the ages of four and five, they are encouraged to plan for their play and follow their interests, although adults do set boundaries for this. In Key Stage 1, children are encouraged to take responsibility and also to do tasks for themselves. Teachers also put boundaries in place so that there is a balance.

Albert Bandura's work on self-efficacy

In addition to personal, social and emotional development as a prime area of learning, the current EYFS also provides some characteristics of learning. They link closely to Albert Bandura's work on supporting babies' and young children's self-efficacy. Practitioners are therefore encouraged to provide children with choices, enable children to be active in their learning and also provide interesting opportunities so that children can be motivated.

In the Key Stage 1 framework, it is also good practice for adults to provide feedback to children so that they know what they will need to do in order to achieve, rather than just saying 'good work'. The Key Stage 1 framework also encourages children to take on responsibility and to set simple goals for themselves.

Charles Cooley's 'the Looking Glass Self' and Susan Harter's model of self-esteem

The current EYFS emphasises the importance of working with children as individuals and valuing each child. The Looking Glass Self theory and Susan Harter's model of self-esteem would suggest that it is important for adults to think about what they say to children and also their reactions towards children, and this is best practice in settings. Adults also spend time with children gaining their feedback and talking to them about their achievements as part of the Key Stage 1 curriculum. It is also good practice for sensitive conversations concerning children to be undertaken out of earshot of the child and other children.

> **Reflect** ❓
>
> Think about the 'hidden messages' that children are learning about themselves in your setting. Are there some children who are learning that they are 'naughty'? How could you help them develop a more positive image of themselves?

LO3 Be able to promote the personal, social and emotional development of children

Have you ever been to a place where you have felt out of place or unwanted? Happily, early years settings work hard to create an environment where children can feel relaxed and secure. In this section, we look at ways in which we can create an environment that will promote the personal, social and emotional development of children.

AC 3.1 Creating an environment that promotes personal, social and emotional development of children

The term environment is a broad one. It includes the physical objects and layout, but also the feeling that is generated by the cultural, social and personal attributes within the setting. There are many ways in which an environment can be created.

Physical environment

The physical environment is important. It is worth thinking about what children and their families see when they arrive.

Displays

Many early years settings will use displays to create a welcoming environment for children. Displays can also help children feel that they belong. Examples of this are displays that have photographs of children in them. Displays can also be used to value children's play as well as artwork. It is common for settings to mount children's artwork attractively but also put up photographs showing children playing or exploring something in the setting.

Displays can also help children feel that their home life and community are being reflected and so, where there are children whose families speak a home language different from that in the setting, there may be displays written in the home language or photographs that reflect the child's home community.

> **In practice**
>
> Ask your placement supervisor if you can create a display which will help children's sense of belonging and feeling valued. If you are working with children from two years old, you may wish to involve children in the making of the display.

Storage for belongings

Children like to have a place for their belongings, such as coats, books or comforters. Many settings will organise hanging pegs or drawers for each child, which might have their name or photograph on it.

Figure 3.12.7 A welcoming environment makes children feel comfortable and secure in the setting

Personal care

When it is nappy-changing time or sleep time, it is usual for children to have their own nappies or bedding so that they can feel that they are special and individual and so promote a strong self-concept.

Learning journeys or similar

Many early years settings use learning journeys with children. These are records and photographs of what a child has done over a period of time. Looking at these with a child can help them to feel valued and also help them to reflect on their progress. This can help children gain in confidence.

> **In your setting**
>
> How does your setting involve children in the observation and assessment process?

Enabling environment

The term 'enabling environment' is used by the EYFS to reflect the importance of creating a physical environment that allows children to do as much as they can for themselves. This means, for example, toys and resources that children can access by themselves and also tidy away. To help create an enabling environment, photographs of equipment might be put onto the side of containers so that children know where to find things.

Role play

We know that role play seems to allow children opportunities to express their feelings. Most children from three years tend to immerse themselves in this type of play. In terms of the physical environment, it is important that props and resources are provided that will support this play. It is also important the props and resources reflect children's home environments. Role play also helps children's social skills as this is often an area in which they play with other children.

Books

Some books can help children to understand and recognise feelings. They can also help children to think about others who may be different from them. An environment that is trying to promote children's personal, social and emotional development will therefore provide books that help children think about their feelings.

Sensory materials, painting and drawing

Dough, water, sand and also opportunities for children to draw and paint are all resources that should be available for children. Sensory materials, drawing and painting allow children to express their feelings and also to develop skills. In addition, sensory materials can help children learn to share and take turns.

Cultural and social aspects

Routines are the way in which the cultural and social aspects of the environment are usually reflected. There are many ways in which routines can promote children's personal, social and emotional development.

Greetings and goodbyes

When children come into a setting with their families, it is important that they are properly welcomed. Usually, this should be done by the child's key person, but everyone that they meet should say hello to them. At the end of the session, it is important again that children hear a positive goodbye as this signals to them that their absence is about to be noted. It is good practice in settings to say a few words of the child's home language as a greeting and a goodbye. This helps the child to feel that their language is recognised.

In practice

Write about how you welcome children and their families into the setting.

Meal times

Meal times should be pleasurable for babies and children. To promote independence and self-efficacy, children should be encouraged to feed themselves and to help themselves to food. Children should also be respected when they indicate that they have eaten sufficiently. Through meal times, children can also learn that other children have different food preferences. They can also learn to enjoy the company of other children. Meal times also help children learn the social skills associated with sharing food with others – for example, waiting to take turns or passing food to each other.

Physical care routines

Dressing, toileting and hand washing are not only important for children's physical well-being, they are also important because they allow children opportunities to learn new skills and to become independent. It is important that equipment such as washbasins and coat pegs allow children easy access. It is also important for adults to allow sufficient time and to encourage children to do as much as they can independently.

Opportunities to be with adults

Children need a lot of time and attention from their key persons and adults. The quality of relationships seems to help children to feel emotionally secure. A routine should therefore provide opportunities for children to spend time enjoying the company of adults.

Personal attributes

The way we work with children can influence how they come to view themselves. It also can make a difference as to how they develop their social skills and behaviours.

Role modelling

We saw in Unit 3.11 that children can learn from watching others. Adults therefore need to create an environment where there is plenty of praise and affirmation. Adults need to show how to listen to others and show respect.

Tone of voice and facial expression

Children are very quick to notice voice tones. They can hear whether or not there is warmth in the voice. Facial expressions are important too. It is worth thinking about what children will see during a session. Will they mainly see adults who are smiling and showing genuine interest in the child?

LO4 Be able to implement an opportunity which promotes the personal, social and emotional development of children

AC 4.1 Planning opportunities to promote personal, social and emotional development

→ In Unit 3.2, we looked at some of the key principles of planning and it will be useful to read these again alongside this unit.

The same principles apply for this unit as Unit 3.2, but the focus here is opportunities that will specifically promote aspects of personal, social and emotional development.

0–1 year 11 months

The main way that we support children in this age group is by spending time with them and making sure that our relationships with them are strong. Any opportunities that we plan with children should therefore focus on supporting relationships. Table 3.12.6 shows some examples of opportunities that might promote aspects of children's personal, social and emotional development. As children in this age group have the tendency to put items in their mouths, any equipment or resources used must always be risk assessed first.

2–2 years 11 months

Children in this age range are known to be impulsive and active and this has to be borne in mind when thinking of play opportunities, especially in terms of safety. Two year olds are also still learning how to take turns and may be able to do this if they are given support by adults. They are also starting to enjoy sensory materials and so opportunities for these can work well as, through sensory materials, children can express their feelings. Children of this age are also interested in looking at photographs of themselves and other children. Table 3.12.7 on the next page shows some examples of opportunities that might promote aspects of children's personal, social and emotional development.

3–5 years

Children in this age range are starting to play co-operatively. Role play is important, as are sensory materials because they allow children to express and explore feelings and emotions. Children are also able to listen to stories and enjoy sharing books with adults. This is another way of helping

Table 3.12.6 Opportunities to promote aspects of babies' and toddlers' personal, social and emotional development

Opportunity	Benefits
Peek a boo and similar types of activities	Peek a boo activities can help children to enjoy being with adults. They also help children to realise that adults are there for them.
Playing with mirrors	Children of this age are fascinated by mirrors. It is a good way of helping children to develop an early sense of identity.
Knock-down play	Babies and toddlers love games that are linked to cause and effect. Putting a stack of beakers together for children to knock down can help children feel powerful and also help them realise that they have control over some objects.
Meal times	At meal times, babies and toddlers can be given choices of foods. They can point to foods that they would like to try and foods can be served in small quantities in different bowls so that children can help themselves. Being able to choose in this way can help babies and toddlers to feel competent.
Musical gadgets	Babies and toddlers enjoy gadgets that make sounds when they press a button or turn a knob. This makes babies and toddlers feel competent and can help them develop a sense of self-efficacy.

Table 3.12.7 Opportunities to promote aspects of personal, social and emotional development in children aged 2–3 years

Opportunity	Benefits
Playing with water and sand	Materials such as sand and water seem to be relaxing for children and also give them a sense of powerfulness as there is no wrong or right way to use them.
Looking at photographs	Children enjoy looking at photographs of themselves when they were younger or ones taken when they have achieved something for the first time, e.g. climbing to the top step of the climbing frame. This is a way to help children feel successful.
Laying the table	Activities that children do alongside adults, such as laying the table, can help children feel confident and capable, provided that adults work with them in ways that encourage them.
Making dough	It is possible to make dough with this age range, which helps them to gain feelings of responsibility and competence. Afterwards they can play with the dough, which is thought to help children release feelings.
Home corner play	Many children in this age range are just starting to enjoy imitating what they see at home. Creating a home corner that reflects children's experiences can help them to express their feelings and try out new roles.

Figure 3.12.8 Sharing books can help children cope with challenging situations or transitions

Table 3.12.8 Opportunities to promote aspects of personal, social and emotional development in children aged 3–5 years

Opportunity	Benefits
Painting and drawing	Many children like drawing and painting as a way of exploring their feelings and also experiences. Look out for a range of different opportunities and choices by, for example, providing a range of textures, colours and tools.
Sharing books	Choosing books to read to children that link to their feelings or fears can be a good way of helping children cope with a transition or past experience. There is a range of stories that consider topics such as not having friends, moving to a new school or living through a parental separation.
Sensory materials and small-world play	Combining sensory materials with small-world play can help children to feel competent as they create fantasy roles for farm animals, play people or cars. Children are also able to express their feelings through this type of play.
Role play	Children can be asked to choose a role-play area that they would like to explore and contribute to its creation. This helps children to gain feelings of competence as well as learn new skills.
Cooking activities	These help children to learn new skills and also help them to feel pride in themselves.

children to learn about others and also think about emotions. Children also enjoy learning new skills as this can make them feel competent.

Table 3.12.8 shows some examples of opportunities that might promote aspects of children's personal, social and emotional development.

AC 4.2 Providing opportunities for personal, social and emotional development

→ In Unit 3.2, we looked at ways of implementing play opportunities with different ages of children. You should revisit that section and read it alongside the following text.

0–1 year 11 months

The focus of promoting personal, social and emotional development with this age range is to help children enjoy and develop strong relationships. You should therefore aim to carry out activities at times when children are not tired and also when there is no rush. A good tip is to mirror the babies' and toddlers' facial expressions and to allow plenty of time for responses. It is also important to carry out activities and opportunities in comfortable places and where there is little distraction. Your body language should

be positive and encouraging – for example, gently clapping when a child knocks down the beakers or smiling when the child turns to you after looking in the mirror.

2–2 years 11 months

Children in this age range, as we have already seen, are very active and also impulsive. To work with this age range, we need to see ourselves as followers rather than leaders! It is important to be patient as, for example, if a two year old is trying to help us lay the table, they may decide to spend a little time playing with the cutlery rather than putting it down! As with babies and toddlers, it is important to choose times when they are not tired and also be very sensitive to their mood. Two year olds need plenty of opportunities to make choices and be independent so do think about how your chosen opportunity will incorporate this.

3–5 years

Children aged 3–5 years are likely to be talking well, especially from four years old. This means that, during planned opportunities, you should encourage children to talk about what they are doing and especially about what they are feeling. It is particularly important to acknowledge children's feelings properly, especially when they are feeling sad or disappointed. A common mistake of adults is to 'cheer' children up rather than to acknowledge how the child is feeling to start with. It is also important during opportunities to praise and acknowledge children when they are being cooperative and taking turns.

In practice

Ask your placement supervisor if you can implement a planned opportunity for children in each of the following age ranges:

- 0–1 year 11 months
- 2–2 years 11 months
- 3–5 years.

Write about the benefits of each opportunity. Carry out the opportunity and reflect on how successful it was in terms of children's interest and enjoyment. Think also about your role and how you worked to ensure that the opportunity promoted children's personal, social and emotional development.

AC 4.3 The benefits to children's holistic learning and development

Children's personal, social and emotional development is important for all aspects of children's overall development. Table 3.12.9 shows how promoting aspects of children's personal, social and emotional development supports other areas of development.

AC 4.4 The early years practitioner's role in promoting personal, social and emotional development in their own setting

How do you show warmth in your interactions with children?

Children can sense whether someone likes them and is interested in them and this often comes from the tone of voice and body language that adults use.

How often do you affirm or acknowledge children?

While it is of course important to praise children for their achievements, it is also important to affirm children for their own sake. Children need opportunities for unconditional love from other adults in addition to their parents. Commenting on what a lovely smile a child has or some aspect of their personality in a positive way can help children to feel valued.

How carefully do you respond to children?

Adults who work well with children tend to be good at responding very sensitively to them. They may, for example, mirror the child's facial expression or listen carefully to what a child is saying without interrupting. This makes

Table 3.12.9 Benefits to children's holistic development when promoting personal, social and emotional development

Aspect of development	Benefit
Managing feelings and behaviour	Children are more likely to find it easier to learn if they can control their behaviour as they will be less distracted. They are also likely to be allowed to explore more challenging materials and activities if adults know that they will respect the rules and boundaries.
Friendships and relationships	Children's learning is often linked to how settled and happy they feel. When children have friends, they are likely to be able to concentrate and gain in confidence. Children who cannot form strong relationships may not join in group play or later on in discussions. They will also miss out on opportunities to learn from each other.
Self-confidence and self-efficacy	Confidence and self-efficacy make a lot of difference to children's holistic development. When children have strong levels of confidence and self-efficacy, they are more likely to be happy and popular and to participate in new opportunities.

Figure 3.12.9 Strong relationships and friendships are important for children's overall development

children feel that they are important and in the long term helps children to feel that they can talk to the adult.

How well do you acknowledge children's negative emotions?

Children cannot be happy all of the time. Adults have to name and acknowledge how a child is feeling rather than just try to fix the problem and chivvy the child along.

How well do you empower children?

For children of all ages to develop self-efficacy and hence confidence, they need opportunities to make decisions and choices, and also to take on some responsibility. It is important that decisions and choices are age/stage appropriate so, while we might ask a three year old to choose between

peas, broccoli or beans, it would be inappropriate to expect them to take on healthy meal planning.

How strong are your relationships with children?

We know that young children need strong relationships with adults. It is worth thinking about how easily you make relationships with children and how strong these are. A sign that you have a strong relationship with a child would include the child actively choosing to spend time with you.

> **In practice**
>
> Reflect on your practice in promoting children's personal, social and emotional development. Consider your strengths, giving examples, and also consider areas that you would like to develop further.

Assessment

To complete this unit, you will need to complete a variety of tasks. It links closely with Unit 1.4 and so it will be worth revisiting. Your assessor may also decide to assess some parts of these units together.

The starting point for this unit is to revisit the stages of children's personal, social and emotional development and also to consider the theoretical perspectives that explain this development. (You need to be secure in this knowledge as it links also to the mandatory task that also has to be completed.) In addition, for Learning Outcome 2, you also have to be able to analyse how these theoretical perspectives link to current early years framework. We look at that in this unit and so you could revisit it.

For Learning Outcome 3, you need to show that you can create an environment that will promote children's personal, social and emotional development. To do this you will need to talk through your ideas with your placement supervisor. You might like to use the suggestions in this book as a starting point for your discussion.

For Learning Outcome 4, you will need to put your knowledge into practice by planning and leading several opportunities that cover the three age ranges given in the assessment practice. You could consider using the ideas given in this book or talk through possible opportunities with your placement supervisor. It will be a good idea to practice the opportunities and to gain feedback from your placement supervisor. In addition, for this learning outcome, you must also be able to explain the links between children's overall development and the promotion of their personal, social and emotional development, which is covered in this unit. Finally, you need to reflect on your own role in relation to promoting children's personal, social and emotional development. To do this, you could gain feedback from experienced colleagues as well as look at the checklist provided at the end of the chapter.

Useful resources

Books and articles

Elfer, P., Goldschmied, E. and Selleck, D. (2003), *Key Persons in the Nursery: Building Relationships for Quality Provision*. London: David Fulton.

Berk, L. (2012), *Child Development*. Oxford: Pearson.

Bowlby, J. (1969), *Attachment and Loss. Vol. I: Attachment*. London: Hogarth Press.

Dowling, M. (2010), *Young Children's Personal, Social and Emotional Development* (3rd edn). London: Sage Publications.

Elfer, P., Grenier, J., Manning-Morton, J., Dearnley, K. and Wilson, D. (2008), 'Appendix 1: The key person in reception classes and small nursery settings', *Social and Emotional Aspects of Development: Guidance for Practitioners Working in the Early Years Foundation Stage*. Nottingham: DCSF Publications, available at http://nationalstrategies.standards.dcsf.gov.uk/node/132720.

Freud, A., in collaboration with D. Burlingham (1973), *The Writings of Anna Freud. Vol. III: Infants Without Families [and] Reports on the Hampstead Nurseries, 1939–1945*. New York: International Universities Press.

Paley, V.G. (1981), *Wally's Stories*. Cambridge, Mass.: Harvard University Press.

Waddell, M. (1995), *Owl Babies*. London: Walker Books.

Winnicott, D.W. (1964), *The Child, the Family and the Outside World*. London: Penguin Books.

Unit 3.13 Support children with additional needs

Have you noticed that new children often need more reassurance? Or that sometimes a child with a communication delay may need more time to process information? These are examples of children who have additional needs. In this unit, we look at how we can support children with additional needs and consider the biological, environmental and developmental factors that might mean that children will need additional support. We also think about how our own experience and attitudes might shape the way we respond. In this unit, we also look at how we identify children with additional needs and how we might work with others to support them. We also look at how you might evaluate the provision for children in your setting.

Learning outcomes

By the end of this unit, you will:

1 Understand biological, environmental and developmental factors which may result in children needing additional support.
2 Understand how personal experiences, values and beliefs impact on the role of the early years practitioner.
3 Understand the principles of inclusive practice.
4 Understand the role of early intervention in partnership working.
5 Be able to support the additional needs of children.
6 Be able to critically evaluate the provision for children with additional needs in own setting.

LO1 Understand biological, environmental and developmental factors which may result in children needing additional support

Nature or nurture? Which one do you think affects children's development more? The reality, as we will see in this section, is that both biological and environmental factors matter and may result in children needing additional support. In this section, we look at the type of factors that might impact on children's development and how these in turn may affect children's learning.

AC 1.1 Biological and environmental

A good starting point when looking at children's additional needs is to understand what the term 'additional needs' means.

The term 'additional needs', in this unit, refers to children who may need additional support for any reason. This includes children who have a disability or medical condition as well as children who may need additional reassurance because they are settling in to a new setting. The reasons why children may at times need additional support can be divided into 'biological factors' and 'environmental factors'.

The term 'biological' refers to the range of ways that nature affects children's development. It is about the factors that are present at birth or present later but are determined biologically. It includes instincts such as the human reflex to breathe as well as genetic factors, such as how tall children grow or what colour hair they have.

The term 'environmental' refers to how the child's development is shaped both positively and negatively by factors that are linked to external aspects, such as society, lifestyle and parenting, rather than nature. It is wide ranging and includes factors such as the number of siblings in a family, the type of parenting style and whether the child's family is religious.

AC 1.2 The impact of biological factors on development

There are many biological factors that can influence children's development. The extent to which they will have an impact is often linked to environmental factors. A good example of this is a child who has asthma. While asthma is a biological factor, its impact on the child could be linked to environmental factors, such as whether an early years setting is dusty. Table 3.13.1 shows examples of biological factors that may affect children's development but also how environmental factors might reduce the impact.

AC 1.3 The impact of environmental factors on development

We have seen that biological factors can impact on children's development, but children's environment can also play a part in their development. Table 3.13.2 shows some examples of how environmental factors can impact on children's development.

In your setting

Make a list of the biological and environmental factors that affect children in your setting.

AC 1.4 The impact of a delayed stage on children's learning

Where a child has a delay in one area of development, there is a likelihood that it will impact on other areas of the child's development and also their learning. This is one of the reasons why it is important for children's additional needs to be recognised early.

→ We look at early intervention in LO4.

Table 3.13.1 Biological factors on children's development and the effect of environmental factors

Biological factor	Potential impact	How environmental factors may mitigate impact
Chronic medical conditions, e.g. epilepsy, asthma, cystic fibrosis, diabetes	Absence from early years settings and school, resulting in children falling behind. Children may have lower self-esteem as they feel different. Drugs may affect concentration.	Early years settings and schools are aware of absence and its impact and therefore give more time and attention to the child. Positive approach of parents and professionals empowers children and supports self-esteem.
Learning difficulty, e.g. Fragile X, Down's syndrome, autism	Children may have lower self-esteem as they feel different. Children may be rejected by other children and so not gain social skills.	Additional support is given to the child to maximise learning opportunities. An inclusive environment is created that supports children's self-esteem and social development.
Physical impairment or disability, e.g. deafness, sight problems, spina bifida	Children may have lower self-esteem as they feel different. Children may miss out on learning opportunities as the equipment or resources may not be tailored to meet their needs. Other areas of children's development may be affected because of impairment, e.g. speech may be affected because of hearing loss.	Adjustments are made to maximise children's independence and access to resources. Adult expectations of children's learning are not lowered. Children are listened to and empowered to make choices. Adults recognise that the impairment may cause developmental delay in other areas and so focus on these.

Table 3.13.2 The impact of environmental factors on children's development

Environmental factor	Impact on children's development
Cramped living conditions/no outdoor space	Children's physical development may be affected. Children may become frustrated and show unwanted behaviours.
Poor diet	Children's growth and health may be affected. Children may find it hard to concentrate and so may not learn as effectively.
Attachment with parents	This can have positive or negative effects on children's development depending on whether the child has a secure attachment with a parent or primary carer. → See also Unit 1.4.
Parenting style	Parenting style can have either a positive or a negative impact on children's development, e.g. where the parenting style is very aggressive, children may show more examples of unwanted behaviour and so may not make strong friendships.

Table 3.13.3 shows how a delay in one area of development may impact on children's learning.

AC 1.5 Short-term factors that affect children's development

There is a range of factors that can affect children's development so that, in the short term, they will need additional support.

→ Many of these factors link closely to the types of transitions that we looked at in Unit 1.4 and you might like to look at that unit again alongside this section.

Illness and accidents

Children who have had or are experiencing a short-term illness are likely to have additional needs. They

Table 3.13.3 The effect of a developmental delay on children's learning

Area of development	Areas of children's learning affected by delay
Physical development	• Opportunities to explore new resources and materials and so learn about textures and concepts such as size and shape • Opportunities to learn self-care skills and to become independent • Opportunities to learn social skills as they may not be able to join other children in play
Communication and language	• Opportunities for children to learn from communicating with adults and children, e.g. sharing a story, joining in a discussion • Opportunities to join other children in play where communication and language are required, e.g. role play • Opportunities to develop social skills as they may not be able to communicate with others
Personal, social and emotional development	• Opportunities to play with other children and develop social skills as other children may reject them • Opportunities to learn from new resources and materials as children may lack confidence to try out new activities • Opportunities to develop physical skills as children with unwanted behaviour may not be trusted to play and use resources safely

may not have the energy to play or to physically move. If they have been away from the setting, they may also have missed out on some learning and may feel a little left out when they return. Such short-term illnesses include diseases such as chickenpox, where a child might be absent from the early years setting or school for a couple of weeks. As well as illness, some accidents may also have a short-term impact, such as a fractured arm, which results in the child wearing a cast. Ill health and accidents affect children's development because they may not be able to socialise and play with other children or they may not feel well enough to concentrate and join in learning activities.

Changes in home circumstances

Changes in children's home circumstances can affect children's development in the short term. They may show more unwanted behaviour or become less settled in the setting. Children may not want to join in with others' play and instead withdraw. Figure 3.13.1 shows examples of changes in children's home circumstances.

Transitions

Some transitions will also cause short-term effects on children's development. These will

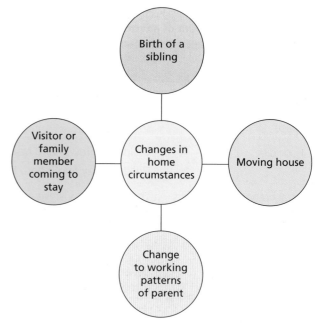

Figure 3.13.1 Changes in home circumstances

include moving to a new setting or having a new key person. These transitions can cause children to become more clingy and less sociable. It may also mean that children have to make new friends and, during this process, may not play with others.

Figure 3.13.2 Children who are undergoing a transition will need more adult attention

Case study

Joelle is a four year old who loves playing outdoors. Four weeks ago, she fractured her leg while playing on a trampoline. She has had to wear a cast on her leg and so has not been able to play with her friends outdoors on the tricycles and climbing frame. She has been feeling very frustrated and also tired as she has been using crutches. The cast on her leg also prevents her from sleeping as well as usual.

1 How might restrictions on Joelle's physical activity affect her physical development?
2 How might her social development be affected?
3 Explain why the impact on her development is likely to be only short term.

AC 1.6 Long-term factors that affect children's development

Some factors affect children in the long term. The range of factors is quite wide and how they affect children's development depends on the level of support that is available. Table 3.13.4 on the following page shows examples of long-term factors and possible effects on children's development.

Test yourself

How might long-term factors be influenced by the quality of support that children receive?

LO2 Understand how personal experiences, values and beliefs impact on the role of the early years practitioner

Can you remember some incidents in your childhood that were significant? It might be moving to a new school or the death or a grandparent. In this section, we look at how personal experiences, values and beliefs impact on how we respond to children and situations.

Table 3.13.4 Long-term factors and possible effects on development

Factor	Effects
Chronic health conditions, e.g. asthma, diabetes, epilepsy	• Tiredness may prevent the child from joining in. • Frequent absence may affect children's opportunities to make friends. • Frequent absence may result in children missing out on chunks of learning.
Divorce or separation of parents	• The impact on children's development depends on whether the separation is hostile or amicable. It also depends on whether children have access to the absent parent. • Divorce or separation can affect children's confidence and they may also show unwanted and frustrated behaviours. They may also lack concentration and interest in the play opportunities and activities available.
Bereavement	• When children lose a close family member or friend, their development may be affected. They may lose interest in play opportunities and may lack concentration and so their learning can be affected. • They may also be clingy and less settled and this can affect their emotional and social development.

AC 2.1 The impact of personal experiences, values and beliefs on professional practice

How we respond to people and situations is a result of a range of factors, including our own personal experiences, values and beliefs. In terms of working with children, these can affect our responses and so it is important to be aware of them and then, if necessary, to change our practice. The ability to analyse and reflect on our personal experiences and consider how they are affecting practice is what makes adults who work with children professionals.

Personal experiences

By the time we work with children, we have clocked up millions of different experiences which will have shaped us in ways that sometimes we may not even realise. If, for example, you moved home several times during your childhood, you might be more empathetic towards a child and her family who have just moved into the area. On the other hand, if you had been bullied at school, you may overreact to a two year old who has snatched a toy from another's hand, when actually this is pretty typical age-related behaviour. While we cannot undo our personal experiences, it is important to recognise their potential impact on our behaviour and thought processes. While personal experiences can make us more empathetic, it is important not to make assumptions that a child in similar circumstances will feel and deal with it in the same way.

Case study

Jodie moved several times as a young child because her mother was looking for work. She remembers hating each move and feeling lonely when she started at new schools. As an adult, she works in a nursery. A new child is starting the nursery. The parent tells her that the family has moved a couple of times already. On the child's first day, Jodie has planned a lot of activities about moving and has found some books to read with the child. She is surprised when the child soon finds another child to play with and is perfectly happy playing in the role-play area. When later on, Jodie starts to read the book about moving, the child asks for another one instead. Jodie feels quite disappointed.

1 How have Jodie's personal experiences shaped her actions?
2 What assumption did Jodie make about this child?
3 Why is it important to recognise our personal experiences?

In practice

Choose a personal experience that has had an impact on you.

Write about how it might affect your practice.

Values and beliefs

As well as our direct personal experiences, the way that we were raised and the community and society that we grew up in will also shape us. This is because we gain our values and beliefs from our parents, school and wider society. While the impact of personal experiences can be easy to pinpoint, it can be harder to recognise the impact of our values and beliefs. This is because many of us continue to live and work in the community and society in which we were raised. Our beliefs and values may seem 'normal' and so we may not even question the impact of them on our practice. A good example of this is the way that, many years ago, most children had married parents, while today the statistics show that many children will be born to cohabiting parents. For adults who grew up in the previous era, this change in family structure might have challenged their values about family life.

In practice

Look at the following five statements and think about your values and beliefs in relation to them.

- Divorce should be made much harder if there are children involved.
- Women are naturally better at child rearing.
- Nature knows best when it comes to premature babies.
- A higher band of tax should be placed on sugary foods such as chocolate.
- It is sad when babies are in day care for 50 hours a week.

How values and beliefs can impact on practice

There are many ways in which our values and beliefs can impact on our professional practice. We may, for example, assume that a family has the same values and beliefs as us and so not have important conversations about issues that affect children's care and education. We may also be judgemental about families who do not share the same lifestyle, beliefs or values as us.

Case study

Kylie is an experienced childminder. Jaden is four years old and has just started with Kylie. He has settled in well and is very happy. His mother has made an appointment, though, to speak to Kylie. Apparently, Jaden has come home a little upset, saying he does not want to eat lunch at Kylie's. Jaden's mother and Kylie have a long talk. It turns out that Kylie's way of serving food is very different from that of Jaden's family. In Jaden's family, vegetables and salad are eaten separately rather than at the same time as the main dish. Kylie thinks that this is a bit odd, but does not say so. Next time Jaden comes around, she lets him serve himself and makes a point of saying how he is missing out by not having everything together.

1 What assumption did Kylie make based on her values and beliefs?
2 How are Kylie's values and beliefs affecting her practice with Jaden?
3 Why is it important for us to recognise that our values and beliefs may not be shared with the families with whom we work?

LO3 Understand the principles of inclusive practice

Can you remember what the term **inclusive practice** means?

→ We looked at inclusive practice in Unit 2.4 and this section should be read alongside it.

In this section we briefly revisit the requirements of legislation in terms of inclusive practice and we also consider the two different models of disability and their implications. We also evaluate inclusive practice in relation to the current frameworks.

Key term

inclusive practice The process of ensuring equality of learning opportunities for all children and young people.

AC 3.1 Current legislation in relation to inclusive practice

➡ In Unit 2.4, we looked at legislation relating to inclusive practice and you should revisit pages 124–25 to look at the main requirements.

The points below summarise the key requirements that early years settings and schools should meet:

- Special education policy has to be in place outlining the procedures for identifying and supporting children with additional needs.
- There should be a designated member of staff who coordinates the provision for children with special needs – the SENCO.
- Reasonable adjustments and adaptations to the layout and equipment have to be made so children are not discriminated against.
- Children's individual care needs have to be considered and met as part of the EYFS.
- Settings should monitor carefully the outcomes of groups of children at risk of discrimination – for example, girls and ethnic minorities.

AC 3.2 Medical and social models of disability

Some children that we work with may have a disability. How we and other professionals work with them can be a reflection of how society views disability. Traditionally, the way that society has viewed disability has been labelled the 'medical model'. The medical model views disability as a problem which needs to be cured or fixed. It also views children with disability as being victims and therefore incompetent. The main criticism of the medical model of working with children is that the focus is always on the disability rather than on the child. The model has also been blamed for the underachievement of children with disabilities as many children with disabilities were educated separately from other children.

Social model of disability

Today, society is starting to view disability differently. The model that is used to support inclusive practice is known as the social model of disability. This model of disability is child centred and focuses on what children can do rather than just on the disability. The model of disability also focuses on the barriers that might prevent children from achieving and suggests that society needs to create environments and ways of working that enable children. The model argues that it is society that disables children by, for example, not putting ramps down to aid mobility or not providing computer programs to children with fine motor difficulties that allow them to dictate their writing.

This model of disability has been very influential and has prompted changes in legislation and the offer of mainstream education for children with disabilities. The language used to describe disabilities has also changed as a result of this model, with terms such as 'suffering from x' being replaced by 'living with x'. However, leading disability campaigners would say that there is still more to do to create a more equal society.

Research it!

Find out more about the medical and social models of disability and their potential impact by visiting www.disabilitywales.org/social-model.

AC 3.3 Inclusive practice and current frameworks for children from birth to seven years

Inclusive practice covers many aspects of work within early years settings, including equality and diversity. In Unit 2.4, we looked at these, but here we focus on inclusive practice in relation to children who have additional needs.

Early years settings and schools have to meet the requirements for inclusive practice that we looked at in Unit 2.4. There are many issues around inclusive practice in relation to the current frameworks. Table 3.13.5 shows some of the key issues and their impact on inclusive practice.

Table 3.13.5 Key issues in relation to inclusive practice

Key issue	Impact on inclusive practice
Physical environment	While settings are required to make reasonable adjustments, some settings are unsuitable for children who have mobility needs as they were built in a time when this was not considered. This means that children may not always be able to access toilets easily or outdoor spaces.
Training	For settings to be inclusive, adults working in the setting need to have the knowledge and training so as to best support them. In some settings, adults may not always know how best to work inclusively with children.
Adult input	Many children with additional needs require more adult input and time. While settings may have additional funding to support children with significant needs, many settings will say that they are not always able to give children the type of input that they need and they cannot afford to pay for additional adults.
Curriculum outcomes	Many adults working with children are concerned that the curriculum outcomes at the end of the Early Years Framework or at the end of Key Stage 1 are a hindrance to inclusive practice as the expectations given are 'one size fits all' and are not necessarily flexible.

In your setting

Talk to your placement supervisor or the person responsible for special educational needs in your setting (SENCO). Find out what they think the challenges are in providing for children who have additional needs.

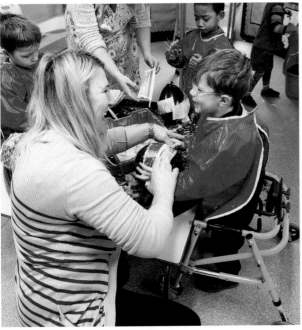
Figure 3.13.3 An inclusive setting allows all children to play

LO4 Understand the role of early intervention in partnership working

Are there children in your setting who have input from other professionals? In this section, we look at the importance of recognising that children have additional needs related to their development and also the importance of early intervention. We also consider the strategies that might be used for early intervention as well as the principles involved in partnership working.

AC 4.1 Children's additional needs expected stages of development

One of the starting points when working with children is to be able to recognise when they may need additional support. One of the indicators that children may need additional support is when they are not showing expected development in relation to their age. It may be that a child who is three years old is not talking clearly even though he is trying to communicate. If this is identified as not being linked to expected development, the child can be given additional support or be referred to other professionals if necessary. Without this recognition, the child might become increasingly frustrated and it may affect other aspects of their development.

Case study

Harry is almost four years old. He is a happy child and settled. Over the last couple of weeks, his key person has noticed that he often says 'pardon' and needs things to be repeated. He does not always respond when his name is called or when he is busy playing. He also seems to be easily frustrated and irritable. She identifies that this is not age/stage-expected development as most children of this age should be responding quickly. She meets with his parents and they agree that outside advice should be sought. A fortnight later, after a hearing test, it is found that he has a build-up of wax in his ear.

1 Why is it important for practitioners to check that children are showing expected development?
2 Is the cause of Harry's additional needs biological or environmental?
3 Explain how his additional need might impact on his overall development?

AC 4.2 Reasons for early intervention when meeting children's additional needs

Over the past few years, it has been increasingly recognised that children who have additional needs should be identified as early as possible. This is because quite often children who have early intervention are more likely to make progress quickly and the extent of the developmental delay can be reduced. There are other reasons too. Many types of additional needs affect children's behaviour and so, while they are not identified, children are likely to be misunderstood. Finally, as we have already seen, where there is a delay or difficulty in one area of development, children's learning and progress in other areas of development can also be affected.

Research it!

It is a statutory requirement for early years settings to carry out a progress check on children between the ages of two and three years. Find out about the reasons for this progress check by visiting www.education.gov.uk and searching for 'EYFS progress check at two'.

AC 4.3 Strategies for early intervention

There is a range of strategies that can be used to help identify children's additional needs and also to support early intervention.

Observation and assessment

→ In Unit 3.14, we look at the importance of observing and assessing children and so it will be worth reading that unit alongside this section.

Observation is about watching children and noticing what they can do and what they choose to do, as well as areas where they have any difficulties. Assessment is about using the observations and drawing conclusions from them. By observing and assessing children, we can check whether there are any aspects of a child's development that are not in line with expected development. We can also look at whether there are any particular areas of play and activity where children need additional support. A good example of this is where we might observe that a four year old tends to play alone and become frustrated when other children join in his play. This might make us consider whether the child has any additional needs in terms of his social skills and we may then consider ways of supporting the child further.

Reflect

Reflect on an occasion when you have observed a child and noticed that the child's response, behaviour or development was not typical of the age group's expected stage of development.

Monitoring and tracking

As well as observing and assessing children's development, early years settings also monitor children over a period of time in order to track their development. This helps adults to recognise children's rate of progress. Monitoring and tracking children's progress are important as sometimes children who are new to a setting may appear not to be showing expected development to begin with, but over the course of a month will start to show expected development.

Figure 3.13.4 It is important to observe children carefully

Where children have additional needs, the starting point is usually for early years settings to provide more adult support and to carefully target activities before referring children. While this extra support is in place, early years settings will then monitor and track the child's progress. If over a period of a couple of months, the extra adult support and activities do not seem to help or the child's rate of progress is less than expected, the early years setting may suggest to the child's parents that other professionals should be contacted.

Working with other professionals

Once it has been recognised that a child may need additional support, early years settings have to work in partnership with parents and decide whether other professionals need to be involved.

→ In Unit 2.5, we looked at the types of professionals who are likely to work with children.

Case study

Cahit has been in the nursery for two weeks. He is new to English and so his key person is spending time with him. He has settled in well and is enjoying being in the nursery. His key person is observing his communication and language carefully and will track his progress in English over the next two months. At present, Cahit is starting to respond to some key words but is not saying very much, which is typical for a child in this situation. His key person is hoping that, over the next few months, he will start to use words and phrases and then move onto sentences.

1 Why is it important that observations of Cahit's language are kept?
2 Why does Cahit's language need monitoring?
3 What would be the effects on Cahit's development and learning if he did not make progress with English?

While some early years settings can make referrals directly to other professionals, they can only do so with the permission of parents. Where a setting cannot make a direct referral, parents are usually signposted to their health visitor or GP, who will start the referral process. In most areas, once a referral has been received, the child will be assessed. At this point, either intervention programmes will be offered or advice will be given as to how the early years setting and parent can support the child's progress. In some cases, it may be decided by professionals, such as the occupational therapist, to continue to monitor the child and review the child's progress at a later date.

Individual education plans

Where additional support is needed, early years settings will draw up individual education plans for children. These set out short-term goals for individual children with strategies and activities that will be used with the children to help them make progress. Plans are drawn up with parents, the child's key person and other professionals if they are involved. It is usually the responsibility of the early years setting's or school's SENCO to coordinate meetings and monitor the plans. As individual education plans are short term, they are regularly reviewed and, if needed, new goals are set.

In your setting

Ask your placement supervisor if you can be shown an individual education plan. Find out when and how your setting uses them.

Statements of additional needs

In some cases, children's additional needs can only be met if there is significant funding in place. This is likely to be the case where children have complex needs. Where it is thought that children will need significant help, a range of assessments by different professionals will take place. The children's needs and how they can be supported are documented and, if approved, the local authority is required to fund the additional support. This process has traditionally been known as 'statementing' but at the time of writing this process is undergoing change. The new process for children with complex needs is likely to result in a document called the 'Education Health and Care Plan' being drawn up.

Research it!

Find out about the new process for documenting and funding children who have significant needs by visiting www.gov.uk/government/policies/increasing-options-and-improving-provision-for-children-with-special-educational-needs-sen.

AC 4.4 Working with others to meet children's additional needs

➡ In Unit 2.5, we looked at the importance of partnership working and so you should read that unit alongside this section.

Partnership working is often used to support children with additional needs. This is because, where a child is not showing expected development or is showing significant signs of emotional insecurity, children will need more targeted support. Other professionals, such as speech and language therapists and psychologists, will be able to identify what the child needs and so, by working with them, we will be able to support children more effectively. While referring to other professionals can often help children with additional needs, it is essential to remember that you are not allowed to refer children to another service without parental permission. This can sometimes be frustrating for practitioners who can clearly see that the child has a need and a parent refuses for the child to be referred. The only exception to this legal requirement is where a child is at serious risk of harm. There are also other principles of working in partnership that we looked at in Unit 2.5, which are listed here:

- confidentiality
- respect for others' ways of working
- recognition that other professionals may not share our aims or way of working
- accuracy of information
- punctuality in terms of attending meetings or providing information.

LO5 Be able to support the additional needs of children

Do you have children in your setting with individual needs? In most settings, there will be a range of children who need additional support from adults and play opportunities that will help them to gain or practise skills. In this section, we look at how you identify the individual needs of children in your setting and how you might respond to children in practice.

AC 5.1 Identifying the individual needs of children in your own setting

We have seen that there are many reasons why children may need some additional support when they are with us. It may be that they are just settling in or that they have a delay in one area of development. The starting point for identifying that children have additional needs is through sensitive observation and assessment as well as conversations with parents. Many practitioners find that it becomes easier with more experience to identify children with additional needs because the more you work with children, the more you become aware of the usual patterns of development and behaviour. A good tip, therefore, is to make sure that you know about expected development and behaviour and are able to link this with different ages of children.

→ In earlier chapters, we have looked at the different areas of development and so you may want to consider revising these.

In practice

Explain how you would identify a child with additional needs in your setting.

AC 5.2 Planning activities in partnership with others

There is no set formula for how to plan activities when working with children with additional needs. This is one of the most important points when working with children who have additional needs. Every child will be individual and so it is important to be ready to change your approach according to the reaction of the child. This is why it is good practice to work with others to recognise the needs of children and also to understand the interests and personality of children when planning activities. While one child might enjoy sharing books with an adult another child might enjoy playing with the sand. Similarly, while one child might be fast to respond to a question, another child might be much slower. This way of working is sometimes referred to as 'child centred' as individual children's needs and interests are the main focus. By working in partnership with others, we are more likely to find out about children's needs and interests. Other professionals may also provide us with suggestions of ideas and approaches which can influence our planning.

Tips to help you to plan activities in partnership with others for children with additional needs.

- Find out from the child's parents and the key person about the child's interest, temperament and usual responses.
- Talk to any other professionals involved with the child including the speech and language therapist and occupational therapist as they may be able to provide further information about the child as well as resources and ideas for activities.
- Plan activities and opportunities using this information.
- During activities and opportunities, observe and respond to the child's reactions.
- Be prepared to adapt your style and the activity according to the child's responses.
- Remember that learning or practising skills can be tiring and so the length of activity should be governed by the child's interest.
- Praise and acknowledge the child's interests.

AC 5.3 Working with others to provide activities to meet children's additional needs

Where children have additional needs, we have seen that there may be a range of others with whom we will work in partnership. Some children will have a specific plan drawn up that will outline the focus for current work, which may be called an individual education plan. Where children need a specific plan, it is likely that we will work with others to plan, but also to provide activities. Some activities might be suggested by other professionals. Where this is the case, it is important to understand clearly the purpose of the activity and how it is to be carried out. Afterwards, it is good practice to give feedback to parents and the other professionals about how the child responded.

Case study

Robert is three years old. He has complex needs that include a communication disorder, but also sensory impairments. A range of professionals supports him and often visits the nursery. They provide suggestions for targeted support that include activities that are often based on the information gained from Robert's parents and also his key person about his needs. Robert has an individual education plan that documents the areas that are being focused on as well as the type of activities that will support these areas. His key person and his parents work closely together and exchange information but also resources. Today his mother has brought in a cardboard tube that Robert has enjoyed looking through and also dropping soft toys down. She wonders whether it might come in handy today.

1 Why does Robert need professionals and parents to work together?
2 Why is it important that Robert's key person carries out activities that are included in the Individual education plan?
3 Why are activities based on Robert's interests?

In practice

Write about how you have worked with others alongside a child with additional needs in your setting. Explain how you ensured that you were child centred in your approach.

AC 5.4 Encouraging parents/carers to take an active role in their child's play, learning and development

We have seen in many units that it is important to work closely with parents and carers. This is particularly important when children have additional needs and where children may not always be able to express what they have done with

us. It is usual for most early years settings to provide home-setting books in which information about the child's day or session can be written and that also allow parents to feed back to us about what they have done with their child at home. It is also useful to share with parents ideas for activities as well as resources that their child has enjoyed. It is usual for parents who have children with additional needs to also give ideas to practitioners as in some cases they have more knowledge about the child's needs than anyone else. This is particularly true of children who have medical conditions.

AC 5.5 Reflect on your own practice in meeting children's additional needs

It is an important part of practice in the early years to be reflective and to think through how well you have worked or are working with children. In some ways the qualities and skills that we need to work with children with additional needs are the same as when working with all children. There are, however, a number of points that you can use to help you reflect on your own practice in meeting children's additional needs beginning with the quality of the relationship that you have with the child and their family:

Relationship with the child and the family
- Does the child respond positively to you?
- Does the child's family respond positively to you?

Respect
- How do you show that you value and respect the child?
- How do you empower the child, e.g. choice, independence?

Knowledge about the child's additional needs
- Have you talked to parents about the child's needs?
- Have you talked to other professionals about this type of need?
- Have you read or researched further about this type of need?

Communication skills
- Have you found a way of communicating effectively with the child?
- Do you show positive non-verbal skills?

- Do you encourage the child to communicate and are you a 'patient' communicator?
- Do you acknowledge the child's communications?

Observing and planning for the child's needs and interests

- How do you ensure that you are accurately observing the child's needs and interests?
- How do you use information gained from these observations to share ideas and information with others?
- How do you use observations and information gained from others to plan activities?

Tips for responding to a child who has additional needs

- Find out from the child's parents and the key person about the child's interests, temperament and usual responses.
- Plan activities and opportunities using this information.
- During activities and opportunities, observe and respond to the child's reactions.
- Be prepared to adapt your style and the activity according to the child's responses.
- Remember that learning or practising skills can be tiring and so the length of activity should be governed by the child's interest.
- Praise and acknowledge the child's interests.

In practice

Write about how you have worked with a child with additional needs in your setting. Explain how you ensured that you were child centred in your approach.

LO6 Be able to critically evaluate the provision for children with additional needs in own setting

Is your setting due an inspection? How a setting supports children with additional needs is one area that is looked at and so it is important that settings regularly evaluate their practice. In this section, we look at what you might consider when evaluating this aspect of your setting's provision.

AC 6.1 Critically evaluate the provision for children with additional needs in own setting

From time to time, it is good practice for settings to reflect on different aspects of their provision. This should be done objectively so that improvements can be made where necessary and so that the setting can build on its strengths. In terms of supporting children with additional needs, there are many aspects to consider when evaluating provision.

Policies and procedures

You should find out about your setting's policies and procedures and how these link to legislation on inclusive practice and the code of practice for children who have special educational needs.

Identification of children with additional needs

You should think about how well your setting identifies children with additional needs, including those whose development is being affected by short-term factors.

Work in partnership with parents

You should think about how information is exchanged with parents and how parents are involved when their children have additional needs.

Work in partnership with other professionals

You should find out about how your setting strives for best practice using advice from other professionals. You should also think about how intervention programmes from other professionals working with individual children are implemented.

Planning for individual children

It is good practice for settings to plan carefully to support children who have additional needs. This can be done through general planning or through individual education plans. Find out how your setting plans for children with additional needs.

Monitoring systems

You should find out about the monitoring systems that your setting uses to check that children are making progress and how observation and assessments are used when children are not showing expected development.

Resourcing – materials and staff

You should think about whether equipment and resources are available that will support children who have been identified as having additional needs. As many children with additional needs require more adult support and therefore time, you should consider whether children have sufficient adult time.

In practice

Write a report that evaluates how your setting supports children with additional needs.

Assessment

This is a wide-ranging unit that considers working with children who may have a range of needs. It links closely with Unit 2.4 so your assessor may assess some parts of both units together. The starting point for this unit is to look at the impact of biological and environmental factors on children's development as well as long- and short-term factors. This is covered in this unit. (You will need to be secure in this knowledge as it links to the mandatory assessment task as well.)

For Learning Outcome 2, you should think about how your own experiences may influence your practice and that of other early years practitioners. You can read about this in this unit, but you should still take time to reflect on your own circumstances as it is key to working effectively with children and their families.

For Learning Outcome 3, you need to look at the current legislation that is in place in relation to children who have additional needs. This links closely to Learning Outcome 1, in Unit 2.3 and so you may revisit this. You also need to look at how the concept of inclusive

practice links to the EYFS and national curriculum. In addition, you need to explain what is meant by the medical and social models of disability.

For Learning Outcome 4, you will need to work closely with your placement supervisor as the assessment criteria lend themselves to focusing on how your setting works with individual children who have additional needs, and how your setting in conjunction with others uses strategies for early intervention. This learning outcome links closely to Unit 2.5 so your assessor may decide to do some joint assessing.

For the Learning Outcomes 5 and 6 you will need to show that you can put theory into practice. You will need the support of your placement supervisor to gain evidence for these assessment criteria. A good tip is to make sure that your placement supervisor or experienced colleagues have seen the assessment criteria. In addition, you should read revisit the information given in this unit to help you reflect on your own practice and that in your setting.

Useful resources

Organisations

The Alliance for Inclusive Education

The Alliance for Inclusive Education is a national campaigning organisation led by disabled people: **www.allfie.org.uk**

Early Support

Early Support provides materials for families and professionals, including a service audit tool, a family pack, information for parents and developmental journals on the deaf, Down's Syndrome and visual impairments: **www.earlysupport.org.uk**

KIDS

KIDS works for disabled children, young people and their families: **www.kids.org.uk**

British Dyslexia Association (BDA)

The BDA is a national charity working for a 'dyslexiafriendly society' that enables dyslexic people of all ages to reach their full potential: **www.bdadyslexia.org.uk**

National Autistic Society (NAS)

The NAS aims to champion the rights and interests of all people with autism, and to provide individuals with autism and their families with help, support and services: **www.nas.org.uk**

Royal National Institute of Blind People (RNIB)

The Royal National Institute of Blind People (RNIB) has produced an excellent booklet, Focus on Foundation, which offers practical advice on the inclusion in early years settings of children who are blind and partially sighted: **www.rnib.org.uk**

Royal National Institute for Deaf People (RNID)

The RNID is the largest charity in the UK offering a range of services for people who are deaf or have a hearing impairment, and providing information and support on all aspects of deafness, hearing loss and tinnitus: **www.rnid.org.uk**

Scope

Scope is a charity that supports disabled people and their families. Its vision is a world where disabled people have the same opportunities as everyone else. Scope specialises in working with people who have cerebral palsy: **www.scope.org.uk**

Books and journals

Alcott, M. (2002), *An Introduction to Children with Special Needs*. London: Hodder & Stoughton.

Contact a Family (2004), *Caring for Disabled Children: A Guide for Students and Professionals*. Available from: **www.cafamily.org.uk/students.pdf**

DfES (2001), *The Special Educational Needs Code of Practice 2001*. Available free at: **www.teachernet.gov.uk**

Dickins, M. and Denziloe, J. (2004), *All Together: How to Create Inclusive Services for Children and Their Families*. National Children's Bureau.

Douch, P. (2006), *It Doesn't Just Happen – Inclusive Management for Inclusive Play*. London: Kids.

Horwath, J. (2001), *The Child's World: Assessing Children in Need*. London: Jessica Kingsley Publishers.

Lindon, J. (2005), *Understanding Child Development: Linking Theory and Practice*. London: Hodder Arnold.

Mortimer, H. (2001), *Special Needs and Early Years Provision*. London: Continuum International Publishing Group.

Wall, K. (2006), *Special Needs and Early Years: A Practitioner's Guide*. London: Paul Chapman Publications.

Wilson, R. (2003), *Special Educational Needs in the Early Years*. Abingdon: Routledge Falmer.

Unit 3.14 Use observation, assessment and planning to promote the development of children

Have you ever watched a baby playing with his hands? Or a couple of children engaged in role play? Observing children and using this information to assess their development, but also to plan for them, are a key part of working with young children. In this unit, we look at the role of observations when working with children and also different types of methods. We also look at some of the issues involved in the observation of children. Finally, we look at different situations in which you might practise your observation skills.

Learning outcomes

By the end of this unit, you will:

1 Understand the role of observation when working with children.
2 Understand observation methods.
3 Understand professional practice in relation to the observation of children.
4 Be able to carry out observations in own setting in line with current frameworks.
5 Be able to work with parents/carers in a way which encourages them to take an active role in their child's play, learning and development.

LO1 Understand the role of observation when working with children

It is a requirement of the EYFS and also good practice in working with older children for regular observations and assessments of their progress to be carried out. In this section, we look at the range of ways in which observations are used.

AC 1.1 Using observations

Observations are considered to be an important part of working with children. When we are working with children, we will be noting what they are doing and responding to them. We may, for example, see that a child's shoes are on the wrong feet or that a child has bags under their eyes and needs a nap. While these informal observations are important, there are times when observations are written down or recorded digitally. There are a number of reasons why recorded observations are needed, as shown in Figure 3.14.1.

Figure 3.14.1 Why observations are used

To plan for individual children's needs

One of the most important reasons why we observe children is to understand more about their interests, their stage of development and also any needs that they may have. Once we have recognised children's needs, interests and stage of development, then

we can use this information to plan resources, play opportunities and activities for them. As children's interests, needs and stage of development change, there is a need to observe children very frequently.

In your setting

Find out how your setting uses observations to support planning.

For early intervention

Some of the observations that we carry out with children will lead to assessments that suggest that children need additional support. In some cases, these observations and assessments will lead to children gaining additional support from adults in the setting, but they may also lead to referrals to other professionals once parental consent has been gained.

→ See also Unit 3.13.

To review the environment

Observations can also be used to help us consider how effectively specific areas within the setting are working. It may be that a mark-making area is hardly used by a group of children and, through observations, we can determine why and also consider how best to improve it.

During transition

When children move from setting to setting during the day or week, it is important for information to be shared with other childcare providers. This can only happen with parental consent, but it can be helpful for other childcare providers to know how the child has been and how the child responds in other settings. When children move from one setting to another (e.g. from nursery to a school), it is usual for observations and assessments to be passed across so that the new setting can quickly meet children's needs. Again, this can only happen if parents give their consent.

In your setting

Find out how your setting exchanges information with other settings to support transition.

When working in partnership

Observations and assessments are also used to work in partnership with parents as well as other professionals. Parents like to know what their children are doing and they are interested in understanding more about their development. Observations and assessments are regularly shared with parents and it is good practice for parents to contribute to them. This is because parents will see different aspects of their child at home.

In addition, observations and assessments are used to work in partnership with a range of professionals who support the child and their family. A speech and language therapist may be interested to know how much communication and language a child uses in the nursery. Again, information can only be shared with parental consent, except when there are safeguarding issues.

→ See also Unit 2.5, page 142.

In practice

Explain how observations are used in your setting for a range of purposes.

LO2 Understand observation methods

Does your setting use learning journeys as a way of recording children's progress? Whatever method they use, all early years settings are required to plan for children's progress and to do this they use a range of observation methods. In this section, we look at the many different observation methods that might be used.

AC 2.1 Observation methods and current frameworks

The EYFS or National Curriculum do not specify any particular observation methods that practitioners should use, although there is a requirement for observations and assessments to be regularly undertaken and for the information

gained from these to be used to plan activities and support.

In practice, most early years settings will use some or all of the following as ways of observing and also assessing development.

Learning journeys

Learning journeys are books or files that record children's progress over time. Practitioners will take photographs or write about times when children have done something which they consider to be significant. Sometimes these are referred to as 'wow' moments. In addition, learning journeys are shared with parents and parents can add in their own observations. It is good practice for learning journeys also to include ideas for planning activities and support based on the observations and 'wow' moments that have been included.

Post-it notes

Some settings will write on post-it notes or stickers to record significant steps or events. These are collated and linked to the areas of learning within the EYFS. In some settings, these will support the learning journey approach, while in others they will be added to children's records.

Checklists

Some early years settings use a checklist approach to record children's progress.

→ For more on checklists, see page 372.

Settings may use commercial checklists or devise their own. Some settings use the non-statutory guidance called Early Years Outcomes and base their observations on the statements within this.

Research it!

Find out about what the EYFS statutory framework says in relation to observation and assessment. Download the EYFS statutory framework from www.foundationyears.org.uk.

Look at paragraphs 2.1 and 2.2.

Figure 3.14.2 Learning journeys often include photographs of children

Summative assessments

It is good practice for all settings to review children's progress based on the observations that have taken place over a period of time. A summative assessment is literally a 'summing up' of the child's progress in the EYFS areas of development. Some early years settings will produce summative assessments like a report, while others will be less formal. It is good practice for parents to contribute to summative assessments and also for summative assessments to be shared with parents.

Statutory summative assessments

There are two points in the EYFS where there is a requirement for early years practitioners to produce a summative assessment.

Two year old progress check

Early years settings that have children aged between two and three years must carry out a summative assessment of children's progress in the three prime areas.

Early Years Foundation Stage profile

At the time of writing reception teachers must carry out a summative assessment using the paperwork provided by the Department of Education at the end of the reception year. This summative assessment provides data for the government as well as information for teachers and parents. Going forward, the government is considering carrying out a summative assessment at the start of the reception year.

> **Research it!**
>
> Find out more about the Early Years Foundation Stage Profile. Go to **www.education.gov.uk**.

AC 2.2 Evaluate observation methods

There is a range of different observation methods that early years and schools can use to find out more about children's development and interests. Each method has advantages and disadvantages. Figure 3.14.3 shows some of the common methods.

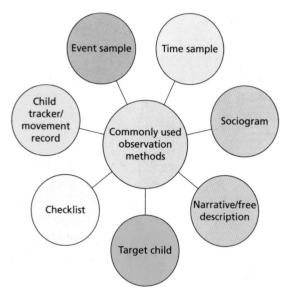

Figure 3.14.3 Commonly used observation methods

Event sample

An event sample is a way of recording how many times a child shows a certain behaviour, action or response. It can be used very flexibly and can help us understand more about how individual children respond as well as whether there are any patterns to their responses or behaviours. Event samples are normally filled in over several days so as to build up a picture of what is happening.

Creating an event sample

Most event samples are created using a grid (e.g. see Table 3.14.1). When the response or behaviour (the 'event') occurs, information is recorded. In the case of a child who often bites, the grid may record

the time of the bite, who was bitten, where the bite took place and the circumstances behind the bite. If there is concern about a child's eating habits, the grid may record the time the child ate, what they ate, where they ate and who was with them.

Advantages

- Event samples are simple to fill in.
- They can be adapted to suit different circumstances.
- They can build up a picture of children's responses or behaviours.
- They can be used to monitor success of any interventions – for example, the number of times a child swears is reducing or the number of interactions a child has with their key person is increasing.

Disadvantages

- Grids have to be carefully designed to collect useful information.
- Other members of the team have to fill it in if the key person is absent.
- It may not explain why the 'events' are occurring.

Time sample

Time samples are often used to look at what children do over a session or a set period of time. The idea is that children's activity is recorded at set times and this builds up to give a picture of children's social groups, interactions and play. It is a very flexible method that early years settings can use to look at a child's activity over a session or an hour. It can also be used to look at areas of provision to see how often they are used and who uses them.

Creating a time sample

The starting point is to decide over what period of time the observation is to take place – for

Table 3.14.1 An event sample grid

Time	Place	Those involved	Circumstances	Other notes

Case study

Josef's mother is concerned that he is not eating enough and she shares her concern with his nanny. The nanny suggests that they draw up an event sample to see just when, what and how much he is eating over a week. The nanny creates a form with columns and over the next week the nanny and the mother fill in the sheet each time that Josef eats or drinks something. By the end of the week, they soon see a pattern of eating and drinking emerging. Josef seems to be refusing food at meal times, but often eats snacks soon afterwards. He also seems not to eat when he is made to sit at the table by himself, but he does eat when someone is sitting with him.

1 Why was an event sample a good method to use to explore Josef's eating habits?
2 Why did the nanny and the mother need to carry it out over a full week?
3 What might be the next steps to encourage Josef to eat more at meal times?

Advantages

● Time samples are easy to use.
● They can be adapted to focus on particular aspects of children's activity.

Disadvantages

● An event of interest may not be captured if it falls outside the recording slot.
● Time samples require good time management skills.
● The observer needs to write concisely and accurately.

Sociogram

Sociograms can be used as a way of finding out about children's friendship preferences. It does this by asking children to name who they play with. A sociogram is not strictly an observation as it requires children to report on their friendships. It is not often used in early years settings because it often generates very unreliable information.

Carrying out a sociogram

To carry out a sociogram, you ask children one by one and in private to name three children who are their friends or whom they like to play with. The information is then collated and shows the names of the children and also who they mentioned as friends. From the data gathered, it is also possible to identify children who are frequently named by others and also children who reciprocate their friendship.

example, an hour or a whole session. If the time sample is done over too short a period, it will not be very effective. Once the time frame has been decided, then the frequency of observation or 'samples' needs to be decided – for example, one minute of observation every ten minutes. A grid then needs to be created that allows the observer to write what the child is doing during the 'sample' (e.g. see Table 3.14.2). It is important for the observer to have a clear idea of what they wish to observe and to make this the focus of the recording, such as interaction levels or physical movements.

Table 3.14.2 A time sample grid

Time	Observation
10.05	
10.15	
10.25	
10.35	
10.45	
10.55	

Table 3.14.3 Example of a sociogram

Name of child	Named friend 1	Named friend 2	Named friend 2
Michaela	Sundus	Sarah	Nilufer
Brian	Sarah	Sundus	Michaela
Viktor	Brian	Nilufer	Sundus
Nilufer	Brian	Sundus	Sarah
Sundus	Michaela	Sarah	Brian
Sarah	Brian	Sundus	Michaela

Look at the example of a sociogram in Table 3.14.3 and answer the following questions:

1 Which child was the most frequently named by other children?
2 Which children may have reciprocal friendships?
3 Which child was not named by the other children?

Advantages

- Sociograms can help practitioners see whether any children are being neglected or rejected by their peers.
- They can be useful during transition to check that children will be with other children with whom they have friendships.
- They show where friendships are reciprocated.

Disadvantages

- Children may name children with whom they have just played.
- Children may forget to name children who are absent.
- Young children may try to please the adult and give names that they think the adult wants to hear.
- Young children's friendships can be very fluid.

Narrative/free description

The narrative or free description method is probably the most used in early years settings. The observer records what the child is doing. The method is very flexible and the observer can focus on any aspect of the child's play, interactions or behaviour. Most early years settings either plan observations to record aspects of the child's learning linked to areas of the EYFS or, after an observation, link what has been recorded to the EYFS.

Carrying out a narrative or free description

To carry out a narrative or free description, all you need are a pen and paper. Watching the child, you record down their activity. It can be helpful to decide in advance what you intend to observe about the child – for example, their physical movements or

their interactions – unless it is the first time that you are working with the child. It is also good practice to put the start time and end time of the observation – for example, 'Start: 10.04 … End: 10.11'. It can be hard to write continuously and so you may decide to record for a few minutes, have a break and then start again. If you decide to do this, you simply show the break in your recordings.

An example of a free description is shown in Table 3.14.4.

Table 3.14.4 Example of a free description

Name of child: Jamie Cullen	Age: 3 years 5 months	Date of observation: 4.11.14
Context: Sand tray. Jamie plus two others.		
Start: 14.45		

Jamie is smiling. He scoops the sand into a bucket. He is talking to the child on his right. He fills the bucket up. He puts the bucket down in the sand and says, 'Now, it's really heavy. Let me try yours.' He takes the other child's bucket and lifts it. 'It is heavier than yours. Much more heavier.' Jamie looks for another bucket. He compares the size of it. He smiles and says, 'This one will be even bigger!' He asks the child on his right if he wants to help him to fill the bucket.

End: 14.53

Advantages

- Narrative/free description is a flexible method.
- No preparation is required.
- It can be used to observe many aspects of children's development.
- It can be used to link specifically to areas of development within the EYFS.

Disadvantages

- It requires speedy writing.
- The observer needs to be good at writing descriptively.
- The observer may not focus on significant developmental points.

Target child

This method is usually used to focus for a short while on a single child's social activity and interaction. Recordings usually take place every

Figure 3.14.4 The free description method of observation requires practice as you have to be able to write what you see very quickly and accurately

minute and thus it provides a detailed account of a child's activity. To help the observer record more effectively, a coding system is used.

How to carry out a target child observation

Begin by looking at the coding system or devise your own coding system. Create a sheet with columns that will provide space for you to record the child's activity minute by minute (e.g. see Table 3.14.5). Put the start time of the observation as well as the date of the observation and the name of the child. Observe the child minute by minute using the coding system. It is useful to use this method over an hour so as to capture plenty of information about the child.

Advantages

- A target child observation can help the observer to understand the extent of children's social interactions with others and levels of activity.

Table 3.14.5 A coding system used for a target child observation

Minute	Location	Activity	Interaction
1			
2			
3			
4			
5			

Coding:

TC = Target child

A = Adult

C = Other children

Arrows used to indicate direction of interaction, e.g.
TC → A = Target child is saying something to the adult,
or →TC← indicating that the child is talking to himself.

- They can be repeated to build up a detailed picture of a child's interactions and activities.

Disadvantages

- The child may not be showing usual responses in the situation observed.
- The observer needs to be familiar with the coding system.

> **Reflect**
>
> How good are you at using coding systems? Would you be better developing your own codes?

Checklist

A checklist is a series of statements or questions about specific skills that children have acquired, in order to check for expected development. Many early years settings use them over a period of time to track children's development. They are often used by health professionals to monitor children's development in relation to expected development. Some checklists are produced commercially; others are created by the early years setting.

How to carry out a checklist

Look carefully at the list of statements on the checklist (e.g. see Table 3.14.6). Decide on whether you will observe as children are playing and engaged in everyday activity or whether you will need to set up a situation to prompt children's activity. For some types of skills on checklists, it may be that the easiest way to collect the information is by asking the child to do a task – for example, 'Can you walk on this line?' Once you have observed the child engaged in the activity or skill, you then make a judgement as to whether or not the child is able to

do it. Some checklists provide an additional column that allows you to record whether the child can do a task with support, which can be very helpful. If you are in doubt as to whether a child has acquired a skill, it is always best to observe again at another point in order for records to be accurate.

Advantages

- Simple to use.
- Can be repeated to check progress.
- can be used to track groups of children

Disadvantages

Provides very limited information e.g. nothing about a child's confidence or motivation. Statements have to be written very carefully to avoid ambiguity

Child tracker/movement record

This method looks at which areas of provision children spend time in and how long they stay there. It is usually carried out for a significant part of a session. While the observer may learn a lot about a child's movements, it is quite simplistic as information about what the child is doing or how they are interacting is not recorded. It also requires a lot of time and so it is not often used in settings.

How to carry out a child tracker/ movement record

Create a diagram of your setting which clearly shows the different areas of your provision – for example, mark-making area, sand tray, toilets, etc. Start off by looking to see where the child is. Mark the spot on the plan and write the time next to it. When the child leaves to go to another area,

Table 3.14.6 Example of a checklist

Skill	Acquired	Emerging	Not yet
Can walk on a line on tiptoe			
Can climb confidently using alternate feet			
Can aim and throw overarm hitting large target at one metre			
Can catch a large ball thrown gently from one metre, using outstretched arms			

Tracking observation sheet

Name of child	Lucien Blackburn
Date of observation	20/03/2014
Start time	10.05
End time	11.40

Comments

Lucien's play centred around block play although he accessed the other areas of the provision to enrich his play.
He was playing with two other children

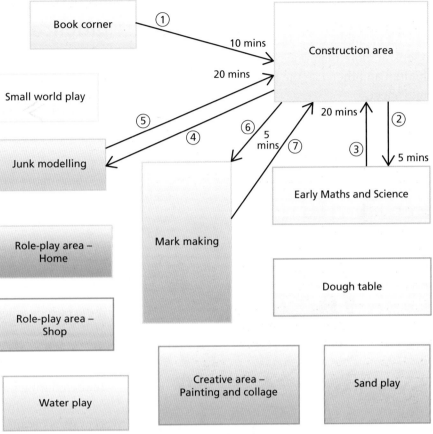

Figure 3.14.5 A tracking observation shows the movements and potential interests of a child

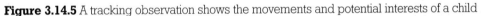

write down the time before drawing a line on the plan that reflects their movement. When they reach another area and settle, record the new time. Continue to do this until the session or the agreed observation time has finished.

Advantages

- Child tracker/movement records can examine which areas of provision seem to engage a child.
- They may highlight where children are not finding the provision stimulating.

Disadvantages

- They do not record the reasons why children are moving from one area to another.
- They do not provide a record of interactions or record of the child's activity.
- They take a lot of time, but do not generate much data.
- They can be difficult for others to interpret.

Test yourself

Look at the following observation methods and explain when they might be used. For each method, give one advantage and one disadvantage:

- checklist
- event sample
- target child.

Other methods of observing children

Early years settings use a range of different methods to gain an accurate picture of children's development. This also includes technology. Popular methods include taking photographs of children during significant moments or to illustrate their play interests, filming children as they play and also recording children's speech and language. These newer methods are often quicker than 'pen and paper', but parents' consent is needed. In addition, many early years settings adapt methods to suit what information they need to collect. They may, for example, use a time sample approach to look at more than one child's activity or film children and then use the footage to fill in a target child sheet.

Figure 3.14.6 Talking into toy phones provides a good opportunity to observe and record children's speech

In your setting

Find out what observation methods your setting mainly uses.

In practice

Ask your placement supervisor if you can observe a child using one of the methods that is used in your setting. What information did you find out about the child? What did you find out about the method that you used?

LO3 Understand professional practice in relation to the observation of children

How would you like the observation records that your assessor completes to be left on a coffee table for anyone to look at? Or how would you like it if your assessor had already made up their mind about how well you work before they watched you? These are some of the issues involved in observing children and, in this section, we look at the importance of being objective and also maintaining confidentiality.

AC 3.1 Objectivity and subjectivity

Observing children is a skill. There are many reasons why observations may not be accurate. These include whether children know that they are being observed, as children may change what they do if they think that they are being watched. This is very important to remember when watching children during role play, for example. One of the main reasons why observations may not always be accurate is because the observer is being subjective. This is sometimes referred to as **observer bias**. Subjectivity means that the observer is being influenced in some way which will affect what they choose to see. There are many possible influences that may cause an observer to be subjective:

- like or dislike of the child
- previous experiences and observations of the child
- overfamiliarity with the child
- knowledge gained from others about the child.

Key term

observer bias When the observer is not objective.

In addition, an observer may be subjective in what they record if they have a particular interest in one aspect of development. This may mean that they miss something else that is relevant.

The opposite of subjectivity is objectivity. Where an observer is recording objectively, they will not show any bias or be influenced by what others say about the child or their own feelings towards the child.

AC 3.2 Reasons for objectivity when recording observations

It is very difficult to be totally objective when recording observations, but it is important that we strive to be. Recognising the influences that may cause us to be subjective can help us to become more objective. This is important as there are many dangers associated with adults being subjective in their recording of observations.

Inaccuracy

Observations of children may not be accurate. An adult who knows a child well may not pick up on aspects of their development as the adult may have become familiar with them.

Case study

Sarah is Ibrahim's key person. She has been working with him since he was a baby. He is now nearly four years old. She regularly observes him in all aspects of his development. Ibrahim's speech is not very clear but Sarah can understand him very well. She has not noted that the clarity of his speech is atypical for his age.

1 Why has Sarah not picked up on the fact that Ibrahim's speech is not typical for his age?
2 Why might this prevent Ibrahim from getting additional support?
3 Why is it important that Sarah starts observing Ibrahim more objectively?

Labelling

Subjective recording of observations may mean that children become labelled and, in turn, positive aspects of their behaviour and development may be missed as the observer may not look out for these.

Incomplete observations

When observers are subjective, they may not focus on certain aspects of children's development, play or interaction that are significant. They may instead continue to look for what they expect to see. This may mean that observations are incomplete.

AC 3.3 Confidentiality during the observation process

All information that we learn about children during our work with them and their families is confidential. This includes information gained from the observations and assessment process. Confidentiality means that you must not talk about or show the information to people who do not have permission to see or hear about the information. People who usually have access to the observations and assessments of children include:

- the child's parents
- the child's key person or co-key person
- the SENCO, if the child has additional needs
- the manager of the setting.

The only reason you may break confidentiality is if the parent gives you consent to do so or where you have concerns about a child's welfare, in which case you should follow the safeguarding procedures in your setting. If you are unsure about whether information about a child is confidential, you should always talk to your placement supervisor or line manager.

Storage of observations and assessments

As the information that is gained about individual children is confidential, early years settings will make sure that children's records are only available for those who have the right to see them. In some settings, children's learning journeys are available in the room, but parents can only look at those that relate to their child. While, in theory, it would be good to keep children's observations and records stored in a secure area, the difficulty that many early years settings have is that they want to share them easily with parents. It is also good practice for children to be able to look at their learning journeys and photographs too.

Using observations for coursework

In terms of showing evidence of your observations and assessments to your assessor for study purposes, the usual procedure is to gain permission from the setting, who in turn should gain consent from the parent. You should then be careful who you choose to observe so as to ensure that the child cannot be identified – for example, you should not choose the only baby under six months in the baby room or the only girl who is two years old. Once the observation has been completed, you should remove all information from the observation that may indicate who the child is, by doing the following:

- Delete the date of birth of the child and instead use their age in years and months.
- Remove any photographs of the child.
- Delete or substitute the name of the child.
- Remove any text that may identify the child (e.g. name of a medical condition, language spoken at home).

In your setting

Find out how your setting keeps observations of children confidential.

LO4 Be able to carry out observations in own setting in line with current frameworks

How often are observations carried out in your setting? In some settings, adults record observations each day. It is also good practice to use observations to reflect on how effective the provision is in settings. In this section, we look at how to carry out observations in a range of different situations.

AC 4.1 Observe in line with current frameworks

It is useful to know how to carry out a range of different observations. Most early years settings carry out the majority of their observations on individual children, but sometimes they may look at groups of children or parts of their provision.

Tips for observations

- Remember to check that you have permission to observe each time you carry out an observation while you are a learner.
- Remember that observations are confidential.
- Always put the date on the observation.
- Think carefully about what you are hoping to learn from an observation.

Observing an individual child

As we saw in LO2, there is a range of methods that you might use to observe an individual child. You will need to consider carefully what you want to learn about the child as a starting point for the observation.

Tips for observing an individual child

- Always ask your placement supervisor for their advice and permission well ahead of carrying out the observation.
- Read up on the expected development for this age group as this will help you understand what you might focus on.
- Decide whether you will observe while talking and playing with the child or from a distance.
- Record the date and time on your observation.

In practice

Carry out an observation looking at one area of a child's development or play. You might like to repeat the observation but choose another age range.

Observing a group of children

It can be hard to observe groups of children, but one way of doing this is by using the free description method. If you find this difficult, consider filming the group's activity and afterwards using the footage to write the free description.

Indoor and outdoor provision

Observations can be used to provide information about the provision and how effective it is. It is not very easy to look at all aspects of the provision simultaneously and so it is worth choosing a specific area. For example, indoors you might look at the mark-making provision, while outdoors you might consider opportunities for role play. There are many things that you might wish to focus on when looking at the provision, such as how much time children spend there or how much interaction children use when in that area. It is important to decide what you wish to focus on ahead of time as this will affect your choice of observation methods. Event samples can work well as a way of monitoring how frequently children use the area and what they do there, while adapting the target child method might be useful if you wish to look at the interactions that a child or group of children have while they are in the area.

AC 4.2 Reflecting on outcomes of observations carried out in your own setting

Observation is just one part of a larger process. The process is often illustrated as a circle or wheel, as shown in Figure 3.14.7.

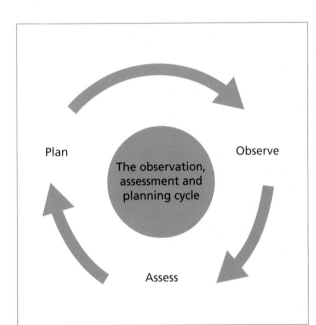

Figure 3.14.7 The observation, assessment and planning cycle

The observation, assessment and planning cycle is important because, while observing children can be interesting, it is essential to use the information afterwards. It may be that, through observing a three year old, we notice that the child has not established a hand preference. An assessment using this information would tell us that most children have developed a hand preference by the age of three. The next step would be to plan some activities to strengthen the hand preference. After a couple of weeks, we might then observe the child again to see whether our activities have been helpful.

Assessment

Assessment is the process of using the information that we have gained from observations to reflect and to reach some conclusions. In some cases, our conclusions might be that we need to observe further because we may recognise that we need additional information or we may think that what we observed was not typical.

Reflecting on outcomes of observations

An individual child

There are several things that you might reflect on using the information that you have gained from an observation of an individual child. Table 3.14.7 shows some of the questions that you might consider.

A group of children

When looking at the outcomes of observations of groups of children, the focus is often on how well the play and resources interested the children and allowed them to play and learn together. Some observations also consider group learning and how well adult-led activities are meeting the needs of the group. Key points to consider when reflecting on outcomes for groups of children include:

- How well were children engaged in the play or the activity?
- Were there opportunities for children to communicate and interact with each other?
- What were the group dynamics and did any children appear to be left out?
- How much support did children need and to what extent did adults provide it?

Indoor and outdoor provision

When assessing the effectiveness of areas within indoor and outdoor provision, there are several things to consider:

- Did many children spend time using the area?
- Who were they and what did they do?
- What was the quality of their play and interactions?
- How long did the children stay and what prompted them to leave?

Table 3.14.7 Reflecting on the outcomes of an observation with an individual child

Play and interests	<ul><li>Did the child seem engaged during the play or activity?</li><li>How long did the child stay playing or engaged in the activity?</li><li>Why did the child leave the activity?</li><li>How well did the child concentrate on the activity?</li><li>What seemed to interest the child?</li><li>Are the available resources and play opportunities suitable and meeting this child's needs?</li></ul>
Emotional development	<ul><li>Did the child seem happy and relaxed?</li><li>Did the child interact with his/her key person?</li></ul>
Social development	<ul><li>Did the child interact or communicate with other children?</li><li>How did they do this and is it typical of expected development?</li><li>How did the child's behaviour link to that expected of their age and stage?</li></ul>
Communication and language development	<ul><li>How often did the child communicate with adults/children?</li><li>How does their language link to that expected of their age and stage?</li><li>How does the production of speech sounds link to that expected of their age and stage?</li><li>Did the child appear to understand other children/adults?</li></ul>
Physical development	<ul><li>What physical skills did the child show?</li><li>How did the child's physical skills relate to those expected of their age and stage?</li><li>Which tools or equipment did the child attempt to use?</li><li>How well did they manage to use the tools or equipment?</li></ul>

- What seemed to appeal most to them during their play?
- How engaged were children while they were in the area?

Using the information gained from the reflection, settings may look to take the following steps:

- Change the layout or increase the resources available for children.
- Consider whether adults need to support children more so that they can access the area.
- Consider whether the resources are sufficiently challenging or suitable for the age and stage of the children.

AC 4.3 Working with others to plan next steps in relation to the needs and interests of children

As part of the process, once we have reflected on the information that we have gained from the observations, we then need to consider the next steps for the child or group of children. This is often done alongside others in group care settings.

Individual children

In most early years settings, the next steps might be to plan activities or to use resources with children. Sometimes, where there are emerging concerns about the child's development, the next step will be to talk to parents with a view to referring the child to other professionals. Table 3.14.8 shows the next steps after considering the questions in Table 3.14.7.

Groups of children

Following on from assessing the possible outcomes of the observation, the next step is to consider the next steps for the group of children. This will very much depend on what has been considered. Here are some possible next steps that might be appropriate:

- Create more challenging play opportunities for children.
- Provide play opportunities that build on children's observed play interests.
- Provide more adult support so that children can communicate and interact with each other further.

Table 3.14.8 Next steps in relation to the needs and interests of an individual child

Play and interests	<ul><li>What other resources could be put out to help the child further explore the activity that is of interest?</li><li>What other play opportunities or activities could be used to extend the child's play interest?</li><li>Does the child need more adult support in order to enjoy the play opportunities?</li><li>Do new resources and play opportunities need to be organised for this child?</li></ul>
Emotional development	<ul><li>Does the settling-in process need to be extended for this child?</li><li>Does the child need more time with their key person?</li></ul>
Social development	<ul><li>Does the child need more support in order to play alongside other children and what activities might be used for this?</li></ul>
Communication and language development	<ul><li>Do adults need to provide more opportunities for this child's interaction?</li><li>What resources could be used to further promote communication and interaction, e.g. toy telephones, role play?</li></ul>
Physical development	<ul><li>Does the child need additional support to help master the use of toys and resources?</li><li>Does the child need a wider range of toys and resources in order to provide more physical challenge?</li></ul>

- Provide more equipment so that all children can join in the play.
- Reconsider adult-led activities to ensure that they are sufficiently participative and age/stage appropriate.

AC 4.4 The early years practitioner's role in meeting the needs and interests of children

It is part of our professional duty when working with children to think about how we might work to meet their needs and interests. Observation, assessment and the subsequent planning of next steps are therefore an important way of ensuring that this takes place. Interestingly, how well we are able to plan for the individual needs and interests of children is a focus of Ofsted.

- How often do you observe individual children in your setting?
- Do you carry out observations that focus on each of the developmental areas as well as the EYFS areas of development?
- Do you focus observations on children's play interests?
- Do you use a range of observation methods and observe children in a range of situations to ensure that your information is accurate?
- Do you take time to assess the outcomes from these observations?
- Do you use sources of information to consider whether children's skills, responses and behaviours link to children's age/stage of development?
- Do you use your observations and assessments to plan individual children's next steps?
- Do you consider children's interests and build on these when planning next steps?

In practice

Using examples, write an evaluation of how you meet children's needs and interests through the observation, assessment and planning cycle.

LO5 Be able to work with parents/carers in a way which encourages them to take an active role in their child's play, learning and development

Have you noticed that the key persons in your setting often talk through the observations that they have made with the child's parents? You might also have seen how parents in your setting share photos and information about their child's development at home too. In this section, we look at how observations, assessment and planning are carried out with parents.

AC 5.1 Encouraging parents/carers to take an active role in their child's play, learning and development

It is good practice and also a requirement of the EYFS that parents are involved in the observation, assessment and planning process. This is because they will see a different side of their child at home than we do in the setting and also they will know what type of things their child enjoys doing. It is therefore important to work in ways that will allow parents to take an active role in this aspect of their child's development.

Learning journeys

As we saw earlier in LO2, learning journeys are the most used method of recording children's developmental progress. They are used by most early years settings and are a good way for parents to learn about, and also become involved in, their child's development. It is usual for most early years settings to include some 'next steps' when they discuss the child with their parents. Some of these next steps might be activities or play opportunities that can be done at home.

Gaining information from home

As well as learning journey approaches, many early years settings take an interest in what children are doing at home. They encourage parents to share photographs and stories of what their child has been doing with them. Through these discussions, the key person can also give further suggestions that parents might like to consider doing with their child.

Assessment

To complete this unit you will need to complete a variety of tasks. This unit is particularly important as it underpins the mandatory task.

Your starting point is to revise the reasons why observations are important when working with children and how the need to observe and assess children links to the current frameworks. This chapter provides information on these aspects.

In addition, to complete Learning Outcomes 2 and 4, you will need to know about the different methods by which you can observe children and the advantages and disadvantages of each. You also need to be able to carry out a range of observation techniques. For Learning Outcome 4, you also have to be able to use the information gained from observing in a range of situations to consider what you have learnt and also to develop plans. (It is important that your

knowledge of observation methods and your ability to use them is secure as this will play a large part in the mandatory task that you also need to complete for this qualification.)

For Learning Outcome 3 you need to be able to consider the issues involved in observing children, which includes objectivity and confidentiality. It may be worth reading about these issues in this chapter before you attempt an assessment.

The final outcome is to show that you can work with parents and encourage them to take an active role. This might mean sharing an observation that you have carried out or working on the planning of activities with parents. As working with parents requires skill and sensitively, you might need advice and guidance from your placement supervisor first.

Useful resources

Books

Berk, L. E. (2006), *Child Development* (7th edn). Boston, MA: Pearson International Edition.

Bertram, T. and Pascal, C. (1997), *Effective Early Learning: Case Studies in Improvement*. London: Hodder & Stoughton.

Harding, J. and Meldon-Smith, L. (1996), *How to make Observations and Assessments*, London: Hodder Arnold.

Sylva, K., Roy, C. and Painter, M (1980), *Childwatching at Playgroup and Nursery School*. London: Sage Publications.

Unit 3.15 Use longitudinal studies to observe, assess and plan for children's needs

How much would you expect a child to change over six weeks? Perhaps a baby might start to lift their head or a two year old might move out of nappies. In this unit, we look at the importance of assessing children's development over a period of time. We also look at the process of using longitudinal studies to meet, assess and plan for children's development and needs. Finally, we look at how you might evaluate the outcomes of the longitudinal study that you carry out as part of the mandatory assessment task that is linked to this unit.

Learning outcomes

By the end of this unit, you will:

1 Understand the purpose of undertaking longitudinal studies.
2 Be able to use observations to assess and plan for the developmental needs of children in line with current frameworks.
3 Be able to critically evaluate the outcomes of longitudinal studies.

LO1 Understand the purpose of undertaking longitudinal studies

Have you noticed just how much a baby changes during the course of a few weeks? By regularly observing a child over a few weeks, we can learn a lot about them and during this time we can also plan for them based on these observations. This is the basis of the type of longitudinal study that you will need to complete for this unit. In this section, we begin by looking at how the longitudinal study can be used to assess children and also how it might benefit the child, the early years practitioner and others involved in the care and education of the child.

AC 1.1 Using a longitudinal study as an assessment tool

A longitudinal study is a way of observing and assessing children's development over a period of time. There are many reasons why a longitudinal study is undertaken. Researchers use longitudinal studies to look at children's development over a long term. They may look at children in certain geographic areas or with specific characteristics, such as being identical twins, over a five-, ten- or fifteen-year period. The information they gain is used to draw conclusions about children's health, development and education outcomes.

> **Research it!**
>
> Find out about the famous longitudinal study known as the Avon Longitudinal Study of Parents and Children. Go to **www.bristol.ac.uk/alspac** and find out about their key discoveries in the 'Media' section of the website.

Longitudinal studies in early years settings

In early years settings, longitudinal studies are used to develop a rounded picture of children's development and are used to actively plan for children's development. By using a range of observational methods and regularly observing children's development, it is possible to make more accurate assessments of children's development. These can be used to check that children are making progress in line with their age and stage of development. Longitudinal studies can also assess children's progress against the areas of learning and development within the Early Years Foundation Stage, which is important as there is an expectation that, by the time children finish the reception year, they should have gained sufficient skills and knowledge to be ready for Year 1. Finally, longitudinal studies can also be used to show evidence to Ofsted that the setting is supporting children to make progress from their starting points.

AC 1.2 The benefits of a longitudinal study

There are many benefits to undertaking longitudinal studies in early years settings.

The benefits of a longitudinal study for the child

Children should be at the heart of everything that we do and so should be the main beneficiary of a longitudinal study. As a result of the longitudinal study, we should know more about the child and particularly their interests. This in turn should help us to respond better to them and also to plan for their needs and interests. It is also good practice for early years settings to involve the child by, for example, talking to them about what we are doing or showing them photographs that we have taken of them as they are playing. Many early years settings that present longitudinal studies as 'learning journeys' also encourage the children to look at them and talk them through what has been written about them. This helps the children to gain a strong sense of competence as they see their progress. It also helps children to develop a sense of pride and belonging.

Figure 3.15.1 This child has learnt to throw as a result of the practitioner observing and planning for their development

In your setting

Find out whether your setting shares learning journeys or other observations with the child.

The benefits of a longitudinal study for early years practitioners

Where the key person is not involved in the longitudinal study because a student or another practitioner is undertaking it, the conclusions from the longitudinal study can help them to find out more about the children for whom they have responsibility. In such cases, a longitudinal study can also provide more objective information as the observer will not necessarily be influenced by pre-existing ideas of the child's interests, stage of development or needs. In some cases, the conclusions from longitudinal studies may also suggest that the child needs additional support or further resources or activities in order to flourish. This again might be helpful for the practitioner.

When it is the practitioner who is undertaking the longitudinal study, the children should be observed through the use of a range of observation methods over a period of time. This can help the practitioner gain a more thorough understanding of the child as it will help them to build up an overall picture of the child's development. In addition, a longitudinal study can support professional development by helping the early years practitioners explore aspects of their practice that might be supporting or hindering the child's development and interests.

The benefits of a longitudinal study for others

There are often many adults involved in a child's care and education. Perhaps the most important of these are the parents. Parents often enjoy looking at longitudinal studies as they show how their child is progressing in particular areas of development. The evaluations from the longitudinal study can also be used for parents and practitioners to work in partnership to support the child's development at home. This is usually done by the key person in early years settings as the EYFS requires the key person to work closely with parents to ensure that children's needs and interests are met. It is also good practice for parents to be involved with the assessment of their children and so they should be contributing their thoughts and ideas too throughout the process. This is a focus of the current inspection cycle.

In your setting

Find out how parents in your setting contribute to the observations and assessments of their children.

In addition to parents, other professionals, such as speech and language therapists and occupational therapists, who work with a child with additional needs will also benefit from finding out how the child is making progress. In particular, they can see from the results of the longitudinal study to what extent their interventions and suggestions are having an impact.

Figure 3.15.2 This parent and key person are sharing information about the child's development

LO2 Be able to use observations to assess and plan for the developmental needs of children in line with current frameworks

Have you noticed that, in your setting, observations and assessments link to the Early Years Foundation Stage framework? You might see that planning for children also shows how the activities and play opportunities that are planned link to areas of learning and development in the EYFS. In this section, we look at how you might carry out longitudinal studies with different ages of children, how you might assess the observations and how best to devise and implement plans to meet children's needs.

AC 2.1 Using methods of observation to assess the changing developmental needs of children

For this unit, you need to show that you can carry out a longitudinal study with an individual child in a real work environment, from one of the following age ranges: 0–1 year 11 months; 2–2 years 11 months; 3–5 years. You must focus on one area of development. For the purposes of this unit, the longitudinal study must cover at least six weeks and you will need to use a range of methods. In order to carry out the longitudinal study, you will need to think carefully about a range of issues.

Permission

You will need to begin by talking to your placement supervisor to ask whether you are able to complete a longitudinal study in the setting. As we saw in Unit 3.14, it is always good practice to ask supervisors' or parents' permission.

Organising your longitudinal study

Longitudinal studies require plenty of preparation and thought. You first need to identify children who might be interesting to observe. It is always easier to carry out observations on children who are likely to attend frequently and also who are unlikely to move during the time period you will be assessing them. For this unit, you need to observe a child within a specific age range and so you should also think about how you will manage this while you are in your work placement.

Methods of assessment

You will also need to think about the methods of assessment that will work well for your longitudinal study. Ideally, you will need to generate as much information as possible and so think about using some methods that are fairly open ended.

→ We looked at different methods of observation and their advantages and disadvantages in Unit 3.14, so you may find it useful to revisit this unit.

Frequency of observations

The strength of a longitudinal study is always determined by the quality of the observations as this is your source material. A good tip, therefore, is to observe as frequently as possible. This is because some observations may not work as intended and so may need to be disregarded. A good example of this is when a child that you are observing becomes tired and, soon after the observation begins, falls asleep!

AC 2.2 Maintaining records of observation, assessment and planning

As part of the longitudinal study, you are expected to use the observations to make assessments and then, from these, to create plans. We will look at how to carry out the assessments and the plans later on in this section. As a longitudinal study does require a lot of organisation, it is worth thinking about how you will manage the records that you are keeping. It is usual for most early years settings to keep children's records in a secure place and it is also usual for the records not to be allowed out of

Figure 3.15.3 Tasks requiring concentration need to be observed when children are not tired

the premises. You will therefore need to discuss with your placement supervisor how you might manage these records to ensure children's confidentiality.

→ In Unit 3.14, we looked at measures that you might take to ensure confidentiality when producing observations and records for your qualification. These measures included anonymising the records so children's names are not used and removing any identifying features, such as the name of the setting.

Tips for practice

- Anonymise all references to the child's name/s.
- Remove references to the name of the setting, although you should include the type of setting (e.g. day care, pre-school).
- Keep records together in a folder.
- Do not leave the records lying around.
- Make the records available only to your tutor, assessor, placement supervisor and the child's parents.

AC 2.3 Evaluating observations

Each time you complete an observation, you should then evaluate it and create an assessment of the child's development, their needs and also how they are doing in relation to the current frameworks. This is good practice in early years settings and will help in the creation of meaningful plans for the child. In addition, for the purpose of this qualification, you should show that you can link what you have seen to relevant theoretical perspectives.

Expected developmental stages

You can use a range of sources to assess children in relation to expected developmental stages. It is always good practice to explain your sources because charts and milestones of expected development can vary. For example:

Figure 3.15.4 Children's skills, such as pointing, should be assessed with reference to specific developmental stages

> During the observation I saw that P pointed to a ball. P is nearly ten months old and pointing is part of his expected development. According to ICAN's stages and sequences of language development, pointing and gestures can be seen from 6–12 months. P is therefore showing expected development.

Current frameworks

You should also in your assessment make links to the EYFS. To do this you will need to have a copy of the statutory framework. It is worth reading the areas of learning and development carefully as well as the Early Learning Goals for each area. In addition, you should also read carefully the characteristics of effective teaching and learning as these also could be referenced.

> When P was pointing to the ball, he was concentrating and very focused. This links to the 'Active learning' characteristic of effective teaching and learning. Being able to concentrate in this way is helpful as it means he can learn more.

Theoretical perspectives

After each observation, you should also consider how what you have seen links to the theoretical perspectives that we have looked at in earlier chapters or other theoretical perspectives that you are aware of. It is important to link to these appropriately.

> When P was pointing to the ball, he wanted to attract the attention of an adult. The adult responded and so P may learn from this that pointing can gain the attention of an adult. This links to the behaviourist perspective of language learning, which suggests that children learn language and communication as a result of positive reinforcement.

Next steps

As part of your evaluation, you should then make some recommendations about how to support the child's development and interests further. These 'next steps' will be the basis of the activities that you create and carry out with the child. It is important that next steps are realistic. A child who is not yet walking but who is moving by holding onto furniture is highly unlikely to be ready to walk in the next week. Instead, the next steps might be to provide more opportunities for **cruising**. It is not uncommon therefore for 'next steps' to be activities that help a child practise an existing skill. For example, the next steps for a child who has a favourite book is to share the book again and see if the child can point to any of the characters or finish off the end of a sentence.

Test yourself

Look at the following observation of a two-year-old child's personal, social and emotional development. See if you can relate the observation to expected development, the EYFS and also a theoretical perspective. Do not forget to put in your source of reference for expected development.

J cries for a moment when his mother leaves. His key person puts out her arms and he comes to her for a cuddle. He is quickly soothed and starts to play with his key person's hair. He pulls her hair and she smiles. He smiles back. He wriggles in her arms and she releases him. He stands for a moment and then points to a book. His key person asks him if he would like her to read to him.

Key term

cruising Where babies who are not yet walking independently hold onto furniture and objects to help them walk.

AC 2.4 Planning to meet the interests and developmental needs of children

After each observation and assessment, you should produce an activity plan. The activity plan should be based on the 'next steps' that you have identified while evaluating the observation. For this unit, guidance has been given as to what your activity plan might include in order to complete the mandatory task. While many early years settings do not produce an activity plan, it can be a useful tool for a learner because it can help you to clarify your ideas and also show others that you have a good understanding and knowledge of how to plan an activity. Let's look now at what each of your activity plans might include.

Aim

You should write down here why you are doing this activity. As well as explaining the skill, knowledge or experience that you want to give the child, include the area of learning and development that it links to within the EYFS and also other areas of learning and development that it might support. If you are carrying out the activity with more than one child, remember that this will give children the opportunity to develop social skills.

> To strengthen P's hand preference by encouraging the use of a stabilising and active hand. This activity links to Physical Development within the EYFS and also to self-confidence and self-awareness within Personal, Social and Emotional Development.

Description of play activity/opportunity

In this section, you should write exactly how the activity is to be carried out so that anyone reading it can understand what the children will be doing. You could also include the resources in here.

> This is a simple activity. The children see if they can pick up small items with the tongs or tweezers and drop them into a beaker. For the small items, I intend to use small stones, chickpeas and also sequins. There will be enough beakers and tongs for each child to have their own.

In practice

Practise this section by writing out a description of a play activity that you have carried out recently with a child or group of children.

How you will provide an enabling environment

In this section, you should write about how you will encourage the child or children to access resources, make choices and be active in their learning. You should also show how you intend to keep children safe and this might include making a note about risk assessment of resources.

> There will be a range of different resources for children to use, including stones, chickpeas, sequins, tweezers and tongs. I have chosen resources that are not known choking hazards, but I will supervise the children during the activity to make sure that they do not put the items in their mouths.

Theoretical perspectives that have influenced your plan

In this section, you should make links to your activity and relevant theoretical perspectives. You could use a range of perspectives in addition to those that link to the area of development that you are focusing on. These could include theoretical perspectives on play.

→ For more on theoretical perspectives on play, see Unit 3.2.

> This activity links to Montessori's approach to play because it is quite structured, but children are independent and active.

In practice

It would be worth practising linking activities to theoretical perspectives. Think of an activity that you have carried out recently with a child or children. Write about how you might link it to a theoretical perspective. Ask your tutor, assessor or placement supervisor for feedback.

Your role/role of others

In this section, you should write about what you or other adults who work with you will be doing. As we saw in Units 3.1 and 3.2, there are many ways of working with children during play. You may, for example, model an action in order that children might copy what you are doing or, on the other hand, you may encourage children by working with them and so scaffold their learning. In some cases, your role may be to set up an activity and, when children are engaging with the activity, sensitively interact with them.

> During this activity, I will begin by modelling the action, but then will take a step back so as to allow children to be able to explore fully the activity. I will sit with the children and be on hand so as to encourage them and draw their attention to the difference between the different materials.

Differentiation

Where you are planning an activity for other children to play alongside the observed child, you should explain how you will ensure that the activity is appropriate for each child who is joining in. In some cases, there may be a child who has an additional need and will need the activity to be adapted slightly. Where you are working with children of different ages, you may also find that their stages of development are different and so again you must explain how you will work to ensure that the activity remains challenging yet enjoyable.

> To make sure that other children will be able to join this activity, I will put out sufficient resources. There will also be a range of materials of different sizes which will allow children with less developed hand–eye coordination or strength to be able to complete the activity. I will also provide a range of different sizes of tongs and tweezers and so this will provide a wide range of skill level.

AC 2.5 Implementing plans

In each of the units that looked at areas of development, we considered tips as to how best to implement activities for children that focused on the particular area of development. Before implementing your activities, it would be worth rereading them. An example of this is that, when supporting communication and language, it is important to give children sufficient time to respond. As with all activities, it is important to make sure that you have spoken to your placement supervisor and talked through the activity so that you can benefit from their expertise and help.

Reflecting on each activity

It is good practice, as we have already seen, to reflect on and evaluate activities. For this unit, you are required to do so as part of the mandatory task.

➡ It may be worth reading Unit 4.1, which is about reflective practice, to help you to reflect on your activities.

The following points can be used to help you reflect on your activity:

- Did the activity allow the child to be active?
- How engaged was the child during the activity?

- Was the activity enjoyable for the child?
- Did the activity achieve its purpose?
- If there was more than one child involved in the activity, how did you ensure that it supported each child's development?
- What did you learn about the child's development during the activity?
- Were there sufficient materials available?
- Were there any aspects of the activity that could be improved?
- What did you learn from carrying out this activity?

In practice

Try practising your reflection skills ahead of completing the longitudinal study. Write a reflective account of an activity that you have carried out. Ask your tutor, placement supervisor or assessor to read through your account and give you feedback.

Figure 3.15.5 Is this child enjoying this activity?

LO3 Be able to critically evaluate the outcomes of a longitudinal study

A longitudinal study needs to be evaluated in order that children's overall learning and progress can be considered. In addition, by critically evaluating the longitudinal study, other important aspects such as the effectiveness of the observations and the scope of the information can be considered. A longitudinal study can also be used to help consider the resources and environment and these can all be considered in a critical evaluation. In this section, we look at how you might critically evaluate your longitudinal study in relation to the task that has been set for this unit.

AC 3.1 Critically evaluate the outcomes of a longitudinal study

For this unit, there is a mandatory task that requires you to critically evaluate the outcomes of the longitudinal study that you have completed.

Figure 3.15.6 shows the many aspects that you need to cover when evaluating your longitudinal study.

Introduction

It is good practice to introduce an evaluation. It is worth writing about how you organised your longitudinal study and how you used it to assess children. You should write about what information has been gained as well as whether there are any areas where more information is needed. You should also write about how, by carrying out the

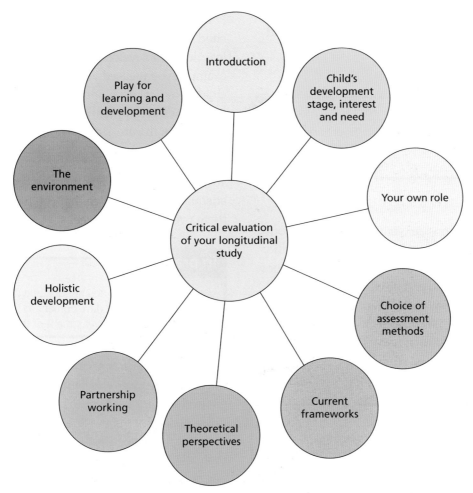

Figure 3.15.6 Aspects to be covered in the critical evaluation of your longitudinal study

longitudinal study, there have been benefits to the child, the early years practitioners and others involved in the care of the child, such as the parents.

→ Before writing this section, you might like to revisit LO1 of this unit, in which we looked at the benefits of longitudinal studies.

Child's development stage, interests and needs

An important focus when writing the critical evaluations is to consider what you have learnt about the child's stage of development. This could include their development in relation to that expected for their age group as well as how well they are making progress. You should consider what factors might have influenced their development and to what extent the longitudinal study is giving an accurate picture of their development. From this, you should then consider what the child's needs are and what type of support or interventions might be needed. You should also identify the child's play and social interests and consider how these might be supported further.

> **Test yourself**
>
> Make a list of sources of expected development that you could use to help you analyse children's expected development.

Own role

You also need to consider your own role. It is worth reflecting on how well you feel you carried out the observations. It is worth starting by considering how well you planned and organised your longitudinal study. Consider what parts of carrying out the study you found easy or difficult and give reasons why. What went well and what have you learnt about organising a longitudinal study?

> **Reflect**
>
> What impact has carrying out this longitudinal study had on your knowledge of child development and assessment methods, and your interest in working with children?

Choice of assessment methods

As part of the critical evaluation, you should also explain why you chose each of the observation and assessment methods. You should also consider how well you think that your choice of observation methods worked and how useful they were in providing information on which you could assess and plan for children's development. For each assessment method, you should think about their advantages and disadvantages. You might also think about whether you found some methods easier than others and give reasons for this. It is also worth reflecting on whether you would use the same assessment methods again and, if so, what you would do differently.

Current frameworks

In the critical evaluation that you write, you must also link what you have learnt about the child's age and stage of development to the Early Years Foundation Stage framework. Think about how this child's development links to the relevant area of learning and development within the EYFS. If, for example, you focused your longitudinal study on a child's physical development, you would consider how their development linked to what might be expected in the areas of learning known as 'Physical development'.

You should consider whether they are making adequate progress given that you have observed them over six or more weeks.

> **In practice**
>
> Use the Early Years Outcomes document to help you link children's stage of development to the relevant area of learning and development of the EYFS.

Theoretical perspectives

In each of the units that looked at individual areas of development such as language, cognition and physical development, we looked at different theoretical perspectives. As part of your critical evaluation, you should consider which theoretical perspectives link to the information that you have gained about the child. You might, for example, have noticed that a child's language is slightly delayed and that the child needs more adult interaction. You could then make the link between the need for interaction and the sociological perspective, which suggests that children develop language partly in response to a social need. It is important to link carefully the theoretical perspective to what you have observed and then also to evaluate to what extent the theoretical perspective matches the information that you have gained.

Test yourself

Write a list of theoretical perspectives that link to the area of development that you focused on in your longitudinal study.

Partnership working

We know that it is good practice to include parents and others involved with children's development in the observation, assessment and planning process. In your critical evaluation, you should write about how you involved others in the assessment and planning process or, if you were unable to involve them, the reasons for this. You should also consider how you might work more closely with others, such as parents, key persons and other professionals, were you to do this again and why such partnerships are important for children's development. You should also consider the barriers for close partnership working and, if you encountered any barriers, how you overcame these.

Holistic development

While the longitudinal study focused on one aspect of the child's development, you should consider what you discovered about other areas of the child's development. You should reflect on how the information that you gained about other areas of the child's development linked to their expected stage of development and also identify any needs that they may have. It would be helpful also to consider how these needs could be met in the future. As well as information about children's developmental age and stage of development, you should also reflect on children's interests and how these too might be supported in the future.

The environment

As part of the critical evaluation, you should also use the information you gained during the longitudinal study to consider how well overall the environment, including the resources, supported the child's development and how well the environment met the child's interests and needs. You could reflect on what other resources might be used in the future to support the child or how the routines or culture of the setting currently support the child.

→ As we looked at the environment in its broadest sense in Unit 3.4, it would be worth revisiting that unit to help you with this section of the critical evaluation.

Play for learning and development

Finally, your critical evaluation needs to consider the impact that play has on the child's development. You could consider how the child currently plays and how the play that is on offer supports their development. You might also consider what other play opportunities might in future benefit the child in terms of their development, needs and interests. You could also make recommendations as to how these could be organised and how exactly they would benefit the child.

Assessment

This unit is assessed through a mandatory task that also links to other units. It is important that you talk carefully with your assessor and placement supervisor before attempting this task.

A good starting point when completing the mandatory task is to practice the different observation methods that we considered in Unit 3.14. This is because strong observations will provide plenty of information that you can evaluate afterwards and also use to plan for the individual child's needs.

You should also carefully read this chapter again so that you are familiar with the range of reasons why longitudinal studies are considered useful.

When carrying out the longitudinal study, it is important to make sure that the child you intend to observe is likely to be in placement for a prolonged period, and that the parent has given permission for you to carry out the observations, assessments, planning and reporting. It is also important to discuss with your placement supervisor which child you should study and, as this is a mandatory task, you might consider following two children in case during your period of study one child stops attending the setting. This also has the advantage of allowing you to decide which of the studies is the strongest and most developmentally interesting.

When completing this task, it is worth looking at the additional grading criteria that are specifically written for the mandatory task as well as the assessment criteria for the unit itself. This is important because the criteria for the mandatory task include, for example, the need to link your assessments to the theoretical perspectives that we looked at in several other units.

Finally, as the mandatory task is a complex task, you will need to show time management and good organisational skills. It is therefore worth drawing up a plan with timings so that you can be sure that you can complete it.

Useful resources

Speak to your tutor for further guidance on useful resources.

Unit 4.1 Engage in professional development

Unit 4.1 Engage in professional development is now part of Theme 2.

Unit 4.1 Engage in professional development

How much have you learnt about children's play, learning and development? How much do you know about the early years framework that is currently being used in England? While, at this point in time, you may feel that you have gained a great deal of knowledge and experience, the reality is that there is plenty still to learn and this will always remain the case. Practices change and so too do curriculum frameworks. In this sector, it is not only the children who keep on learning! Engaging in professional development is therefore an essential part of our work with children. It keeps us up to date and also helps improve our practice. In this unit, we look at what is meant by professional development, the theories of reflective practice and also how to use professional practice to support your own development.

Learning outcomes

By the end of this unit, you will:

1 Understand professional development.
2 Understand theoretical perspectives in relation to reflection.
3 Be able to use reflective practice to contribute to own professional development.

LO1 Understand professional development

AC 1.1 What is professional development?

The term 'professional development' is used to describe the process by which adults keep reflecting on their practice and also keep up to date in their knowledge and skills. Professional development is important in early years for many reasons, as outlined below.

Quality provision

One of the reasons why professional development and reflective practice are considered important is that they can improve the quality of our work with children. By thinking carefully about what we do and its impact on children's enjoyment and development, we can keep improving our practice.

Research

Sometimes research will indicate that some ways of working with children are particularly important. This means that practices change to reflect the research. An example of this is the way that neuroscience has shown how young babies and toddlers need plenty of stimulation in order for their brains to develop.

Policy

The way that we work with children can also be changed because of government policy. This includes changes that are made to statutory frameworks. An example of such a change is that now it is a legal requirement for all children to have a key person, whereas before many settings did not do this.

In your setting

Talk to experienced practitioners in your setting about the changes that they have seen in the early years framework since they began work. How have the changes affected their day-to-day work?

Influences from the work of other early years educators

There is more than one way to work with young children. Practices can sometimes change because of the influence of other early years settings and other countries' models of early education. A good example of this is the way that many settings now use learning journeys, the concept of which we 'borrowed' from early education in New Zealand.

Research it!

The Forest School approach has become very popular. Find out about the origins of Forest Schools by visiting www.forestschoolassociations.org/history-of-forest-school.

Social changes

Sometimes we have to keep our knowledge up to date or change the way we work because circumstances change. Social changes such as more mothers returning to work in the 1990s meant that more babies came into day care settings. This in turn meant that adults had to think carefully about their practices in relation to working with babies.

Personal interest

As well as professional interest being needed in order that practice in early years settings can reflect changes in thinking and policy, there are personal reasons why everyone should engage in professional development. Firstly, it is good for us to learn new skills to help us stay motivated. This in turn means that we can be fresh and interested in children and so work well and sensitively with them. It is also important to engage in professional development in order to remain in employment and also to gain promotion.

AC 1.2 Identifying professional development opportunities

There are many ways in which we can develop our practice. These include going on training and taking further courses of study, but also visiting other settings to learn from their practice. There are thus many opportunities for professional development, but one of the challenges is to know what the focus of our professional development should be. There are several methods by which we can work out what the next steps for our professional development should be. All are widely used in early years settings.

Peer observation

Peer observation means that colleagues you work with watch you work and then give you feedback. For peer observation to work well, it is important that you trust the person who is observing and giving you feedback to be sensitive, but at the same time honest. It can be useful to agree with the person observing you over which areas they might focus on, such as your interactions with children or how you support child-initiated play. Some settings have developed peer observation sheets, which make it easier for the observer to carry out observations and also to provide feedback. The advantage of peer observation is that the person who observes you knows you well

and you will be able to talk through with them what they have seen.

Appraisal

It is good practice for early years settings who employ staff teams to carry out an appraisal every year or, in some cases, twice a year. An appraisal is a summing up of how you are working professionally and includes your strengths, weaknesses and areas for future development. Appraisals are usually carried out by the manager or deputy of the setting.

The appraisal process usually includes observations of you working, as well as opportunities for those working with you to make comments about your work. Another key feature of the appraisal process is your comments and thoughts about how your work, what you enjoy doing and also where you feel you could improve. As part of the appraisal process, you are likely to have a long discussion with your appraiser, who will talk through your work, and

Figure 4.1.1 Peer observation is a useful tool for developing your practice

together you will agree on areas on which you might like to focus. Following on from the discussion, it is also good practice for a development plan to be drawn up containing your goals, along with strategies and activities that will help you achieve these goals. It is also good practice for there to be regular meetings to monitor your progress towards the agreed goals.

Self-evaluation

As well as using other people to help you think about areas for further professional development, you can also review your own practice to evaluate your strengths and weaknesses. This should help you think about your next steps. This is called self-evaluation. Self-evaluation requires that you are able to think objectively about your practice and in some ways it is quite difficult to do accurately. Here are some questions that can be used to support self-evaluation.

● What areas of my work interest me and would I like to know more about?
● What areas of my work or situations do I find less interesting and so would benefit from additional input?
● What areas of my work do I find stressful and would I benefit from learning about other strategies and ways of working?
● What curriculum areas do I feel less confident in observing, assessing and planning for and so would benefit from more knowledge?
● What age groups do I find the most challenging to work with and so would benefit from learning more about their development and play needs?
● Where would I like to be working in the future and what additional knowledge, skills and experience would I need to gain?

LO2 Understand theoretical perspectives in relation to reflection

Have you ever handled a situation with a child badly? You may have felt afterwards that you did not listen or that you overreacted. Working with children is difficult and so it is important for everyone to be able to reflect on their practice afterwards in order to improve their responses or the overall way in which they work. There are different theoretical perspectives as to how you might do this. In this section, we look at the different theoretical perspectives on reflection and how these link to professional development.

AC 2.1 Theoretical perspectives on reflection in professional development

There are two theories that have been particularly influential in helping people to understand the reflective process.

Kolb's learning cycle

Kolb proposed a learning cycle which can be used to help us reflect on our learning and, therefore, is used for reflective practice. Kolb suggested that, for effective learning, four processes need to take place, as shown in Figure 4.1.2.

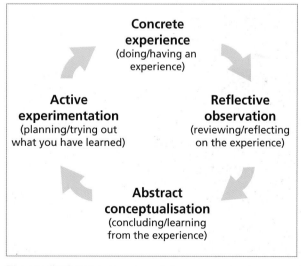

Figure 4.1.2 Kolb's learning cycle

- **Concrete experience**: this is about doing something. In an early years setting, this could mean teaching children to play a game of snap.
- **Reflective observation**: this is about reviewing and reflecting on the experience. This might mean that the practitioner thinks about which elements of the game of snap seemed to work well and which elements were less successful.
- **Abstract conceptualisation**: this is about developing new ideas. In our example of playing a game of snap, it might mean that we decide to use pictures on cards that link to children's experiences and to have extra cards that match to prevent children from becoming bored.
- **Active experimentation**: this is about putting into practice our new ideas. We may, for example, play the game of snap again with the new pictures and more opportunities for children to find a 'snap'.

The process that Kolb proposed is represented as a cycle because once we have tried out our new ideas, we may need to reflect once more.

Links to professional development

This learning cycle has been used as a basis for many models of reflective practice and so has been very influential. The idea is that, using this cycle, you can think about areas of your practice that need developing by reflecting on what you do and then putting into action changes, before reviewing them again.

(Interestingly, Kolb later suggested that most people were not able to master and learn from each step and so used his learning cycle 'steps' as a basis for his work on learning styles.)

> **In practice**
>
> Write about how you have used Kolb's reflective cycle to improve an element of your practice in your setting.

Gibbs' reflective cycle

Graham Gibbs adapted Kolb's work to create a more structured approach which could be used after situations have arisen to help adults reflect on their responses, but also to come to some conclusions about what they could do differently in the future. Figure 4.1.3 shows his reflective cycle.

How the cycle works

Following a situation or incident, which could be positive or negative, the adult thinks about what happened and their feelings, and also evaluates it. They go on to analyse why it occurred and also what conclusions could be reached. Finally, an action plan is drawn up. The case study below shows Gibbs' cycle being used in a nursery.

How Gibbs' cycle links to professional development

In the conclusion stage of the cycle, one of the conclusions that might be reached is that more training is needed or that more opportunities to learn from others would be useful. This would then be fed into the action plan and therefore link to professional development.

> **Case study**
>
> Lucie has hidden some dinosaurs in the sand tray. She is hoping to encourage the children to count them as she finds them. The children are excited, but instead of counting them, they just play with them. She is disappointed, but takes time to think about why this is. She decides that, while the sand/dinosaur combination works well, she needs to improve the focus on the numbers. She then has an idea. She decides that if the dinosaurs were grouped in small bags with numbers on them, children might notice them more. The next day she puts her idea into action. She is pleased to see that the children enjoy opening the bags and some children also point to the number on the bag before counting out how many dinosaurs are inside.
>
> 1 How has Lucie's reflection helped children's learning and development?
> 2 Explain how Lucie's thinking links to Kolb's learning cycle.
> 3 Why is it important for adults working with children to reflect on their practice?

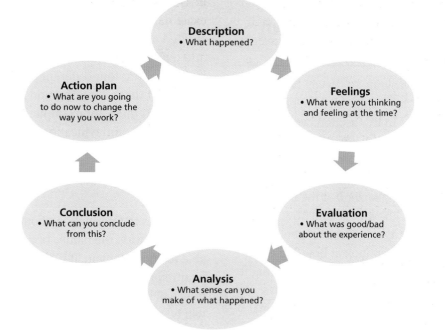

Figure 4.1.3 Gibbs' cycle of reflection

Case study

Jaimee works with two year olds. This afternoon one of the two year olds keeps taking pieces from the jigsaw puzzle and dropping them in the water tray. Jaimee tells the two year old to stop doing this. The two year old carries on. Jaimee becomes very cross and takes the two year old over to another part of the room. The two year old cries. Other children in the room also cry because Jaimee has raised her voice. Jaimee's supervisor afterwards talks through the incident. She uses Gibbs' cycle to help Jaimee reflect on what has happened.

Description

She starts by asking Jaimee to talk about what happened and asks her not to justify her actions, but simply to describe the incident.

Feelings

She then asks Jaimee to talk about how she was feeling at the time. Jaimee says that she felt angry and frustrated but also tired.

Evaluation

Her supervisor then asks Jaimee to evaluate the incident in terms of the quality of the practice. Jaimee is clear that she had upset the children and that this incident was poor practice. She should have handled the situation differently

Analysis

The supervisor then asks Jaimee to think about what the underlying issues were. Jaimee was not sure, but thinks that her being tired was one of them as she was less patient. Her supervisor also asks her about her knowledge of child development and also managing behaviour. Jaimee realises that her lack of knowledge could have been a factor.

Conclusions

The supervisor asks Jaimee to think about the conclusions that could be drawn and how these might be used to help Jaimee improve her practice. Jaimee says that she would like more information about two year olds and particularly promoting positive behaviour. Jaimee also concludes that, if she is working on a long shift, she needs to rethink her lifestyle outside work so that she is less tired.

Action plan

The supervisor and Jaimee agree on an action plan so as to prevent this situation from occurring again. It includes Jaimee going on some training and also the supervisor modelling how to defuse situations with two year olds.

1 Why was it important for this incident to be reflected upon?
2 How do you think this process made Jaimee feel?
3 How has this process supported Jaimee's overall professional development?

LO3 Be able to use reflective practice to contribute to own professional development

What strengths and weaknesses do you have as a practitioner? What do you think you need to do next in your career? In this section, we look at how to use reflective practice. We start with how to develop a curriculum vitae, before considering your own professional development needs and how you might support these. We also look at the importance of maintaining subject knowledge and how, with others, you might agree your own personal development plan. We then look at how, once you have had further learning opportunities, you might put these into practice. Finally, we look at ways in which you might record your own professional development as it progresses.

AC 3.1 Develop a curriculum vitae

A curriculum vitae is usually referred to more simply as a CV. It is an important document that is often used when applying for jobs or contracts. A CV shows a potential employer or business what skills, knowledge and experience you have.

Creating a CV

Your starting point when creating a CV to is bring together different pieces of information. This might require hunting for certificates, finding out exact names of places where you have worked or studied and working out specific dates for jobs and qualifications. Information that you present is divided into four different categories. It is important that all information given is accurate and so you must, for example, know the full title of any childcare and education qualification that you have taken and the dates of any employment you have had.

Referees

In addition to information about yourself, you also have to provide the names of two people who are able to vouch for you. It is important to choose your referees carefully. You need to be sure that they will be positive about you and also that they will be professionally credible. It is good practice to ask someone whether they will be a referee for you before putting their names down. Most learners will ask their tutor or assessor and also their placement supervisor to be referees.

Choosing a format

There are many different formats that can be used to create a CV. It is worth looking at different ones before deciding on how you wish to present your information. In theory, CVs should be concise as they are summaries. The most common type of CV puts information in chronological order.

Table 4.1.1 Information to include on a CV

Type of information	Details
Personal information	• Full name • Date of birth • Contact details, including full address, phone number and email address
Education and qualifications	• Where you studied • Dates and correct titles of qualifications, with grades • If you are currently studying, you should put 'ongoing' • Training that you have attended, with dates and correct titles
Employment history and experience	• Dates and titles of any jobs that you have had, including your key responsibilities, e.g. handling cash, talking to customers
Skills and personal attributes	• Skills that you have gained and examples of how you can demonstrate these • Personal attributes and examples in practice
Referees x 2	• Name, professional role and contact details for each referee, including a contact number

Keeping a CV up to date

Once you have created a CV, you should keep it up to date. This saves time if you wish to apply for a new post, but it has other benefits too. By keeping you CV up to date, you will automatically find yourself thinking about your skills, knowledge and experiences.

AC 3.2 Your professional development needs as an early years practitioner

Many early years practitioners develop their own personal development plan. This is often done with the active support of their early years settings and it is closely linked to the appraisal process that we looked at earlier. The starting point for developing a personal development plan is to start by understanding your own professional needs. As we saw in LO1, there are several ways in which you might gain feedback to help you further understand your needs. If you are studying, you will also be able to talk to your tutor or assessor about your strengths and weaknesses. In addition to feedback from others, you should also do some self-evaluation. Table 4.1.2 shows some of the key aspects of working with children, which may help you to analyse your own development needs.

In practice

Think about one of the sections in Table 4.1.2. What are your strengths? Where might you be able to improve your practice?

Table 4.1.2 Analyse your own professional development

Relationships with children	Consider how well you form relationships with children: ● Do children enjoy your company? ● Are you able to form relationships with children of different ages? ● Do you understand children's behaviour and how it links to their age and stage of development? ● Do you have knowledge about reasons why children may not show typical behaviour and the range of approaches that might be used to support them further?
Relationships with parents	Consider how well you form relationships with parents: ● Do you feel confident talking to all parents? ● Are you able to maintain a friendly yet professional manner?
Relationships with colleagues	Consider how well you work with colleagues: ● Do they enjoy working with you? ● Are you considered to be part of the team? ● Are you able to ask questions or to put forward your point of view appropriately?
Supporting children's play	Consider how well you are able to support the many different ways in which children play: ● Are you confident about supporting play with different age groups of children? ● Do you have the knowledge to know what play opportunities are suitable for different age groups? ● Are you able to plan for different children and maintain a play environment?
Supporting children's communication and language	Consider how well you interact with children: ● Do you listen carefully to children and follow up on their thoughts and ideas? ● Are you able to interact sensitively with children in ways that allow them to express themselves? ● Do you understand how children develop language and the factors that might influence the development of language? ● Do you have knowledge about how to support children who may have language delay, e.g. use of Makaton?

→

Table 4.1.2 Analyse your own professional development   (contd.)

Supporting children's physical development and health	Consider how well you support children's physical development and health: ● Do you have the knowledge you need to support children's physical development at different ages? ● Do you know how to plan play environments to support children's physical development? ● Are you able to provide opportunities for physical development and support children of different ages? ● Do you know about factors that influence children's physical development and how these may be supported? ● How sensitively can you support children's physical care routines? ● Do you have detailed nutritional knowledge and the skills to prepare food for different ages of children?
Supporting the early years curriculum	Consider how well you can plan and deliver the early years framework: ● Are you confident that you can assess children precisely in each of the areas of the early years framework? ● Are you able to plan effectively for each of the areas of learning and development in the early years framework? ● Do you understand the inspection framework for the early years sector? ● Are you able to evaluate your practice against the framework that will be used?
Progression	Consider how you intend to progress your career further and use this to work out what additional knowledge, skills and experience you will need: ● Would you like to eventually take on a leadership role, e.g. room leader, manager? ● Would you like to start your own business, e.g. childminder, set up a nursery? ● Would you like to work in a specialised role, e.g. SENCO, play therapist or working with parents as an outreach worker? ● Would you like to work in a specialised centre with children with additional needs, e.g. speech and language unit, special school? ● Would you like to become an inspector of early years provision?

AC 3.3 Learning needs, professional interests and development opportunities

The next step in developing a professional development plan is to use the information that you have gained from your analysis to consider your learning needs, but also what interests you have, based on your strengths. You also need to start researching what development opportunities are available in your local area.

Types of development opportunities

There is a wide range of different learning opportunities for you to consider.

Courses leading to a qualification

It may be that you should consider taking a course of further study that will lead to a recognised qualification. There is a range of ways in which you can take further qualifications, including distance learning courses, enrolling at a local college or university or taking up a work-based course. As courses leading to a qualification can be expensive, it is important to consider whether you have enough time to study and also whether you are sufficiently motivated to complete the course you choose. There are many advantages of courses leading to further qualification. You are likely to become a better practitioner, meet new people working in early years and also be able to apply later on for roles that are more demanding.

Training courses

In most local areas, there are short training courses. Many training courses last a few hours, but some can be longer. Short training courses are normally organised by local authorities but also by local networks. Training courses are helpful to learn more about a specific aspect of working with children, such as promoting behaviour or creating opportunities for mathematics. Short training courses are also good ways of meeting other people from different early years settings. At the end of a training course, a certificate of attendance is usually given but, with the exception of first aid and food hygiene courses, they do not normally lead to a qualification.

Research it!

Find out what short training courses are available in your local area. Who organises them and how much do they cost?

Conferences and professional exhibitions

There is a range of one-day conferences and exhibitions that are held every year that attract national speakers. Attending a conference might involve some travelling, but it can be interesting to hear the views of early years experts and also leaders in the field of education. While most conferences and seminars at exhibitions charge for attendance, some local authorities also arrange conferences at minimal or no cost.

Shadowing

Shadowing means watching other practitioners work and learning from them. It can be a cheap and effective way of gaining new skills and ideas and also reflecting on your own practice. Shadowing can take place within your setting or you could arrange to do this at another setting.

Visits to other settings

It is always useful to see a wide range of different early years settings. It can help us to pick up new ideas and also other ways of working. Most practitioners find it a very useful way to help them reflect on their development and also to think about their **pedagogy**.

Key term

pedagogy Beliefs that underpin how an early years educator works with children.

Reading

There is a range of professional journals and newspapers for the early years and also the wider education sector. A good way of learning more about any aspect of early years is therefore to pick out articles and read them. Ideally, it is useful to discuss them afterwards with others as, through the process of discussion, we can often become more reflective in our practice.

Joining organisations

There are some professional organisations that can support professional development. Most charge a membership fee, but in return, members often have access to training, resources and usually a website.

Research it!

Find out about the following organisations by visiting their websites:

Professional Association for Childcare and Early Years: **www.pacey.org.uk**

The Pre-School Learning Alliance: **www.pre-school.org.uk**

National Day Nurseries Association: **www.ndna.org.uk**

AC 3.4 Maintain knowledge on curriculum subjects that are of personal interest

We saw in LO1 that there are many reasons why all adults working with children should continue their professional development. In many early years settings, individual members of staff tend to take on responsibility for specific curriculum subjects. How this happens depends on the early years setting, but mostly people take on the role because they are particularly interested in the subject area. It then becomes their role within the early years setting to share information with their colleagues. The most common ways of maintaining subject knowledge are through reading, networking with other colleagues and also attending training courses. In addition, there are websites and organisations that have been set up to support specific curriculum subjects or aspects of early years practice. A good example of this is the National Association of Language Development in the curriculum (www.naldic.org.uk), which provides advice and resources about English as an additional language.

In practice

Which area of learning and development or aspect of early years are you interested in? Can you find a website or organisation that provides more information about this area? Visit the website and write about what information you have found out that might support your practice.

AC 3.5 Working with others on a personal development plan

When drawing up a personal development plan, it is worth getting help from others. This might happen anyway because your setting may develop plans as part of their appraisal process. If you have not drawn up a plan before, you could also work with your tutor or assessor, who will be able to help you.

Gaining the advice and input of others is useful as they can help you decide on your priorities and help you to set timescales. In some early years settings, there is a fund that is set aside to send staff on training and so, by working with others, you may also be funded for some aspects of your plan.

People who may help you develop your personal development plan

Colleagues

Colleagues may give you suggestions and advice based on knowing you well and also watching you work. They may also have recently undertaken training or other development and so will be able to recommend what they found useful.

Line managers

As we have seen already, you may have an appraisal with your manager and this is likely to lead to

suggestions and advice about what you need to do to improve your knowledge, skills and experience further.

In-service trainers

In some settings, the staff team will have the opportunity to be trained together in what is known as inset or **in-service training**. Most in-service or inset training helps staff to focus on particular aspects of their work. In-service trainers may be able to suggest further courses, training or resources that would support the aims of your personal development plan.

Key term

in-service training Training that is organised by management for staff teams.

External trainers

External trainers are usually self-employed and their services are bought in by local authorities or early years settings. They usually have a national overview and are likely to be specialists in certain areas of child development or early years. As with in-service trainers, they may be able to suggest further courses or resources.

Agreeing a personal development plan

There is no set formula for personal development plans, although the following information is usually included on the plan:

- the areas of your work for development
- the reasons for development
- the type of learning opportunities that will be arranged
- the timescale for arranging and completing the learning opportunities
- how the plan will be monitored and the date of review.

In your setting

Does your setting use personal development plans to support staff's further knowledge and skills?

Tips on making the most of learning opportunities

- **Open-mindedness**: it is important to be open-minded when you are learning. This is one of the most essential things as, if you are not open-minded at the start to new ideas, you may not be able to benefit.
- **Participating**: it is also important to be active in your learning. This might mean joining in discussions or asking questions. Participating in your learning is also likely to make the learning both enjoyable and memorable.
- **Networking**: where your learning opportunity gives you a chance to meet other practitioners from early years settings or other professionals, you can add to your learning by talking to them and finding out about their work. This can help you see things from others' points of view and it may also lead to an exchange of ideas.

- **Note-taking**: most people learn best when they take some notes. There are many different ways to take notes. Some people draw diagrams, others write questions and some people simply record key points. Note-taking is particularly important if you are due to report back to your setting or if you are going to be writing an assignment or essay.
- **Reflecting**: as you learn new information, it is important to reflect on how this might affect your practice. You might write notes to yourself to record this reflection as part of your note-taking.
- **Further reading**: it is helpful if you read around the subject after you have finished the learning opportunity. Some tutors may provide you with additional information, such as books or websites that you can use to enrich your learning.

AC 3.6 Using learning opportunities for professional development

We have seen that there are many different learning opportunities. How much you gain from the different learning opportunities depends on several things.

In addition to the key tips it is also important to get the basics right, such as arriving on time and not being too tired so that you can properly concentrate.

In practice

Write about a learning opportunity that you have participated in. Explain how you used it to support your professional development.

AC 3.7 Reflective practice and improved ways of working

In LO2, we looked at two different theoretical perspectives for reflecting on practice. One of the key benefits of reflective practice is the way that it can improve practice using these types of models. Reflective practice means thinking about each aspect of our work with children and considering how children respond, how we respond and, where

necessary, exploring other ways of working. By going on a training course or other learning opportunities, we may be given suggestions that will help us think about our practice.

Using learning opportunities to reflect on practice

It is important after a learning opportunity to spend time using the information gained to think about what we are currently doing and how it links to the learning that we have gained. It may be, for example, following a literacy training course, that we reflect on the number and quality of the books available in the story area. We may observe how children use them before starting to introduce new books and looking at their impact.

Allowing time

When changing our practice, it is worth remembering that it can take time for both us and children to adapt to new ways of working. At first, changes may not look as if they have been successful and so it can be tempting to think that they are not working. By allowing sufficient time for everyone to get used to them and then reflecting on practice, we can decide if further changes are needed or if they are indeed improving children's learning and supporting their needs.

Case study

Jodie works at the Browning Ponds pre-school. She has noticed during story time that some children are not always engaged. She has asked her manager if she can attend a course on promoting literacy. During the course, she learns that large story times are not as effective as small groups and, where possible, it is good practice to share stories with children individually or in pairs.

Following the course, she observes more closely what happens at story time and also which books different children seem to enjoy. She talks in a team meeting about changing the approach to story time. The team agree and the next day, at story time, the children are divided into smaller groups, with each staff member taking a group. The children look confused and some children try to run from group to group. The staff team have another meeting and decide to stay with the system for a further week before making any more

changes. Over the week, the children start to settle and staff report back that children are much more talkative and engaged in the stories. They also say that they are enjoying the system more.

Jodie continues to observe the practice but decides on reflection that they could also add in some story boxes that could be placed in different areas of the room, and also outside. She hopes that this might encourage children to look at books independently.

1 How did Jodie use the learning opportunity to improve practice in her setting?
2 Why was it important for the team to allow time before judging the success of the changes to practice?
3 How has Jodie continued to use reflection to improve practice?

In practice

Write about the way that you have used a learning opportunity to reflect on your practice and make changes.

AC 3.8 Recording personal development progress

It is important to record your progress. Whatever the learning opportunity, you should always keep a record of the date, the type of learning opportunity and a title if necessary. If you use a website, it may also be worth recording the name of the website or printing out or storing the information that you have found in case, when you revisit, it is no longer available. If you have created a personal development plan, you could add in notes about how the learning opportunity has changed your practice. In addition, you may be asked to write a reflective account by your tutor or manager about how your practice has developed as a result of learning more.

Assessment

In order to complete this unit you need to show that you understand and can use reflective practice to contribute to your own professional development. A good tip is to allow plenty of time to complete the unit, as while it is straightforward, you need to create a plan and show that you are carrying some parts of it out.

The starting point for this unit is to understand what is meant by the term 'professional development' and the different methods that you can use to identify different professional opportunities. This was covered in this chapter. For Learning Outcome 2, you need to consider different theoretical perspectives. You may also find it interesting to see if you can talk to your placement supervisor and apply them to your practice ready for Learning Outcome 3.

For Learning Outcome 3, you need to show that you can put the skills of reflective practice into practise. You may find the support of your assessor and placement supervisor as well as experienced colleagues useful, so it will be worth sharing with them the assessment criteria for the learning outcome. This is important because you have to identify areas on which you can work and also work with others to agree a personal development plan, which you will need to maintain and review. You also have to show that you have taken up learning opportunities that were identified in the plan.

Finally, as part of this learning outcome, you also have to develop a curriculum vitae, or CV. It is worth exploring different styles of these by carrying out an internet search or seeing if your computer provides different templates.

Useful resources

Organisation

TACTYC Association for the Professional Development of Early Years Educators

An early years organisation for anyone involved with the education and training of those who work with young children: **www.tactyc.org.uk**

Books

Gibbs, G. (1988), *Learning by Doing: A Guide to Teaching and Learning Methods*. Oxford: Further Educational Unit, Oxford Polytechnic.

Kolb, D.A. (1984), *A source of Learning and Development*. New Jersey: Prentice Hall.

Schön, D. (1983), *The Reflective Practitioner*. New York: Basic Books.

Glossary

anaemia A disease caused by a lack of iron.

auditory discrimination The ability able to pick out particular sounds in words or music

auditory discrimination The ability able to pick out particular sounds in words or music

behaviourist Behaviours, skills or characteristics that are learnt as a result of reinforcement.

binocular vision Single vision, although each eye is seeing a slightly different view.

cognition The processing and interpreting of information which supports the learning of concepts and the development of ideas and thoughts

cognitive skills Skills associated with cognition, such as the ability to understand number

constipation Difficulty in passing a bowel movement.

constructivist Behaviours, skills or knowledge that are learnt as a result of cognitive processing.

cruising Where babies who are not yet walking independently hold onto furniture and objects to help them walk

diarrhoea Bowel movements that are liquid rather than solid

disclosure A safeguarding allegation means the giving out of information that might commonly be kept secret, usually voluntarily or to be in compliance with legal regulations or workplace rules. (Allegation used to be known as disclosure.) For example, a child tells an adult something that causes him or her to be concerned about the child's safety and well-being

diversity The differences in values, attitudes, cultures, beliefs, skills and life experiences of each individual in any group.

early intervention This approach seeks to offer extra help and support to a family before the child starts to lag behind in development or experience neglect or abuse. Early intervention is about working co-operatively with parents and carers, giving them a chance to make choices about which services they need

emollient cream A product that moisturises skin and is used in the treatment of eczema

emotional well-being An umbrella term that covers many aspects of emotional development, including relationships, self-esteem, happiness and resilience

environmental perspective Theories of development that suggest that what happens to children outweighs nature's impact

Epi-Pen A device used to inject adrenaline when a child is having a severe allergic reaction

equality Allowing the same access for every child and family to full participation for all services.

fine and gross motor skills These relate to the way in which we move. Gross motor skills are large movements, such as running, skipping and hopping, or throwing and catching, and fine motor skills are small movements, such as using scissors, a pencil or a knife and fork

guidelines This refers to the local authority's published supporting document for practitioners when looking at issues of safeguarding, welfare and child protection. This will be up to date with current legislation and in line with the guidance and procedures of the Local Safeguarding Children's Board (LSCB). It should also contain information about how to share sensitive information with others as well as how the early years practitioner can keep themselves safe

holistic learning and development Children's overall development and learning rather than a single aspect

immune system Processes in the body designed to fight infection

inclusive practice The process of ensuring the equality of learning opportunities for all children and young people

informed consent When anyone, child or adult, is given sufficient information to be able to make a genuine decision to say 'yes' or 'no' to a request

inhaler A device used to deliver medication to the lungs.

innateness Behaviours, skills or characteristics that are instinctive.

in-service training Training that is organised by management for staff teams

inter-agency protection plan If a child's health or development has been significantly impaired as a result of physical, emotional or sexual abuse or neglect, an inter-agency protection plan may be drawn up. The plan will identify the steps that the family needs to take to safeguard the child, with the support of Children's Services and other agencies. The child's safety, health, development and well-being will be regularly monitored throughout the plan.

key person system A system within an early years setting in which care of each child is assigned to a particular adult, known as the key person. The role of the key person is to develop a special relationship with the child, in order to help the child to feel safe and secure in the setting. The key person will also liaise closely with each child's parents.

legislation Requirements and rules that have become law.

life limiting When a medical condition reduces the life expectancy of a child

malnourished A diet lacking in some of the minerals, vitamins and other nutrients required by the body

mouthing Exploring an object by putting it in the mouth to touch and taste

nutrients Foods that contain chemicals that the body requires

observer bias When the observer is not objective

others Relates to parents, carers and other professionals

paediatric ward The ward on a hospital that specialises in nursing children

pedagogy[definition to come]

pincer grasp Using the thumb and index finger to make a squeezing movement.

pointing Using index finger to touch or to show something.

policies Principles that the early years setting intends to follow.

policy A safeguarding policy is a statement that makes it clear to staff, parents and children what the organisation or group thinks about safeguarding, and what it will do to keep children safe

prime areas of learning and development Areas of development which are seen by the EYFS as being a priority as they support children's later development

procedures Ways in which policies will be put into practice.

regulations Specific legal requirements.

roles and responsibilities Working within organisational policies and procedures

safeguarding This term includes: all the steps you would take in an early years setting or school to help children to feel safe and secure; protecting children from neglect or abuse; ensuring that children stay safe, healthy and continue to develop well

scaffolding Setting opportunities that are relevant, meaningful and purposeful for the children with varying adult intervention

self-talk Where young children use language to talk aloud.

SENCO Special educational needs co-ordinator

sensory development The process by which the body learns to process information gained from touch, taste, sight, sound and smell

separation anxiety A term used to describe the stages of distress that occur if a baby or child is separated from their primary attachment

sociological Behaviours, skills or characteristics that are learnt as a result of being with others

spiral curriculum The concept that a subject may be repeatedly taught but in increasing depth

strategies Recognised approaches which can be applied to mathematical learning

sustained shared thinking An interaction between adult and child that allows for the development of ideas

vocalisations A range of sounds, including babbling, that are made before children are ready to make words.

Useful resources

Organisations

5x5x5creativity

This is an independent, arts-based action research organisation and has been influenced by theory in Reggio Emilia in Italy: **www.5x5x5creativity.org.uk**

Action for Sick Children

The UK's leading health charity, specially formed to ensure that sick children always receive the highest standard of care possible. Provides useful information for parents and professionals on all aspects of healthcare for children: **www.actionforsickchildren.org.**

The Alliance for Inclusive Education

This is a national campaigning organisation led by disabled people: **www.allfie.org.uk.**

Anna Freud Centre

The centre was established in 1947 by Anna Freud to support the emotional well-being of children through direct work with children and their families, research and the development of practice, and training mental health practitioners: **www.annafreud.org**.

British Dyslexia Association (BDA)

The BDA is a national charity working for a 'dyslexiafriendly society' that enables dyslexic people of all ages to reach their full potential: **www.bdadyslexia.org.uk**

British Heart Foundation National Centre (BHFNC)

The BHF publishes the UK Physical Activity Guidelines for Early Years: **www.bhfactive.org.uk**

Contact a Family

This website is for families who have a disabled child and those who work with disabled children or who are interested to find out more about their needs: **www.cafamily.org.uk**

Early Support

This organisation provides materials for families and professionals, including a service audit tool, a family pack and information for parents on certain disabilities and impairments: **www.earlysupport.org.uk**.

Health and Safety Executive (HSE)

HSE is the national independent watchdog for work-related health, safety and illness: **www.hse.gov.uk**.

Health Play Staff

Aims to promote the physical and emotional wellbeing of children and young people who are patients in hospital, hospice or receiving medical care at home: **www.nahps.org.uk**.

High/Scope

High/Scope is an American approach to early education and care, with several decades of research into its effectiveness. The website includes books, DVDs and news of training events and conferences in the UK: **www.high-scope.org.uk.**

JABADAO

A national charity which works in partnership with the education, health, arts and social care sectors to bring about a change in the way people work with the body and movement: **www.jabadao.org**

Kate Greenaway Nursery School and Children's Centre

This website includes news and policies for a centre based in central London: **www.kategreenaway.ik.org**.

KIDS

KIDS works for disabled children, young people and their families: **www.kids.org.uk**.

Kidscape

This charity was established specifically to prevent bullying and child sexual abuse. The website includes resources for parents, children and professionals, and details of campaigns and training events: **www.kidscape.org.uk**.

National Autistic Society (NAS)

The NAS aims to champion the rights and interests of all people with autism, and to provide individuals with autism and their families with help, support and services: **www.nas.org.uk**

National Parent Partnership Network and Parent Partnership Services (PPS)

These are statutory services offering information advice and support to parents and carers of children and young people with special educational needs (SEN): **www.parentpartnership.org.uk**.

The National Strategies (Early Years)

The government's programme for developing practice in the early years, including statutory requirements, advice on best practice, and research findings: **www.education.gov.uk** and search for early years.

Ofsted

Ofsted is the Office for Standards in Education, Children's Services and Skills. Ofsted inspects and regulates services which care for children and young people, and those providing education and skills for learners of all ages: **www.ofsted.gov.uk**.

Play England

Promotes free play opportunities for all children and young people, and works to ensure that the importance of play for children's development is recognised: **www.playengland.org.uk**

RIDDOR

RIDDOR puts duties on employers, the self-employed and people in control of work premises (the Responsible Person) to report certain serious workplace accidents, occupational diseases and specified dangerous occurrences (near misses): **www.hse.gov.uk/riddor**.

Royal National Institute for Deaf People (RNID)

The RNID is the largest charity in the UK offering a range of services for people who are deaf or have a hearing impairment, and providing information and support on all aspects of deafness, hearing loss and tinnitus: **www.rnid.org.uk**

The Royal Society for Public Health

www.rsph.org.uk

Royal National Institute of Blind People (RNIB)

The Royal National Institute of Blind People (RNIB) has produced an excellent booklet, Focus on Foundation, which offers practical advice on the inclusion in early years settings of children who are blind and partially sighted: **www.rnib.org.uk**

Scope

Scope is a charity that supports disabled people and their families. Its vision is a world where disabled people have the same opportunities as everyone else. Scope specialises in working with people who have cerebral palsy: **www.scope.org.uk**

Siren Films

High-quality DVDs showing the importance of attachments and key people in the EYFS: **www.sirenfilms.co.uk**

Start4Life and Play4Life

The early years section of the Department of Health's (DH) Change4Life campaign, aimed at health care and childcare professionals. Active play resources are available which can be downloaded from **www.dh.gov.uk** (search Start4Life).

TACTYC Association for the Professional Development of Early Years Educators

An early years organisation for anyone involved with the education and training of those who work with young children: **www.tactyc.org.uk**

Books, articles and journals

Alcott, M. (2002), *An Introduction to Children with Special Needs*. London: Hodder & Stoughton.

Axline, V. (1971), Dibs, *In Search of Self: Personality Development in Play Therapy*. London: Penguin.

Berk, L. (2012), *Child Development*. Oxford: Pearson.

Bertram, T. and Pascal, C. (1997), *Effective Early Learning: Case Studies in Improvement*. London: Hodder & Stoughton.

Blythe, S.G. (2006), *The Well-Balanced Child: Movement and Early Learning*. Stroud: Hawthorn Press.

Bowlby, J. (1969), *Attachment and Loss. Vol. I: Attachment*. London: Hogarth Press.

Brooker, E. (2002), *Starting School: Young Children Learning Cultures*. Maidenhead: Open University Press.

Bruce, T. (1996), *Helping Young Children to Play*. London: Hodder & Stoughton.

Bruce, T. (2004), *Developing Learning in Early Childhood*. London: Paul Chapman Publishing.

Bruce, T. (2005), *Early Childhood Education and Care* (3rd edn). London: Hodder Arnold.

Bruce, T. (2009), 'Learning through Play: Froebelian Principles and their Practice Today', *Early Childhood Practice: The Journal for Multi-professional Partnerships* 10(2): 58–73.

Bruce, T. (ed.) (2010), *Early Childhood: A Guide for Students* (2nd edn). London: Sage.

Bruer, J.T. (1999), *The Myth of the First Three Years: A new understanding of early brain development and lifelong learning*. New York: Free Press.

Contact a Family (2004), *Caring for Disabled Children: A Guide for Students and Professionals*. Available from: **www.cafamily.org.uk/students.pdf**

Conteh, J. (ed.) (2006), *Promoting Learning for Bilingual Pupils 3–11: Opening Doors to Success*. London: Sage.

Cooper, L. and Doherty, J., (2010) *Physical Development (Supporting Development in the Early Years Foundation Stage)*,Continuum

Crawley, H. (2006) 'Eating well for under 5s in child care.' The Caroline Walker Trust: **www.cwt.org.uk/pdfs/Under5s.pdf**

Dearnley, K., Elfer, P., Grenier, J., Manning-Morton, J. and Wilson, D. (2008) 'Appendix 1: The key person in reception classes and small nursery settings', in *and Emotional Aspects of Development: Guidance for Practitioners Working in the Early Years Foundation Stage*. Nottingham: DCSF Publications, available at http://nationalstrategies.standards.dcsf.gov.uk/node/132720.

DfES (2001), *The Special Educational Needs Code of Practice 2001*. Available free at: **www.teachernet.gov.uk**

Dickins, M. and Denziloe, J. (2004), *All Together: How to Create Inclusive Services for Children and Their Families*. National Children's Bureau.

Douch, P. (2006), *It Doesn't Just Happen – Inclusive Management for Inclusive Play*. London: Kids.

Dowling, M. (2010), *Young Children's Personal, Social and Emotional Development* (3rd edn). London: Sage Publications.

Elfer, P. and Dearnley, K. (2007), 'Nurseries and emotional well-being: Evaluating an emotionally containing model of continuing professional development', *Early Years: An International Journal of Research and Development* 27(3): 267–79.

Elfer, P., Goldschmied, E. and Selleck, D. (2003), *Key Persons in the Nursery: Building Relationships for Quality Provision*. London: David Fulton.

Freud, A., in collaboration with Dorothy Burlingham (1973) *The Writings of Anna Freud. Vol. III: Infants Without Families [and] Reports on the Hampstead*

Nurseries, 1939–1945. New York: International Universities Press.

Gibbs, G. (1988), *Learning by Doing: A Guide to Teaching and Learning Methods*. Oxford: Further Educational Unit, Oxford Polytechnic.

Greenland, P. (2000), *Hopping Home Backwards*. Leeds: Jabadao, **www.jabadao.org**.

Harding, J. and Meldon-Smith, L. (1996), *How to make Observations and Assessments*, London: Hodder Arnold.

Horwath, J. (2001), *The Child's World: Assessing Children in Need*. London: Jessica Kingsley Publishers.

Hughes, B. (1996a), *Play Environments: A question of quality*. PLAYLINK.

Isaacs, S. (1945), *Childhood and After: Some Essays and Clinical Studies*. London: Agathon Press.

Kalliala, M. (2006), *Play Culture in a Changing World*. Oxford: Oxford University Press.

Kolb, D.A. (1984), *A source of Learning and Development*. New Jersey: Prentice Hall.

Langer, E. (1997), *The Power of Mindful Learning*. Harlow: Addison-Wesley.

Lindon, J. (2006) Equality in Early Childhood: Linking Theory and Practice, London: Hodder Arnold.

Matthews, J. (2003), *Drawing and Painting: Children and Visual Representation* (2nd edn). London: Paul Chapman Publishing Ltd.

Meggitt, C. (2012), *An Illustrated Guide to Child Development* (3rd edn). Oxford: Heinemann.

Mortimer, H. (2001), *Special Needs and Early Years Provision*. London: Continuum International Publishing Group.

Nyland, B., Ferris, J. and Dunn, L. (2008), 'Mindful hands, gestures as language: Listening to children', *Early Years* 28(1): 73–80.

Ouvry, M. (2004), *Sounds like Playing: Music in the Early Years Curriculum*. London: BAECE/Early Education.

Paley, V.G. (1981), *Wally's Stories*. Cambridge, Mass.: Harvard University Press.

Palmer, S. and Bayley, R. (2004), *Foundations of Literacy: A Balanced Approach to Language, Listening and Literacy Skills in the Early Years*. Edinburgh: Network Educational Press.

Pound, L., (2013) *Quick Guides for Early Years: Physical Development* Hodder Education

UK Physical guidelines for early years **www.bhfactive.org.uk/userfiles/Documents/ guidelineswalkers.pdf**

Schön, D. (1983), *The Reflective Practitioner*. New York: Basic Books.

Siraj-Blatchford, I. (2009), 'Conceptualising Progression in the Pedagogy of Play and Sustained Shared Thinking in Early Childhood Education: A Vygotskian Perspective', *Education and Child Psychology* 26 (2).

Siraj-Blatchford, I. Sylva, K., Melhuish, E.C., Sammons, P. and Taggart, B. (2004), *The Effective Provision of Pre-School Education (EPPE)*. London: DfES/Institute of Education, University of London.

Sylva, K. and Lunt, I. (1982), *Child Development: A First Course*. Oxford: Blackwell.

Sylva, K., Roy, C. and Painter, M (1980), *Childwatching at Playgroup and Nursery School*. London: Sage Publications.

Tovey, H. (2007), *Playing Outdoors: Spaces and Places, Risk and Challenge*. Oxford: Oxford University Press.

Trevarthen, C. (2004), *Learning about Ourselves from Children: Why a Growing Human Brain needs Interesting Companions*. Perception-in-Action Laboratories, University of Edinburgh.

Waddell, M. (1995), *Owl Babies*. London: Walker Books.

Wall, K. (2006), *Special Needs and Early Years: A Practitioner's Guide*. London: Paul Chapman Publications.

Whitehead, M. (2010), *Language and Literacy in the Early Years 0–7 (4th edn)*. London: Sage.

Wilson, R. (2003), *Special Educational Needs in the Early Years*. Abingdon: Routledge Falmer.

Winnicott, D.W. (1964), *The Child, the Family and the Outside World*. London: Penguin Books.

Websites

BBC CBeebies
www.bbc.co.uk/cbeebies

BBC Games
www.bbc.co.uk/cbbc/games/index.shtml

Berit's Best Sites
www.beritsbest.com

Enchanted Learning Online
www.enchantedlearning.com/categories/preschool.shtml

Kids @ National Geographic
www.nationalgeographic.com/kids

Kids Domain
www.kidsdomain.com

Kid's Wave:
www.safesurf.com/safesurfing

Microsoft Kids Website
www.kids.msn.com

Peter Rabbit
www.peterrabbit.com

PBS Kids
http://pbskids.org

Thomas the Tank Engine
www.hitentertainment.com/thomasandfriends/uk

Index

equality 124–7, 129–39, 410
Equality Act 2010 124
Equality and Human Rights Commission (EHRC)
    131
Erikson, E. 333–5, 337
estimating 239, 251
event sample 266, 368
exercise
    benefits of 23
    inclusive provision 30–1
    national initiatives 24
    planning activities 27–29
    requirements for 23
    risk assessment 27
    supporting 26–7, 29
    see also physical development
expansion 228
expected development 355, 387
experiences
    of children 333
    of practitioner 352
expressive arts and design 196, 217–19
expressive language 296
extended families 148
extraversion 332
eye contact 290
face washing 36
face-to-face communication 151–2
facial expressions 340
facilitating 218
family breakdown 61
family doctor (GP) 146
family outreach worker 146
family structures 147–8
feelings 329
    see also emotional wellbeing; personal, social and
        emotional development
fine motor movements 263, 313, 317, 323–4, 410
finger rhymes 305, 308
fire 119
    hazards 113
first words 223
five a day campaign 3
flooding 119
flu 70, 72
fluency 224

folic acid 5–6
food
    allergies 14, 15
    during illness 76
    groups 6–7
    hazards 113–14
    hygiene 40–1
    intolerances 14, 15
    labelling 3–4
    poisoning 71, 72, 73
    preparing and serving 16, 41
    recording intake 15, 16
    reheating 41
    storing 41
    see also healthy eating; nutrition
Food Hygiene (England) Regulations 2006 106, 109
Forest Schools 182–3, 184
formal operational stage 284
formula feed 15, 16, 41
foster families 148
free description 266–7
free-flow play 178
friendships 166, 330, 344
Froebel, F. 179, 184
frustration 175
fussy eaters 62
gas leak 119
gender concept 136, 166, 330–1
German measles 70, 71, 73, 74
Gesell, A. 319–20
Gibbs, G. 400
    cycle of reflection 400–1
gloop 288
goodbyes 340
grammar 296
grapheme 230
greetings 340
gross motor movements 263, 313, 317, 323–4, 410
group learning 205
groups, belonging to 200
guidelines 410
guilt 335
hair care 37, 50
hand, foot and mouth 70, 72, 73
hand washing 35–6, 39–40, 50
hand-eye coordination 313